Routledge Revivals

Salvation of the Soul and Islamic Devotion

First Published in 1983, *Salvation of the Soul and Islamic Devotion* demonstrates that salvation is a central concept of the religion of Islam, even though its meaning, causes and results according to Islam may differ from what is taught by Christianity and other world religions. The first chapter of the book presents the Islamic doctrine of salvation as set forth in the Quran and prophetic tradition. The meaning of salvation is explored, and the means to it on both human and divine sides are considered with special emphasis upon Islamic devotions. The remaining eight chapters deal with both obligatory and supererogatory devotions prescribed by Islam, concentrating on the methods of their correct performance, on which salvation is largely dependent.

The material used in this book has been derived entirely from the original Islamic sources written in Arabic. Efforts are made to make the book useful to both Muslim and non-Muslim readers of English interested in the Islamic theory of salvation and acts of devotion.

Salvation of the Soul and Islamic Devotion

M. A. Quasem

Routledge
Taylor & Francis Group

First published in 1983
by Kegan & Paul International

This edition first published in 2023 by Routledge
4 Park Square, Milton Park, Abingdon, Oxon, OX14 4RN

and by Routledge
605 Third Avenue, New York, NY 10017

Routledge is an imprint of the Taylor & Francis Group, an informa business

Publisher's Note

The publisher has gone to great lengths to ensure the quality of this reprint but points out that some imperfections in the original copies may be apparent.

Disclaimer

The publisher has made every effort to trace copyright holders and welcomes correspondence from those they have been unable to contact.

A Library of Congress record exists under ISBN:

ISBN: 978-1-032-51462-8 (hbk)
ISBN: 978-1-003-40232-9 (ebk)
ISBN: 978-1-032-51463-5 (pbk)

Book DOI 10.4324/9781003402329

SALVATION OF THE SOUL AND ISLAMIC DEVOTIONS

by

MUHAMMAD ABUL QUASEM
B.A.HONS., M.A., PhD.(EDIN), KAMIL(DAC)

Associate Professor
Department of Theology and Philosophy
National University of Malaysia

KEGAN PAUL INTERNATIONAL
London, Boston, Melbourne and Henley

This edition first published in 1983
by Kegan Paul International
39 Store Street, London WC1E 7DD, England
9 Park Street, Boston, Mass. 02108, USA
464 St Kilda Road, Melbourne,
Victoria 3004, Australia and
Broadway House, Newtown Road,
Henley-on-Thames, Oxon RG9 1EN, England
Printed in Great Britain by
Redwood Burn Limited, Trowbridge, Wilts

Library of Congress Cataloging in Publication Data

Muhammad Abul Quasem.
Salvation of the soul and Islamic devotions.
Bibliography: p.
Includes index.
1. Islam – Customs and practices. I. Title.
BP174.M83 1983 297'.446 83–17584

ISBN 0–7103–0033–6

بسم الله الرحمن الرحيم

In the name of God, Most Gracious, Ever Merciful

وينجي الله الذين اتقوا بمفازتهم لايمسهم السوء ولا هم
يحزنون.ـ قران ٣٩:٦١

God will save the righteous and bestow success on them; no evil will afflict them, nor will they grieve. — Qur'ān 39:61

واعبد ربك حتى يأتيك اليقين.ـ قران ١٥:٩٩

Worship your Lord [by performing devotional acts] until death overtakes you. — Qur'ān 15:99

CONTENTS

PREFACE page 12

TRANSLITERATIONS 16

ABBREVIATIONS 17

CHAPTER 19

I SALVATION

1. The Concept of Salvation in the Qur'ān and Prophetic Tradition, 19. 2. The Means to Salvation: the Means to Salvation on the Human Side, 29. Faith and Salvation, 31; Devotional Acts and Salvation, 35; the Parts of Devotional Acts and Salvation, 40; the Means to Salvation on the Divine Side — Intercession and Divine Mercy, 43.

II CLEANLINESS 50

1. Kinds of Water with which Cleanliness can be Achieved, 50. 2. The Small Quantity of Water from which an Animal has Drunk, 51. 3. The Use of Clean Pots and Clothes mixed with Unclean Ones, 52. 4. A Small Well into which Unclean Matter or Anything Else has Fallen, 53. 5. Cleanliness after Relieving Oneself, 55. 6. Ablution (*Waḍū'*): the Pillars of Ablution, 58; the Stipulations for Ablution, 59; Some Necessary Acts in Ablution, 60; Sunna Acts in Ablution, 61; Praiseworthy Acts in Ablution, 62; Disliked Acts in Ablution, 63; the Three Kinds of Ablution, 64; Things Nullifying Ablution, 65; Things which do not Nullify Ablution, 66. 7. Bath: Causes of Obligatory Bath, 66; Things which do not Necessitate Bathing 67; Obligatory Acts in a Bath, 68; Sunna Acts in a Bath, 68; Praiseworthy and Disliked Acts in a Bath. 69; when Bathing is Sunna, 70; when Bathing is Praiseworthy, 70; 8. Ablution with Clean Sand (*Tayammum*): Stipulations for the Validity of Ablution with Sand, 71; the Causes of, and Stipulations

for, the Obligation of Ablution with Sand, 74 ; the Pillars of Ablution with Sand, 74 ; Sunna Acts in Ablution with Sand, 74 ; Praiseworthy Acts in Ablution with Sand, 74 ; what Nullifies Ablution with Sand, 75 . 9. Wiping over Boots: Stipulations for Wiping over Boots, 76; Duration of Wiping over Boots, 76 ; Obligatory Acts in Wiping over Boots, 77 ; Sunna Acts in Wiping over Boots, 77 ; what Nullifies Wiping over Boots, 77 . 10. Wiping over a Bandage, 78 . 11. Menstruation, Bleeding after Child-birth, Istiḥāḍa and the State of Legal Impurity: Acts Unlawful in Menstruation and in Bleeding Period after Child-birth, 79 ; Unlawful Acts in the State of Major Legal Impurity, 80 ; Unlawful Acts in the State of Minor Legal Impurity, 81 ; Rules on Istiḥāḍa and Excuses; 81 . 12. Filth and Cleanliness from it: Serious Filth and Light Filth, 81 . 13. Cleanliness of Hides of Dead Animals, 83 .

III RITUAL PRAYER 85

1. Stipulations for the Obligation of Ritual Prayer, 85 . 2. Times of Ritual Prayer, 85 . 3. The Times when Ritual Prayer is Disliked, 87 . 4. Call to Ritual Prayer (*Adhān*), 88 . 5. Stipulations for the Validity of a Ritual Prayer and its Pillars, 91 . 6. Ritual Prayers with Filthy Clothes, 93 . 7. Facing the Direction of the Ka'ba, 95 . 8. Required Acts in a Ritual Prayer, 96 . 9. Sunna Acts in a Ritual Prayer, 97 . 10. Praiseworthy Acts in a Ritual Prayer. 100 . 11. How to Compose a Ritual Prayer, 101 . 12. Leading of a Ritual Prayer (*Imāma*): Stipulations for Leading a Ritual Prayer, 106; Stipulations for Following the Imām, 106; Reasons for Non-performance of a Ritual Prayer in Congregation, 108 ; the Man Most Deserving of Leading a Ritual Prayer, and Ordering of Lines of Devotees, 108 ; Acts to be performed by the Follower after the Imām's Completion of a Ritual Prayer, 110. 13. Praise of God after Obligatory Ritual Prayer, 111. 14. Acts Corrupting a Ritual Prayer, 112. 15. Acts which do not Corrupt a Ritual Prayer, 116. 16. Acts Legally Disliked in a Ritual Prayer, 116 . 17. Setting up of a Barrier and Repelling One Passing in front of the Devotee, 120. 18. Acts not Legally Disliked for a Devotee, 120. 19. Acts Requiring the Nullification of a

Ritual Prayer and Acts Permitting it, 121. 20. The Odd Prayer (*Ṣalāt al-Witr*), 122. 21. Supererogatory Ritual Prayers, 125. 22. Ritual Prayer for Greeting the Mosque, Ritual Prayer Following the Sunrise, and Keeping Vigil at Night, 127. 23. Supererogatory Ritual Prayer by One Sitting or Riding, 130. 24. Obligatory and Required Ritual Prayers by One Riding or in a Vehicle, 131. 25. Ritual Prayer in a Boat, 132. 26. Tarāwīḥ Prayer, 132. 27. Ritual Prayer inside the Ka'ba, 133. 28. Ritual Prayer by a Traveller: Definition of Travel, 134 ; Stipulations for the Validity of Intention of Travel , 135. 29. Ritual Prayer by a Sick Man, 137. 30. Falling of Ritual Prayer and Fasting from One's Responsibility, 139. 31. Performance of Ritual Prayers at Later Times (*Qaḍā'*), 140. 32. Attainment of an Obligatory Ritual Prayer with the Imām, 142. 33. Prostration due to Forgetfulness, 144 . 34. Doubt in Ritual Prayer, 147. 35. Prostration due to Recitation of Certain Qur'ānic Verses 148. 36. Prostration for Expressing Gratitude to God, 151. 37. An Effective Measure against every Serious Misfortune, 152. 38. The Friday Assembly Prayer: Stipulations for the Friday Assembly Prayer, 152 ; Sunna Acts in the Addresses of Friday Assembly Prayer, 154; Required Acts in Preparation for Friday Assembly Prayer, 154; Disliked Acts in Friday Assembly Prayer, 155. 39. 'Īd Prayers: Stipulations for 'Īd Prayers, 156; Praiseworthy Acts on the Day of 'Īd al-Fiṭr, 156 ; Times and Methods of 'Īd Prayers, 157. 40. Ritual Prayers for Removal of Fear and Eclipse of the Sun and the Moon, 160. 41. Ritual Prayer for Rain, 160. 42. Ritual Prayer in Fear, 162. 43. Legal Rules concerning Funerals: Duties towards a Dying Man, and Preparing the Dead for Burial, 162; Ritual Prayer over a Bier, 167; Who will Lead the Ritual Prayer over a Deceased Person, 169; Bearing of a Bier to the Graveyard and the Burial, 171; Visiting the Grave, 174. Legal Rules concerning the Martyr, 174.

IV FASTING 177

IV 1. Definition, 177. 2. Stipulations for Fasting: when Fasting is Obligatory, 177 ; Stipulations for Observance of Fasting, 178 ; Stipulations for the Validity of Fasting,

179. 3. The Pillar of Fasting, 179. 4. Kinds of Fasting, 180. 5. Making the Intention of Fasting, 182. 6. The Sight of the New Moon for Fasting and for Festival Days, and Fasting on Days Doubtful to be Days of Ramāḍan, 183. 7. Acts which do not Corrupt Fasting, 185. 8. Acts which Corrupt Fasting and Require both Atonement and Re-observance, 187. 9. Atonement for Corruption of Fasting, 187. 10. Acts which Corrupt Fasting but do not Require Atonement, 189. 11. Fasting Part of the Day, 190. 12. Acts Disliked, Acts not Disliked and Acts Praiseworthy to a Fasting Individual, 190. 13. Accidental Circumstances and Fasting, 191. 14. Accomplishment of Vows, 193. 15. I'tikāf — Seclusion for Complete Devotion in a Mosque. 194.

V DIVINE TAX (*ZAKĀ*) 197

1. Stipulations for, and Rates of, Divine Tax, 197. 2. Persons to whom Divine Tax can be Paid, 202. 3. Divine Tax of the Day of 'Īd al-Fiṭr, 204.

VI PILGRIMAGE 207

1. Definition, 207. 2. Stipulations for the Obligation of the Pilgrimage, 207. 3. Stipulations regarding the Necessity of Performance of the Pilgrimage, 208. 4. Stipulations for the Validity of Performance of the Pilgrimage, 208. 5. Required Acts in the Pilgrimage, 209. 6. Sunna Acts in the Pilgrimage, 210. 7. How to perform the Activities of the Pilgrimage One after Another, 214. 8. Ifrād Form of the Pilgrimage, 225. 9. The Qirān Form of the Pilgrimage, 226. 10. The Tamattu' Form of the Pilgrimage, 227. 11. 'Umra — the Lesser Pilgrimage, 228. 12. The Best Day, 228. 13 Commission of Offences in Pilgrimage, 229. 14. Animals for Sacrifice in Pilgrimage, 231. 15. Visit to the Tomb of the Prophet, 232.

VII THE RECITATION OF THE QUR'ĀN 246

1. Three Motives of Qur'ān-recitation, 246. 2. When Qur'ān-recitation is Unlawful, 247. 3. Required Acts in Qur'ān-recitation 248. 4. Sunna and Praiseworthy Bodily Tasks in Qur'ān-recitation, 248. 5. Sunna and Praiseworthy Mental Tasks in Qur'ān-recitation, 253.

VIII REMEMBRANCE OF GOD (*DHIKR ALLĀH*) 258

1. Two Forms of Remembrance of God, 258. 2. Stipulations for Remembrance of God, 259. 3. Most Important Formulae of Remembrance of God: the Formulae of Oneness of God, 260; the Formulae of Glorification, Praise and Magnification of God, 261.

IX SUPPLICATION (*DU'Ā'*) TO GOD 263

1. The Meaning of Supplication to God, 263. 2. Praiseworthy Methods of Supplication, 264. 3. Most Important Supplication Formulae: Supplication Formulae of taking Refuge with God, 267; Supplication Formulae for Forgiveness of Sin, 269; Formulae of Invoking Blessings upon the Prophet, 271.

CONCLUSION 273

BIBLOGRAPHY 277

INDEX 281-289

PREFACE

Islam is an all inclusive religion in the sense that it is guidance for mankind in *all* aspects of his life. This all inclusive guidance is absolute in as much as it is valid in all places and in all times until Doomsday. The Arabic term *shumūl* is usually used to mean the all inclusive nature of Islam. It has, however, not been used in the Qu'rān; what is employed in the Qur'ān is the phrase *kull shay'*[1], meaning everything, i.e. the core principles of knowledge of every problem of human life. The Qu'rān contains such principles in order to assist man in the conduct of his life at both the theoretical and practical levels. The life and teachings of the prophet of Islam (may peace be upon him!), as recorded in the standard works of his biography as well as in the six canonical works on Tradition (*ḥadīth*), clearly demonstrate how comprehensive a religion Islam is. Western orientalists had, for a long time, held a distorted view on the nature and scope of the religion of Islam; recently, however, their mistake is corrected to a certain degree so that many of them have now come to hold that Islam is a complete code of life.

The all inclusive teachings of Islam aim at preparing man for his well-being or happiness in the world to come. A fundamental belief of Islam is that a man's life in this world continues eternally after his death, and that the final goal of this life is well-being or happiness in his life after death. This is also a central teaching of all other revealed religions in their original form, i.e. the form in which they were revealed. Well-being or happiness in the world to come consists in absence of misery and presence of enjoyment in their different forms at different stages of the life after death. This is the meaning of man's salvation (*najāt*) in the Qur'ān and Tradition. The aim of this study is first to present this doctrine of salvation and then to give a detailed account of Islamic devotional acts (*'ibādāt*) as a means to it. This study does not seriously consider the theories of salvation formulated by different classes of Muslim intellectuals, such as the jurists, theologians, philosophers, and ṣūfīs; it occasionally refers to these theories only in passing. It confines itself to the Qur'ānic

[1] Qur'ān 12:111, 17:12.

theory on the ground that this theory is the root or basis of all other theories, although some of them, e.g. philosophic and Mu'tazilite theories, mark sharp deviations from it on certain crucial points.

A central teaching of the Qur'ān and Tradition is that the means to salvation are faith (*īmān*) and action (*'amal*). The term action, though very comprehensive in Islam, means, in the context of salvation, two things: just behaviour towards other people and devotional acts prescribed by Islam which are of two kinds, namely, obligatory and supererogatory. Just and unjust behaviour of a man has not been treated in detail in the present study, for their detailed treatment may by itself form the subject matter of an independent work. The present study concerns only the devotional acts from the standpoint of salvation; it aims at giving a very comprehensive and systematic treatment of the methods of performance of all obligatory and supererogatory devotions in the perfect manner so that they may serve as a means to salvation. In addition, it mentions, though only occasionally, the consequences of individual acts of devotion in this world as well as in the world to come. Neither the psychology of devotional acts nor their philosophy nor their sociology has been dealt with in this study although these have some concern with salvation; this is because the psychology, philosophy and sociology of Islamic devotions are so rich in content that taken together they can be treated in a separate work. Of the two means to salvation faith is more fundamental than action; it is presupposed by action; it is, therefore, considered necessary to give an outline of Islamic faith in a section of the book.

The material for this study has been derived entirely from the original, Islamic sources written in the Arabic language. The first chapter dealing with the doctrine of salvation is based on the Qur'ān and Tradition interpreted in keeping with the opinion of Ahl as-Sunna wa l-Jamā'a who form the main body of Muslims. The text of chapters 2-6 may be considered something like the reproduction of a well known work on the Ḥanafī school (*madhhab*) of Islamic jurisprudence, *Nūr al-Īḍāḥ wa Najāt al-Qulūb*,[2] by the Egyptian scholar ash-Shurunbalālī. This book is a collection of the most correct methods of obligatory devotional acts scattered throughout many important, lengthy works on the Ḥanafī school of jurisprudence — a collection made for the convenience of readers interested in Islamic devotions.[3] It has long been used as a text book

[2]Ḥasan ibn 'Ammār ash-Shurunbalālī, *Nūr al-Īḍāḥ wa Najāt al-Qulūb*, Egypt, 1965.

[3]*Ibid.*, p. 3.

in the University of al-Azhar as well as in the religious institutions of India, Bangladesh, Pakistan and many other countries where the Ḥanafī school of jurisprudence is followed almost exclusively. Since a great part of material for chapters 2-6 is derived from this book it is considered unnecessary to cite references to it. A small part of the material used in these chapters has its source in a few other works: the Qur'ān, the six canonical works on Tradition, ash-Shurunbalālī's *Marāqī al-Falāḥ* which is a commentary on *Nūr al-Īḍāḥ*, al-Marghinānī's *al-Hidāya, al-Ghazālī's Iḥyā' 'Ulūm ad-Dīn*, Ibn Qayyim's Zād al-Ma'ād, and Shāh Walī Allāh's *Ḥujjat Allāh al-Bāligha*. References to these works have duly been given. The last three chapters are based on the Qur'ān, the six canonical works on Tradition, especially the *Ṣaḥīḥ* of al-Bukhārī and the *Ṣaḥīḥ* of Muslim, and the first part of al-Ghazālī's *Iḥyā' 'Ulūm ad-Dīn*. So far as the methods of devotional acts are concerned the present study fully follows the Ḥanafī school of jurisprudence which is considered to be more rational than any other school of Islamic jurisprudence.

All prayer formulae cited in this study are given in Arabic, because some of them need to be recited by Muslims in that language, while in the case of others it is preferable to recite them in Arabic. All formulae are translated into English with a view to assisting the reader who cannot understand Arabic to know their meaning and significance; recitation of a prayer formula with an understanding of its meaning earns more merit than its recitation without understanding. Most of the prayer formulae cited in Arabic are transliterated in order to facilitate their reading by those who cannot read Arabic correctly. The methods of transliteration are mostly the same as those followed by the Department of Arabic & Islamic Studies, University of Edinburgh, where the author did his doctoral studies about ten years ago. The Qur'ānic verses quoted are cited in both Arabic and English translations. In numbering the verses the official Egyptian edition of the Qur'ān is consistently followed; this should be borne in mind by the reader when he endeavours to locate in his edition of the Qur'ān the various verses referred to in this study. Efforts are made to find out the sources of Traditions sometimes quoted and at times only referred to in this study, for this seems important from the viewpoint of both research and practice of devotions by appropriate people. It is hoped that the book will prove useful to both Muslim and non-Muslim readers of English interested in the Islamic concept of salvation and acts of devotion. It will provide them with a knowledge of the concept of salvation set forth in the Qur'ān and Tradition; it will also give them knowledge of the minute details of methods of correct performance of Islamic devotions which forms a means to salvation.

I am unable to express my gratitude to God through Whose help the preparation of this book for publication has become possible. I should like to record my thanks to Mr. Peter Mooney and Dr. Harold Crouch of the National University of Malaysia for going through the manuscript and making valuable comments and suggestions and for reading the proofs despite their many engagements.

National University of Malaysia M.A. Quasem

Muḥarram 1400
November 1980

TRANSLITERATIONS

Consonants

ء	ʾ (except when initial)	ز	z	ق	q
ب	b	س	s	ك	k
ت	t	ش	sh	ل	l
ث	th	ص	ṣ	م	m
ج	j	ض	ḍ	ن	n
ح	ḥ	ط	ṭ	هـ	h
خ	kh	ظ	ẓ	و	w
د	d	ع	ʿ	ي	y
ذ	dh	غ	gh		
ر	r	ف	f		

Short Vowels

ـَ : a　　ـُ : u　　ـِ : i

Long Vowels

ـَي or ـَا : ā　　ـُو : ū　　ـِي : ī

Dipthongs

ـَي : ay　　ـَو : aw　　ـُوّ : uww　　ـِيّ : iyy

The letter ة is sometimes transliterated into ‘t’ and sometimes omitted.

ABBREVIATIONS

The abbreviations listed below are used for the journals and encyclopaedias referred to in this study.

A.	—*Arabica*
D.I.	—*Der Islam*
E.I.[2]	—*The Encyclopaedia of Islam*. New edition.
E.I. (S)	—*The Shorter Encyclopaedia of Islam*
J.A.O.S.	—*The Journal of American Oriental Society*
J.P.H.S.	—*Journal of Pakistan Historical Society*
I.S.	—*Islamic Studies*
P.A.P.S.	—*Proceedings of American Philosophical Society*
S.I.	—*Studia Islamica*
I.Q.	—*The Islamic Quarterly*
E.R.E.	—*The Encyclopaedia of Religion and Ethics*
M.W.	—*The Muslim World*
I.C.	—*Islamic Culture*

SALVATION OF THE SOUL AND ISLAMIC DEVOTIONS

I

SALVATION

THE CONCEPT OF SALVATION IN THE QUR'ĀN AND PROPHETIC TRADITION

The concept of salvation is to be found in the Scriptures of all developed religions, revealed and man-made. It is strongly emphasized in them and its treatment is elaborated to a great extent, on the ground that every Scripture is guidance for mankind and what this guidance aims at is his salvation, whether in this world or in the world to come. Thus salvation is the central theme of all important Scriptures, including the Qur'ān, the Scripture of Islam. In works other than Scriptures the problem of salvation is also discussed, but it is discussed in some of them as a central concept and in others as only linked up with such a concept. These works are of different categories, such as juristic, theological, philosophic and mystical. Their emphasis on salvation is of varying degrees, and their discussion of it is also of varying length and nature. Thus the mystics' stress on salvation, happiness and similar concepts is much stronger than that of philosophers.[4] A study of the doctrine of salvation put forward in different Scriptures as well as in other works is an important undertaking and worthy of a life's study, but our aim here is only to give an account of the Qur'ānic concept of salvation, because it is with this concept that Islamic devotions are most intimately connected. Since prophetic tradition is but an explanation of the Qur'ān an account of Qur'ānic teaching on salvation must incorporate ideas from prophetic tradition as well.

In the Qur'ān is to be found the discussion of two forms of salvation, namely, that which occurs in man's life in this world and that which takes place in the world to come. The former is found in deliverance from all that threatens or impairs life, such as oppression, injustice, calamity, divine chastisement, troubles and distresses of every kind.[5] It is granted by God on account of man's

[4] Muhammad Abul Quasem, *The Ethics of al-Ghazālī*, 2nd ed., New York, 1978, pp. 53-78 where al-Ghazālī's theory is set forth in some detail.

[5] Qur'ān 28:25, 17:67, 11:58, 21:76, 11:116.

faith, piety and devotions.[6] Salvation in the Hereafter is found in deliverance from misery or punishment and attainment of happiness or reward from God.[7] This is the meaning usually understood when the term 'salvation' is used in the Qur'ān and Tradition. The phrase 'doctrine of salvation' or 'concept of salvation' is also understood to refer to this meaning and not the other just mentioned. This kind of salvation pertains to *sam'iyyāt* or matters which are to be known from the Qur'ān or the Prophet. It is the main concern of Islamic devotions and so needs to be treated here in some detail. Just as both forms of salvation are discussed in the Qur'ān, so too they are dealt with in the Judaic and Christian Scriptures.[8]

The terms used in the Qur'ān and Tradition for what is meant by the word 'salvation' are *najāt* (salvation), *fawz* (success), *falāḥ* (prosperity), and *sa'āda* (happiness). The first term, together with its different derivatives, is frequently used for both kinds of salvation.[9] *Fawz* and its derivatives, however, often refer to salvation in the Hereafter only.[10] The use of *falāḥ* and its many derivatives is similar to that of *najāt*.[11] *Sa'āda* does not occur even once in the Qur'ān; its derivatives, *su'idū* and *sa'īd*, have occurred in it in the eschatological sense.[12] In Tradition, of course, *sa'āda* occurs in this sense very frequently as do its different derivatives.[13] Where a word connotes salvation in this world it is to be found to have some relationship with salvation in the world to come, for the Qur'ān and Tradition consider this world as only a preparatory ground for the future world. Muslim ascetics and jurists use *najāt* more frequently than other Qur'ānic words, and they use it mostly in the eschatological sense. Ṣūfīs and Muslim philosophers of the medieval times, however, prefer *sa'āda* to other terms, the former emphasizing its other-worldly meaning while the latter stressing upon its this-worldly connotation. There are reasons for these variations in use of terms by different classes of Muslim intellectuals; discussion of them here seems irrelevant.

Coming from terms to meaning, one finds two general features of the Qur'ānic view on salvation in the Hereafter. One is that salvation

6Qur'ān 41:18, 11:66.

7Qur'ān 19:72, 61:10, 40:41.

8T.B. Kilpatrick, "Salvation (Christian)", *ERE*, II, 110-31; M. Joseph, "Salvation (Jewish)", II, 138-48.

9Qur'ān 28:25, 17:67, 11:58, 21:76, 19:72, 61:10, 40:41.

10Qur'ān 3:185, 4:73, 13, 23:111, 59:20, 78:31, 3:188, *passim*.

11Qur'ān 2:64, 23:1, 7:8, 87:14, 91:9, 18:20, 6:135, *passim*.

12Qur'ān 11:105, 108.

13Al-Bukhārī, *Ṣaḥīḥ*, Qadar, 15, 'Ilm, 33; Muslim, *Ṣaḥīḥ*, Qadar, 3; Ibn Māja, *Sunan*, Muqaddama, 17.

and its opposite state, damnation, are of the soul as well as of the body. Man is a combination of soul and body; if both are equally important to form one whole man, this is called monism; if, however the soul is considered to be the real man, while the body to be only its necessary instrument or tool, this is dualism. This dualism is implied in Qur'ānic verses,[14] but clearly spoken of in prophetic Tradition. It is true of man in this world as well as in the Hereafter. The resurrected man will have both body and soul; his essence will be the soul, while his body its tool, its follower or its servant; it is the soul which will be saved or damned, while the body will only follow it in this respect. In the life of this world it is the soul which knows God or is ignorant of Him, which is drawn near to God or is veiled from Him; the body is only its instrument which the soul uses for its purposes. Therefore, it is the soul which will be saved or damned, and the body will also be so as being its tool which works for it.[15] Thus there is an important sense in which salvation may be said to be of the soul, even though the body will also be saved. It is in this sense that the phrase 'salvation of the soul' occurs in the title of this work. Similar phrases also occur in Christian Scriptures.[16]

The Qur'ānic teaching that both soul and body will be saved or damned is followed by Muslim jurists, theologians, including the Mu'tazilites, and ṣūfīs, but not the medieval Muslim philosophers who denied the physical aspect of the Hereafter altogether, affirming only the spiritual side of it. Their arguments have been fully refuted by al-Ghazālī;[17] yet following them some Muslim intellectuals of modern time deny the Qur'ānic concept of the bodily aspect of the life after death. Like Islam, Judaism and Christianity in their original form taught about both physical and spiritual resurrection and reward and punishment in the Hereafter. It is only later, in medieval times, that some Jews and Christians gave a spiritual interpretation of the future world. One of these Jews was Maimonides who was greatly influenced by medieval Muslim philosophers in this and many other respects. In modern times many Jews and Christians,

[14]Christian Scriptures also emphasize the soul and speak of the instrumental nature of the body. See Romans 6:13; Matthew 5:8; Hebrews 12:14; Acts 15:9, 35ff. ; I Corinthians 6:19.

[15]Abū Ḥāmid Muḥammad al-Ghazālī, *Iḥyā' 'Ulūm ad-Dīn*, Beirut, n.d., III, 2; Quasem, *Ethics*, pp. 46f., 73.

[16]Hebrews 10:39 —" ... but of them that believe to the saving of the soul;" James 1:21 — "... which is able to save your souls."

[17]Abū Ḥāmid Muḥammad al-Ghazālī, *Tahāfut al-Falāsifa*, ed., al-Yasū'ī, Beirut, 1962, pp. 235-53.

deviating from the Scriptural teaching, conceive of the Hereafter as only spiritual in nature.

The second general feature of the Qur'ānic concept of salvation and damnation in the Hereafter is their occurrence in successive stages. The future life starts from immediately after a man's death, and continues, through a few stages, eternally, without an end. The first stage is the grave period, also called the ***barzakh*** period,[18] which will end with the start of the Day of Resurrection. The second stage is the period of Resurrection and Judgement in a few distinct phases. The last stage is the period of dwelling in Paradise or in Hell. It is at this last stage that salvation and damnation will take place in their full form. During the preceding stages it is only the foretastes of these that are experienced, the degree of foretastes depending upon the degree of salvation and damnation at the final stage. The Qur'ānic concept of salvation by stages is intimately connected with the concept of the physical nature of the Hereafter, and hence the medieval Muslim philosophers' denial of the latter involves their denial of the former. The refutation of their arguments by al-Ghazālī in his *Tahāfut al-Falāsifa*[19] is of tremendous importance for Islam in this connection as well. Muslim jurists, theologians and ṣūfīs follow the Qur'ānic concept of salvation and damnation by stages.

But what is salvation at the last stage and what are its foretastes at the preceding stages? The answer to these questions can be attempted here very briefly in view of the short space available. At the last stage of the Hereafter salvation will be found in deliverance from punishment or misery in Hell and in attainment of reward or happiness in Paradise. A certain degree of this misery or happiness is experienced by every deceased person first at the grave period and then at the period of Resurrection and Judgement. This is what is meant by foretaste of salvation and damnation in Islam. The exact nature of happiness and misery at these stages will not be the same; rather it will vary because of variation in thetemporal andspatial nature of these stages. Thus concerning the grave stage the Qur'ān says that believers remain firm in their belief when they are interrogated by al-Munker and an-Nakīr,[20] that those who turn away from the rememberance of God have had a straitened life in the grave,[21] and that Hell is exposed to infidels morning and evening.[22] Of the many Traditions which elaborate on this teaching of the Qur'ān three

[18]Qur'ān 23:100, 25:53. [19]pp. 235-53.

[20]Qur'ān 14:27; Abū Ṭālib al-Makkī, *Qūt al-Qulūb*, Egypt, 1961, II, 256.

[21]Qur'ān 20:124. [22]Qu'rān 40:46.

may be quoted here as follows:

> "The grave is either like a ditch from the ditches of Hell, or like a luxuriant garden from the luxuriant gardens of Paradise."[23]

> "Seventy dragons are given power over an infidel in the grave, and bite and sting him till the Last Hour comes. If one of these dragons were to breathe over the earth, it would bring forth no green things."[24]

> "When a man is placed in his grave and his companions leave him, [his soul is returned to his body] and he hears the beat of their sandals. Then two angels, [one called al-Munkar and the other an-Nakīr], come to him and, having made him sit up, say, 'What was your opinion of this man, of Muḥammad?' The believer replies, 'I give witness that he is God's servant and messenger.' Then he is asked, 'Look at your abode in Hell for which God has substituted for you an abode in Paradise.' He will see them both. The hypocrite and infidel are asked, 'What was your opinion of this man?' He replies, 'I do not know. I held the opinion others held.' He is told, 'You neither knew nor did you follow [the believers].' He is then given a blow with iron hammers and utters a shout which is heard by all near him, with the exception of men and jinn."[25]

> "When one of you dies his dwelling place is exposed to him morning and evening. If he is from among the dwellers of Paradise, his dwelling place is from Paradise; if he is from the dwellers of Hell, his dwelling place is from Hell. He is told, 'This is your dwelling place so that you will be sent to it on the Day of Resurrection.' "[26]

Vision of a dwelling place in Paradise or in Hell produces an immense joy or sorrow in the deceased's mind. Repetition of this vision every morning and evening results in repetition of joy or sorrow throughout the grave period. This is in addition to punishment stated in other Traditions. The ṣūfīs add to all this a certain kind of

[23] At-Tirmidhī, *Sunan*, Qiyāma, 26.

[24] *Ibid.*, 126; ad-Dārimī, *Sunan*, Riqāq, 94; Ibn Ḥanbal, *Musnad*, III, 38.

[25] Al-Bukhārī, *Ṣaḥīḥ*, Janā'iz, 67, 86; an-Nasā'ī, *Sunan*, Janā'iz, 110; Abū Dāwūd, *Sunan*, Sunna, 24; Ibn Ḥanbal, *Musnad*, III, 4,126.

[26] Al-Bukhārī, *Ṣaḥīḥ*, Janā'iz, 90; Muslim, *Ṣaḥīḥ*, Janna, 65f.; at-Tirmidhī, *Sunan*, Janā'iz, 170; an-Nasā'ī, *Sunan*, Janā'iz, 116.

purely spiritual happiness and misery.[27] The medieval Muslim philosophers also believe in it, but not in physical happiness and misery.[28] This kind of purely spiritual form of happiness and misery is true no doubt, but its discussion here is unnecessary because the Qur'ān and Tradition are not very explicit on it. The foretastes of salvation and damnation in the form of physical reward and punishment mentioned above are not visible if the grave is dug, for the eyes of this world are unfit to see the affairs of the future world, which occur through the power of the Almightly and according to the pecualiar divine arrangements.[29]

At the stage of Resurrection and Judgement consisting of several phases, happiness and misery experienced as foretastes of salvation and damnation are more mental than physical. This stage begins with the rising of the dead from their graves on hearing the fierce sound of the trumpet blown by the angel Isrāfīl.[30] Everyone will be confused, nervous and terrified by this sound. In this mental state, when all will be led to the field of Judgement, the believers will go on foot, and the infidels on their faces.[31] This is a kind of bodily punishment to infidels, in addition to mental suffering. All creatures — men, angels, jinn, Satans, beasts, insects and so on — will assemble in the field of Judgement.[32] The sun will be near to men's heads, and its heat will increase greatly. There will be no wind and no shade whatsoever, except the shade of the throne of God. Only those who are drawn near to God (*al-muqarrabūn*) will be allowed under this shade.[33] This is a foretaste of the highest grade of salvation. People will perspire profusely through excess of sorrow. Sweat will flow in the field of Judgement and rise to some people's knees, to others' navels, and to still others' ears; these variations will depend upon variations in people's status with God.[34] All this is a foretaste of salvation and damnation. In that sorrowful state every human being will be brought to the Judgement seat where God Himself, without any veil and without any translator, will question him about everything, small and great, secret and public. God will conclude His questioning of an infidel by saying, "We disregard you today as you disregarded the meeting of this day of yours. Your resort is

[27]Al-Ghazālī, *Iḥyā'*, IV, 500ff. [28]*Idem., Tahāfut*, pp. 235-53.

[29]*Idem., Iḥyā'*, IV, 500.

[30]Qur'ān 18:99, 33:101, 36:51, 39:68, 69:13, 20:102, 78:18.

[31]Qur'ān 17:97, 25:34; al-Bukhārī, *Ṣaḥīḥ*, Riqāq, 81; Muslim, *Ṣaḥīḥ*, Musafirīn, 54.

[32]Qur'ān 38:19, 19:85, 20:102, 19:68, 6:128, 81:5.

[33]Al-Bukhārī, *Ṣaḥīḥ*, Adhān, 36; Muslim, *Ṣaḥīḥ*, Zakā, 91; at-Tirmidhī, *Sunan*, Zuhd, 53; an-Nasā'ī, *Sunan*, Quḍāt, 2.

[34]Al-Bukhārī, *Ṣaḥīḥ*, Riqāq, 47; Muslim, *Ṣaḥīḥ*, Janna, 60; at-Tirmidhī, *Sunan*, Qiyāma, 2; Ibn Māja, *Sunan*, Zuhd. 33; al-Ghazālī, *Iḥyā'*, IV, 514.

Hell."[35] At that moment how great will be his sorrow and grief! To a believer, however, God will be lenient: He will keep his faults secret and will not disclose them to all creatures present. God will ask him secretly, "Did you do such-and-such deeds?" He will reply, "Yes." God will say, "I kept them secret in the world and I forgive them today." At this his joy will know no bounds, and all others will envy him. This is an effect of future salvation.

After divine questioning, people's fates will be decided. Those who have no good whatever will be announced 'damned'. Concerning those who have no evil at all it will be declared, 'Salvation after which is no damnation.' The majority who mingle good with evil will come to the Balance where their actions will be weighed. The records of actions will fly and fall to the right hands of those who will be 'saved' and to the left hands of those who will be damned, even though temporarily.[36] One whose good acts outweigh the evil will be announced 'saved', but if the evil predominates one will be declared 'damned'.[37] This moment of declaration of salvation or damnation will be one of extreme joy or sorrow. Judgement will be made individually, and this is a reason why Islam is called an individualistic religion. This is true of Christianity as well. Some of those who are declared 'damned' will be saved by God's mercy or through the intercession of prophets, saints and other pious men. This will be discussed in a subsequent section.

All people then will proceed to the Bridge suspended over Hell to be crossed by everyone.[38] It will have hooks and thorns which will catch people at right and left. Those who are declared 'damned' will fall down the gulf of Hell. Others will pass over the Bridge in varying speeds: some like lightning, some like wind, some like a running horse, some will run, some will walk, and some will crawl with much difficulty;[39] these variations will depend on variations in the strength of faith and in the number and types of good works performed. Having crossed the Bridge all these people will enter into Paradise. They are the saved without being damned. Those who will fall down into Hell are the damned eternally or for a period of time, and their number will be 999 out of every thousand people.[40]

With men's entry to Paradise and Hell the last stage of the

[35]Qur'ān 7:51, 45:34. [36]Qur'ān 84:7, 10,69: 19,25, 45:28, 17:13.

[37]Qur'ān 7:8f., 101:6, 23:103, 101:8; al-Ghazālī, *Iḥyā'*, IV, 520. Mu'tazila heretics denied the weighing of actions on rational grounds. They interpret the Qur'ānic verses and prophetic traditions on this point. Ash'arite theologians refuted the arguments of Mu'tazilites.

[38]Qur'ān 37:23. Mu'tazila heretics denied the existence of the Bridge as well. Their arguments were refuted by Ash'arite theologians.

[39]Al-Bukhārī, *Ṣaḥīḥ*, Riqāq, 56; Muslim, *Ṣaḥīḥ*, Īmān, 299.

[40]Al-Bukhārī, *Ṣaḥīḥ*, Anbiyā', 7; Muslim, *Ṣaḥīḥ*, Fitan, 116.

Hereafter starts, and it is at this stage that salvation and damnation occur in their full degree. Damnation lies in one's entry to Hell, while salvation is found in deliverance from it and attainment of Paradise.[41] Attainment of Paradise without dwelling in Hell at all is called salvation free from damnation — a thing to be achieved by those who are declared 'saved' and those who are forgiven in the field of Judgement. But if the attainment of Paradise is after suffering in Hell for some time,[42] the length of which is to be commensurate with the degree of weakness in faith and with the number of sins committed, it is called salvation after damnation. It is to be attained by those believers who are declared 'damned' and who are not forgiven, through intercession, before entry to Hell. They will not be dwelling in Hell eternally, because they have faith in God the reward of which can only be given after deliverance from Hell. Only infidels will be suffering in Hell forever. Physical punishment in Hell is of different durations, types and degrees of intensity, and a damned man will suffer from the appropriate punishment in these respects. Hell has seven grades[43] which may be regarded as seven grades of damnation. These are commensurate with the seven bodily members by which sins are committed. Major elements of bodily torment are blazing fire, boiling water, smelly pus , poisonous snake-bite, hot coal tar, and so on, More intense than physical punishment is spiritual suffering caused by being veiled from God,[44] grief and remorse over the loss of delights in Paradise and over the misspent life.[45]

Opposite to Hell in all respects is Paradise which has eight gates commensurate with the principal acts of obedience to God. There are innumerable grades of happiness in Paradise,[46] depending upon innumerable differences in people's devotions and character-traits. These grades can be subsumed under a lower and a higher which may be regarded as the two grades of salvation or happiness. At the lower grade lies physical enjoyment of Huris, food, drink, beautiful palaces, and all other kinds of fleshly delights. Details of this enjoyment are to be found in the Qur'ān and Tradition, and show some similarity with the views of Rabbinic teachers — views rejected later

[41]Al-Ghazālī, *Iḥyā'*, IV, 543.

[42]Mu'tazila heretics hold that the man who enters into Hell will remain there for ever. Ash'arite theologians maintain that after suffering the appropriate torment every believer will find deliverance from Hell, and refute the arguments of Mu'tazilites. Detailed discussion of this and other controversies between these two classes of Muslim theologians is outside the scope of the present study.

[43]Qur'ān 15:44, 16:29.

[44]Qur'an 83:15.

[45]Qur'ān 19:39, 69:50, 2:167, 39:56, 6:31.

[46]Qur'ān 17:21, 6:132.

by Maimonides, Joseph Albo and others in favour of purely spiritual joy. Spiritual happiness consists in looking upon the glorious face of God for evermore. It is the highest grade of happiness and far more intense than physical enjoyment. It will give so intense a degree of pleasure that all other delights of Paradise will be forgotten in it.[47] The Prophet said,

> "No other thing will be more liked to dwellers of Paradise than looking upon the face of God."[48]

It is concerning the beatific vision that the Prophet said,

> "God (exalted is He!) says, 'I have prepared for My virtuous servants that which no eye has seen, no ear has heard, and nor has entered into the mind of any human being.' "[49]

These words of God are also found to be recorded in previous Scriptures.[50] The beatific vision is also referred to in the Qur'ānic verses.

> "No soul knows what supreme bliss is kept hidden from them, as a reward for what they used to do."[51]
> (فلا تعلم نفس ماأخفى لهم من قرةأعين، جزاء بماكانوا يعملون.)

> "For those who do good, there will be a good recompense and more besides [i.e. vision of God]."[52]
> (للذين احسنوا الحسنى وزيادة.)

The ṣūfīs lay supreme importance upon these Qur'ānic verses and prophetic traditions, for it is they who are most concerned with the highest form of salvation. Their aim is the vision of their Beloved and not the fleshly delights of Paradise the existence of which, of course, they do not deny[53] as did the medieval Muslim philosophers.

Between Paradise and Hell there is a place called A'rāf where there will be neither reward nor punishment of any kind. Some people, who will be neither condemned to Hell nor entitled to Paradise on the ground that they neither disobeyed God nor obeyed Him, will

[47] Al-Ghazālī, *Iḥyā'*, IV, 543.

[48] Muslim, *Ṣaḥīḥ*, Īmān, 297; at-Tirmidhī, ***Sunan***, Janna, 16; Ibn Māja, ***Sunan***, Muqaddma, 13.

[49] Al-Bukhārī, *Ṣaḥīḥ*, Tawḥīd, 35; Muslim, *Ṣaḥīḥ*, Īmān, 312; Ibn Māja, ***Sunan***, Zuhd, 139.

[50] Isaiah 64:4; I Corinthians 2:9. [51] Qur'ān 32:17. [52] Qur'ān 10:26.

[53] Al-Ghazālī, *Iḥyā'*, IV, 543; al-Makkī, *Qūt*, II, 257.

be dwelling in A'rāf.[54] They cannot be called saved in the usual Qur'ānic sense of the term, because even though the fundamental idea in salvation is safety from punishment in Hell, this safety alone is not salvation; for salvation it needs to be conjoined with reward in Paradise. Some ṣūfīs,[55] however, regard them as saved, emphasizing the fundamental idea in salvation which is safety from punishment. They make a distinction between salvation and success in that while the former consists in safety the latter in entitlement to reward after it. The word 'prosperity' is considered by them as a synonym of 'success'.[56] In the Qur'ān, however, this distinction is not obvious.

From the above account it will be seen that salvation in the Qur'ānic sense is attainable only in the life to come, and that the decision on it will also be made in that life; it is impossible, then, to say anything categorically concerning the ultimate fate of an individual believer, even though some indication of it can be found.[57] Salvation in the Hereafter is a continuous process, beginning from the life immediately after death and culminating in the life in Paradise; in this process it is a receiving, not a becoming; it is the receiving of the fruit of faith and action performed in this life. In Christianity, by constrast, salvation is achieved in this world through the redemption by Christ and the faith and works (or action) of the individual; but it has also its future meaning to a certain extent. It is a becoming; it is moral transformation; it is a change from sin to holiness; it is only from sin in its four aspects, namely, the pleasure of sin, the penalty of sin, the power of sin, and the presence of sin: these are distinct phases or stages of salvation. The underlying idea is that sin is destructive to man's spiritual life, his true life, in as much as it destroys his communion with God in righteousness and love; therefore he must be delivered from it first of all. Such deliverance is possible here and now. When it is made actual a new spiritual life is achieved through which the interrupted communion or fellowship with God is restored. Thus salvation is primarily deliverance from sin. Islamic teaching is that sin stands between man and God no doubt, but he is not dead in it; so no new birth of

[54]Qur'ān 7:46,48.

[55]Al-Ghazālī, *Iḥyā'*, IV, 30f.

[56]*Ibid.*, p. 31; al-Makkī, *Qūt*, II, 540.

[57]If an individual finds the path of good easy to follow, this indicates that he will be among the saved. If, however, when he intends to do something good, he faces obstacles and averts it, whereas if he does not intend to do evil it becomes easy for him so that he does it, this is a clear indication that he will be one of the damned. Al-Ghazālī says that this is an inference, just as fire is an inference from smoke (al-Ghazālī, *Iḥyā'*, IV, 535). The concept of this symptom was originally given by the Prophet; see al-Bukhārī, *Qadar*, 20; Ibn Ḥanbal, *Musnad*, IV, 427.

the spirit is needed; he must, however, repent. Man is not by nature in a position from which he needs to be redeemed. He commits sin from which he must repent; his repentance is not salvation, but only a means to it; salvation is safety from the punishment of sin in the life after death. The problem of the means to salvation should thus be discussed now in some detail.

THE MEANS TO SALVATION

The Means to Salvation on the Human Side

The Qur'ān teaches that the means to salvation in the Hereafter on the human side are belief or faith (*īmān*)[58] and action (*'amal*): salvation cannot be achieved without these two means. Both of them are mentioned in most of the verses of the Qur'ān containing references to salvation;[59] in a few such verses, however, only faith is mentioned explicitly, but action is implicit in them. That faith and action are the requirements of salvation on the human side is also the teaching of the prophetic tradition which is but an elaboration of what is briefly taught by the Qur'ān. The prophetic tradition presents us with details of faith and action as means to salvation. Closely following this teaching of the Qur'ān and Tradition, Islamic jurisprudence, theology and ṣūfīsm have unanimously agreed that faith and action are the only two means to salvation. In working out the details of these means, however, they differ slightly among themselves. Thus jurisprudence accepts the outward meanings of the teachings of the Qur'ān and Tradition, without feeling the need to exblore their deep, inward meanings. Ṣūfīsm, in addition to outward meanings, looks for inward meanings; it also adds material learnt from experience[60] but not inconsistent with the Qur'ānic teachings. Islamic theology adds arguments to these teachings and is concerned more with defence of common men's beliefs against the heretical innovations than leading them to practice.[61] While jurusprudence, theology and ṣūfīsm equally emphasize faith and action as the two basic requirements of salvation, Islamic philosophy of the medieval times believed that faith or knowledge alone was the means to salvation and that action was not needed very

[58]The word 'belief' is used in this book as a synonym of the term 'faith'. The question whether they have exactly the same meaning or not need not be discussed here. Saving faith in the Biblical sense is always more than belief; see James 2:19 .

[59]Qur'ān 2:25, 4:57, 122, 173, 5:9, 13:29, 14:23, 18:107, 22:14, 23, *passim*.

[60]Abū Ḥāmid Muḥammad al-Ghazālī, *al-Munqidh min aḍ-Ḍalāl*, ed. 'Abd al-Ḥalīm Maḥmūd, Cairo, 1955, p.111.

[61]*Ibid.*, p. 90.

much.[62] This reflects the influence of Greek thought on Islamic philosophy. It is a sharp deviation from the Qur'ānic teaching and condemned by ṣūfīs as delusion. Ṣūfīs put a great emphasis upon the Qur'ānic teaching that faith and action are both needed if man is to ascend from the rank of lower animals to that of those who behold the beauty of the glorious face of God.[63] Jesus, Moses and all other previous prophets of God also taught faith and action to be the only two means to salvation on the human side. It is only later that other thoughts, such as the atonement (in Christianity) and the ancestral merit (in Judaism) were invented and sought to be somehow justified by the teachings of Jesus and Moses themselves. Islam rejects these other thoughts as later inventions.

Concerning the relationship between faith and action as the two means to salvation on the human side the Qur'ān teaches that the former precedes the latter in order as well as in importance.[64] Islam, like other religions, whether revealed or man-made, has two aspects: doctrinal and practical. The former is identical with faith or the theoretical or inward aspect of Islam, while the latter is the same as works or action or the outward aspect of Islam. Faith precedes action: it is, as it were, the nucleus, the centre, the most fundamental part of Islam. Action follows faith; it is prescribed in keeping with faith; it is the outcome of faith. In the absence of the faith aspect there can be no Islam at all, and consequently no salvation even after damnation for a long time;[65] but if the action aspect is totally neglected Islam can still be said to exist even though in an imperfect form, and so salvation is possible although after damnation for a long time.[66] This is the teaching of the Qur'ān and Tradition. Of the two means to salvation faith is more basic and more important than action. By faith man enters into the Islamic life — a thing which has some similarity with what is called 'justification' in Christianity, for justification is by faith.[67] By action he progresses in this life; this corresponds to the Christian concept of 'sanctification.'

The treatment of all aspects of Qur'ānic teaching on faith and action as the two means to salvation is not appropriate to this study; what is appropriate is only to present that aspect which concerns the

[62] *Idem.*, *Ayyuhā l-Walad*, tr. George H. Scherer, Beirut, 1933, p. 54.

[63] *Idem.*, *al-Arabaʿīn fī Uṣūl ad-Dīn*, Egypt, 1344 A.H., p. 293.

[64] It is for this reason that faith precedes action in numerous Qur'ānic verses where both of them are mentioned.

[65] Qur'ān 24:39.

[66] Al-Bukhārī, *Ṣaḥīḥ*, Jihād, 102; Muslim, *Ṣaḥīḥ*, Īmān, 47; at-Tinmidhī, ***Sunan***, Īmān, 17; Ibn Ḥanbal, *Musnad*, III, 467.

[67] Acts 13:39; Romans 5:1; Galatians, 3:8.

relationship of devotional acts with salvation. Since, however, action presupposes faith for its validity and efficacy and since devotional acts form, as will be shown shortly, part of action in general, it is necessary first to give a brief outline of faith with reference to salvation. It is only after this that the relationship of devotional acts with salvation may be considered.

Faith and Salvation

The faith taught by the Qur'ān and Tradition is very simple to understand and to form within oneself; its understanding is much easier than that of the Christian faith which involves the Trinity, sin, atonement and so on. It has three basic ingredients — so basic that absence of any one of them negates the presence of faith as a whole. Each basic ingredient has certain other beliefs attached to it, and these beliefs are such that they only perfect the basic ingredient, add meaning and significance to it; without them also the basic element can exist, though imperfectly. The three basic elements are not of the same importance: one of them is the most fundamental and forms the basis of the other two. All three elements are needed for salvation.

1. The most fundamental ingredient of Islamic faith is belief in the oneness of God. The Qur'ān bears constant witness to the absolute unity of God; indeed its major aim is to call mankind to this unity.[68] This most basic element finds its essential expression in the hundred and twelfth sura of the Qur'ān which runs thus:

> "Proclaim: He is God, the Single; God, the Self-existing and Besought of all. He does not beget, nor is He begotten; and there is none like Him."[69]
>
> (قل هوالله أحد. الله الصمد. لم يلد، ولم يولد. ولم يكن له كفوا أحد.)

Thus the crux of Islamic faith is that God is one; there are no two gods or more in whatever relationships they may exist mutually. The Qur'ān asserts that oneness of God was the original teaching of all previous revealed religions, including Christianity and Judaism, and that later on, their votaries changed that teaching for certain reasons.[70] Just as Jesus did not seek to create a wholly new faith by destroying "the law or the prophets,"[71] so the faith of Islam is not

[68] Muhammad Abul Quasem, *The Jewels of the Qur'ān: al-Ghazālī's Theory*, 2nd ed., Kuala Lumpur, Malaysia, 1980, p. 21.

[69] Qur'ān 112:1-4.

[70] Qur'ān 2:85, 4:46, 5:13, 41.

[71] Matthew 5:17f.; Qur'ān 5:46.

something entirely new; it is the confirmation and restoration of the *original* belief of the previous revealed religions in the oneness of God.[72] God is not like the impersonal Absolute of philosophy; rather He is personal: He is eternal, Self-subsisting, All-creating and All-sustaining reality; He has the attributes of power, knowledge, will, hearing, seeing and speaking. His attributes are such as befit Him; they are not like human attributes.[73] Associated with faith in oneness of God is faith in the angels, a type of intelligent being different from man, whom God created out of light. Human beings, except prophets, cannot see them in their original nature, but can see them when they take material form. They perform various functions on behalf of God. They are fully dependent upon God in their functions — they do only what they are commanded to by the one God. Among the angels, four — Isrāfīl (Raphael), Jibrā'īl (Gabriel), Mikā'īl (Michael), and 'Azrā'īl (Azrael) — are the greatest.

2. The second fundamental ingredient of Islamic faith is belief in the prophecy of Muḥammad. He was the last prophet. Every previous prophet of God was sent to a particular people, but Muḥammad was sent to all human beings of the world until Doomsday. This universality is explicit in the Qur'ān[74] and Tradition.[75] The message of God passed by Muḥammad to the whole of mankind is the Qur'ān revealed to him through the angel Gabriel who used to convey divine messages to previous prophets. Thus belief in Muḥammad's prophecy is bound up with belief in the Qur'ān as the speech of God addressed to all human beings of the world.

Associated with these beliefs is faith in all prophets of all previous revealed religions and in all Scriptures revealed to them. From the time of Adam to that of Muḥammad 124,000 prophets were sent by God; they all, including Jesus and Moses, were true prophets.[76] They all were human beings fully: Jesus, the Qur'ān asserts, was son of Mary and not of God; he was created by God in the same way as Adam was created from soil; he was the word of God in the sense that God said 'be' and he was without father;[77] there was no divine partnership in him;[78] he was a loyal servant of God who never claimed that he was divine in any sense. Muḥammad, though the last in

[72] Qur'ān 2:130, 135, 5:95, 4:125, 6:161, 19:123, 22:78 where Islam is regarded as continuation of the purely monotheistic religion of the prophet Abraham.

[73] Al-Ghazālī, *Iḥyā'*, I, 108-10.

[74] Qur'an 34:28.

[75] Al-Bukhārī, *Ṣaḥīḥ*, Tayammum, 1; ad-Dārimī, *Sunan*, Siyar, 28.

[76] Qur'ān 2:136, 3:84, 4:163.

[77] Qur'ān 3:59, 4:171, 5:114, 19:34, 61:60.

[78] Qur'ān 5:116, 4:171, 5:73.

an uninterrupted chain of the prophets, was the greatest of them all in merit in the estimation of God. The previous revealed Scriptures are 104, four of which are long, while the remaining revelations are referred to as only Leaves (*ṣuḥuf*).[79] The four long Scriptures are the Torah, the Gospel, the Psalms, and the Qur'ān. Of the Leaves, ten were revealed to Adam, fifty to Shīth (Seth), thirty to Idrīs (Enoch), and ten to Abraham.[80] These previous revelations, so long as they remained unaltered, were the same as the Qur'ān in essential beliefs; they too taught oneness of God, prophecy and the life after death. But because of alterations made in them by their followers differences occurred between them and the Qur'ān.

The two above mentioned ingredients of faith form the well-known *shahāda*, the confession of faith. The *shahāda* is so essential a part of faith that it alone, without the remaining part, is generally known as faith or *īmān*. It is a witness to the faith expressed in:

> "I give witness that there is no god but God, and I give witness that Muḥammad is His servant and messenger "
> (اشهد ان لاالـه الاالله، واشهد ان محمدا عبده ورسولـه.)

3. The third fundamental ingredient of faith is belief in life after death. All prophets of God taught this belief. Arguments are put forward in numerous Qur'ānic verses to prove the reality of life after death.[81] The Qur'ān also gives details of man's states in that life. Traditions supply greater details of these states but not arguments for the reality of the world to come. The life after death starts from immediately after a man's death and continues eternally, without an end. The body is destroyed after death, but the soul survives, On the Day of Resurrection a body will be created and the soul united with it. Thus the resurrected man will have both body and soul and will be immortal in this form. The deceased remains in the grave and is either punished or enjoys happiness according to the life he lived in this world. On the Day of Resurrection the reckoning of whatever he did in this life — small or great — will take place, and he will either be admitted to Paradise or condemned to Hell. Belief in these main points about the Hereafter is sufficient for salvation; knowledge of more details of it is not essential, but only useful. The physical nature of future life is so strongly emphasized in the Qur'ān and Tradition that its denial is considered as infidelity (*kufr*), which causes eternal damnation.

[79] Abū Ja'far Muḥammad ibn Jarīr aṭ-Ṭabarī, *Tārīkh al- Umam wa l-Mulūk*, Egypt, n.d., I, 86.

[80] *Ibid*.

[81] E.g. Qur'ān 7:57, 22:6, 41:39, 46:33, 15:40.

That the three fundamental beliefs discussed above — belief in oneness of God, prophecy of Muḥammad and life after death — together with the other beliefs associated with them, form the faith of Islam is stated in numerous Qur'ānic verses, three of which may be quoted as follows:

> "The righteous are those who believe in God, the Last Day, the angels, the Book, and the prophets."[82]
>
> (ولكن البر من امن باالله واليوم الاخر والملئكة والكتاب والنبيين.)
>
> "Anyone who disbelieves in God, His angels, His Books, His messengers, and the Last Day, has surely strayed far away."[83]
>
> (ومن يكفر بالله وملئكته وكتبه ورسله واليوم الاخر، فقد ضل ضلالا بعيدا.)
>
> "All — the Messengers and the believers — believe in God, His angels, His Books, and His messengers, affirming: we make no distinction among any of His messengers."[84]
>
> (كل امن بالله وملئكته وكتبه ورسله؛ لانفرق بين احد من رسله.)

Faith just outlined is, according to the Qur'ān, the only wholly valid faith to be found on the surface of the earth since the advent of Islam until Doomsday. Faiths of previous revealed religions are not entirely free from corruption now and so cannot be a means to salvation. That the faith of Islam is the only completely valid faith is clearly stated in the following two Qur'ānic verses:

> "Surely the true religion in the estimation of God is Islam."[85]
>
> (ان الدين عند الله الاسلام.)
>
> "Whoever seeks a religion other than Islam, it shall not be accepted from him, and in the life to come he will be among the losers."[86]
>
> (ومن يبتغ غير الاسلام دينا، فلن يقبل منه، وهو في الاخرة من الخاسرين.)

Formation of faith described above in a nutshell is possible in one of three ways which have relevance to salvation. Faith must be absolutely certain if it is to serve as a means to salvation. Certainty of faith, however, has different degrees. The lowest degree exists when

[82] Qur'ān 2:177.
[83] Qur'ān 4:136.
[84] Qur'ān 2:285.
[85] Qur'ān 3:19.
[86] Qur'ān 3:85.

a man fully believes in God, the prophecy of Muḥammad and the Last Day by hearing these from an authority. It is in this way that common men form their faith which is sufficient for salvation free from damnation. This salvation, however, is of a low degree, since the certainty of faith is also low. Many Qur'ānic verses mean this way of formation of faith. The Prophet was also fully content with people's faith acquired in this way. A more certain faith is generally believed to be that which is formed by way of arguments of theology. This faith, theologians claim, causes a high degree of salvation. The most certain faith is that of a ṣūfī based on his mystical intuition (*kashf*). The ṣūfī's intuitive knowledge of God, prophecy and affairs of the Hereafter is extremely clear and comprehensive. Such knowledge makes his faith most certain, and it is this faith which causes the highest grade of salvation.

Devotional Acts and Salvation

With the inculcation of faith outlined above a man gets entry into Islam and thus fulfils the most basic requirement of salvation. This faith must continue to exist throughout his life; it must remain in his mind at the time of his death.[87] Faith alone, however, is not sufficient: from the entry into Islam through faith he has to make progress and develop the faith through action performed in the light of the teachings of the Qur'ān and Tradition. Faith and action correspond to what is called in Christianity 'justification' and 'sanctification' respectively. Action has in it an element of faith and thus presupposes faith; without faith it is invalid.[88] It in turn contributes to the strengthening of faith. Thus faith and action taken together perfect the life and bring about salvation.

Action prescribed by Islam is relevant to the entire practical aspect of a man's life. This is because Islam is divine guidance for the life of a man in its entirety at both the theoretical and practical levels. It is for this all inclusiveness that Islam is called a complete code of life and a religion which differs from some other religions which regulate only part of the life of human being. Action as a means to salvation concerns domestic, social, political, economic, devotional and all other practical aspects of a man's life. This can be clarified by an example. A Muslim's work in a factory or in a paddy field in order to earn his livelihood appears to be a secular act, but it is not really so; in reality it is a religious act, altough its merit is less than that of his performance of a ritual prayer recommended by

[87] Al-Bukhārī, *Ṣaḥīḥ*, Janā'iz, 1. [88] Qur'ān 24:39.

Islam. The latter is remembrance of God itself and thus directly improves his relationship with God, and so its place is at the top of religious acts. The former is a means to the latter and thus has a religious quality, but because it is only a means the degree of its religious quality is lower.[89]

Thus all activities of a Muslim may fall under the heading 'religious acts'. Their categorization is made in various ways. The broadest and commonest way is one done by considering the relationship of acts with objects to which they are directed. From this perspective acts are divided into two categories, namely, man-directed and God-directed. The former are those which are performed in relationship with one's fellow men, whether at home or in society or elsewhere. These acts are called *mu'āmalāt* in Islamic literature. A non-Muslim may regard them as secular acts, but in Islam these have a religious nature because they are ordained by God and have to be performed under His guidance. Thus a Muslim's attitude towards his fellow human beings has in it an element of his attitude towards God; to be good or bad to other people in one's social behaviour is the fruit of his strong or weak faith in God.

As for the God-directed acts they are also prescribed by God and have to be performed under His guidance. Most of them, e.g. ritual prayer, fasting, pilgrimage, Qur'ān-reading, have no relationship with anyone other than God: these are performed only for pleasing God. Some God-directed acts have primary relationship with God, but secondary concern with men. An example of these acts is divine tax (*zakā*) which is paid primarily to please God but secondarily to please the beneficiaries. Because of exclusively or primarily divine concern the God-directed acts are called devotional acts or simple devotions (*'ibādāt*) in Islam. They are more important than man-directed act — the reason why their treatment in Islamic literature precedes that of the acts directed towards men. God-directed acts form worship itself, and to them is the direct reference of the Qur'ānic verse:

> "I only created jinn and man that they might worship Me "[90] (وماخلقت الجن والانس الا ليعبدون).

Correct performance of God-directed acts is a means to salvation, and this is the main concern of the present study. Salvation is also dependent upon proper performance of man-directed acts. This

[89] Many Muslims fail to realize this relation of means and end. They regard all acts as having equal religious value.

[90] Qur'ān 51:56.

means that in a man's behaviour with his fellow human beings the requirement of justice and equity as taught by Islam must be fulfilled — injustice and oppression must be avoided. The question of guarding against injustice will not be dealt with in detail in this work, for the main concern of this book is with devotions.

Islamic devotions are of two types, namely obligatory and supererogatory. Obligatory devotional acts are ritual prayer (*ṣalā*), fasting, divine tax (*zakā*), and pilgrimage to Mecca. Ritual prayer is obligatory five times a day; more than this is supererogatory. Fasting during one full lunar month Ramaḍān is obligatory; to fast on other great days of the year is supererogatory. Divine tax is obligatory on a rich Muslim annually; his payment of more than the fixed rate is supererogatory; donations by a person who is not obliged to do so is also a supererogatory act. Pilgrimage to Mecca is obligatory once in a person's lifetime provided he fulfils certain stipulations; his performance of it more than once is a supererogatory act; likewise it is a supererogatory act if it is performed by a person on whom it is not obligatory. Thus the four obligatory devotional acts sometimes become supererogatory.

These four acts of devotion together with just behaviour with one's fellow men form the second primary means to salvation, the first being faith. Without them salvation wholly free from damnation cannot be achieved. Just as continuation of faith until death is essential, so is perseverance in these devotions (as well as in just behaviour). This is explicit in the following Qur'ānic verse:

> "Worship your Lord until death overtakes you "[91]
> (واعبد ربك حتى يأتيك اليقين).

The Prophet, when asked concerning the means of other worldly happiness, said,

> "Happiness lies in worship of God in a long life."[92]

A break in perseverance in devotions or worship, which occurs in the case of many people, does not negate salvation totally: it can be made good through repentance (*tawba*). Neglect of any of the four obligatory devotions even once is a grave sin, but this sin, like all other grave sins, can be remedied by repentance which consists of three elements, namely, remorse (*nadam*) over the past shortcomings in devotions, reparation of them, and resolve not to neglect devotions in future.[93] When all these elements are present, repen-

[91] Qur'ān 15:99.

[92] Ibn Ḥanbal, *Musnad*, III, 332.

tance is accepted by God, and it is about this repentance that the Prophet said,

> "One who has repented from sin is like one who has no sin."[94]

This agrees with Christianity which teaches that if all the elements are found in a repentance sins are blotted out.[95]

The 'saving' merit of the four obligatory devotions accrues from their perfect performance which, of course, is impossible in the case of most people. Imperfections occur in devotions for several reasons the most important of which are: Satanic influence, evil nature of the carnal soul (*nafs*),[96] and weakness of faith. Satan gives evil suggestions to man's mind against engagement in devotions; if these suggestions are repelled and devotions are started, evil suggestions are given again with the result that the devotee fails to perform them perfectly. The carnal soul is by nature reluctant to perform devotional acts which is something not very easy; it, moreover, is incited to evil by Satan. The evil of the carnal soul is also spoken of in Christian Scriptures.[97] Weakness of faith causes lack of enthusiasm in devotions and of proper attention to them after they are started. Imperfections in the obligatory devotions caused mostly by these factors can be made good by occasional performance of them as supererogatory devotions in the way just mentioned. In the case of gross imperfections, there is a severe need of their performance as supererogatory, otherwise salvation will be impossible. If imperfections are little, as in the case of saints and ascetics, performance of obligatory acts as supererogatory will effect the higher grade of salvation. Concerning making good by acts of supererogation the Prophet said that on the Day of Judgement when a man's obligatory works will be found wanting God will ask, "Has My servant got any supererogatory devotions?"

Aside from the four obligatory devotions which can also be performed as supererogatory, there are three devotional acts which are always supererogatory. They are Qur'ān-recitation, remembrance of God (*dhikr Allāh*), and supplication (*du'ā'*) to Him. Qur'ān-recitation by a Muslim is an act of devotion even if he does not

[93]The need of repentance for salvation is also emphasized in Christian Scriptures (Luke 5:32, 13:3, 5; Acts 17:30, 26:20; Mark 1:15; II Corinthians 7:10; II Timothy 2:25; II Peter 3:9) and Judaism. The three elements of repentance in Islam are also the elements of saving repentance in Christianity.

[94]Ibn Māja, *Sunan*, Zuhd, 30.

[95]Acts 2:38, 3:19.

[96]Al-Ghazālī, *Iḥyā'*, IV, 404-408.

[97]Romans 8:7; Jeremiah 17:9.

understand its meaning. Just as the meaning of the Qur'ān is divine, so is its language. This is a special feature of the Holy Book of Islam; no other Scripture of world religions possesses this characteristic. Remembrance of God by praising Him and mentioning His names is regarded, in certain circumstances, as the best of all supererogatory acts of devotions, provided it is performed continually and with full attention of the mind.[98] Supplication to God is called by the Prophet "the marrow of devotional acts,"[99] because what should exist in the devotee's mind are self-abasement and helplessness, and divine greatness and might, and these are necessarily present in any true supplication. As an independent act of devotion it is treated in detail in Islamic literature.

These three devotions are independent acts of supererogation, even though parts of them are included in the four obligatory devotions discussed above. Just as the obligatory devotions, when performed as supererogatory acts, aim at making good the imperfections occuring in them when performed as obligatory, so also are the three purely supererogatory devotions: they aim at making good the shortcomings that occur in obligatory acts. In addition to this compensatory aim which is ultimately for making salvation *possible* only, the three supererogatory acts aim at creating and establishing a very close relationship between man and God — a relationship by which the higher grade of salvation is achieved. God is very compassionate; out of compassion He has recommended the performance of these three devotions so that by it man may achieve nearness to Him and consequently the higher degree of salvation. This is explicit in a holy Tradition (*al-ḥadīth al-qudsī*) which runs thus:

> "God (blessed and exalted is He!) says, 'Nothing brings men near to Me like the performance of that which I made obligatory upon them, and through supererogatory acts My servant [i.e. man] comes even nearer to Me until I love him. When I have bestowed My love on him, I become [as if] his hearing with which he hears, his sight, with which he sees, his tongue with which he speaks, his hand with which he grasps, and his feet with which he walks.'"[100]

The degree of nearness to God mentioned in this 'holy Tradition' marks the highest growth in Islamic life which causes the highest grade of salvation. This is achieved by means of perseverance in both obligatory and supererogatory devotional acts and in justice to other

[98]See *infra*, p. 259. [99]See *infra*, pp. 263f.
[100]Al-Bukhārī, *Ṣaḥīḥ*, Riqāq, 38; Ibn Ḥanbal, *Musnad*, IV, 256.

people, after the entry into Islam through faith. The basic requirement, however, is faith. Thus faith and action (i.e. devotions and just behaviour) taken together form the means to salvation on the human side. For convenience we call them the two means, but really they form one means: they are indistinguishable. Action (including devotions) alone is useless; faith alone cannot cause salvation free from damnation; (it can cause salvation after damnation).

The Parts of Devotional Acts and Salvation

It has been mentioned above that a devotional act which is obligatory as a whole, e.g. an obligatory ritual prayer, differs, in respect of value and importance for salvation, from a devotional act which as a whole is supererogatory, e.g. a supererogatory ritual prayer, although they both are means to it. Differences in effecting salvation also occur as regards parts of a devotional act, whether obligatory or supererogatory. An act of devotion, e.g. a ritual prayer, is a totality, a whole consisting of several parts which are words, gestures, bodily acts, mental attitudes and so on. These parts are not of the same category, even though the devotional act as a whole is obligatory or supererogatory; rather some of them are obligatory, some required, some praiseworthy and so on. Different categories of parts have different degrees of merit in effecting salvation. We shall briefly mention here all these categories together with brief definitions of them. We shall also indicate their relationships with salvation.

1. The first category consists of the obligatory (*farḍ*) parts of a devotional act. These parts are also called the pillars (*arkān*) of an act of devotion. Non-observance or incorrect observance of any one of them even though for an excuse, e.g. forgetfulness, renders the entire devotional act null and void. Wiping the head, for instance, is obligatory in a ritual ablution; its omission, for whatever reason, invalidates ablution as a whole.

2. The second category consists of the required (*wājib*) parts. Their commission earns reward from God and their omission causes punishment in the Hereafter. Omission of any one of them *forgetfully* in a devotional act makes the act imperfect, but not invalid as in the case of the omission of an obligatory part; this imperfection can, however, be made good, before completing the devotional act, by performing the Prostration for Forgetfulness--a thing which is not possible in the case of the omission of an obligatory part. For *deliberate* omission of a required part the devotional act must be repeated. If the act is not repeated, or if, in the case of the omission

of a required part forgetfully, the Prostration for Forgetfulness is not performed, the devotional act is to be regarded as having been performed only imperfectly.

3. The third category is that of sunna. Sunna literally means a way, a path which may be good or evil. Technically it means the religious path trodden by the Prophet without being considered by him as required or obligatory. Sunna is of two kinds: emphasized (*mu'akkada*) and praiseworthy (*mandūb, mustaḥab*). An act is emphasized sunna if the Prophet persisted in it; it is only once or twice in his lifetime that he omitted it without an excuse. An act is praiseworthy sunna if he did not persist in it but did it many times in his lifetime. Praiseworthy sunna is sometimes referred to as simply sunna. Commission of an emphasized sunna act earns reward from God; its omission causes, not punishment, but reproach of Him. In the case of the praiseworthy sunna, reward is obtained by its commission, but neither reproach nor punishment is caused by its deliberate omission.

4. At the fourth level are placed those parts which are called the good manners or etiquette (*ādāb*) of a devotional act. These parts are those which the Prophet performed only once or twice in his lifetime. Their observance is a means of reward from God but their omission is not blameworthy. Examples are: reading the formulae of glorification of God (*tasbīḥāt*) many times in the bowing and prostrations of a ritual prayer; reading the Qur'ān in a ritual prayer more than that measure of it which is sunna.

Those parts of a devotional act which are called sunna, whether emphasized or not, and the parts regarded as the etiquette of an act are sometimes put under the more general category of supererogatory (*nafl, (tatawwu'*) parts of a devotional act.

5. At the lowest level are placed those parts which are called permissible or allowed (*mubāḥ, jā'iz*) in a devotional act. They cause neither divine pleasure nor divine displeasure. Legally they are neutral acts.

There are certain things which are irrelevant to a devotional act. They form its negative aspect just as the parts making it up form its positive aspect. In the negative aspect too there are several grades which are as follows:

1. At the highest grade are those things which are called unlawful (*ḥarām*), forbidden (*mamnū'*), not allowed, or not permissible (*ghayr jā'iz*). A thing is unlawful in a devotional act if its unlawfulness is established by a proof that is absolutely certain. A devotional act in which such a thing occurs must be repeated.

2. The second grade consists of those things which are called disliked (*makrūh*). The disliked things are of two kinds, namely, gravely disliked (*makrūh taḥrīmī*) and slightly disliked (*makrūh tanzīhī*). The former is nearer to the unlawful than to the lawful, while the latter is nearer to the lawful than to the unlawful. Both cause divine displeasure and punishment in the Hereafter: for the former the degree of punishment is greater than that for the latter. A devotional act in which anything disliked, whether gravely or slightly, is done is to be regarded as correct but disliked ; it should be repeated.

The above mentioned grades relating to the positive and negative aspects of a devotional act can be represented in the form of the following diagram:

Positive aspect

		Obligatory (فرض)	1
		Required (واجب)	2
Supererogatory (تطوع، نفل)	Sunna (سنة)	emphasized sunna (سنة موءكدة)	3a
Supererogatory (تطوع، نفل)	Sunna (سنة)	praiseworthy (مندوب، مستحب)	3b
Supererogatory (تطوع، نفل)		Good manners or etiquette (آداب)	4
Supererogatory (تطوع، نفل)		Permissible or allowed (مباح، جائز)	5

Negative aspect

	Unlawful (حرام، ممنوع، غيرجائز)	1
Disliked (مكروه)	gravely disliked (مكروه تحريمى)	2a
Disliked (مكروه)	slightly disliked (مكروه تنزيهى)	2b

Clear understanding of these grades is a prerequisite to an apprehension of books on Islamic devotional acts where the parts of these various grades are discussed very frequently without an explanation of their meaning. This understanding is also essential for the practice of devotional acts properly. Many devotees who lack this understanding often become victims of illusion: sometimes, neglecting an obligatory act, they engage themselves in a supererogatory act; sometimes they become so deeply involved in a supererogatory act that they cross the proper limit to the blameworthy access.[101] What is necessary for a worshipper is to maintain order among various good acts. All obligatory acts must be preferred to all supererogatory acts.

[101] Al-Ghazālī, *Iḥyā'*, III, 400f.

A devotional act is only perfected by the observance of all its parts, obligatory and supererogatory: the imperfection that usually occurs in obligatory parts is made good by the supererogatory parts; if the imperfection is little the supererogatory parts cause an increase in the spiritual condition of the devotee. An individual who limits himself to the obligatory parts only is in danger, for he has nothing to compensate for the defect that usually occurs in them. A devotee who, in addition to the performance of all obligatory parts almost perfectly, performs all supererogatory parts in proper manner is gradually drawn near to God as stated in a Tradition.[102]

Devotional acts produce good effect on the soul of a person who performs them with a fully sincere intention (*ikhlāṣ*)—an intention with which no worldly motive is mixed.[103] In fact it is for their effects on the soul of a devotee that they are prescribed by God. As a result of a man's performance of them, the soul becomes illumined and the faith (*īmān*) strengthened and alive. Consequently he obtains salvation in the Hereafter.[104]

The Means to Salvation on the Divine Side: Intercession and Divine Mercy

Faith and action, including devotions, are treated in the preceding section as the two means to salvation on the human side. There are two more things — intercession and divine mercy — which will also cause salvation of believers in the world to come. Neither of these two causes is wholly separate from faith and action; rather each of them involves faith and action somehow or other. They are the two means to salvation on the divine side. Intercession may appear at first sight to be something not divine, but since on analysis it is found to be dependent upon God's mercy needed for its initiation and for its acceptance, it is to be regarded as a cause of salvation on the divine side. Intercession and divine mercy in relation to salvation are, like faith and action, clearly set forth in the Qur'ān and prophetic tradition; they are very easy to understand and to acquire and not complicated like the Christian concept of intercession and divine grace in relation to salvation. A brief account of them we propose to give here. From this account it will be seen that intercession and divine mercy in Islam have not much similarity with the Christian

[102]Al-Bukhārī, *Ṣaḥīḥ*, Riqāq, 38; Ibn Ḥanbal, *Musnad*, IV, 256.

[103]For the Qur'ānic emphasis upon sincerity see Qur'ān 39:2, 11, 14, 7:29, 4:14, 65, 98:5, 39:3.

[104]For a brief account of al-Ghazālī's view on Islamic devotions see Muḥammad Abul Quasem, "Al-Ghazālī's Theory of Devotional Acts", *IQ*, XVIII, 48-61.

notions of them. In fact, these two are among those problems where comparison can hardly be made between Islam and Christianity.

In Islam intercession as a means to salvation connotes one's prayer to God for the forgiveness of others in the Hereafter. In Christianity, however, it has a wider significance, and expresses the more general idea of Christ's acting for others, of his being surety for them. Islamic theory is that for salvation intercession will take place at two stages: on the Day of Judgement and after the sinners' entry to Hell. On the Day of Judgement it will take place first before the divine questioning; it is the prophet Muḥammad who will intercede first for the forgiveness of his community. Accepting this intercession, God will grant him permission to take, to Paradise through its right gate (*al-bāb al-ayman*) built for them especially, all those people of his community who are entitled to it without giving an account of their actions.[105] Then when, following the weighing of actions in the Balance, the verdict of damnation will be passed to numerous groups of believers who commit major sins,[106] intercessors, including all prophets, will intercede for the forgiveness of many of them.[107] God out of mercy will accept their intercession and save a large number of sinners. This salvation is free from damnation. The second stage of intercession is after the sinners being like coal as a result of constant burning in Hell-fire for a long time.[108] When they are suffering thus , intercessors will pray to God for the rescue of many of them. The result of this will be divine forgiveness of them before the end of their redemptive punishment. This is salvation after damnation.

Who will intercede in the Hereafter? Not only the angels and all prophets, but also those believers who have high status with God, such as saints, ṣūfīs, religious scholars, and other pious men, will be able to intercede for others. They will intercede for the forgiveness of only those sinful believers for whom God will grant them permission,[109] and permission will be granted for intercession for believers only. Thus belief or faith lies at the background of intercession. The concept of intercession in Islam presupposes not only a

[105] Al-Bukhārī, *Ṣaḥīḥ*, Tafsīr Sūra 17.5; Muslim, *Ṣaḥīḥ*, Zuhd, 14; at-Tirmidhī, *Sunan*, Qiyāma, 10; Ibn Ḥanbal, *Musnad*, II, 436.

[106] The Prophet said, "My intercession is for those people of my community who commit major sins." See at-Tirmidhī, *Sunan*, Qiyāma, 11; Abū Dāwūd, *Sunan*, Sunna, 31; Ibn Māja, *Sunan*, Zuhd, 37; Ibn Ḥanbal, *Musnad*, III, 213.

[107] Al-Ghazālī, *Iḥyā'*, IV, 530.

[108] Muslim, *Ṣaḥīḥ*, Īmān, 306; al-Bukhārī, *Ṣaḥīḥ*, Riqāq, 56; Ibn Māja, *Sunan*, Zuhd, 37; Ibn Ḥanbal, *Musnad*, III, 79.

[109] Qur'ān 2:255, 10:3, 19:87, 20:109, 21:28, 34:23, 53:26.

doctrine of God, but also a doctrine of man and his relation to his fellow men. That relation is best described by the word 'solidarity'. Faith is the bond of solidarity between the intercessor and those for whom he pleads, and yet the former differs from the latter in that he is nearer to God. The qualification for the work of intercession is thus twofold. Aside from faith, there are certain acts which facilitate intercession. These are supererogatory ritual prayer,[110] love for the prophets and a strong desire to follow their sunna, to please the pious and thus to obtain the blessings of their prayer, and so on.[111] Thus, in addition to faith, action is involved in intercession. Where salvation will occur through intercessory prayer, faith and action will be there as the two means to it on the human side.

The initiation of intercessory prayer in the Hereafter is dependent upon the permission of God moved by His mercy; its acceptance by Him is also through His mercy or grace; this mercy, however, is indirect since it is operative through the mediation of others. Even faith and action, the two means to salvation on the human side, which occur through human endeavour are ultimately dependent upon divine mercy for their occurrence and efficacy. God's acceptance of repentance as the sinner's expiation is also through His grace. Thus divine grace or mercy plays a major role in salvation even where the means to it are worked out through human endeavour. The Prophet said,

> "Without the mercy of God no one can attain salvation by virtue of his action." His companions asked, "Not even you, O the messenger of God!" He replied, "Not even I. God will, however, cover me with mercy?"[112]

Besides operating through the mediation of others, divine mercy will also be operative directly in the Hereafter at two stages: on the Day of Judgement and after the sinners' entry to Hell. Islamic teaching is that the mercy of God in general predominates over His wrath.[113] Only one per cent of His mercy is bestowed upon all His creatures in this world, the rest, i.e. ninety-nine per cent, being reserved for the world to come.[114] God's compassion for man is

[110] Al-Makkī, *Qūt*, II, 202.

[111] Al-Ghazālī, *Iḥyā'*, IV, 526; al-Makkī, *Qūt*, II, 260.

[112] Al-Bukhārī, *Ṣaḥīḥ*, Riqāq, 18; Muslim, *Ṣaḥīḥ*, Munafiqīn, 77; Ibn Māja, *Sunan*, Zuhd, 20; Ibn Ḥanbal, *Musnad*, II, 235.

[113] Al-Bukhārī, *Ṣaḥīḥ*, Tawḥīd, 15, 55, 22, 28; Muslim, *Ṣaḥīḥ*, Tawba, 14ff., Ibn Māja, *Sunan*, Zuhd, 35.

[114] Al-Bukhārī, *Ṣaḥīḥ*, Adab, 19, Riqāq, 19; Muslim, *Ṣaḥīḥ*, Tawba, 17ff.; at-Tirmidhī, *Sunan*, Da'wāt, 99; Ibn Māja, *Sunan*, Zuhd, 35.

much more than a woman's compassion for her small baby.[115] This emphasis of Islam upon divine mercy in general is in agreement with Psalm 136 where "his mercy *endureth* for ever" occurs twenty-six times.[116] Islamic view is that on the Day of Judgement divine mercy will be bestowed upon believers directly, without the mediation of anyone, at divine questioning, at the weighing of actions in the Balance, and at passing over the Bridge — three most critical moments of the Day of Judgement. A form of bestowal of mercy at the weighing of actions in the Balance is multiplication of good deeds in order to outweigh the bad, as in the Qur'ānic verses:

> "If there be a good deed, He will multiply it and bestow from Himself a great reward."[117]
> (وان تك حسنة يضاعفهام ويوءت من لدنه اجرا عظيما.)

> "Whosoever does good will have ten times as much, and whosoever does evil will only be requited with the like of it; and no wrong will be done to them."[118]
> (من جأ بالحسنةم فله عشر أمثالها. ومن جأ بالسيئةم فلا يجزى الامثلهام وهم لا يظلمون.)

The bestowal of divine mercy directly after the sinners' entry to Hell will follow the deliverance of many sinners from there through intercession. It will start with the words of God:

> "The angels have interceded; prophets have interceded; and believers have interceded; now there remains only the Most Merciful of those who show mercy."[119]

Then He will order the transfer, from Hell to Paradise, of every believer in whose mind will exist good (*khayr*) equal to the weight of a gold coin. Immediately this order will be executed. Then He will order the deliverance of every believer in whose mind will exist good equal the weight of half a gold coin. This order too will be carried out without delay. Then He will order the deliverance of every believer in whose mind will exist good equal to the weight of a particle. As a result of the execution of these three orders a large number of sinful believers will find deliverance from Hell after being damned for a long time, but before the expiry of the duration of punishment due to them. There will still remain in Hell many believers who never

[115] Al-Bukhārī, *Ṣaḥīḥ*, Adab, 18; Muslim, *Ṣaḥīḥ*, Tawba, 22; Abū Dāwūd, *Sunan*, Janā'iz, 1; Ibn Māja, *Sunan*, Zuhd, 35.

[116] Psalm 136:1-26.

[117] Qur'ān 4:40.

[118] Qur'ān 6:160.

[119] Al-Bukhārī, *Ṣaḥīḥ*, Tawḥīd, 34; Muslim, *Ṣaḥīḥ*, Īmān, 302; an-Nasā'ī, *Sunan*, Īmān, 18; Ibn Māja, *Sunan*, Muqaddama, 9; Ibn Ḥanbal, *Musnad*, III, 17.

did any good in their life and who have now become like coal as a result of constant burning in Hell-fire. With one handful, God Himself will bring all these people out of Hell and throw them into the River of Life (*nahr al-ḥayāt*) flowing near the gates of Paradise. From this river they will come out being like pearls and having necklace-like marks around their necks, by which marks they will be recognized in Paradise as "those who are delivered by the Most Merciful" (*'utaqā' ar-Raḥmān*). God will ask them to enter into Paradise to enjoy its delights and, above all, His pleasure eternally.[120] With the deliverance of these believers from Hell the process of granting salvation will come to an end, for there will be no more believers in it — all its dwellers are infidels for whom there is no deliverance.[121]

Thus in the case of direct divine mercy also faith lies at the background. Action too has relevance in as much as it moves mercy promptly; variance in action causes variance in promptness of mercy; where action is lacking completely, divine mercy is bestowed at last. In the case of intercession also faith and action are found to be involved. These, then, are needed everywhere. The existence of them or at least of faith only at the background of divine mercy, direct or indirect as in intercession, is in accordance with the requirement of justice.[122] Justice requires that some merit must be there to elicit and to justify the mercy of God, otherwise it will be an arbitrary thing, depending upon the moods of divine feeling.

[120] *Ibid.*

[121] Qur'ān 2:161, 3:91, 4:48, 116:137, 167, *passim*.

[122] Al-Ghazālī, *Iḥyā*, IV, 30.

DEVOTIONAL ACTS IN ISLAM

قـــال النبي، صلى الله عليه وسلم:

بني الا سلام على خمس: شهادة ان لااله الاالله، وان محمدا عبده ورسوله؛ واقام الصلواة؛ وايتاء الزكاة، وحج البيت؛ وصوم رمضان.

(The Prophet (may God bless and greet him!) declared: Islam is based on five things: the testimony that there is no god but God and that Muḥammad is His servant and messenger; the performance of ritual prayer; the payment of divine tax; the pilgrimage; and the fast during [the lunar month] Ramaḍān.) [1]

[1] Al-Bukhārī, *Ṣaḥīḥ*, Īmān, 1,3; Muslim, *Ṣaḥīḥ*, Īmān, 19-22; at-Tirmidhī, *Sunan*, Īmān, 3; an-Nasā'ī, *Sunan*, Īmān, 13.

NOTE

The major part of one of the two means to salvation on the human side, as explained in the preceding chapter, consists of devotions, both 'obligatory' and 'supererogatory'. The 'obligatory' devotions are ritual prayer, fasting, divine tax and the pilgrimage, while the 'supererogatory' ones are Qur'ān-recitation, remembrance of God and supplication to Him. The efficacy of devotions for salvation is dependent upon their correct performance, as prescribed by the Sharī'a, the revealed law of Islam. Thus the treatmment of their correct performance logically follows that of salvation, and it is to this treatment that the rest of the present study is devoted.

Physical cleanliness is a prerequisite to most Islamic devotions: it is 'obligatory' in some of them and 'praiseworthy' in others. It is valued in Islam even if it is achieved, not as a means to devotions, but for its own sake. It has two aspects, namely, the things with which it is achieved, such as water, clean sand and so on, and the methods by which it is effected. A detailed treatment of it in both its aspects must precede that of devotions.

II
CLEANLINESS

ان الله يحب التوابين ويحب المتطهرين.ـــ قران ٢:٢٢٢

Surely God loves those who turn to Him often and He loves those who clean themselves. — Qur'ān 2:222

قال النبي، صلى الله عليه وسلم: الطهور شطر الايمان.

The prophet Muḥammad (may God bless him and greet him!) said, "Cleanliness is one half of the faith." [2]

KINDS OF WATER WITH WHICH CLEANLINESS CAN BE ACHIEVED

There are seven kinds of water with which cleanliness (*ṭahāra*) can 'correctly' be achieved. They are the water of rain [3], the water of the sea, the water of the river, the water of the well, the water derived from the melting of ice, the water derived from the melting of hail, and the water from a spring.

These seven kinds of water are again put under five categories in accordance with the special quality possessed by each of them.

The first category of water is that which is legally clean itself and which cleanses others; cleansing with it is 'not disliked' by the law.[4] This water is ordinary water, i.e. the water which has not become contaminated by coming in contact with something else.

The second type of water is also that which is legally clean itself and which cleanses others; but cleansing with it is 'slightly disliked' by the law. This water is that small quantity of water from which a cat or a similar animal has drunk.

The third category of water is that which is legally clean itself but which cannot cleanse others; it is water which has already been used for the removal of the state of minor legal impurity (*ḥadath*)[5] or

[2] Muslim, *Ṣaḥīḥ*, Ṭahāra, 1; Dārimī, *Sunan*, Ṭahāra, 2.

[3] Qur'an 8:11.

[4] The word 'law' used in this book means Islamic religious law derived from the Qur'ān, words, deeds and approvals of the prophet Muḥammad, the consensus of the Muslims, and the analogy.

for any meritorious act such as the performance of ablution (*waḍū'*) with the proper intention despite one's having already performed ablution [6] . Water is legally considered to be already used merely by its separation from the body of the person who has used it.

It is 'not correct' to effect cleanliness with the water of a tree or of a fruit, even although this water comes out by itself without applying pressure. Nor is cleanliness correctly achieved with water the nature of which is lost as a result of cooking something in it or as a result of the predominance of something else in it. This predominance, in the case of the mingling of a solid substance with water, occurs if the water loses its properties of thinness and liquidity. There is, however, no harm if all the properties of the water are lost by its mingling with a solid substance such as saffron, fruit or the leaves of a tree. Predominance, in the case of the mingling of a liquid substance with water, occurs [a] if there appears in the water one property of a liquid substance which has only two properties, e.g. milk which has colour and taste but not much smell, and [b] if there appear in the water two properties of a liquid substance which has three properties, e.g. vinegar. In the case of the mingling of water with a liquid substance which has no quality whatever, e.g. water which has already been used, or rose-water the smell of which has been removed, predominance is determined by weight. Thus should there be two *riṭls* of already used water mixed with one *riṭl* of ordinary water, ablution is 'not correct'. But ablution is 'correct' should the proportion be the opposite.

The fourth category of water is unclean water; it is a small, stagnant quantity of water into which some unclean matter has fallen. A small quantity of water is that amount of water which occupies a space of less than ten square cubits. This quantity of water becomes legally unclean by the fall of unclean matter into it even although the sign of the unclean matter is not visible in it. Unclean water also includes running water in which the signs of unclean matter that has fallen into it are visible. The sign of unclean matter is its tastes, colour or smell.

The fifth type of water is that water concerning the cleanliness of which there is doubt; it is the water from which a donkey or a mule has drunk.

THE SMALL QUANTITY OF WATER FROM WHICH AN ANIMAL HAS DRUNK

[5] There are two states of legal impurity — minor and major (*janāba*). The former is that which contradicts ritual ablution, and the latter necessitates a bath.

[6] See *infra*, p.64.

A small quantity of water, [i.e. the water which occupies a space less than ten square cubits], from which an animal has drunk may be of four kinds. Such water is called *sū'r*.

The first is that which is clean itself and which cleanses others. It is that small quantity of water from which a man, whether major (*bāligh*)[7] or minor, or a horse, or any other animal the meat of which is lawful to eat, has drunk.

The second is that which is unclean. Its use for cleanliness is 'not permissible' by the law. Nor can it be drunk. It is that small quantity of water from which a dog,[8] or a pig,[9] or any of the ferocious animals such as the cheetah or wolf has drunk.

The third is that water the use of which is 'slightly disliked' by the law when other water that is legally clean is available. It is that small quantity of water from which has drunk a pet cat or a domestic fowl which has escaped from its confines, or a ferocious bird such as a small hawk or gerfalcon or a rat, but not a scorpion.

The fourth kind is that water the cleanliness of which is doubtful. It is that small quantity of water from which a mule or a donkey has drunk. In the absence of other water that is clean, one has to perform ablution with it and also ablution with sand (*tayammum*) and then to perform ritual prayer (*ṣalā*).

THE USE OF CLEAN POTS AND CLOTHES MIXED WITH UNCLEAN ONES

If pots, containing water, of which most are clean [but some unclean], are mixed together, a person has to select, for use in performing ablution and in drinking water, those which he imagines to be clean after a great deal of consideration. But if most of the pots are unclean, he should not think much about them, but abstain from them all, and perform ablution with sand. For selecting clean pots for the purpose of drinking only, however, he should consider them very carefully.

If two pots filled with water — one being clean and the other

[7] For the definition of the term 'major' or 'mature' in Islamic religious law see *infra*, p.60.

[8] The prophet Muḥammad said that the utensil into which a dog has put its mouth is unclean and that in order to make it clean it must be washed either three times or five times or seven times. It is 'praiseworthy' that in one of the times of this washing, the utensil should be rubbed with soil. See al-Bukhārī, *Ṣaḥīḥ*, Waḍū', 33; Muslim, *Ṣaḥīḥ*, Ṭahāra, 89f.

[9] Not only the saliva but the entire body of a pig is considered by the law as unclean even though it is reared in a farm which is very neat and clean. Uncleanliness is inherent in the very nature of the pig. See Qur'ān 6:145.

unclean — are mixed together, and an individual, without thinking much about which of them may be clean, makes ablution by making use of both pots and then performs ritual prayer, this is 'correct' provided he wipes his head at two different places. If he wipes the head at one place only, the matter dwindles between what is 'permissible' and what is 'not permissible'.[10]

If the unclean and clean pots are of an equal number, no consideration is necessary to select the clean ones; one should abstain from them all and should make ablution with sand.[11]

In the case of pieces of cloth mixed together, a person has to think much about which piece is clean or unclean [and then select that piece which he imagines to be clean and cover his private parts with it when performing ritual prayer].

[If there are two pieces of cloth, and the individual, after considering much about them, selects one as clean and performs a ritual prayer wearing it; then, intending to perform another ritual prayer, he selects the other piece as clean; this second ritual prayer is 'not correct'. All his ritual prayers would have been 'correct' only if he had worn that piece which he had selected first.[12]

If two upright men have given contradictory opinions on some water so that one affirms the cleanliness of the water while the other denies it, the water will be treated as clean, relying on the original nature of water which is clean.[13]

A SMALL WELL INTO WHICH UNCLEAN MATTER OR ANYTHING ELSE HAS FALLEN

If any unclean matter has fallen into a small well which occupies a space less than ten square cubits, it will have to be emptied even although the unclean matter is little (except a little dung), e.g. a drop of blood or of wine, for even this small portion of unclean matter has rendered the whole well unclean. It will also be emptied [a] if a pig which in its entirety is legally considered unclean, has fallen into it even though it came out alive and its mouth did not touch the water of the well, or [b] if a dog or a goat or a man has died inside it, or [c] if an animal, however small, has died and its body distends in it thereby spreading the filth throughout the well. Should the complete emptying of the well not be possible, two hundred medium-sized[14] buckets of water must be taken out of it in these cases.

10 Maḥmūd 'Abd al-Wahhāb ash-Shurunbalālī, *Marāqī al-Falāḥ: Sharḥ Matn Nūr al-Īḍāḥ*, Egypt, n.d., p. 18.

11 *Ibid.* 12 *Ibid.* 13 *Ibid.*

Should a domestic fowl or a cat or the like die inside a small well, it is necessary to take forty buckets of water following the removal of the animal from the well. To draw out fifty or sixty buckets is, of course, 'praiseworthy'. If a rat or a similar animal dies inside the well but its body is not distended, twenty buckets of water will have to be drawn out. [8] The drawing out of the buckets of water in all these cases results in the cleanliness of the well, the bucket and its rope, and the hand of the man who draws out the water.

The well does not become unclean by the presence in it of the dung of a hoofed animal, i.e. a camel or goat, the dung of a horse, mule, donkey or cow. The well, however, becomes unclean if this dung is of such a quantity that one who looks at the well considers it a large quantity, or if no bucket of water drawn out is free from dung.

The water of a well does not become legally filthy by the falling of the dung of a pigeon or a sparrow into it. Nor does it or any other liquid thing become unclean by the death inside it of any living being in which there is no flowing blood, e.g. a fish or a frog or of aquatic animals, or of a bug or a fly or a wasp or a scorpion. Nor does it become unclean by the fall into it [a] of a man or an animal, the meat of which can legally be eaten, provided it comes out alive and there was no filth on its body, or [b] of a mule or a donkey or a ferocious bird or any wild animal. This is the correct view.

Should the saliva of any animal which has fallen into the well reach the water, a legal ruling will be given on the water in keeping with the ruling on the cleanliness or uncleanliness of the saliva.

The discovery of a dead, but not swollen, animal in the well, if the time of its falling into it is not known, makes the well unclean until a day and a night have passed. But if the body of the animal

[14] Islam is a religion which enjoins moderation or the mean state of all affairs. In Islam there is place neither for too much of hardship nor for too much of lavishness, neither for excess nor for deficiency. Moderation is considered by Islam to be the most reasonable course of action and to enable man to achieve that at which the Islamic religion aims. A man has an outward aspect and an inward aspect, and moderation is to be observed in relation to both. His outward aspect is mainly the concern of Islamic law (*fiqh*) and hence in this field one often finds the prescription of moderation and the middle course. The inward aspect of a man is mainly dealt with in ṣūfism and Islamic philosophy and hence in these two disciplines also we find that moderation or the mean is taught emphatically. Besides law, ṣūfism and philosophy, the mean and moderation are prescribed in clear terms in the Qur'ān and prophetic tradition. Thus the Prophet said, "The best of all affairs is their mean (*wasaṭ*)." "Surely God likes easiness in every affair" (al-Bukhārī, *Ṣaḥīḥ*, Adab, 35; Muslim, *Ṣaḥīḥ*, Salām 10). God commanded the observance of the mean through many Qur'ānic verses, e.g. 17:29, 25:67, 7:31, 48:29.

discovered is swollen, the well is to be regarded as unclean until three days and three nights have elapsed.

[A man who has found traces of sperm in his clothing must repeat all the ritual prayers which he has performed wearing it from the time he last went to sleep.] [15]

CLEANLINESS AFTER RELIEVING ONESELF (*ISTINJĀ'*)

On passing urine, a person has to seek freedom from the leakage of urine, until the sign of leakage disappears and his mind becomes quiet concerning the leakage. This freedom can be achieved by following one's habitual methods — by walking a few steps or by making a sort of half-cough or by reclining or by similar acts. It is 'not correct' to start performing ablution until the mind is quiet about the stopping of the leakage of urine.

It is the 'confirmed sunna' to cleanse the filth which comes out through the genitals or the anus provided it has not crossed the boundary of the orifice. If it has crossed and the space it has smeared is equal to the size of a silver coin, it is 'required' to remove it with water. If the place smeared is more than the size of a silver coin, the removal of the filth by washing it with water is 'obligatory'.

When bathing to remove the state of major legal impurity after the ceasing of mentruation or the end of the childbirth bleeding period, it is 'obligatory' to wash with water the filth which is at the orifice even though it is very small in quantity.

Cleanliness after relieving oneself is to be accomplished by wiping the filth with a cleansing stone or something similar which is clean, cleanses others and is not precious or honourable. To wash the filth with water is better. Best of all is to use both stone and water, i.e. to wipe the filth with the stone first and then to wash it with water. [16] It is, however, 'correct' to use either water or a stone.

What is sunna is only to achieve cleanliness. To use a *specific number* of stones or of any thing similar is only 'recommended' by the law [17] and not an 'emphasized sunna', [because the Prophet said, "One who wants to use stones should use an odd number of them. One who has done this has done a good work, but one who has

15 Ash-Shurunbalālī, *Marāqī*, pp. 21-22.

16 Because the dwellers in the village Quba' in Medina used to combine both water and stone during the lifetime of the Prophet, they were praised in the Qur'ān (9:108). So this combination has become sunna for all the time. This is the correct view and on this legal decision (*fatwā*) has been given.

17 The Prophet said, "One who uses stones should use an odd number of them." See al-Bukhārī, *Ṣaḥīḥ*, Waḍū', 25, 26; Ibn Māja, *Sunan*, Ṭahāra, 23, 44.

not done this has not done any thing wrong"].[18] Thus, as a 'recommended' act, a person will use three stones even though cleanliness can be achieved with the use of less than three.

The manner of cleanliness after relieving oneself is this. A man will wipe the filth with the first stone from the front of the place of the filth to the rear. With the second stone, he will wipe the filth from the rear to the front. The third stone he will use for wiping the filth from the front to the rear. This procedure is to be followed when his testicles are hanging loosely lest they might be defiled. If they are not hanging loosely, wiping will proceed from the rear to the front because this procedure effects cleanliness more. A woman will begin by wiping the filth from the front to the rear, in case the filth might defile her genitalia. After wiping the place of filth with three stones in this way, the individual will first wash his hand with water and will then rub the place of the filth with water by using the inner side of one finger, or two or even three if necessary. The method of using the finger is as follows: A man will slightly elevate his middle finger above his other fingers when starting the cleansing process; then, after washing to a certain extent, he will slightly elevate his second little finger. He should not limit himself to the use of only one finger. A woman will slightly elevate her second finger and middle finger together at the start of the cleansing, in case she might experience sexual pleasure from rubbing her genitalia. Increase may be made in the number of stones used and in washing in order that no smell of the filth remains. A person not fasting should fully relax his hips so that the filth in the orifice may be removed fully. A fasting man, however, must not do this in case the water used enters and thus corrupts his fasting. On completion of cleanliness with water, a person will wash his hands a second time and, if he is fasting, dry his hips before standing up, in case the water still present at the genitals or the anus enters, thereby corrupting his fasting. This drying is also 'praiseworthy' for one not fasting.

It is 'not permissible' to uncover, in the presence of others, the private parts of the body (*'awra*) in order to effect cleanliness after relieving oneself. [To reveal the private parts when there are on-lookers is strictly 'forbidden' by the law. Without uncovering one's private parts, one should somehow wipe the orifice from under one's cloth with a stone or similar object.]

If the filth has crossed the orifice, and the place over which it has spread is more than the measure of a silver coin, and it is not

[18] Al-Bukhārī, *Ṣaḥīḥ*, Waḍū', 25f.; Muslim, *Ṣaḥīḥ*, Ṭahāra, 20, 22, 24; at-Tirmidhī, *Sunan*, Ṭahāra, 21; Ibn Māja, *Sunan*, Ṭahāra, 23, 44.

removed despite the availability of water or other object with which it can be removed; ritual prayer is not valid. One must try to find the correct objects for its removal without revealing one's private parts to the eyes of any on-lookers.[19]

It is 'disliked' by the law to accomplish cleanliness by the use of bone,[20] the food of man or any lower animal, baked brick, earthenware, coal, glass, gypsum, anything worthwhile such as a piece of brocade and cotton or by the use of the right hand except when there is an excuse for not using the left hand. [The Prophet said, "When anyone of you urinates, he should not wipe his genital by using his right hand, and when he defecates, he should not wipe the filth by using the right hand....]"[21]

A person should enter a lavatory with the left foot first. When entering, he should seek the protection of God from the rejected Satan by reading the prayer formula:

> God, I seek the protection of You against the rejected Satan, the filthy, the impure, the abominable, the pernicious[22].
>
> (اعوذ بالله، من الرجس النجس، الخبيث المخبث، الشيطان الرجيم)
>
> *(A'ūdhu bi-Allāhi, mina r-rijsi n-najasi l-khabīthi l-mukhbithi, ash-Shayṭāni r-rajīmi.)*

He should sit supporting himself on the left leg and should not speak except through absolute necessity. It is 'gravely disliked' to sit, when relieving oneself, facing the qibla or with one's back to

[19] Cf. Ibn Māja, *Sunan*, Ṭahāra, 22. [20] Ibn Māja, *Sunan*, Ṭahāra, 16.

[21] In Islam there is a principle for use of the hands. Although as parts of the same body the two hands are the same, they differ in respect of the purpose of their creation. When creating them God has given the right hand excellence over the left. Therefore anything superior, such as eating, drinking, wearing the dress, touching the Qur'ān, should be done with the nobler hand, while in doing anything inferior, e.g. cleansing of filth, taking off of shoes and dress, the inferior hand is to be used. What things are superior and so should be done with the right hand were most correctly apprehended by the Prophet through the light of prophecy (*nūr an-nubuwwa*). In the light of such apprehension he prohibited the use of right hand for cleansing purposes and for taking off the shoes and dress, and the use of the right foot for entering the lavatory; this is because the right hand and the right foot need to be honoured. But he asked us to use the right foot for coming out of the lavatory, because to leave a place of filth is something good for which the right foot deserves to be used. The Prophet was the man able to understand this sort of delicate matter. See ash-Shurunbalālī, *Marāqī*, p. 27.

[22] Ibn Māja, *Sunan*, Ṭahāra, 9; at-Tirmidhī, *Sunan*, Ṭahāra, 4; al-Bukhārī, *Ṣaḥīḥ*, Waḍū', 9.

it, even though one is in a lavatory inside a house.[23] [One who has done this forgetfully should, if possible, turn to face another direction as soon as one is aware of it. This is because of the honour of the Holy Ka'ba.] Likewise, it is 'gravely disliked' to sit facing the sun or the moon because these are two great signs of God or the windward direction in case the splashes of urine may make one defiled.

It is 'disliked' by the law to urinate or to defecate in water, in the shade where people sit, in a hole because a snake or the like may cause harm from the inside of it, on the road, or under a fruit tree. To urinate while standing is also 'disliked' by the law;[24] it is, however, 'permissible' if there is a real excuse, e.g. pain in the back which makes it impossible to sit.

[It is 'praiseworthy' to enter into a lavatory wearing a cloth not used for the performance of ritual prayer; if such a separate cloth be not used, one should safeguard oneself against the filth. It is 'disliked' by the law that a person should relieve himself when having with him anything which contains the name of God or of His messenger Muḥammad or a Qur'ānic verse.[25] It is 'forbidden' to think of God while a person is relieving himself — thus for no reason will he utter الحمد لله (*al-ḥamdu li-Allāhi*: praise be to God). He will not reply to the salutation of someone else to him, nor reply to one who is calling to ritual prayer (*mu'adhdhin*), nor gaze unduly on his private parts, nor play with his private parts.]

One should come out of the lavatory with the right foot first and then read the prayer formula:

> Praise be to God Who has removed from me that which is harmful and has left me that which is useful to my health[26](الحمد لله الذى اذهب عنى الاذى وعافانى).
> *(Al-ḥamdu li-Allāhi l-ladhi adhhaba 'annī l-adhā wa 'āfānī).*

ABLUTION (*WAḌŪ'*)

The Pillars of Ablution

The pillars of ablution are four in number.[27] They are the 'obligatory' parts of ablution. They are as follows:

[23] Ibn Māja, *Sunan*, Ṭahāra, 16.

[24] To urinate while standing is prohibited by the Prophet. See at-Tirmidhī, *Sunan*, Ṭahāra, 8; Abū Dāwūd, *Sunan*, Ṭahāra, 16.

[25] Abū Dāwūd, *Sunan*, Ṭahāra, 10; Ibn Māja, *Sunan*, Ṭahāra, 11.

[26] Cf. at-Tirmidhī, *Sunan*, Ṭahāra, 5; Ibn Māja, *Sunan*, Ṭahāra, 10.

[27] These are mentioned in the Qur'ān 5:6.

The first pillar is the washing of the face. The limit of the face lengthwise is from the beginning of the upper surface of the forehead to the lower part of the chin, and breadthwise it is that part which exists between the two lobes of the ears. The second pillar is the washing of the hands up to the elbows. The third pillar is the washing of the feet up to the ankles. The fourth pillar is the wiping of one fourth of the head with the hands wetted with water freshly taken. [The law defines the head as that part of the body which is above the ears, so that the wiping of the part just below the ears is not legally correct].

The reason for making ablution is to acquire a legal state of fitness for performing the rites which are 'not lawful' without ablution. [These rites are ritual prayer, the circumambulation of the Ka'ba, the touching of the Qur'ān, and so on.] This is the reason of this world for ablution. The other-worldly reason is the obtainment of reward in the Hereafter.

The Stipulations for Ablution

The stipulations which must be fulfilled by a person, if ablution is to be 'required' of him, are eight in number. They are as follows:

[1] Sanity (*'aql*). A person who is sane is 'required' by the law to make ablution for the performance of certain rituals.[28] [2] Maturity. Those who have become mature are 'required' to perform ablution. Legal maturity comes with physical puberty when it is presumed, unless there is evidence to the contrary, that the person concerned has attained that degree of sound and mature judgement which enables him or her properly to manage his or her own affairs. Physical puberty is a matter to be established by appropriate evidence, but the law presumes that it cannot occur before the age of nine in the case of girls and twelve in the case of boys, and that it

[28] Three categories of people are exempted from the Islamic religious obligations: the insane, the minor and the faint. The general rule is that whatever a man does or says, whether good or bad, small or great, is recorded by the two angels placed at his two side (Qur'ān 6:61, 10:21, 43:80, 82:11); the angel placed at his right side is called *ṣāḥib al-yamīn* who records only his good utterances and good actions, while the angel placed at his left side is called *ṣāḥib ash-shimāl* and he records only his bad actions and bad utterances. The insane, the minor and the faint are exceptions to this general rule — nothing which they do or say is recorded by the angels —; this is explicit in prophetic tradition (al-Bukhārī, *Ṣaḥīḥ*, Ḥudūd, 22; at-Tirmidhī, *Sunan*, Ḥudūd, 1; an-nasā'ī, *Sunan*, Ṭalāq, 21). The reason is obvious: they lack the capacity to know what is good and what is bad, what is 'obligatory' and what is not. The law says that the capacity to know concerning these things must be possessed by one if one is to be obliged to perform the religious duties (*mukallaf*).

must have occurred by the age of fifteen for both sexes. [3] Islam. Only Muslims are 'required' to perform ablution. [4] Ability to use that quantity of clean water which is sufficient for washing the limbs of ablution once at least. [5] To be in the state of minor legal impurity. A person who is not legally impure, i.e. who is already in ablution, is not 'required' to perform ablution.[29] [6-7] Absence of menstruation and the period of childbirth bleeding. [8] When there is only sufficient time left for a ritual prayer or of any other rite requiring ablution, then ablution must be performed immediately.

Stipulations for the validity of ablution are three in number. They are the following.

[1] The application of clean water to the totality of the epidermis of one's bodily organs that must be washed in ablution. If a place as small as the size of a needle-point remains dry, ablution is not correct. [2] The absence of menstruation, period of childbirth bleeding and the state of minor legal impurity, which all contradict ablution. [3] The removal of that which prevents the water from reaching the outer layer of the skin, e.g. wax or fat. [If anything inhibits the washing of organs which must be washed, ablution is not correct. Oil and similar preparations applied to the body are not, however, regarded as preventing water reaching the outer layer.]

Some 'Necessary' Acts in Ablution

The washing of only the external part of a thick beard [— so thick that the outer layer of the skin is not visible —] is 'necessary'. This is the most correct of all legal opinions given on this point. If the beard is sparse, it is 'necessary' to make the water reach the outer layer of the skin. It is not 'necessary' to make the water reach the hair which hangs down from outside the circumference of the face. Nor is it 'necessary' that the water should reach those parts of the lips which remain concealed when they are closed in the usual manner. [Similarly water 'need' not reach the interior part of the eyes.]

If the fingers are held tightly together so that water does not reach between them, or if the nail has become long so that it covers the tip of the finger preventing water from getting underneath it, or if in the tip there is something like doughpaste, [fat, and so on] which prevents water from reaching it — in all these cases, it is 'necessary'

[29] If, however, he makes ablution he will obtain reward for this. Ablution itself is a good work drawing man near to God (*qurba*), even though it is meant to serve as a means of performing devotional acts. Making ablution despite one's already being in ablution is 'praiseworthy'.

to wash the covered parts after the removal of the substance. Dirt from the nose, the dung of fleas or similar things in the tips of the fingers are not considered by the law to prevent water from reaching them [because these are too small to prevent water and because these are not too sticky; so washing is correct despite the presence of these substances. The colour which remains on the nail of a person who out of necessity has adopted the profession of colouring, is not regarded as preventing water from reaching the body — a view on which legal decision has been given].

It is 'necessary' to move tight rings around the fingers. [Likewise, earrings 'need' to be moved around because otherwise the water may not go into the holes made for these earrings.]

Should the washing of fissures in the heels be harmful, it is 'correct' just to let water go over any medicine that has been applied to them.

There is no need to repeat the washing or the wiping of the hair of the head in ablution, after the hair is shaved. Nor is there any need to repeat the washing after cutting one's nails or moustache.

Sunna Acts in Ablution

There are eighteen sunna acts in ablution. They are as follows: [1] Washing the hands up to the wrists at the start of ablution. [2] At the start of this washing, to utter the name of God,[30] i.e. to say:

> In the name of God, Most Gracious, Ever Merciful.[31]
> (بسم الله الرحمن الرحيم)
> (*Bi-smi Allāhi r-raḥmāni r-raḥīmi*).

[3] Cleansing the mouth, when commencing ablution, with a tooth-stick (*miswāk*), or with a finger when a tooth-stick is not available. [The Prophet said,

> "One ritual prayer after the use of a tooth-stick is better than seventy ritual prayers without the use of it."[32] "Had it not been for my fear to overburden my people, I would have commanded them to use a tooth-stick before every ritual prayer."[33]]

[30] The Prophet said, "There is no ablution to him who does not call upon the name of God." See Ibn Māja, *Sunan*, Ṭahāra, 41.

[31] Qur'ān 1:1.

[32] Aḥmad ibn Ḥanbal, *Musnad*, 169.

[33] Aḥmad ibn Ḥanbal, *Musnad*, 167, 170. Not only in ablution, but at other times also the use of a tooth-stick is 'praiseworthy'. These times are: on waking from sleep, just before starting a ritual prayer, before entering into a house or a people's gathering, and before reading the Qur'ān or a book on prophetic tradition. The

[4] Rinsing the mouth three times even though using only a single handful of water. [5] Drawing water inside the nostrils with three fresh handfuls of water. [6] Exaggeration in rinsing, i.e. to make the water reach near the throat, and in drawing the water inside the nostrils, i.e. to allow the water to reach the cartilage of the nose. This exaggeration is to be made only by those who are not fasting. [7] After washing the face, the wetting of a thick beard three times with a palmful of water from below the beard and combing with the fingers. [8] Wetting with the fingers the skin between the fingers and the toes. [9] Washing the limbs three times. [10] Wiping the entire head once and wiping the ears even though it is with the water taken for wiping the head. [11] Rubbing the limbs washed in ablution. [12] Washing the limbs one after another quickly so that one limb should not become dry before washing the other. [12] Making the intention (*niyya*) of ablution in the beginning. [14] Observance of the gradual order of acts of ablution, as mentioned in the Qur'ān,[34] i.e. first to wash the face, then to wash the hands, then to wipe the head, and finally to wash the feet. [15] Starting every act in ablution from the right side of the body. [16] Beginning washing the fingers and the toes from their tips. [17] Beginning wiping the head from its frontal part. [18] Wiping the neck, not the throat. Some authorities maintain that these last mentioned four acts are 'praiseworthy', not sunna.

'Praiseworthy' Acts in Ablution

The 'praiseworthy' acts in ablution are fourteen in number. They are the following:

[1] To sit on an elevated place so that the used water may flow away easily. [2] To face the direction of the Holy Ka'ba in Mecca, because this state is most conducive to the acceptance by God of all prayers read when making ablution. [3] Not to seek assistance from others in the performance of ablution. This is because devotional acts should be performed through one's own effort. [4] Not to utter any word which is not a part of supplications and praises of God. [5] To combine the mental intention of ablution with the verbal utterance of the words of intention. Mental intention consists in a person's *resolve* that he is making ablution in order to remove the

Prophet said, "The use of a tooth-stick cleanses the mouth and pleases the Lord" (al-Bukhārī, *Ṣaḥīḥ*, Ṣawm, 27; an-Nasā'ī, *Sunan*, Ṭahāra, 4). This statement of the Prophet includes all conditions. Shaykh Aḥmad az-Zāhid has collected all excellences of the use of the tooth-stick in his book *Tuḥfat as-Sālik fī Faḍā'il as-Siwāk*.

[34] Qur'ān 5:6.

state of minor legal impurity, or to acquire legal fitness for the performance of ritual prayer or any other rite, or to obey the command of God. The words of this intention are:

نويت ان اتوضوء لـرفع الحدث، او لاستباحة الصلوة، او
لاطاعة امر الله ۰

(Nawaytu an atawaḍḍaū' li-raf'i l-ḥadathi, aw li-istibāḥati ṣ-ṣalāti, aw li-iṭā'ati amri Allāhi)

[6] To supplicate to God by the recitation of those prayer formulae which are transmitted from the Prophet, his companions and their followers. [7] To utter the name of God when performing each act related to every part of the body during ablution.

[8] To insert the little finger into the holes of the ears when wiping the ears. This perfects the act of wiping. [9] To move a loose ring around the finger when washing the fingers so that washing may be complete. [10] To use the right hand in rinsing the mouth and in drawing water inside the nostrils. [12] To perform ablution before the start of the time of a ritual prayer. This is for those who have no excuse. [13] To complete ablution by the recitation of the two sentences of confession of the faith while standing and facing in the direction of the Holy Ka'ba in Mecca. The two sentences are:

> I testify that there is no god but God, and I testify that Muḥammad is His servant and messenger.
> (اشهد ان لا اله الا الله، واشهد ان محمدا عبده ورسوله)
> *(Ashhadu an lā ilāha illā Allāhu, wa ashhadu anna Muḥammadan 'abduhu wa rasūluhu)*

[14] After ablution, to drink from the suplus water of ablution while standing and then to pray:

> God, make me one of those who turn to You in repentance, and make me one of those who clean themselves.
> (اللهم، اجعلني من التوابين، واجعلني من المتطهرين)
> *(Allāhumma, aj'alnī mina t-tawwābīna, wa aj'alnī mina l-mutaṭahhirīna)*

'Disliked' Acts in Ablution

The performance of the following six acts in ablution is 'disliked' by the law:

[1] Extravagance in the use of water. [2] Miserliness in the use of water so that washing becomes like wiping. [3] Splashing the face with water. [4] Utterance of a word other than those constituting

prayers and praises of God. [5] Seeking assistance from others in making ablution when there is no excuse for it. [6] Wiping the head three times with fresh water.

The Three Kinds of Ablution

Ablution is of three kinds — 'obligatory', 'required', and 'praiseworthy'.

First, ablution is 'obligatory' for a person who is in the state of minor legal impurity and who wants to perform a ritual prayer, even though it is 'supererogatory',[35] or to perform the ritual prayer over the bier, or to perform the prostration due to Qur'ān-recitation,[36] or to touch the Qur'ān even though a single verse of it,[37] whether written on a wall or a coin or some similar thing. Second, ablution is 'required' for the circumambulation of the Holy Ka'ba.[38]

Third, ablution is 'praiseworthy' [a] for sleeping in the state of legal purity, [b] when one wakes up from sleep, [c] for continuance in ablution, [d] for the obtaining of reward of performance of ablution despite one's already being in ablution, [e] after back-biting, falsehood, calumny or any other sin, [f] after the composition of a verse of evil poetry, [g] after loud laughter which is not during ritual prayer, [h] after washing or carrying a dead body, [i] at the time of every ritual prayer, [j] just before bathing for the removal of the state of major legal impurity, [k] for a person in the state of major legal impurity, when he wants to eat, drink or perform sexual intercourse, [l] at the arousal of anger, [m-n] for the noble acts of reciting the Qur'ān from memory, and for reading a Tradition or narrating it, [o] for the study of a book of religious knowledge, [p] for the call to ritual prayer (*adhān*), [q] for the call to the actual start of a ritual prayer (*iqāma*), [r] for addressing a gathering, [s] for visiting the tomb of the Prophet, [t] for the ritual of halting at 'Arafa during the time of pilgrimage to Mecca, [u] for the ceremony of running between the hill Safa and the hill Marwa, [v] after eating the meat of a slaughtered animal, and [x] after an act concerning which religious scholars differ whether or not ablution is necessary for it, e.g. touching a woman.

[35] Qur'ān 5:6.

[36] In the Qur'ān there are fourteen verses in which the word 'prostration' (*sajda*) occurs and which are such that a person who recites any one of them himself or hears another person recite it, is 'required' by the law to prostrate himself before God. For making this prostration ablution is 'obligatory' upon him.

[37] Qur'ān 56:79.

[38] At-Tirmidhī, *Sunan*, Ḥajj, 112; an-Nasā'ī, *Sunan*, Manāsik, 136; al-Bukhārī, *Ṣaḥīḥ*, Ḥajj, 78. For details about circumambulation of the Ka'ba see *infra*, pp. 244-34.

Things Nullifying Ablution

There are twelve things which nullify ablution. They are as follows:

[1] Anything which comes out through either the anus or the genitals makes ablution null and void. The air which comes out through the genitals, however, does not nullify it; this is the most correct view. [Air coming out through the anus, of course, does nullify ablution.] [2] Giving birth to a child without any visible blood also nullifies ablution. [3] Any filth flowing out of a place of the body other than the genitals or the anus, e.g. blood and pus. [This flowing is defined by the law as the crossing of the filth from it to its surrounding area even though it is very slight.] [4] Vomiting food or water or blood clots or bile provided it fills the mouth. Filling the mouth is defined as that in which the mouth cannot be shut except with difficulty; this is the most correct view. Vomiting several times is considered one occurrence provided their cause is the same. [5] Blood which is equal to, or greater than, the saliva which accompanies it. [This is to be known from the colour of the saliva; the yellow colour proves the predominance of saliva over blood; a slightly red colour indicates that the saliva is in equal proportion to the blood; a fully red colour proves that it is the blood which predominates.] [6] Sleep in which one's hips have not remained firmly on the ground. [7] The sleep of a sitting person during which his hips have risen up from the ground before his waking up, even though he did not fall down. This is a clear legal view. [Slight drowsiness during which one hears what is said near him does nullify ablution.][39] [8] Faintness. [9] Insanity. [10] Drunkenness. [11] Loud laughter done deliberately or forgetfully by an awake, mature person during that ritual prayer which has bowing and prostation,[40] even though by this laughter he had intended to withdraw himself from that ritual prayer, i.e. he did this after the last sitting when nothing of the ritual prayer remains except salutation. [Loud laughter is defined by the law as that which is heard by those near him. Laughter is defined as that which is heard by himself only; this nullifies ritual prayer but not the ablution. A smile is that in which only the teeth are seen but no sound is heard; it nullifies neither ritual prayer nor ablution.][41] [12] Touching a woman's genitalia [or

[39] Ash-Shurunbalālī, *Marāqī*, p. 41.

[40] This excludes ritual prayer over the bier and prostration due to Qur'ān-reading. Loud laughter inside these two acts nullifies them but not the ablution.

[41] Ash-Shurunbalālī, *Marāqī*, p. 40.

her hip] with the erected penis without any covering. [Likewise, when a man touches another man's penis or hips with his erected penis without any covering, or a woman touches another woman's genitalia with sexual excitement without any covering, ablution is nullified] [42] .

Things which do not Nullify Ablution

There are ten things which do not nulify ablution. They are as follows:

[1] Bleeding which has not flowed from its place. [2] The loss of a small piece of flesh from the body without the flowing of blood. [3] Coming out of a worm from an wound, from the ear, or from the nose. [4] Touching the penis, the anus, or the woman's genitalia. [5] Touching a woman. [6] Vomiting which is not equivalent to a mouthful. [7] Vomiting phlegm even though it is great in quantity. [8] Swaying of a drowsy man by which his hips are inclined. [9] The sleeping of a sitting man whose hips are firmly on the ground or against some other object, such as a wall or a pillow, even though he is reclining upon something which, if it were removed, would cause him to fall down. [10] The sleep of a person performing a ritual prayer even though it is in that state of bowing or prostration which is sunna.

BATH (*GHUSL*)

وان كنتم جنبا فاطهروا. — قران٦:٥

If you are in the state of major legal impurity, clean yourselves by bathing. — Qur'ān 5:6

Causes of an Obligatory Bath

Taking a bath becomes 'obligatory' for a person if any of the following seven things happen to him:

[1] The emission of sperm with excitement even without sexual intercourse [as in the case of nocturnal emission (*iḥtilām*). If sperm comes out with excitement as a result of mere thought about sex or merely looking upon an object of sex or by manipulation of the genitals, then a bath is also 'obligatory'. The emission of sperm without excitement does not require one to bathe. All this is true for man and woman alike]. [43]

[2] The insertion of the front part of the penis of a man with sexual desire, i.e. the circumcised part of his penis, inside the

[42] *Ibid.* [43] *Ibid.*, p. 42.

genitalia or anus of a living human being. [Both persons involved in this act must bathe. If the front part of the penis wrapped with plastic or similar covering is placed inside the woman's vagina or anus, a bath is 'obligatory' upon both even though no emission has occurred and no pleasure has been felt.]

[3] The emission of sperm as a result of sexual intercourse with a dead body or with an animal. [4] A man's discovery of a thin watery substance after waking from sleep even though he does not remember any sexual dream, provided his penis was not in an excited state before he fell asleep. [If it was in an excited state, the watery substance is to be taken to be not sperm but juice from some gland, and consequently a bath is not necessary.] [5] The finding of wetness on clothing or in the body which one imagines to be sperm, after one's recovery from intoxication or faintness. [6] The cessation of menstruation. [7] The end of the period of childbirth bleeding.

It is a collective obligation (*farḍ kifāya*) [44] to wash the body of a person who has died — a collective obligation in the sense that it is obligatory upon all individuals of the society, but if a single one of them performs this 'obligatory' act, all other individuals are relieved of the responsibility.

Things which Do not Necessitate a Bath

There is no need to take a bath if the following ten things are found. [1] The emission of *madhī*. [*Madhī* is a white, thin, watery substance which comes out through the genitals when one is in excitement. It does not come out with excitement, nor is it poured forth like sperm; sometimes one is not aware of its coming out.] [2] The emission of *wadī*. [It is a water-like substance coming out through the genitals; it has no smell and is usually emitted after the passing of urine but sometimes before it too.] [3] Dreaming of having sexual intercourse with someone but finding, on waking, no wetness or any sign of emission. [4] Giving birth to a child without any visible blood occurring. This is the correct view. [5] The insertion of the penis wrapped with plastic or similar thing fully preventing the feeling of pleasure. [6] Having an injection. [7] The insertion of a finger or a similar object into the vagina or the anus.

[44] Obligation is of two kinds: collective and individual. An individual obligation (*farḍ 'ayn*) is an obligation on every individual, and it must be fulfilled by every individual. A collective obligation is an obligation on every individual of the society, but if only one individual fulfils it, it ceases to be the responsibility of all other individuals. Washing the dead body of a Muslim and the ritual prayer over the bier are examples of this latter type of obligation.

[8-9] Sexual intercourse with an animal or with a dead person without emission. [10] Penetration of a virgin girl whose virginity is not removed thereby, and no emission has occurred.

'Obligatory' Acts in a Bath

The 'obligatory' acts in an 'obligatory' bath are eleven in number. They are enumerated as follows:

[1] Washing the mouth, [2] washing the interior of the nose, and [3] washing the entire body. Washing these is 'obligatory' only once. [4] Washing the inner side of the circumcisable part of the penis provided this can be done without difficulty. [5] Washing the inner side of the navel. [6] Washing a small hole or opening in the body which is not filled with the flesh. [7] Washing the inner side of a man's hair and undoing it completely, i.e. whether water has penetrated to the roots or not. It is, however, not necessary to undo the braids of a woman's hair if the water has already penetrated to the roots. [8-10] Washing the beard, moustache and eyebrows together with the outer layer of the skin of the places where these have grown, even though the hair is very thick.[45] [11] Washing the external parts of the genitals.

Sunna Acts in a Bath

Twelve acts are sunna in a bath. They are the following: [1] Starting the bath with the utterance of the name of God, i.e. with the utterance of the formula:

> In the name of God, Most Gracious, Ever Merciful
> (بسم الله الرحمن الرحيم)
> (*Bi-smi Allāhi r-raḥmāni r-raḥīmi*).

[2] Making the intention of the bath to the effect that it is taken for the removal of the state of major legal impurity. The making of the intention as well as uttering the name of God should be done when washing the hands up to the wrists. [3] Washing the hands to the wrists. [4] Then the washing off of filth if there is any on the body. [It is to be washed off before washing the whole body, otherwise the filth will defile the entire body.] [5] Then the washing of the genitals, even though there is no filth on them.

After the performance of all these acts, the person bathing will make ablution as he does for ritual prayer. So he will [6] wash three times all the parts of the body to be washed in ablution, and [7] wipe

[45] Qur'ān 5:6.

the head, but [8] defer for the time being the washing of the feet if he is standing with his feet in water.

[9] Then he will pour water over his *entire* body three times. If he is immersed in running water or in some other water which is legally similar to it, e.g. a well occupying the space of ten square cubits, he has completed the sunna, for such immersion effects as much washing as is done by washing three times. [10] Starting the pouring of water over the body from the head. [11] Then washing the right shoulder first and then the left shoulder. [12] Rubbing over the body thoroughly.

'Praiseworthy' and 'Disliked' Acts in a Bath

The 'praiseworthy' acts in a bath are the same as those in ablution. The only difference is that facing the direction of the Holy Ka'ba which is 'praiseworthy' in ablution is not 'praiseworthy' in a bath, for a bath is mostly taken when uncovering the private parts of the body.

[It is 'praiseworthy' not to speak when bathing even though speaking takes the form of prayer and praise of God, for the time of bathing is one of the washing away of filth. It is also 'praiseworthy' to bathe in a place where none can see the private parts of the bather. The Prophet said,

> "God is Ever Living and Ever Concealed from the eyes of people, and He likes those who acquire the qualities of modesty and concealment; so when anyone of you wants to bathe, let him observe secrecy."[46]

If, when bathing along with other men, one does not find an opportunity to observe secrecy, one should choose a place which is least exposed. A woman should do the same when bathing together with other women. A woman will bathe last if she is bathing with men. It is a sin to look at the private parts of a person who has uncovered them for the purpose of washing the body.]

All acts which are 'disliked' by the law in ablution are also 'disliked' in a bath. [These acts have already been mentioned in the chapter on ablution. In addition to them it is 'disliked' to read any prayer formula while bathing. Bathing while naked is also 'disliked' by the law. Extravagance and miserliness in the use of water are both 'disliked'; it is the middle course which is prescribed.]

[46] Abū Dāwūd, *Sunan*, Ḥammām, 1; an-Nasā'ī, *Sunan*, Ghusl, 7; ash-Shurunbalālī, *Marāqī*, p. 47.

When Bathing is Sunna

It is sunna to take a bath for the performance of four acts. [1] Performance of the Friday Assembly Prayer.[47] [2] Performance of the ritual prayers of the two 'Īds — 'Īd al-Fiṭr (the Festival Day on the expiry of the lunar month Ramaḍān), and 'Īd al-Aḍḥā (the Festival Day of the Sacrifice of Animals). [3] Entering into the ritual of *iḥrām* [whether for the greater pilgrimage (*ḥajj*) or the lesser pilgrimage (*'umra*). The bath on entering into *iḥrām* is only for the general cleanliness of the body and hence it should be taken even by a menstruating woman and by a woman in the period of childbirth bleeding]. [4] For a pilgrim at 'Arafa, not outside it, after the sun passes its meridian. This bath is sunna because of the excellence of the time for the ritual of halting at 'Arafa.

When Bathing is 'Praiseworthy'

It is 'praiseworthy' to take a bath in the following conditions: [1] A person accepting Islam while being pure from the state of major legal impurity, from menstruation and from childbirth bleeding. [It is 'praiseworthy' for him to bathe, because the general cleanliness of the body is fitting for the acceptance of a new faith.] [2] A person who has become mature by the reckoning of age [which is fifteen for both boys and girls. An individual who has not yet experienced nocturnal emission or has not yet emitted sperm in any other way or has not yet menstruated, but has reached the age of fifteen, must be regarded as mature by the age. It is 'praiseworthy' for such a person to bathe]. [3] A person who has just recovered his normal state from insanity, faintness or drunkenness. [4] After the cupping of blood. [5] After washing a dead body. [6] In the Night of Immunity (*laylat al-Barā'a*), i.e. the night of the fifteenth day of the lunar month Sha'bān. In this night a bath should be taken for the performance of devotional acts and also for showing honour to the night.[48] [7] In the Night of Decree (*Laylat al-Qadr*) provided one has found it

[47] The Prophet said, "One who has made ablution on Friday [for the Assembly Prayer] has performed an excellent act, and one who has taken a bath [for the same purpose] has done a more excellent work." The Prophet also said, "Taking a bath on Friday is 'required' of every major person." See Muslim, *Ṣaḥīḥ*, Jumu'a, 7; an-Nasā'ī, *Sunan*, Jumu'a, 6, 11; al-Bukhārī, *Ṣaḥīḥ*, Jumu'a, 6.

[48] In Islam this is one of the great nights of the year. A man's sustenance, lifetime and other important affairs are usually believed to be determined by God in this night. Throughout this night every Muslim should be engaged in 'supererogatory' devotional acts, such as ritual prayer, Qur'ān-reading, glorification of God, and invoking blessings upon the prophet Muḥammad. He should clean himself completely by taking a bath just after the Sunset Prayer.

[with certainty or with great probability. This is a holy night. No one knows its exact date but it must be the night of an odd numbered day of Ramaḍān. It is more likely to be in the last ten days of Ramaḍān as the night of the 21st, or 23rd, or 25th, and so on. Knowledge of its exact date can be obtained through mystical intuition (*kashf*) coupled with discovering its signs. The finding of mere signs yields the most probable knowledge of it. These signs are that it is bright, not hot and not cold, and that in its morning, the sun rises without rays. If one finds this night, one should take a bath for the performance of 'supererogatory' devotional acts throughout it and for showing honour to it].

[8] For entering into Medina. For magnification of the excellence of this holy city and for arriving in the presence of the Prophet, one should take a bath before entering. [9] For the performance of the rite of halting at Muzdalifa in the morning time, i.e. between daybreak and sunrise, of the Day of Sacrifice of Animals (*yawm an-naḥar*), i.e. the ninth day of the month Dhū l-Ḥijja. [10] When entering the holy city of Mecca for the rite of any circumambulation of the Holy Ka'ba, especially the Visiting Circumambulation (*ṭawāf az-ziyāra*). For complete cleanliness, a bath is 'praiseworthy' when entering Mecca for this purpose.

[11-16] For the performance of the ritual prayers for the removal of an eclipse of the sun or the moon, for seeking rain, for the removal of a fear, of darkness in the daytime, or of a strong wind, such as a cyclone or tornado.

[A bath is also 'praiseworthy' for a person repenting from sin, a person returning home from the journey, a woman whose blood of *istiḥāḍa* has stopped, a pilgrim intending to perform the rite of casting pebbles at the Jamras, and a person whose body has come into contact with some filth but its exact whereabout is unknown.]

ABLUTION WITH CLEAN SAND (*TAYAMMUM*)

فلم تجدوا ماءً فتيمموا صعيدا طيبا. — قران ٦:٥م ٤٣:٤

"If ... you find no water [for ablution or bath], then have recourse to clean dust." — Qur'ān 4:43, 5:6

Stipulations for the Validity of Ablution with Sand

Ablution with clean sand is correct if the following eight stipulations are fulfilled by an individual making it.

First, making an intention, which consists in a mental resolve to perform the act of ablution with sand. It is not the mere verbal utterance of the formula of intention. The time for making an intention is when a person puts his palms over the sand or a similar substance with which this ablution (*tayammum*) can be made. The stipulations for the validity of this intention are: the person's being a Muslim, his sanity, and his knowledge of the reason why he is making the intention.

The intention of ablution with sand made for the performance of ritual prayer is valid if it fulfils one of three stipulations: it is made [i] for the removal of the state of legal impurity, or [ii] for the obtainment of legal fitness for the performance of ritual prayer, or [iii] for the performance of a devotional act which is prescribed as an independent, not a subordinate, act and which is not a correct act without cleanliness. [Thus, in the case of this last stipulation, the intended devotional act should be either ritual prayer or a part of it in itself. Making an intention in this case is this: I intend to make ablution with sand for ritual prayer, or for the ritual prayer over the bier, or for prostration due to Qur'ān-reading, or for simply Qur'ān-reading when the person is in the state of major legal impurity; each one of these acts needs cleanliness and is an independent act.] Because of the three stipulations just mentioned, a person cannot perform a ritual prayer if he has made his ablution with sand with the intention of performing ablution with sand only, or with the intention of reading the Qur'ān if he was in the state, not of major, but of minor legal impurity when he made his ablution with sand. [If a person in the state of major legal impurity has made ablution with sand for touching the Qur'ān or for entering into the mosque or for instructing another man in the methods of ablution with sand, he is 'not permitted' by the law to perform ritual prayer with this ablution with sand. Likewise, ablution with sand made for visiting graves, for calling people to ritual prayer (*adhān*), for calling people to the actual start of a ritual prayer (*iqāma*), for salutation, for reply to salutation, or for accepting Islam, is not valid for the performance of a ritual prayer.]

Second, the existence of an excuse 'permitting' ablution with sand. Examples of an excuse are: [a] a person's being a mile distant from water even though he is in a town; [b] sickness which is likely to aggravate or to delay a cure if water is used; [c] such cold as may cause death or sickness; [d] fear of an enemy whether man or animal, whether the fear is for the person himself, or his property, or a woman's fear of a wicked man near the water supply; [e] fear of thirst if the water present is used for ablution — thirst at present or in the near future, whether for himself or for companions or for an animal; [f] a need for the available water for making bread but not for cooking curry; [g] the absence of tools for drawing water from a well; and [h] fear of missing, even though partly, the ritual prayer over a bier or for an ‘Īd if he is engaged in making ablution with water. Ablution with sand is also ‘permitted’ if one’s ablution with water is nullified during one’s ritual prayer over a bier or for an ‘Īd when there is a great crowd of people preventing one going out for ablution with water.

The fear of missing the Friday Assembly Prayer or of not having enough time for a daily ritual prayer, if one is engaged in making ablution with water, is not included in an excuse ‘permitting’ ablution with sand, because the Friday Assembly Prayer has a substitute which is the Afternoon Prayer (*Ẓuhr*), and daily ritual prayer can be observed later (*qaḍā’*). This, however, does not minimize the importance of the Friday Assembly Prayer. There is a Tradition which runs thus:

> قال رسول الله صلى الله عليه وسلم: من ترك الجمعة ثلاثا من غير عذر طبع الله على قلبه.
>
> (The messenger of God — may God bless him and greet him! — said, “God puts a seal upon the mind of one who leaves the Friday Assembly Prayer unperformed three times successively without any real excuse.”)

Third, making ablution with sand by using something clean derived from the earth, e.g. soil, stone and sand; it cannot be made by using such materials as wood, gold, silver, or iron.

Fourth, wiping each place of wiping completely. [The places of wiping in ablution with sand are the face and the hands up to the elbows. For wiping these places in their entirety, one will move around one’s ring, comb the skin between the fingers with the fingers, and wipe the whole of the outer layer of the skin of the face and all the hair.]

Fifth, wiping with the use of the entire palm or the greater part of it. If wiping is accomplished with two fingers it is ‘not correct’, even though this is done repeatedly until the entire place of wiping is wiped. This is different from wiping the head in ablution with water.

Sixth, the performance of ablution with sand by patting the inner side of the palms over the soil twice, even though the patting is made over the same portion of soil. Patting is not needed if, with the intention of ablution with sand, one wipes the soil already present on one’s body.

Seventh, when making ablution with sand, freedom from menstruation, childbirth bleeding, and the state of minor legal impurity — things which negate ablution with sand.

Eighth, the removal of that which prevents wiping the outer layer of the skin, e.g. wax and fat, for with the presence of these things on the face or on the hands wiping will be the wiping of these things, not the wiping of the skin of the body.

The Causes of, and Stipulations for, the Obligation of Ablution with Sand

The reasons why ablution with sand is necessary and the stipulations for the necessity of ablution with sand are the same as those for ablution with water. They are mentioned in our discussion on ablution with water and need not be repeated here.

The Pillars of Ablution with Sand

There are two pillars of ablution with sand. They are the wiping of the hands up to the elbows and the wiping of the face.

Sunna Acts in Ablution with Sand

The sunna acts in ablution with sands are seven in number. They are as follows:

[1] At the start of ablution with sand, utterance of the name of God, i.e. to utter:

> In the name of God, Most Gracious, Ever Merciful
> (بسم الله الرحمن الرحيم)
> *(Bi-smi Allāhi r-raḥmāni r-raḥīmi)*.

[2] The observance of the order in the acts of ablution with sand. This order is: first to wipe the face and then to wipe the hands. [3] The performance of these acts uninterruptedly. [4] Bringing the palms forward and backward after patting them over the soil. [5] Shaking off from the palms after patting them over the soil, in case the face and the hands are soiled. [6] Keeping the fingers wide open when patting them over the soil.

'Praiseworthy' Acts in Ablution with Sand

It is 'praiseworthy' to delay the making of ablution with sand by a person who hopes that water will be available before the time for the ritual prayer is exhausted. Delay is 'necessary' for a person whom someone has promised to supply with water even though he fears that because of the delay he may miss the performance of the ritual prayer at its proper time. It is also 'necessary' to make a delay (as long as there is no fear of missing the ritual prayer in time), if one who is naked is promised that he will be supplied with a cloth to be used in the ritual prayer, or if one who has no water is promised that he will be supplied with the means of getting it, such as a rope and bucket; if, however, there is any doubt, one should make ablution with sand.

It is 'necessary' to look for water by going to a distance of four hundred footsteps provided one imagines that water is near and provided there is safety. If these two stipulations are lacking, it is 'not necessary' to look for water. It is also 'necessary' to seek water from one's companions if one is at a place where people are not usually niggardly. Should the companion not give the water without the usual price, one is 'required' by the law to buy it provided one has money in excess of one's maintenance.

With a single ablution with sand, a person is 'allowed' by the law to perform any number of 'obligatory' and 'supererogatory' ritual prayers. [It is, however, better to repeat ablution with sand for each 'obligatory' ritual prayer. The performance of ablution with sand before the start of the time of a ritual prayer is correct.]

If there are wounds in half or more than half of a person's body, he will make ablution with sand, even though he is in the state of major legal impurity. But if more than half is sound, he will wash the sound part and wipe over the wounded part.

One is 'not allowed' by the law to wash the body and also to make ablution with sand both together.

What Nullifies Ablution with Sand

The acts which nullify ablution with water also nullify ablution with sand. These acts have already been mentioned in the chapter on ablution with water. In addition, the ability to use, though once, that quantity of water which is sufficient for ablution with water renders ablution with sand null and void.

A person whose hands and legs are cut off and on whose face are wounds, will perform ritual prayers without ablution with sand and will not repeat the ritual prayers after the wounds are healed.

WIPING OVER BOOTS

It is legally correct [49] for both men and women to wipe over boots

[49] Prophetic traditions on the permissibleness of wiping over boots are narrated by more than eighty companions of the Prophet. These traditions have attained to the status of *mutawātir*.

covering the ankles for cleanliness against [50] the minor legal impurity, i.e. that impurity for the removal of which ablution is necessary, even though the boots are made of a thick substance other than leather; it is all the same whether or not these boots have leather soles. Men and women are 'allowed' by the law to wipe over boots whether they are stationary (*muqīm*) or on a journey and whether they need wiping or not,

Stipulations for Wiping Over Boots

Wiping over boots is 'permissible' by the law if it fulfils seven stipulations. These stipulations are as follows:

First, the boots are put on after the washing of the feet, even though this putting on is done before the completion of ablution with water. However, this ablution must be completed before the occurrence of anything which nullifies ablution.

Second, the boots must cover the ankles from the sides. Third, the boots are such that it is possible for him who has put them on to walk at ease. Thus it is 'not permissible' to wipe over boots made of glass or wood or iron. Fourth, each of the two boots must be free from an opening equal to the measure of three smallest toes. Fifth, boot must be not less than the breadth of the three smallest fingers. the feet. Sixth, the boots are such that water cannot penetrate into the feet through them. Seventh, the length of the frontal part of the boot must be not less than the breath of the three smallest fingers. This length is that measure of the place of wiping on which wiping is 'obligatory'. Should this length be absent, wiping over the boots is 'not permissible' by the law, even though the part at the heel of the foot is present, for this part is not the place where wiping is 'obligatory'.

Duration of Wiping over Boots

A stationary person (*muqīm*) is 'allowed' by the law to wipe over his boots during the period of a day and a night. A person on a journey can wipe during the period of three days together with their nights. The beginning of this duration is counted from the time when the minor legal impurity has occurred after putting on the boots in the state of cleanliness.

A stationary person who has wiped over his boots and then has become a traveller before the expiry of the duration 'allowed' to the stationary, is 'allowed' by the law to complete the duration meant for

[50] Wiping over boots is not correct for the obtainment of cleanliness against the major legal impurity — an impurity for which a ritual bath is necessary.

a traveller, for what is to be considered is the last part of the duration. A traveller who has become stationary after wiping over his boots during the period of a day and a night is 'required' to take off his boots; he is 'not permitted' to wipe during the period of three days and nights for he is no longer a traveller; but if he has become stationary *before* wiping during the period of a day and a night, he will complete this period, for this period is meant for a stationary period.

'Obligatory' Act in Wiping over Boots

The obligatory act in wiping over boots is to wipe once over the outward side of the frontal part of every foot — only the length of three smallest fingers. [Making this measure wet with a piece of cloth or by pouring water over it is 'permissible'. It is 'not correct' to wipe over the inward side of the feet or back of the feet or the both sides of the feet or over the leg. Wiping is to be done only once; more than once is not sunna.]

Sunna Act in Wiping over Boots

The sunna act in wiping over boots is to wipe over them starting from the heads of the toes and proceeding to the leg, by using the fingers wetted with water and spread wide.

What Nullifies Wiping over Boots

There are four things which make wiping over boots null and void. They are as follows:

[1] Everything which nullifies ablution with water also nullifies wiping over boots, because the latter is but a substitute of the former. The things which nullify ablution with water are mentioned in a previous section. [2] The pulling off of a boot even though this is effected by the coming out of only the greater part of the foot to the leg of the boot. By this the boot is moved from its proper position. [3] Penetration of water into the greater part of any one of the two feet inside the boot; this is the correct view. In this case it is 'necessary' to take off the boots and wash both feet. [4] Expiry of the duration fixed for wiping over boots provided there is no fear that, after taking off of the boots, the feet will be destroyed by terrible cold. Should there be such a fear wiping can be continued. After the last mentioned three things the person's wiping over the boot is null and he will wash his feet only. He is not 'required' to repeat the remaining parts of his ablution.

It is 'not permissible' to wipe, when performing ablution, over the turban, cap, veil and pullover.

WIPING OVER A BANDAGE

If a person's blood is drawn as a medical treatment or he has received a wound or his limb is broken, and he has bound the places affected with rags or bandages, and he is unable to wash the affected limbs in ablution or to wipe them — in all these cases it is 'necessary' to wipe over the greater part of the rags or the bandages. It is sufficient to wipe over that part of the body which appears between the bandages put by the drawer of blood and the like.

Wiping over a bandage is like washing that place of the body which is under the bandage; it is not a substitute for washing. Hence it is not limited in duration, as is the wiping over boots. There is no stipulation that the bandage should be made when the person is in the state of legal purity. It is 'permissible' to wipe over the bandage on one leg and to wash the other. Wiping is not nullified by the fall of the bandage before the healing of the wounds. Replacement of a bandage wiped over with another is 'permissible', and after replacement it is not 'necessary' to repeat the wiping done over the previous bandage. Repetition, however, is better.

If a person suffering from opthalmia is asked by the physician not to wash his eyes, or if a person has applied medicine or chewing-gum or some similar thing to his broken nose and it is harmful to take it away — in all these cases it is 'permissible' for him to wipe. Should the wiping be harmful in these cases, he will leave wiping undone.

There is no need of making intention in the case of wiping over boots, of wiping over a bandage, or of wiping the head in ablution, for all these are as good as washing with water.

MENSTRUATION, CHILDBIRTH BLEEDING AND ISTIḤĀḌA

ويسئلونك من المحيض. قل هى اذى، فاعتزلوا النساء فى
المحيض، ولاتقربوهن حتى يطهرن. فاذا تطهرن فاتوهن من
حيث امركم الله. ان الله يحب التوابين ويحب المتطهرين.—
قران ٢:٢٢٢

They enquire from you as to [consorting with their wives during their menstruation. Tell them: it is harmful, so keep away from women during their menstruation and do not consort with them until they are clean. But when they have become clean consort with them as God has commanded you. Surely God loves those who turn to Him often and He loves those who clean themselves. — Qur'ān 2:222

The Blood of menstruation, childbirth and istiḥāḍa flows out through the women's genitals. Menstruation is the blood secreted from the uterus of a woman who has attained to the age of maturity which the law presumes to be not less than nine, who is not suffering from certain particular diseases, who is not pregnant, and who has not reached the age of barrenness which the law presumes to be usually fifty-five. The shortest duration for menstruation is three days. The medium duration is five days together with the nights, and the longest is ten days. [Hence if a woman stops bleeding before the expiry of three days or continues it after ten days, it is not menstruation.]

The blood of the childbirth bleeding period is that which comes through a woman's genitals, following her giving birth to a child. The longest duration for this bleeding is forty days. There is no limit to its shortest duration.

Istiḥāḍa is the blood which comes out through a woman's genitals, originating from a vein and not from the uterus; it has no smell. It stops in a period less than three days, or continues after ten days in the time of menstruation and after forty days in the case of childbirth bleeding.

The shortest duration for a woman's being clean between her two periods of menstruation is that of fifteen days. There is no limit set to its longest duration, except for those women who have reached the stage of istiḥāḍa. [For such women, menstruation will be counted as ten days, the duration of being clean as fifteen days, and the childbirth bleeding as forty days; the days in excess of these are regarded as the days of istiḥāḍa.]

Acts 'Unlawful' in Menstruation and in Childbirth Bleeding

It is 'unlawful' to perform the following eight acts during menstruation and childbirth bleeding period:

[1] Performance of ritual prayer. [2] Observance of fasting. [3] Recitation of even a single verse of the Qur'ān.[51] [4] Touching of a Qur'ānic verse,[52] whether it is written on a sheet of paper or on a coin or on a wall. To touch a verse from the outside of a case or a veil, however, is not 'unlawful'. [For touching a book on the commentary of the Qur'ān, ablution is 'required'.] [5] Entering into the mosque. [The Prophet said,

[51] The Prophet said, "Neither a menstruating woman, nor a person in the state of major legal impurity will read anything of the Qur'ān. Women with childbirth bleeding are like menstruating women in this respect." See at-Tirmidhī, *Sunan*, Ṭahāra, 98; Ibn Māja, *Sunan*, Ṭahāra, 105.

[52] God said, "No one except the purified can touch it." See Qur'ān 56:79.

[53] Abū Dāwūd, *Sunan*, Ṭahāra, 92; Ibn Māja, *Sunan*, Ṭahāra, 126.

"I do not make the mosque 'lawful' to a person in the state of major legal impurity or to a menstruating woman.[53] Women with childbirth bleeding are to be treated as like them."]

[6] Circumambulation of the Holy Ka'ba in Mecca. The circumambulation is like ritual prayer in this respect and so it cannot be performed by menstruating women and women with childbirth bleeding. [7-9] Sexual intercourse and any other sexual enjoyment with that part of her body which lies from below her navel to below her knee.[54]

It is 'lawful' to have sexual intercourse, without bathing, just when bleeding has stopped on the expiry of the longest durations fixed for menstruation and for childbirth bleeding.[55] It is, however, 'praiseworthy' not to have sexual intercourse until she bathes. But if bleeding has stopped on the completion of her usual duration for it but before the expiry of the longest possible duration for it, sexual intercourse is 'not lawful' until [a] she bathes, or [b], if there is an excuse, does *tayammum* (i.e. purifies with clean sand) and performs a ritual prayer even though it is 'supererogatory', or [c] until a ritual prayer becomes due on her responsibility. This last alternative is such that, after the stopping of bleeding on completion of her usual duration, she finds such a time as is sufficient for bathing and starting a ritual prayer by uttering *Allāhu akbar* and doing more than this, but she does not bathe or does not purify herself with clean sand until the time for that ritual prayer is exhausted. [Just after the exhaustion of the time, it is 'lawful' to have sexual intercourse.]

Menstruating women and women with childbirth bleeding who miss fasting will observe it later when they are clean; but they will not perform ritual prayers they miss, later when they are clean.

'Unlawful' Acts in the State of Major Legal Impurity

If a person has incurred the major legal impurity — an impurity for which bath is obligatory —, it is 'unlawful' for him to perform the following five activities:

[1] Performance of ritual prayer. This is 'unlawful' because cleanliness is a stipulation for ritual prayer.[56] [2] Recitation of a verse of the Qur'ān. [3] Touching of a Qur'ānic verse.[57] However, touching a Qur'ānic verse from outside a case is 'not unlawful'. [4] Entering into the mosque. [5] Circumambulation of the Ka'ba in

[54] Qur'ān 2:22; Abū Dāwūd, *Sunan*, Ṭahāra, 82; Aḥmad ibn Ḥanbal, *Musnad*, I, 14; Muslim, *Ṣaḥīḥ*, Ḥayḍ, 3.

[55] Qur'ān 2:222.

[56] Qur'ān 5:6.

[57] Qur'ān 56:79.

Mecca. This is equal to ritual prayer, and therefore can not be performed at the state of major legal impurity.

'Unlawful' Acts in the State of Minor Legal Impurity

If a person has incurred the minor legal impurity — an impurity for the removal of which ablution is necessary —, it is unlawful for him [1] to perform ritual prayer, [2] to circumambulate the Holy Ka'ba in Mecca, and [3] to touch the Qur'ān even though a single verse of it. Touching the Qur'ān from outside a case, however, is 'not unlawful'.

Rules on Istiḥāḍa and Excuses

The legal rulings on the blood of istiḥāḍa are indentical with the rulings on perpetual haemorrhage of the nose: it does not prevent the performance of ritual prayer, fasting, or sexual intercourse, for it is not a filth. The woman suffering from istiḥāḍa and the person who has such an excuse as looseness of urine or stomach trouble or perpetual haemorrhage of the nose, must make ablution for the *time* of every 'obligatory' ritual prayer, and, with that ablution, perform, during that time, (a) any number of 'obligatory' ritual prayers, i.e. the obligatory ritual prayer of that time as well as the 'obligatory' ritual prayers which were not performed in their due times, (b) 'supererogatory' ritual prayers, [and (c) 'required' acts, e.g. the Odd Prayer (*Ṣalāt al-Witr*), the 'Īd Prayers, circumambulation of the Ka'ba, touching of the Qur'ān, and so on], which they wish. The ablution of those who have an excuse becomes invalid with the passing of that time only, even though nothing nullifying it other than this excuse has occurred.

A person is legally considered excused only if his excuse prolongs throughout the time of a ritual prayer — there being no removal of the excuse in that time for such measure of time as allows one to make ablution and to perform a ritual prayer. This is the stipulation for the establishment of an excuse. The stipulation for the continuation of an excuse is that, after its establishment, it should be present in every time of ritual prayer even though once. The stipulation for the cessation of an excuse is that one complete time of a ritual prayer is free from the excuse. These, then, are the three stipulations.

FILTHS AND CLEANLINESS FROM THEM

Serious Filth and Light Filth

Filth is legally divided into two kinds: serious and light. Examples of the former are: wine [58], the blood poured forth [59], flesh of a dead animal which has flowing blood [60] and its hide before tanning it, the urine of those whose flesh cannot be eaten legally, e.g. man, wolf and rat, dung of the dog, dung of ferocious animals, e.g. cheetah and pig, the saliva of ferocious animals, the dung of domestic fowls, duck and goose, and finally all those things the coming out of which from the human body nullifies ablution, e.g. flowing blood, sperm, *madhī, wadī*, istiḥāḍa, blood of menstruation, blood of childbirth and vomiting of a mouthful. Examples of light filth are: the urine of the horse, the urine of those animals the flesh of which can be eaten legally, e.g. sheep and deer, and the dung of a bird the flesh of which cannot be eaten legally, e.g. falcon. However, the dung of the horse, donkey, ass, cow and goat are serious filth. The blood of fish, and the saliva of the donkey and the ass are clean legally.

Serious filth of the measure of a silver coin — i.e. its weight in the case of filth which has body and its size in space in the case of filth which is liquid — is forgiven. Light filth occupying less than a fourth of a complete piece of cloth or the entire body is forgiven. So also are forgiven splashes or urine so little as the heads of needles, even though urine is a serious filth.

If a filthy bed or filthy soil becomes wet by the wetness of the sweat of a man sleeping on them or by the wetness of the feet of one who has walked on them, and the trace of the filth appears on the body of the man who slept or at the feet of the man who walked, the body and the feet are to be regarded as filthy. If, however, the trace of filth does not appear, these are not to be considered as filthy, as in the case of a dry, clean cloth wrapped in a wet filthy cloth the wetness of which is such that it is not exuded when it is pressed.

A wet cloth does not become filthy if it is spread out on soil unclean with dried filth, e.g. dried urine, and the soil has become

[58] Wine is a serious filth according to Islamic law. In the Qur'ān (5:90-93) the drinking of wine is strictly prohibited: God said, "O you who believe, wine, gambling, idols and divining arrows are but abominations (*najas*) and Satanic acts. So turn wholly away from each of them that you may prosper. Satan desires only to create enmity and hatred between you by means of wine and gambling and to keep you back from the remembrance of God and from ritual prayer. Will you, then, desist? Obey God and obey the Messenger [i.e. Muḥammad] and be ever on your guard [against wine and gambling] ....".

[59] Qur'ān 56:145 . The following types of blood are not considered by the law as unclean: a little blood which remains in the meat of a slaughtered animal and inside its veins, blood present in its liver and spleen, a little blood the coming of which does not nullify one's ablution, the blood of the flea and the lice even though this blood is much in quantity, the blood of the fish, and the blood of the martyr for himself.

[60] The flesh of a dead fish and of a locust is not filthy, because the law considers

soaked from the wetness of the cloth, but no trace of the filth is visible on the cloth. A piece of cloth does not become filthy if the wind blown over a filth reaches it; if, however, any trace of the filth is visible on the cloth the cloth becomes filthy.

A thing filthy with a visible filth, e.g. blood, becomes clean by the removal of the filth itself even though by washing once — this is the correct view. Should any trace of the filth, e.g. colour or ordure, remain after washing, cleanliness is not affected by this if it is difficult to remove the trace.

A thing filthy with an invisible filth becomes clean by washing it three times together with pressing it each time. If one who has forgotten the location of an invisible filth in his cloth, has washed one side of the cloth without thinking much concerning the location, the cloth is to be regarded as clean, and ritual prayer may be performed wearing it; [if later it becomes clear that the location of the filth is at the other side of the cloth, the ritual prayer will be repeated.]

Filth, whether visible or invisible, on a piece of cloth or on the body is cleansed with water and with any other clean, liquid thing which removes filth, e.g. rose water and vinegar. Boots and similar things, e.g. shoes, are cleansed by washing with water and by rubbing with soil if the filth on them has a body even though this filth is wet. A sword or a similar thing, e.g. a mirror, is cleansed by wiping the filth with soil or a rag. It is all the same whether this filth is wet or dry or urine or stool or the like.

When the trace of filth has disappeared from the soil and the soil has become dry, it is 'permissible' to perform ritual prayer on it, but not to use it in ablution with clean sand. Trees, grass, etc. which have grown on a filthy ground are clean when the filth is dried up and its trace is removed.

Filth becomes clean if its essence is changed into something else, as in the case where a filth is turned into salt or dust, or where fire has reduced it to ashes.

A piece of cloth or a bodily organ on which dried sperm is visible, becomes clean by rubbing it out with the hand. Anything filthy with wet sperm becomes clean by washing the sperm with water.[61]

CLEANLINESS OF HIDES OF DEAD ANIMALS

these to have no flowing blood when they are alive.

61 This ruling is based upon Traditions recorded in: at-Tirmidhī, *Sunan*, Ṭahāra, 85; an-Nasā'ī, *Sunan*, Ṭahāra, 187; Abū Dāwūd, *Sunan*, Ṭahāra, 134; Muslim, *Ṣaḥīḥ*, Ṭahāra, 105, 106; Ibn Māja, *Sunan*, Ṭahāra, 82.

The hide of a dead animal even though it is the dog becomes clean through its real tanning. The hide of a pig or of a man does not become clean through any kind of tanning.

Slaughtering approved by the Sharī'a (i.e. the Islamic revealed law) purifies the hide, but not the meat, of an animal the meat of which is not 'lawful' to eat. The case of a pig is of course an exception; its hide is not purified by this slaughtering. This is the most correct of those views on which legal decision has been given.

Any part of an animal, except the pig, to which the blood cannot reach, does not become legally unclean after the animal dies. Examples of such a part are the hair, feathers, horn, hoof, and bone so long as no greasiness is present in them.

Nerve is unclean according to the correct view. That part of the skin of an animal in which exists musk is clean absolutely, as is the musk itself. It is 'lawful' to eat musk. The fragrant perfume obtainable from a deer is clean; the ritual prayer of a man who has applied it to his body is correct.

III
RITUAL PRAYER

ان الصلاة كانت على المومنين كتابا موقوتا.ـ قران ٤:١٠٣

Ritual prayer is an obligation on the believers to be observed at its appointed time. — Qur'ān 4:103

STIPULATIONS FOR THE OBLIGATION OF RITUALPRAYER

There are three stipulations for ritual prayer (*ṣalā*) to be 'obligatory'. They are as follows. [1] Islam. A person must be a Muslim if ritual prayer is to be 'obligatory' upon him, because devotional acts are not addressed to a man who has not yet accepted Islam. [2] Maturity. Only those who have attained the age of maturity can be under an 'obligation' to perform ritual prayer. Children are not obliged to perform it. [3] Sanity. Ritual prayer can only be 'obligatory' upon those who are sane.

Children of seven will be commanded to perform ritual prayer. If, at the age of ten, they do not perform it they will be struck with the hand mildly, but not with a stick. The prophet Muḥammad said,

> "Command your children to perform ritual prayer when they are seven, and beat them for neglecting it when they are ten...." [62]

TIMES OF RITUAL PRAYER

Performance of ritual prayer five times daily is made 'obligatory' by the presence of these times. Performance of a ritual prayer becomes 'obligatory' in the first part of its time, but it can be delayed to a later part of it.

There are five times of 'obligatory' ritual prayer. They are as follows. [1] The time of the Dawn Prayer (*Ṣalāt al-Fajr*) starts from the true daybreak and ends with a little before the sunrise. [2] The time of the Noon Prayer (*Ṣalāt aẓ-Ẓuhr*) starts from the time when the sun passes its meridian, and ends when the shadow of a thing

62 Aḥmad ibn Ḥanbal, *Musnad*, II, 180.

becomes its double in length or equal to it excluding the shadow of the equator. This latter view is chosen by the jurist aṭ-Ṭaḥāwī,[63] and it is also the opinion of Imām Abū Yūsuf[64] and Imām Muḥammad.[65] [3] The time of the Late Afternoon Prayer (*Ṣalāt al-'Aṣr*) starts from after the time when the shadow of a thing becomes equal to itself or double of itself, excluding the shadow of the equator, and ends with the setting of the sun.

[4] The time of the Sunset Prayer (*Ṣalāt al-Maghrib*) begins from the sunset and ends when the red evening twilight in the horizon is set. On this view legal decision has been given. [5] The time of the Evening Prayer (*Ṣalāt al-'Ishā'*) and the Odd Prayer (*Ṣalāt al-Witr*) starts from the setting of the red evening twilight in the horizon and continues until the true daybreak. The Odd Prayer cannot precede the Evening Prayer because the maintenance of the order between these two ritual prayers is necessary. One who does not find the time of these two ritual prayers is not 'required' to perform them. This happens in certain countries where in the shortest night of the year, daybreak occurs before the setting of the red evening twilight in the horizon.

Two 'obligatory' ritual prayers cannot be combined in a time for any excuse, such as rain and journey. Combination of them is only permissible to a pilgrim at 'Arafa, provided he performs them with the greatest imām and provided he is in *iḥrām*. So he will combine the Noon Prayer and the Late Afternoon Prayer in the first part of the time of the Noon Prayer. He will also combine the Sunset Prayer and the Evening Prayer in the time of the Evening Prayer at Muzdalifa. It is 'not permitted' by the law that the Sunset Prayer be performed by a pilgrim along the way to Muzdalifa.

[63] Imām Abū Ja'far aṭ-Ṭaḥāwī (d. 321 A.H./933 A.D.) was one of the older jurists and theologians of the Ḥanafī school of Islamic religious law. Although he belonged to this school, he sometimes diverged from its established views. A number of his books have survived.

[64] Imām Abū Yūsuf Ya'qūb (d. 182 A.H./798 A.D.) was one of the founders of the Ḥanafi school. The caliph Hārūn ar-Rashīd conferred upon him the title of 'Judge of the Judges' (*qāḍī al-quḍāt*) for the first time in Islam. His literary output was considerable. His doctrine, on the whole, presupposes the doctrine of Abū Ḥanīfa, whom he regarded as his master. But there are points where he diverged. See Ibn an-Nadīm, *Fihrist*, pp. 502-503, 415; Schacht, "Abū Yūsuf", *EI*², I, 164-165.

[65] Imām Muḥammad ash-Shaybānī (d. 189 A.H./805 A.D.) was one of the founders of the Ḥanafī school. Like Abū Yūsuf, he wrote extensive literary works. He and Abū Yūsuf have come to be known as the two main companions of Abū Ḥanīfa, and together with him they form the triad of the highest authorities of the school. See Ibn an-Nadīm, *Fihrist*, pp. 496-97, 504, 507-509, 514, 516, 519, 523, 568; W. Heffening, "Al-Shaibānī", *EI*, 271.

Delay in the performance of the Dawn Prayer until the dawn shines is 'praiseworthy' for a man. [For a woman, however, its performance early in the morning when the dawn has not yet become very bright, is 'praiseworthy'.] It is 'praiseworthy' for man and woman alike to delay the Noon Prayer to a certain extent during the hot summer season, but to hasten it during the winter season except on a cloudy day when it should be delayed. It is also 'praiseworthy' to delay the Late Afternoon Prayer in all seasons as long as no change has taken place in the brightness of the sun. [To delay it to the time of this change is 'gravely disliked' by the law.] Hastening its performance on a cloudy day is 'praiseworthy'. To hasten the Sunset Prayer in all seasons is 'praiseworthy', except on a cloudy day when it should be delayed until the time when one is sure that the sun is set. [Delay on other days is 'disliked' by the law.] It is 'praiseworthy' to delay the Evening Prayer until the end of the first one-third of the night. To delay it until midnight is 'permissible', but after the midnight is 'gravely disliked' by the law. In a cloudy night of course, its early performance is 'praiseworthy'. Likewise, it is 'praiseworthy' to delay the Odd Prayer to almost the end of the night; this is for one who is confident of waking so late.

THE TIMES WHEN PERFORMANCE OF A RITUAL PRAYER IS 'DISLIKED'

There are three times in which it is not correct to perform any 'obligatory' or 'necessary' ritual prayer which became due upon a person *before* the start of these times. ['Obligatory' ritual prayers are those performed five times daily. The 'necessary' ritual prayers are: the Odd Prayer, those ritual prayers which a person vowed to God absolutely, the two *rak'as* of ritual prayer performed after the circumambulation of the Ka'ba, the 'supererogatory' ritual prayer one has deliberately nullified after starting it at a time not 'disliked' by the law, and the prostration due to the recitation of a certain Qur'ānic verse recited at a time other than the 'disliked' time. The three times in which these 'obligatory' and 'necessary' ritual prayers are incorrect, are as follows.]

[1] From the time when the sun is rising to the time when it has risen one or two spear lengths high. [2] When the sun is on its meridian. [3] From the time when the sun has become yellow and its rays weak to the moment when it has actually set. [Thus the Dawn Prayer of a person performing it while the sun is rising is invalid.]

If any ritual prayer has become 'necessary' *in* any of these three times, its performance during this time is legally correct. Thus if at any of these times a bier is brought and the ritual prayer is performed over it, or a Qur'ānic verse of prostration is recited and the prostration is duly made, all these cases are to be regarded as correct. Likewise, it is correct to perform the Late Afternoon Prayer of a particular day at the time of the sunset of the same day; even though this is correct it is 'disliked' by the law, because of the delaying of this ritual prayer to the sunset time.

Performance of a 'supererogatory' ritual prayer at any of these three times is 'gravely disliked' by the law even though this prayer has a cause. Examples of this prayer are: the ritual prayer one has vowed to God to perform, and the two sunna *rak'as* following the circumambulation of the Ka'ba.

It is 'disliked' to perform any 'supererogatory' ritual prayer other than the two sunna *rak'as* of the Dawn Prayer, in the time from after daybreak to the performance of the obligatory *rak'as* of the Dawn Prayer. Likewise, it is 'disliked' to perform any 'supererogatory' ritual prayer [1] after the 'obligatory' *rak'as* of the Dawn Prayer, [2] after the 'obligatory' *rak'as* of the Late Afternoon Prayer [even though the sun is not yet about to set], [3] before the 'obligatory' *rak'as* of the Evening Prayer, [4] from the time when the imām (i.e. one who leads a ritual prayer) comes out to the pulpit in order to address the congregation until he completes the ritual prayer, [5] when the call for the actual start of an 'obligatory' ritual prayer (*iqāma*) is being made — the two sunna *rak'as* of the Dawn Prayer can, however, be performed when the *iqāma* is being made provided one is sure that their performance will not cause one to miss the 'obligatory' *rak'as* in congregation —, [6] before an 'Īd Prayer even though at home, [7] after an 'Īd Prayer in the place where this prayer is performed, [8] between the two 'obligatory' ritual prayers performed combinedly at 'Arafa, [9] between the two 'obligatory' ritual prayers combined at Muzdalifa, [10] when the time for the 'obligatory' *rak'as* of a ritual prayer is short [thus not allowing one to perform any 'supererogatory' prayer], [11] when one needs to relieve oneself, [12] when food is brought to one's presence, and [13] when anything is present which prevents the mind from concentration on the ritual prayer and impairs the submission of the mind to God in it.

CALL TO RITUAL PRAYER

قال النبي صلى الله عليه وسلم: اذا حضرت الصلاة فليوءذن لكم احدكم وليوءمكم اكبركم.

The Prophet (may God bless him and greet him!) said, "When the time of an obligatory ritual prayer is come let one of you call you to it and let the greatest of you lead it for you." [66]

The call to ritual prayer (*adhān*) and the call to the actual start of a ritual prayer (*iqāma*) are both 'emphasized sunna' for 'obligatory' ritual prayers [and also for the Friday Assembly Prayer], even though one performs the 'obligatory' ritual prayers alone, and whether one performs them in their scheduled times or later and whether one performs them as 'stationary' or as a traveller. All this is for a man. For a woman the call to ritual prayer and the call to the actual start of a ritual prayer are both 'disliked' by the law.

In the beginning of *adhān*, *Allāhu akbar* (الله اكبر) is to be uttered four times, [67] and at the end of it this sentence is to be repeated twice like all other sentences of *adhān*. No undue stress of words should be made in the two sentences of the testimony, i.e. in *ashhadu an lā ilāha illā Allāhu*(اشهد ان لا اله الا الله)and *ashhadu anna Muḥammadan rasūlu Allāhi*.(اشهد ان محمدا رسول الله). *Iqāma* is also like this. In the *adhān* for the Dawn Prayer, *aṣ-ṣalātu khayrun mina n-nawmi*(الصلاة خير من النوم)is to be added twice after *ḥayya 'alā l-falāḥi*. (حي على الفلاح). In *iqāma*, *qad qāmati ṣ-ṣalātu* (قد قامت الصلاة) is to be added twice after *ḥayya 'alā l-falāḥi*. In *adhān* every sentence will be uttered with a pause, but in *iqāma* it will be uttered with haste.

Adhān in a language other than the Arabic, e.g. Persian, is not correct even though people understand that this is *adhān*. It is 'praiseworthy' that the man who calls people to ritual prayer (*mu'adhdhin*) be pious, knower of the sunna acts in *adhān* and of the proper times of ritual prayers, in ablution, and facing the direction of the Ka'ba — however if he is riding or on a vehicle it is not 'praiseworthy' for him to face the ka'ba. It is also 'praiseworthy' that he puts his two fingers in his two ears, turns his face to the right side when saying *ḥayya 'alā ṣ-ṣalāti*(حي على الصلوة)and to the left side when saying *ḥayya 'alā l-falāḥi*, turns round in the monastery [if

[66] Al-Bukhārī, *Ṣaḥīḥ*, Adhān, 17, 18, 49, 140; Muslim, *Ṣaḥīḥ*, Masjid, 292, 293. Concerning the excellence of a man who performs the call to ritual prayer the Prophet said, "Every jinni or man or thing which hears the voice of a man calling people to ritual prayer, will bear witness for him on the Day of Judgement" (al-Bukhārī, *Ṣaḥīḥ*, Adhān, 5). In the following Qur'ānic verse (41:33) God has praised those who perform the call to ritual prayer: "Who speaks better than one who invites people to God, does good and affirms: surely I am one of the Muslims?" This verse is revealed concerning those who perform the call to ritual prayer.

[67] The reason for repetition of words of *adhān* is to impress the importance of ritual prayer in the minds of people.

the call is not felt complete as a result of the turning of the face to the right side and the left side], that he allows between the *adhān* and the *iqāma* as much interval as is required for pious men to be present in the congregation but at the same time should not miss the 'praiseworthy' part of the time for the ritual prayer. In the case of the Sunset Prayer, this interval should be that measure in which one can read three Qur'ānic verses of small length [or one verse], or can walk three steps. In the case of all 'obligatory' ritual prayers, the man who calls to ritual prayer should, after the *adhān*, gather the people by saying, for example, 'ritual prayer, ritual prayer, O the performers of ritual prayer'.

It is 'disliked' that one modulates one's voice in *adhān*, that one in the state of the minor legal impurity should perform *adhān* and *iqāma*, and that one who is in the state of the major legal impurity performs these. It is also 'disliked' that *adhān* should be performed by a boy whose faculty of intellect has not yet started functioning, by a person who is insane or drunk, by a woman, by a wicked person, and by a sitting individual. Speaking during *adhān* and *iqāma* is 'disliked' by the law. If one speaks it is 'praiseworthy' to repeat the *adhān* but not the *iqāma*. *Adhān* and *iqāma* for the Noon Prayer on Friday in a town are 'disliked' by the law. They both will be performed for a ritual prayer which could not be performed in its scheduled time. Likewise, both will be performed for the first of the several ritual prayers which could not be performed in their due times; it is 'disliked' not to perform *iqāma*, but not *adhān*, for these ritual prayers except the first one, provided these prayers are performed at one time.

If a person hears the sunna part of *adhān*, he will stop his works and say what the *mu'adhdhin* says.[68] When the *mu'adhdhin* says *ḥayya 'alā ṣ-ṣalāti* and *ḥayya 'alā l-falāḥi,* he should say *lā ḥawla wa lā quwwata illā bi-Allāhi l-'aliyyi l-'aẓīmi* (لاحول ولا قوة الا بالله العلي العظيم : there is no ability and there is no power except with God, the All-high, the All-great). When the *mu'adhdhin* says, in the *adhān* for the Dawn Prayer, *aṣ-ṣalātu khayrun mina n-nawmi,* the person will say *ṣadaqta wa bararta* (صدقت وبررت: you have spoken the truth and have done good) or *mā shā'a Allāhu* (ما شا الله : whatever God wants becomes). On completion of an *adhān*, both the *mu'adhdhin* and the person who hears the *adhān* will pray to God through the Means, by reading the formula:

[68] The Prophet commanded, "When you hear the call to ritual prayer, repeat what the caller says." See al-Bukhārī, *Ṣaḥīḥ*, Adhān, 7; Muslim, *Ṣaḥīḥ*, Ṣalā. 10.

God, the Lord of this perfect call and of this ritual prayer to be established, grant Muḥammad the Means and excellence, and raise him to the commendable station You promised to him.[69]

(اللهم رب هذه الدعوة التامة والصلاة القائمة ات محمدا الوسيلة والفضيلة وابعثه مقاما محمودا الذى وعدته).

(*Allāhumma, rabba hādhihi d-da'wati t-tāmmati, wa ṣ-ṣalāti l-qā'imati; āti Muḥammadani l-wasīlata wa l-faḍīlata; wa ab'athhu maqāman maḥmūdan alladhī wa-'adtahu.*)

STIPULATIONS FOR THE VALIDITY OF A RITUAL PRAYER AND ITS PILLARS

For the validity of a ritual prayer twenty-seven things are necessary. They are called the stipulations of ritual prayer. They are as follows:

[1] Cleanliness from the state of major and minor legal impurity, and from menstruation and childbirth bleeding. [2-4] Cleanliness of one's entire body and the dress, and of the place of ritual prayer from that measure of filth which is not forgiven. It is essential to secure cleanliness even of the place of one or both the feet, the hands, the knees and the forehead. This is the most correct view. [5] Covering the private parts of the body, even though the devotee is performing the ritual prayer in darkness. [The use of silken cloth, stolen cloth, and land owned by others renders the ritual prayer 'disliked' but not invalid. It is 'praiseworthy' to perform ritual prayer by using three of one's best clothes — shirt, trousers and turban or cap; to limit to the trousers only, despite one's ability to use the other two, is 'disliked' by the law.] [6] Facing the *qibla*. A person who is in Mecca and who sees the Holy Ka'ba,[70] must face the Ka'ba itself; but for those who do not see it, even though they are in Mecca, it is 'obligatory' only to face the direction of the Ka'ba.

69 The Prophet said that on the Day of Judgement it will be lawful for him to intercede to God for one who prays after *adhān* by reading this formula prayer (al-Bukhārī, *Ṣaḥīḥ*, Adhān, 8; Abū Dāwūd, *Sunan*, Ṣalā, 37). The Prophet also said, "When you hear the voice of him who calls to ritual prayer, repeat what he says. Then invoke blessings on me, for God sends blessings ten times to a person who invokes blessings on me once. Then pray to God that He should grant me the Means which is a status in Paradise that befits only one believer from among the servants of God [i.e. men], and I hope that I shall be that person. My intercession to God will be lawful for him who prays that God should grant me the Means." See al-Bukhārī, *Ṣaḥīḥ*, Adhān, 7; Muslim, *Ṣaḥīḥ*, Ṣalā, 10,11; also see *infra*, pp. 235f.

70 The Holy Ka'ba is the house ascribed to God (*bayt Allāh*) standing, under the sky, in the open courtyard of the Sacred Mosque in Mecca.

This is the correct view.

[7] Presence of the time of the five obligatory ritual prayers. [8] The firm conviction of the devotee that the time of the ritual prayer he is performing has already started. [9] Making of intention for the ritual prayer. [This consists in mental resolve and not in mere verbal utterance of a formula of intention.] [71] [10-11] Uttering *Allāhu akbar* (God is the greatest) at the start of the ritual prayer, without separating it from the making of intention [by any act, e.g. speaking]. [12-14] Uttering this *Allāhu akbar* by standing before bending the back for the bowing, not to utter it before the making of intention, and to utter it so loudly that the devotee himself can hear this — this is the most correct view.

[15] In a ritual prayer in congregation, the follower's making the intention of following the imām, (i.e. one who leads a ritual prayer), in addition to his making the basic intention of the ritual prayer. [16] When making the intention of an 'obligatory' ritual prayer, to specify that it is an '*obligatory*' ritual prayer. [17] Similarly, when making the intention of a ritual prayer which is 'required', specification of it as a *required* ritual prayer.

[18] Standing in the case of the performance of all 'obligatory' as well as 'required' ritual prayers. [19] Reading the Qur'ān even though it is a single, small verse consisting of only two words. [72] This must be made in two *rak'as* of an 'obligatory' ritual prayer and in all the *rak'as* of a 'supererogatory' ritual prayer and the Odd Prayer. No verse of the Qur'ān is fixed for the validity of a ritual prayer. In a ritual prayer in congregation, one who is following the imām will not read any Qur'ānic verse, but will listen to the reading of the imām or keep silent if the imām reads secretly. [73] The follower's reading is 'gravely disliked' by the law.

[20] Bowing (*rukū'*). Bowing is perfect if the head and the hips of the devotee are put on an equal level. [21] Prostration on a thing on which the forehead can completely settle. Prostration is correct if it is made on the devotee's palm or a side of his cloth, provided the

[71] In the case of each of several devotional acts prescribed by Islam — ritual prayer, fasting, divine tax, pilgrimage, and so on — it is necessary to make the appropriate intention at the start of it. The reason for this is: devotional acts must be performed with a single motive, i.e. the motive of obedience to God (Qur'ān 18:110), and this motive can be fixed in the devotee's mind through the making of the intention at the start of them. If no intention be made, or if the intention be made, not of pleasing God, but of something else, e.g. social approval, devotional acts will not be accepted by God. The Prophet said, "Acts are dependent solely upon their intentions;" see al-Bukhārī, *Ṣaḥīḥ*, Bad' al-Waḥy, 1; Muslim, *Ṣaḥīḥ*, Imāra, 155.

[72] Qur'ān 73:20.

[73] Qur'ān 7:204.

place on which the forehead is put is clean. It is 'necessary' to prostrate by using the hard part of the nose and of the forehead. Prostration by the use of the nose only is not correct, except when there is an excuse in the forehead. The place in which prostration is made must not be more elevated than the place of the feet by more than half a cubit; if it is elevated by more than half a cubit, prostration on it is not correct, except in a great crowd where one prostrates on the back of another who is performing the *same* ritual prayer. In the state of prostration, one must put on the ground one's hands, the knees — this is the correct view — and part of the toes; it is not sufficient for the validity of prostration that one puts the outer part of one's feet on the ground. Bowing must precede prostration.

[22] Rising from the prostration to that extent which approaches the position of sitting — this is the most correct view — and then to return to a second prostration [because the second prostration is 'obligatory' like the first one]. [23] The last sitting — that measure of it in which the Witnessing *(at-tashahhud)* can be read. [24] Making the last sitting after all pillars of a ritual prayer.

[25] Performance of all pillars of a ritual prayer in the waking state. [Thus if bowing or prostration or standing is made in the state of sleeping, the ritual prayer is not to be considered correct.]

[26] Full knowledge of the procedure of a ritual prayer and all its 'obligatory' characteristics — a knowledge which enables the devotee to distinguish these characteristics from the sunna characteristics. [27] The conviction of the devotee that the ritual prayer he is performing is as a whole an *'obligatory'* one. This conviction should enable him not to make the intention of a 'supererogatory' ritual prayer for an 'obligatory' one.

Of the twenty-seven acts mentioned above, four are regarded the pillars of a ritual prayer. They are: standing, reading of a Qur'ānic verse, bowing, and prostration. Some authorities maintain that the last sitting — that measure of it which is needed for reading the Witnessing *(at-tashahhud)* — is also a pillar. The remaining of the twenty-seven acts are stipulations, some of which being stipulations for the validity of the start of a ritual prayer — and these are those which are outside it — while others are stipulations for the validity of the continuance of a ritual prayer.

RITUAL PRAYER WITH FILTHY CLOTHES

Ritual Prayer on a brick the upper part of which is clean but not the lower part is correct, because it is so thick that its two sides can be regarded as two pieces of cloth. Similarly, ritual prayer is correct on a piece of clean cloth the lining of which is filthy, provided this cloth is not quilt, and on the clean side of such a cloth or bed or any similar thing that if this side moves the other side also moves — this is the correct view. It is correct to perform ritual prayer if the turban of its performer is such that its one side, which is kept aloof from his body, is filthy and the other side, which is clean, is kept on his head, and that when the clean side is moved the filthy side is not moved. If, however, the filthy side moves, ritual prayer is not correct.

One who has no means to remove the filth from one's cloth, will perform ritual prayer wearing the filthy cloth. No repetition of this prayer is necessary. Likewise, no repetition is necessary if a person, having found nothing to cover his private parts even although it is silken-cloth or herb or clay, performs a ritual prayer naked. But if he finds something to cover his private parts and the one-fourth of it is clean, his performance of a ritual prayer in the state of being naked is not correct. Should less than one-fourth be clean, he has the option of using it or of performing the ritual prayer naked. A ritual prayer in which a compeletely unclean cloth is used, is better than a ritual prayer one performs being naked. Should a person find only such a thing by which he can cover part of his private parts, he must use it covering the genitals and the anus; if it is sufficient to cover only one of these, the authorities differ — some maintain that the anus should be covered, while others say that it is the genitals which should be covered.

For a naked man it is 'praiseworthy' to perform a ritual prayer in the state of sitting, by indicating, bowing and prostrating with his eyes and spreading the legs towards the direction of the Ka'ba. If he performs it [a] in the state of standing by indicating as aforesaid, or [b] in the state of standing by bowing and prostrating, this is to be regarded as correct.

The private parts (*'awra*), in the case of a man [whether free or slave], is that part of the body which lies between his navel and the end of his knees. In the case of a slave woman, her belly and back are to be added to this part. For a free woman, the private parts are her entire body, except the face, the palms together with their back parts, and the feet, both their inward and outward sides. [Thus the forearms of a free woman are included in her private parts. Likewise, is that part of her hair which covers her head; so the uncovering of one-fourth of the hair is a bar to the validity of her ritual prayer. Looking at her hair is also unlawful.]

Uncovering of at least one fourth of a limb included in the private parts of a man or woman during a ritual prayer, prevents the validity of this prayer. [The knee and the thigh taken together constitute one limb. A woman's ankle together with her leg, her ear as separate from her head, her loose breasts, a man's penis alone, his testicles as separate from his penis — are all to be regarded as separate limbs. The part lying between the navel and the pubic bone is one complete limb. If the uncovering has occurred in various limbs of the private parts and the sum total of the uncovered places equals one fourth of the smallest of the uncovered limbs, this makes invalid the ritual prayer in which this uncovering has taken place.]

FACING THE DIRECTION OF THE KA'BA

فول وجهك شطر المسجد الحرام، وحيث ماكنتم فولوا
وجوهكم شطره. — القران ٢:١٤٤

When performing ritual prayer turn your face towards the Sacred Mosque in the open courtyard of which stands the Holy Ka'ba.— Qur'ān 2:144

It has already been mentioned that to face the direction of the Holy Ka'ba is one of the stipulations of ritual prayer. But a person who is unable to face the Ka'ba by himself because of a disease, or because he is unable to descend from his riding animal or moving vehicle by himself, or because he is afraid of an enemy, will face that direction which he can and which is safe for him.

The person to whom the direction of the Ka'ba has become uncertain, and there is no one correctly to inform him of the direction, nor is there any pulpit of the mosque indicating the direction [or any other indicator], will try his best and think to decide on the matter. If later he realizes that his decision was wrong, it is not necessary for him to repeat the ritual prayer he performed facing the direction he decided by thinking independently. If, however, he realizes the wrongness of his decision while he is still engaged in the ritual prayer, he must turn to the correct direction immediately and build the ritual prayer on that part which he has accomplished relying on his previous decision. If he started the ritual prayer without thinking much about the direction of the Ka'ba, and after completing the prayer he has come to know that he faced the correct direction, his ritual prayer is correct; but if he knows it while he is still engaged in the ritual prayer, his prayer is corrupted, as in the case where he does not know at all that he faced the right direction. In a ritual prayer in congregation in the darkness of the night, if different people face different directions after thinking independently, and they do not know to what direction their imām (i.e. one who is leading their ritual prayer) has faced, this is correct, [except for him who has performed the ritual prayer by being in front of the imām].

'REQUIRED' ACTS IN A RITUAL PRAYER

Eighteen acts are 'required' in a ritual prayer. They are as follows:

[1] Reading the Opening Sūra (*al-Fātiḥa*) of the Qur'ān.[74] [2] Adding to the Opening Sūra any other Qur'ānic sūra or three small verses in the first two *rak'as* of those 'obligatory' ritual prayers which consist of more than two *rak'as* and in all *rak'as* of the Odd Prayer and 'supererogatory' ritual prayers. [3] Fixing the reading of the Opening Sūra in the first two *rak'as* of the 'obligatory' *rak'as* of a ritual prayer. [4] Preceding the reading of the Opening Sūra to that of the additional sūra or the verses.

[5] The use of both the nose and the forehead in prostration. [If only the nose is used in a ritual prayer, this prayer is not correct.] [6] In every *rak'a*, performance of the second prostration before passing on to those acts of the ritual prayer which are other than prostration. [7] Performance of all pillars of the ritual prayer peacefully and at ease. [Thus bowing and prostration must be made so peacefully that all limbs of the devotee come to rest and their joints are at ease; standing after bowing, sitting between the two prostrations of each *rak'a*, and rising from the bowing must all be made in a state of serenity and ease.]

[8-9] The first sitting [which is at the end of the first two *rak'as* of a ritual prayer], and the reading of the Witnessing in this first sitting — this is the correct legal opinion. [10] Reading the Witnessing in the last sitting. [11] After the reading of the Witnessing, to stand up, without any delay, for starting the third *rak'a*. [12] Uttering the word *as-salām* (peace) two times — once to the right side and once to the left, but not the word *'alaykum* (on you). [13] Reading the *du'ā' Qunūt* in the Odd Prayer. Likewise, is the utterance of *Allāhu akbar* in the two 'Īd Prayers.[15] Specification of the words *Allāhu akbar* for the start of every ritual prayer, except the two 'Īd Prayers. [16] The utterance of *Allāhu akbar* for the bowing of the second *rak'a* of the two 'Īd Prayers.

[17] Imām's reading the Qur'ān loudly in the two 'obligatory' *rak'as* of the Dawn Prayer, in the first two *rak'as* of the 'obligatory' *rak'as* of the Sunset Prayer and the Evening Prayer, even though when these are performed later than their scheduled times, in the Friday Assembly Prayer, in the two 'Īd Prayers, in the Tarāwīḥ

[74] At-Tirmidhī, *Sunan*, Mawāqīt, 69, 115; Ibn Māja, *Sunan*, Iqāma, 11.

Prayer and in the Odd Prayer in the lunar month Ramaḍān. [Reading of the Qur'ān is considered to be done loudly if it is audible to others.] The imām's reading the Qur'ān secretly in all the *rak'as* of the Noon Prayer and the Late Afternoon Prayer [even though they are combined at 'Arafa], in all the 'obligatory' *rak'as* following the first two 'obligatory' *rak'as* of the Sunset Prayer and the Evening Prayer, and in all the *rak'as* of a 'supererogatory' ritual prayer performed at day time. [18] A person performing an 'obligatory' ritual prayer alone has the option of reading the Qur'ān loudly or secretly in those *rak'as* where the imām must read loudly; he is like one who performs a 'supererogatory' ritual prayer at night, [such a one also has the same option]. If the imām leaves undone the reading of the sūra in both the first two *rak'as* of the 'obligatory' *rak'as* of the Evening Prayer, it is 'necessary' for him to read that sūra in the last two *rak'as* of this Prayer, together with the Opening Sūra, loudly — first the Opening Sūra will be read and then the additional sūra. If the reading of the Opening Sūra is left undone by mistake in the first two *rak'as*, it will not be repeated in the next *rak'as*; [rather the prostration of forgetfulness is to be made].

SUNNA ACTS IN A RITUAL PRAYER

Fifty-one acts are sunna in a ritual prayer. They are as follows:

[1] Lifting the hands for saying *Allāhu akbar* at the start of the ritual prayer. A man will lift the hands to the ears. A free woman will lift them up to her shoulders. [2] Spreading the fingers when uttering this *Allāhu akbar*. [3] In a ritual prayer in congregation, the closeness of the follower's utterance of this *Allāhu akbar* with the imām's utterance of it. [4] A man's putting his right hand over his left hand below his navel. The manner of putting the hand is that he puts the inward part of his right palm over the outward part of his left palm, catching the wrist with the middle finger and the thumb in such a way as to appear like a ring. [5] A woman's putting her hands over her chest, without catching the wrist so as to make it appear like a ring.

[6] Praising God [after putting the hands over the wrists. This is to be accomplished by reading a special formula to be mentioned shortly.] [7] Seeking the protection of God from Satan at the start of reading Qur'ānic verses. [This too is to be done by reading a special prayer to be cited shortly.] [8] Uttering the name of God at the start of every *rak'a,* before the reading of the Opening Sūra. [9] Saying *āmīn* (i.e., God, accept our prayer) on completion of the Opening Sūra. [10] Praising God by saying *rabbanā wa laka l-ḥamdu*. [This

is to be done by those who perform the ritual prayer alone and by those who follow the imām]. [11] Utterance of all these — praising God, seeking the protection of God, uttering the name of God, saying *āmīn* — secretly.

[12] Uttering the *Allāhu akbar* of the beginning of the ritual prayer in the state of equilibrium, without bowing the head. [13] In a ritual prayer in congregation, the imām's loudly uttering *Allāhu akbar* and *sami'a Allāhu li-man ḥamida.* [14] Spreading the feet for the measure of four fingers when standing.

[15] Selecting the sūra to be added to the Opening Sūra, from the long sūras in the case of the Dawn Prayer and the Noon Prayer, from the medium sūras in the case of the Late Afternoon Prayer and the Evening Prayer, and from the short sūras for the Sunset Prayer. This division is applicable when the devotee is a 'stationary' (*muqīm*) person. If, However, he is on a journey he is at liberty to read the sūra of any length he wishes. [16] Lengthening the first *rak'a* of the 'obligatory' *rak'as* of the Dawn Prayer only. [To make the second *rak'a* of any 'obligatory' ritual prayer longer than the first by a reading of more than two verses, is 'disliked' by the law. In the case of 'supererogatory' ritual prayer, however, these regulations do not apply.]

[17] Uttering *Allāhu akbar* of the bowing. [18] Glorifying God [by saying *subḥāna rabbī l-'aẓīm*] in the bowing three times. [In a ritual prayer in congregation, if the imām lifts his head from the bowing before his follower has completed the reading of this formula three times, the correct view is that he should follow the imām by lifting up his head from the bowing even though he did not complete the formula thrice.] [18] Catching the knees with the hands in the state of bowing. [19] Spreading the fingers in this catching. A woman, however, will not spread her fingers. [20-22] In the state of bowing, to set up the legs, to flatten the back and to make the head and the buttocks at the same level. [23-24] Lifting up the head from the bowing and then to stand up at ease.

[25-26] When prostrating, to put the knees on the ground first, then to put the hands and then the face. Withdrawing these in a contrary way when standing up from the prostration. [27-28] Uttering *Allāhu akbar* when prostrating and when rising up from the prostration. [29] Prostrating between the palms. [30] Glorifying God by saying *subḥāna rabbī l-a'lā* three times in prostration. [31-34] In prostration, a man's keeping the thigh away from his belly, his elbows away from the sides of his body, and his arms away from the ground, if there are no too many devotees. A woman, in

prostration, will lower her body, and adjoin her belly with her thighs. [35] Perfection of the rising up from prostration. [36-37] Sitting between two prostrations and putting the hands on the thighs in the state of this sitting, just as a devotee does this when he reads the Witnessing. [38-39] In this sitting, to spread out the left leg but to raise the right, making the toes face the direction of the Ka'ba. A woman will sit leaning on her hip-bones, put her one thigh on another, and bring out her feet from below her right hip-bone. [40] Indicating — this is the correct view — with the forefinger of the right hand when reaching the words of witnessing the oneness of God occurring in the Witnessing. The procedure of indicating is that the forefinger will be lifted up when negating the existence of any god but God by uttering *lā ilāha* (لا إله: there is no god), and be lowered down when affirming the existence of God alone by uttering *illā Allāhu* (إلا الله: but God). [41] Reading the Opening Sūra of the Qur'ān in all *rak'as* following the first two *rak'as*.

[42] Invoking blessing upon the Prophet in the last sitting of the ritual prayer. There is a special formula for this which will be cited shortly. [43] To follow this invoking by a prayer to God using a formula of prayer which resembles the words of the Qur'ān and Tradition but not the words of people. This formula will be mentioned soon. [44] Looking first at the right side with a salutation (*salām*), and then at the left side with a salutation. [45] These two salutations the imām will make to people who are following him, the guardian angels[75] who are with himself and with each of his followers, and the pious jinn[76] who might be following him in the ritual prayer. This is the most correct view. [46] The follower will make his salutation to the imām when saluting to the right side, if the imām is on that side, or to the left side, if the imām be on this side. If the

[75] The guardian angels record whatever a man says or does and also safeguard him from harmful things. There is disagreement of opinion on their number.

[76] Jinn constitute a class of intelligent beings created by God. They are bodies composed of vapour or flames, intelligent, imperceptible to our senses, capable of appearing under different forms and of carrying out heavy labours. They are created of smokeless flame (Qur'ān 55:15), while mankind, and the angels, the other two classes of intelligent beings, are created of clay and light respectively. They are capable of salvation; since they fall under religious obligation (Qur'ān 51:56, 55:39, 60:128, 6:130) the pious of them sometimes perform ritual prayer in the mosque along with men. Some jinn will enter Paradise while others will be cast into Hell (Qur'ān 7:38, 7:179). They can mix with men. There are stories of love between jinn and human beings. There are many stories, too, of relations between saints and jinn; see Ibn an-Nadīm, *Fihrist*, pp. 209, 291, 539, 728-29, 756-57, 760, 823; D.B. Macdonald, *Development of Religious Attitude and Life in Islam*, Beyrouth, 1965, pp. 144 ff.; *idem*., H. Masse *et al*, "Djinn", *EI*² II, 546-50.

imām is in front of him straight, he will make it to the imām in both salutations. In addition to the imām, the follower will also make it to all other devotees present, the guardian angels as well as the pious jinn. [47] A person performing the ritual prayer alone will make salutations to the angels alone, for there is no one else whom he can intend in salutations. [48] The tone of the second salutation should be lower than that of the first. [49] The follower's salutation should be attached to his imām's salutation, not after it. [50] Salutation should be started from the right side. [51] The person who joins the imām in a ritual prayer after a part of it has already been performed (*masbūq*) by the imām, will not stand up to perform that part alone until the imam completes his salutations.

'PRAISEWORTHY' ACTS IN A RITUAL PRAYER

There are certain acts in a ritual prayer which are regarded as 'praiseworthy'. These acts are meant for the perfection of the ritual prayer but not for its validity. They are as follows:

[1] Man's bringing his palms out of his sleeves when uttering *Allāhu akbar* at the start of a ritual prayer. [In the presence of an obstacle, e.g. cold, bringing out of the palms is of course not 'praiseworthy'. A woman will not bring out her palms; on the contrary, she will cover them for fear of uncovering of her forearms.] [2-6] The devotee's looking at the place of his prostration when he is in the state of standing, at the outward part of his feet when he is bowing, at his nose when he is in prostration, at his bosom when he is in the condition of sitting, and at his shoulders when he is saluting with a view to withdrawing from the ritual prayer. [All this is meant in order that his mind may not be diverted to anything other than God. The Prophet commanded:

> "Worship God as if you see Him when you are worshipping; even if you do not see Him He certainly sees you."][77]

[7] Checking of coughing as far as possible. [Coughing, without any necessity, when one is engaged in a ritual prayer corrupts the prayer.] [8] Repressing the mouth when yawning. If complete repression is not possible, the mouth should at least be covered with the hand or with the sleeve. The Prophet said,

> "Yawning in ritual prayer results from the influence of Satan. So when one of you yawns let him repress it as far as possible." [78]

[77] Al-Bukhārī, *Ṣaḥīḥ*, Īmān, 37; Muslim, *Ṣaḥiḥ*, Īmān, 1, 5-7.

[9] In a ritual prayer in congregation, the standing up of all present in order to start the ritual prayer, just when the man performing *iqāma* (i.e. one who calls to the actual start of the ritual prayer) utters *ḥayya 'alā l-falāḥi.* [10] The imām's starting the ritual prayer just when the man performing *iqāma* utters *qad qāmati ṣ-ṣalātu.*

HOW TO COMPOSE A RITUAL PRAYER

When a man wants to perform a ritual prayer, he should bring his palms out of his sleeves. [This need not be done if there is any obstacle, e.g. cold. A woman will not do this even though there is no obstacle.]

Then he will lift the palms up, opposite to his ears, and will utter *Allāhu akbar* (الله اكبر: God is the greatest). The utterance of *Allāhu akbar* must be coupled with the making of intention (*niyya*) for the ritual prayer. [A woman will lift her hands up to her shoulders only. At the state of lifting the hands, whether by a man or a woman, the inner side of the palms should be in the direction of the Ka'ba; the fingers will be neither spread nor closed together]. It is correct to start the ritual prayer by reading a sentence expressing the meaning of *Allāhu akhbar* in any language other than Arabic, e.g. English; this is only for those devotees who are unable to read *Allāhu akbar* in Arabic; if a devotee reads this in a language other than Arabic despite being able to read in Arabic, his ritual prayer is not valid. No reading of the Qur'ān in a language other than Arabic is correct in a ritual prayer, because the Qur'ān consists of both expression and meaning, — this is the most correct view.

Just after uttering *Allāhu akbar*, the man will, without any delay, put his right hand on the left below the navel; [a woman, however, will put them on her chest]. In this condition he or she will read:

سبحانك اللهم وبحمدك. وتبارك اسمك. وتعالى جدك.
ولا اله غيرك.

(*Subḥānaka, Allāhumma, wa bi-ḥamdika. Wa tabāraka ismuka. Wa ta'ālā jadduka. Wa lā ilāha ghayruka.*)

(Glorified are You, O God! Praise belongs to You! Blessed is Your name! Exalted is Your dominion! There is no god besides You!)

This formula prayer should be read by everyone performing ritual

[78] Muslim, *Ṣaḥīḥ*, Zuhd, 59; Dārimī, *Sunan*, Ṣalā, 106.

prayer, whether he be alone or an imām or a follower of an imām, and whether the devotee be male or female.

Then the devotee will seek the protection of God from Satan, the rejected, by reading:

اعوذبالله من الشيطان الرجيم.
(*A'ūdhu bi-Allāhi mina sh-Shayṭāni r-rajīmi*)
(I seek the protection of God from Satan, the rejected).

This formula is to be read secretly. It is meant for the start of reading Qur'ānic verses in a ritual prayer, and hence [a] it will be read by the *masbūq* [i.e. one who is performing, after the imām has completed the ritual prayer, that part of it which he failed to perform with the imām because he came late], but not by one who is following the imām from the begining of the ritual prayer (*muqtadī*); and [b] it will be delayed until after the reading of additional *Allāhu akbar* in the first *rak'a* of the two 'Īd Prayers.

After this the devotee will secretly read the name of God, reading: بسم الله الرحمن الرحيم.
(*Bi-smi Allāhi r-raḥmāni r-raḥīmi*)
(In the name of God, Most Gracious, Ever Merciful).

In every *rak'a*, whether 'obligatory' or 'supererogatory', he will read this formula just before the Opening Sūra only.

Then the devotee will read the Opening Sūra. In a ritual prayer in congregation, the imām and the follower will secretly read امين (*āmīn*) at the end of the Opening Sūra. The word 'secretly' means that the voice should be audible only to the devotee himself.

Then he will read one complete sūra of the Qur'ān, or three small verses, or one long verse.

Then he will utter (*Allāhu akbar*), bowing, with ease, putting the head and the buttocks on the same level, catching the knees with the hands, and spreading the fingers. [The utterance of *Allāhu akbar* should start with the start of bowing. A woman will not spread her fingers.] In bowing, glorification of God will be made at least three times by reading: سبحان ربى العظيم, (*subḥāna rabbīl-'aẓīmi*: glorified is my Lord, the Greatest). Then he will lift his head and stand up at ease, reading: سمع الله لمن حمده. ربنا لك الحمد (*sami'a Allāhu li-man ḥamida. Rabbanā laka l-ḥamdu*: God hears one who praises Him. Lord, to You alone belong all types of perfect praise). This is for the imām and for one who performs ritual prayer alone. The follower of the imām, however, will be content only with the utterance of *rabbanā laka l-ḥamdu*.

Then the devotee will utter *Allāhu akbar*, falling down in prostration. When prostrating, he will put on the ground first his knees then the hands and then the face between his palms; he will prostrate with the nose and the forehead, and in a state of ease and serenity; he will glorify God at least three times by reading: سبحان ربي الاعلى (*subḥāna rabbī l-a'lā*: glorified is my Lord, the Most Exalted!). In prostration he will keep his belly aloof from his thighs and his arms aloof from the armpits, if there is no crowd; he will face the fingers and the toes to the direction of the Ka'ba; fingers will be closed together, not spread out. A woman, however, will lower her body, adjoin her belly with her thighs, and close the arms with the armpits. The devotee will sit between the two prostrations, putting his hands on his thighs, and being in a state of ease and serenity. Then he will utter *Allāhu akbar* for the second prostration, and prostrate in the state of ease; in this prostration too he will read *subḥāna rabbī l-a'lā* three times at least, keeping his belly aloof from his thighs and the forearms aloof from the armpits. Thereafter he will lift his head from prostration uttering *Allāhu akbar* and stand up, without supporting his hands against the ground and without sitting. Up to this is the completion of the first *rak'a*.

The second *rak'a* is like the first *rak'a*, except that in the beginning of it there is no reading of the formula of praise of God (*thanā'*), and no seeking the protection of God by saying *a'ūdhu bi-Allāhi mina sh-shayṭāni r-rajīmi*.

It is not sunna to lift the hands opposite to the ears, except when starting every ritual prayer, when uttering *Allāhu akbar* for reading the *du'ā' Qunūt* in the Odd Prayer, when uttering the additional *Allāhu akbar* in the two 'Īd Prayers, when seeing the Holy Ka'ba, when kissing the sacred Black Stone, when standing upon the hill Safa and the hill Marwa on the occasion of the ceremony of running (*sa'ī*), when performing the ritual of halting at 'Arafa and halting at Muzdalifa, when standing after the rite of casting pebbles at the first Jamra and the middle Jamra at Mina, when praying for rain or for other things, and when supplicating, after glorifying God, at the end of ritual prayers.

On completion of the second prostration of the second *rak'a*, the devotee will spread out his left leg and sit on it, but raise the right leg facing its toes to the direction of the Ka'ba; he will put the hands on the thighs near the knees, spreading the fingers. This is for a man. A woman, however, will sit supporting on her hip-bones. In this state of sitting, the devotee, even if he is a follower of imām, will read the Witnessing (*at-tashahhud*) narrated from Ibn Mas'ūd. [79] When reading the Witnessing he will indicate with the forefinger of the right hand, lifting it when reading the word *lā* (لا) and lowering it when reading *illā Allāhu* (الا الله). Nothing will be added to the Witnessing in the first sitting. The Witnessing is:

التحيات لله والصلواة والطيبات. السلام عليك ايها النبى ورحمة الله وبركاته. السلام علينا وعلى عباد الله الصالحين. اشهد ان لا اله الا الله واشهد ان محمدا عبده ورسوله.

(*At-taḥiyyātu li-Allāhi, wa ṣ-ṣalāwātu wa ṭ-ṭayyibātu. As-salāmu 'alayka, ayyuhā n-nabiyyu, wa raḥmatu l-Allāhi wa barakātuhu. As-salāmu 'alaynā, wa 'alā 'ibādi Allāhi ṣ-ṣāliḥīna. Ashhadu an lā ilāha illā Allāhu, wa ashhadu anna Muḥammadan 'abduhu wa rasūluhu.*)

(All types of perfect greetings are due to God and also are all prayers and all that is good. Salutation is to you, O the Prophet and also are God's mercy and blessings. Salutation is to us and to the pious servants of God. I bear witness that there is no god but God, and I bear witness that Muḥammad is His servant and messenger.)

The devotee will read the Opening Sūra in all *rak'as* after the first two *rak'as*. On completing all *rak'as*, he will sit in the manner of first sitting and read the Witnessing mentioned above. Then he will invoke blessings upon the Prophet by reading the formula of blessing:

اللهم صل على محمد وعلى ال محمد كما صليت على ابراهيم وعلى ال ابراهيم. اللهم بارك على محمد وعلى ال محمد كما باركت على ابراهيم وعلى ال ابراهيم. انك حميد مجيد.

(*Allāhumma, ṣalli 'alā Muḥammadin, wa 'alā āli Muḥammadin; kamā ṣallayta 'alā Ibrāhīma wa 'alā āli Ibrāhīma. Allāhumma, bārik 'alā Muḥammadin, wa 'alā āli Muḥammadin; Kamā bārakta 'alā Ibrāhīma, wa 'alā āli Ibrāhīma. Innaka ḥamīdun majīdun.*) [80]

[79] 'Abd Allāh ibn Mas'ūd (d. 32 A.H.) was one of the greatest companions of the Prophet. The Prophet taught him the Witnessing we now read in ritual prayer and hence it is called the Witnessing of Ibn Mas'ūd. For his biography see Ibn Ḥajar, *Tahdhīb*, VI, 27-28.

[80] There are other formulae of invoking blessings upon the Prophet, but this formula is the best. See al-Bukhārī, *Ṣaḥīḥ*, Anbiyā', 15; an-Nasā'ī, *Sunan*, Sahw, 52.

(God, grant mercy to the prophet Muḥammad and to the members of the family of Muḥammad, as You granted mercy to the prophet Abraham and to the members of the family of Abraham. God bless Muḥammad and the members of the family of Muḥammad, as You blessed Abraham and the members of the family of Abraham. Surely You are All laudable, All-glorious).

The reading of this formula of invoking blessing upon the Prophet will be followed by reading any prayer formula which resembles the prayers mentioned in the Qur'ān and Tradition. The formula usually read is:

اللهم اني ظلمت نفسي ظلما كثيرا، وانه لايغفر ذنوب الا انت.
فاغفرلي مغفرة من عندك، وارحمني. انك انت الغفور الرحيم.

(*Allāhumma, innī ẓalamtu nafsī ẓulaman kathīran; wa innahu lā yaghfiru adhdhunūba illā anta. Fa-ghfir lī maghfiratan min 'indika, wa rḥimnī. Innaka anta l-ghafūru r-raḥīmu.*)

(God, I have done wrong to my soul tremendously, and no one except You can forgive sins; so forgive me completely through Your special favour and bestow mercy upon me. Surely it is You Who are the Most Forgiving, Ever Merciful).

Then the devotee will salute to his right side first and then to the left side, reading: السلام عليكم ورحمة الله.

(*As-salāmu 'alaykum, wa raḥmatu Allāhi.*)

(May peace be upon you and also God's mercy!)

He will make salutations to all those who are with him. The details of this have been given in a previous section.

LEADING OF A RITUAL PRAYER (*IMĀMA*)

قال رسول الله صلى الله عليه وسلم: صلواة الجماعة تفضل صلواة الفذ بسبع وعشرين درجة.

The prophet Muḥammad (may God bless him and greet him!) said, "A ritual prayer in congregation is twenty-seven degrees more excellent than a ritual prayer performed by a single person." [81]

[81] Al-Bukhāri, *Ṣaḥīḥ*, Adhān, 29; Muslim, *Ṣaḥīḥ*, Masājid, 245, 247.

Stipulations for Leading a Ritual Prayer

Leading a ritual prayer (*imāma*) is more excellent than calling people to ritual prayer (*adhān*). Ritual prayer in congregation (*jamā'a*) is 'emphasized sunna' for men who have no excuse. [Once, when some people remained absent from a certain ritual prayer in congregation, the Prophet warned,

> "I have intended to order a man to lead the ritual prayer and myself go to those who did not attend it and burn their houses."[82]

A healthy man's leading a ritual prayer is correct if he fulfils the following six stipulations: [1] Islam, i.e. to be a Muslim. [2] Maturity which has been defined in a previous section. The imām (i.e. one who leads a ritual prayer) must be mature. A child cannot legally lead a ritual prayer. [3] Sanity. [4] One leading a ritual prayer must be a male person. [5] The man leading a ritual prayer must be able to recite the Qur'ān in it from memory, of any verse the reading of which makes ritual prayer correct. [6] Freedom from excuses such as constant haemorrhage of the nose, and stammering in which [a] one repeats letters of words whenever one speaks and [b] one's tongue moves from one letter to another resembling it. The man leading a ritual prayer must not lack any stipulation meant for the validity of a ritual prayer, e.g. cleanliness and covering of the private parts.

Stipulations for Following the Imām

A person's following the imām (one who leads ritual prayer) is legally valid if he fulfils fourteen stipulations which are as follows:

[1] The follower (*muqtadī*) makes the intention of following the imām in close touch with the utterance of *Allāhu akbar* made at the start of the ritual prayer. [Making of this intention is in addition to the making of the intention for the ritual prayer itself.] [2] A woman's following a male imām is correct only if he makes the intention of leading the ritual prayer performed by women. [This is true in the case of the Friday Assembly Prayer as well as the two 'Īd Prayers.]

[3] The follower stands in such a state that the imām's heel is ahead of that of his own. [4] The condition of the imām is not inferior to that of the follower. [Thus it must not happen that the

[82] Al-Bukhārī, *Ṣaḥīḥ*, Adhān, 29; an-Nasā'ī, *Sunan*, Imāma, 49; Ibn Māja, *Sunan*, Masājid, 17.

imām is performing a 'supererogatory' ritual prayer, while his follower's ritual prayer is an 'obligatory' one, or that the imām is a man suffering from a complaint legally considered to be an excuse, while the follower is free from any such excuse.] [5] The imām is not performing a particular 'obligatory' ritual prayer, whereas the follower is performing another 'obligatory' ritual prayer. The imām and the follower must be engaged in the same ritual prayer. [6] The imām is not a 'stationary' man, while the follower is on a journey after the time in a ritual prayer consisting of four *rak'as*. Nor is such a follower a *masbūq*, i.e. one who joined the imām not from the start of the ritual prayer but later.

[7] There is no row of women between the imām and the follower. [8] Nor is there any river between the imām and the follower — a river in which small boats sail. [9] Nor is a path along which carts or cars or similar vehicles pass. [10] There is not a big wall between the imām and the follower causing the latter not to be aware of the former's passing from one act of the ritual prayer to another. If there is a wall which causes no confusion as to hearing the utterances of the imām or to seeing him, but the situation is such that it is not possible to reach him, the following of the follower is correct; this is the correct legal opinion.

[11] The imām is not riding on an animal nor is on a vehicle, while the follower is on foot, or vice versa. Nor is the imām riding on an animal or on a vehicle, while the follower is on another animal or another vehicle. However, in the case of the follower's being on the same animal or vehicle as the imām, his following is to be considered legally correct. It should not happen that the follower is in a boat and the imām is in another boat which is not attached with it. If they are attached together, however, it is correct to follow the imām.

[14] It is not that the follower is aware of proceeding from the imām such an act as corrupts ritual prayer in the follower's opinion, e.g. flowing blood or mouthful vomiting, and is sure that the imām did not repeat his ablution after it.

Following the imām is correct if a man who has cleansed himself through ablution with water follows an imām who has purified himself through ablution with clean sand; if a man who has washed his bodily parts in ablution follows an imām who has wiped over some of them, e.g. over boots or a bandage; if a man performing the ritual prayer by standing follows an imām performing it by sitting or by crooked-backed; if a man performing the ritual prayer by indicating follows an imām who is similar to him in this respect; and if a man engaged in a 'supererogatory' ritual prayer follows an imām engaged in an 'obligatory' ritual prayer.

Should it become clear that the ritual prayer of the imām was nullified by the non-observance of a stipulation or a pillar of the prayer, it is necessary for him to repeat this prayer. In that case he must notify, as far as possible, the followers to repeat their ritual prayer as well.

Reasons for Non-performance of a Ritual Prayer in Congregation

The Duty of attending ritual prayer in congregation ceases to be a responsibility for anyone of the following eighteen reasons.

[1] Rain, [2] severe cold, [3] fear of an oppressor, [4] strong darkness, [5] imprisonment, [6] blindness, [7] paralysis, [8-9] the cutting off of a hand or a leg, [10] sickness, [11] prevention from attending the congregation, [12] thin mud, [13] old age, [14] a discussion of Islamic jurisprudence in a group which causes one not to attend congregation, [15] the arrival of food which one is eager to eat, because in this case one cannot concentrate on the ritual prayer, [16] the start of a journey, [17] attendance upon a sick man who is harmed if one leaves him in order to perform ritual prayer in congregation, [18] and gusty wind at night, but not during the day.

A man who has the intention of attending congregation but could not actually attend it because of any of these excuses, obtains the reward of performance of ritual prayer in congregation by virtue of his intention. The prophet Muḥammad said,

> "Actions depend on their intentions, and most surely every one obtains that for which he has made the intention." [83]

The Man Most Deserving of Leading a Ritual Prayer. Ordering of Lines of Devotees

Should the dweller in a house in which people have gathered, or the man in charge of leading ritual prayer, i.e. the imām of the locality, or the man of authority, i.e. the political ruler or the magistrate or the judge, be not present among those who have assembled, then the man who deserves to lead the ritual prayer most is the one who is the most learned in the rules of ritual prayer though not of other subjects. [The judge or the magistrate has the preference over the imām of the mosque; this is clearly stated in a prophetic tradition]. [84]

[83] Al-Bukhārī, *Ṣaḥīḥ*, Bad' al-Waḥy, 1; Muslim, *Ṣaḥīḥ*, Imāra, 155.

[84] Muslim, *Ṣaḥīḥ*, Masājid, 290, 291; at-Tirmidhī, *Sunan*, Ṣalā, 6; an-Nasā'ī, *Sunan*, Imāma, 3, 6; Ibn Māja, *Sunan*, Iqāma, 46.

Next to the most learned man is he who is the best in Qur'ān-reading by observing its rules; next to him is the most pious man; next is the oldest man; next is the man whose character is the best, for such a man will be lenient to the devotee; next is he whose countenance is most beautiful; next is the one who is the noblest in lineage; next is the one whose voice is the sweetest; next is the man whose clothes are cleanest.

Should all people present be equal in qualities, either lots will be cast or the people will select someone to lead their ritual prayer. If they differ in their opinion, it is the majority opinion which should be accepted. If the majority chooses one who is not the best, it does something wrong but has not committed a sin thereby.

It is 'disliked' by the law that the following people should lead a ritual prayer. [1] A slave. [2] A blind man. [3] A villager who is ignorant. [4] A bastard son who is ignorant of religion and who is not pious. [5] A man who commits major sins even though he is learned in religion. [6] A heretic, i.e. one who believes in, or does, anything which has no basis in the teachings of the Qur'ān and sunna.

It is 'disliked' by the law that the imām should lengthen the ritual prayer he is leading, to such an extent that it would be felt burdensome by the followers. [The Prophet said, "Let one who leads a ritual prayer make it light."][85] Likewise, it is 'disliked' that naked persons and women should perform ritual prayer in congregation. [In the case of women the reason is fear of disturbance.] If women perform ritual prayer in their own congregation, their female imām will stand in the middle of them, keeping her heels slightly ahead of their heels.

Should the follower, whether an adult or a child whose sense of discrimination has started functioning, be only one he will stand by the right side of the imām and behind his heels. [It is 'disliked' by the law that he should stand by the left side of the imām or behind him.] If the followers are more than one, they will stand behind the imām.

In a ritual prayer in congregation the first line of the devotees will be that of male adults. Behind them will stand boys, behind whom will be the line of the hermaphrodites, behind whom will stand women if they are present. [It is sunna that the imām should ask the devotees to make the lines straight. The Prophet commanded:

85 Muslim, *Ṣaḥīḥ*, Ṣalā, 183; al-Bukhārī, *Ṣaḥīḥ*, Adhān, 63; at-Tirmidhī, *Sunan*, Ṣalā, 61.

"Make your lines straight so that your minds may be straight to God; be very close touching the bodies of others so that divine mercy may be bestowed upon you."[86]

"Make Your lines straight, stand touching the shoulders of other devotees, close up the vacant place in the line ..., and do not leave places for Satan. God establishes relationship with him who joins the line in ritual prayer and He cuts off relationship with him who cuts off the line [by leaving space in it]."[87]

The first line is the best of all lines in a ritual prayer in congregation; next to this is the second, then the third, and so on. The Prophet says that divine mercy is bestowed first on the imām; then it passes over to one who is opposite to him in the first line, then to those who are on his right side, and then to those who are on his left side; then it passes over to the second, and other lines in the same way.[88]

Acts to be Performed by the Follower after the Imām's Completion of a Ritual Prayer

If the imām has saluted and thus withdrawn from the ritual prayer, but the follower has not yet completed the reading of the Witnessing, it is necessary for the follower to complete the reading of the Witnessing. [If, however, the follower has completed the Witnessing but has not yet read the formula of invoking blessings on the Prophet and other prayer formulae, he will neglect these and salute with the imām. If the imām has risen up for the third *rak'a* but the follower has not yet read the Witnessing, he should complete it; if, however, he does not complete it but rises up with the imām, it is 'permissible' by the law.]

In a bowing or a prostration, if the imām raises his head before the follower has read the formula of glorification of God three times, the follower will obey the imām, i.e. will raise his head with the imām, without reading it three times.

If the imām forgetfully adds a third prostration or stands up after the last sitting, the follower will not obey him, [but wait and salute along with the imām if the imām returns without doing prostration of the *rak'a* for which he forgetfully stood up or if he sits down after thus standing]. But if the imām has made prostration of the *rak'a* for which he forgetfully stood up, the follower will not wait for him

86 Al-Bukhārī, *Ṣaḥīḥ*, Faḍā'il Aṣḥāb an-Nabī, 8; Muslim, *Ṣaḥīḥ*, *Ṣalā*, 122.

87 An-Nasā'ī, *Sunan*, Imāma, 31; Abū Dāwūd, *Sunan*, Ṣalā, 93.

88 Ash-Shurunbalālī, *Marāqī*, p. 122.

but will salute alone and thus withdraw from the ritual prayer.

If the imām forgetfully stands up before the last sitting, the follower will not obey him but will wait; if the follower salutes before the imām has made a prostration of the additional *rak'a* for which he stood up forgetfully, the follower's 'obligatory' ritual prayer is corrupted thereby.

It is 'disliked' by the law that the follower should salute after the imām has read the Witnessing but before he has saluted — 'disliked' because he has not fulfilled the succession of the salutation of the imām.

PRAISES OF GOD AFTER 'OBLIGATORY' RITUAL PRAYER

It is sunna to stand up for the start of the sunna *rak'as* immediately after the completion of the 'obligatory' *rak'as*. However, between the sunna *rak'as* and the 'obligatory' *rak'as* it is 'praiseworthy' to read only the following single prayer formula; it is an established fact that the Prophet used to defer the start of the sunna *rak'as* by the reading of this formula only.[89] The formula is:

> God, You are peace, from You originates peace and to You returns peace. Blessed are You, O Possessor of majesty and honour.
>
> (اللهم انت السلام ومنك السلام واليك يعود السلام. تباركت ياذا الجلال والاكرام)
>
> (*Allāhumma, anta s-salāmu, wa minka s-salāmu, wa ilayka ya'ūdu s-salāmu. Tabārakta yā dha l-jalāli wa l-ikrāmi*)

Shams al-A'imma al-Ḥalwāni maintains that there is no sin in reading praises of God between the 'obligatory' *rak'as* and the sunna *rak'as*.

It is 'praiseworthy' for the imām that, after salutation, he moves towards his left side in order to perform those 'supererogatory' *rak'as* which are after the 'obligatory' *rak'as*, and that, on the performance of the 'supererogatory' *rak'as*, he sits facing the congregation. In that state all should pray for forgiveness from God three times by reading the formula: *astaghfiru Allāha ta'ālā* (استغفر الله تعالى : I seek the forgiveness of God, exalted is He!), should read the Verse of the Throne (*Āyat al-Kursī*)[90] and the two Qur'ānic sūras by which one seeks the protection of God,[91] should glorify God thirty-three times [by reading the formula: *subḥāna*

[89] *Ibid*. p. 124. [90] Qur'ān 2:255.

[91] These are the last two sūras of the Qur'ān consisting of five and six verses respectively.

Allāhi (سبحان الله: glorified is God!)], should praise God thirty-three times [by reading *al-ḥamdu li-Allāhi* (الحمد لله: praise be to God!)], and should magnify God thirty-three times [by reading the formula: *Allāhu akbar* (الله اكبر: God is the greatest)]. All this constitutes ninety-nine times. After this, will be read: *lā ilāha illā Allāhu waḥdahu, lā sharīka lahu. Lahu l-mulku, wa lahu l-ḥamdu. Wa huwa 'alā kulli shay'in qadīrun* (لا اله الا الله وحده لا شريك له. له الملك وله الحمد. وهو على كل شيء قدير : there is no god but God alone. He has no partner. To Him belongs the dominion and to Him belongs praise; and He has the fullest power over everything). This completes one hundred times. [The Prophet said that the sins of any one who reads these praises one hundred times on completion of every ritual prayer, are forgiven even though they are as many as the scum of the sea.][92] Thereafter all will pray to God for the good of themselves and the good of other Muslims, by reading prayer formulae which are transmitted from the Prophet.[93] When praying they will raise their hands equal to their chests in all humility and submission to God. The prayer will be concluded by wiping the face with the *inward* sides of the palms. The Prophet said,

> "When you pray to God pray with the inward sides of your palms, and do not pray using their back sides. When you have completed the prayer wipe your face with them."[94]

ACTS CORRUPTING A RITUAL PRAYER

Ritual prayer is corrupted by any of about sixty-eight acts. They are as follows:

[1] Utterance of a word even although forgetfully or by mistake. [2] Such a supplication as resembles our ordinary speech, e.g. 'God, help me to repay my debt', 'God, assist me to marry so-and-so', and 'God, grant me a high post'. [3] Salutation with the intention of greeting someone even although forgetfully. [4] Replying, with the tongue, to someone's salutation. [5] Replying to someone's saluta-

92 Al-Bukhārī, *Ṣaḥīḥ*, Da'wāt, 65; Muslim, *Ṣaḥīḥ*, Dhikr, 28, Masājid, 146; Abū Dāwūd, *Sunan*, Tasbīḥ, 24; at-Tirmidhī, *Sunan*, Witr, 15; an-Nasā'ī, *Sunan*, Sahw, 96; Ibn Māja, *Sunan*, Adab, 56.

Every Muslim should read these formulae, one hundred times in total, on completion of each ritual prayer.

93 One may invoke in one's own way, but it is better to use those invocations which are transmitted by Tradition. A number of them have been mentioned by al-Ghazālī so that men may read them after each ritual prayer and in the morning and evening. See al-Ghazālī, *Iḥyā'*, I, 313-23.

94 Ibn Māja, *Sunan*, Iqāma, 119.

tion by shaking hands with him.

[6] Too much action. [The law defines too much action as an act which gives its observer the impression that the doer of the act is certainly not engaged in a ritual prayer.] [7] Turning the chest away from the direction of the Ka'ba. [8] Eating anything from the outside of the mouth, even though it is very small. [9] Eating that which is between the teeth and which is at least of the measure of a pea. [10] Drinking anything. [11] A half-cough without any excuse. [A half-cough done for an excuse, e.g. difficulty caused by phlegm in reading Qur'ānic verses, does not nullify the ritual prayer.] [12-14] Saying 'ugh', groaning exclaiming 'ah!', and weeping — for physical pain or for a misfortune, but not for remembrance of Paradise or Hell in which case ritual prayer is not corrupted. [15] Replying to a sneeze by saying *yarḥamuka Allāhu* (يرحمك الله :may God bestow mercy upon you!)[95] [16] Replying to one, who has asked if God has any partner, by saying 'there is no god but God'.

[17] Replying to bad news by saying *innā li-Allāhi, wa innā ilayhi rāji'ūna* (انا للهم وانا اليه راجعون: surely we belong to God, and surely it is to Him that we are returning).[96] [18] Replying to happy news by saying *al-ḥamdu li-Allāhi* (الحمد لله: praise be to God!). [19] Replying to suprising news by saying *lā ilāha illā Allāhu* or by saying *subḥāna Allāhi* (سبحان الله: glorified is God!). [20] Utterance of any part of the Qur'ān with the intention of replying to a questioner, e.g. to utter the verse, "O Yaḥyā, hold fast the book..."[97], to a man looking for a book or a similar thing. [If by utterance of a Qur'ānic verse, what the devotee intends is not a reply to an enquirer but to make him aware that he is engaged in ritual prayer, his prayer is not corrupted thereby.]

[21] Availabiltiy of water for, and ability to use it by, a devotee who started a ritual prayer by making ablution with clean sand. [22-23] Termination of the duration of wiping over boots, or the taking off of the boots on which one wiped when making ablution. [24] Learning a Qur'ānic verse by an unlettered devotee. [25] A

[95] Islamic etiquette is that on sneezing, a Muslim should say: *al-ḥamdu li-Allāhi* (praise be to God!). Another Muslim hearing him say this, should pray: *yarḥamuka Allāhu*. This is his duty towards the sneezing man. A Muslim has twenty-five duties towards another Muslim. Fulfilment of them strengthens the tie of brotherhood and also earns reward from God.

[96] One of the attributes of a good believer is that whenever any misfortune befalls him, he directs his mind towards God by reading this formula. This is explicit in the Qur'ān (2:156). If, however, misfortune visits him when he is engaged in a ritual prayer he must not read it, for it will nullify his ritual prayer.

[97] Qur'ān 19:12.

naked devotee's finding something with which his private parts can be covered. [26] Obtaining the ability for bowing and for prostration, by a person performing the ritual prayer by indicating because he lacked this ability. [27] Remembering those ritual prayers which the devotee failed to perform in their due times and which he must perform later in a gradual order. [28] The imam's appointing as his deputy a man who is not fit for leading a ritual prayer, e.g. an unlettered man or a man having an excuse. [29-31] The rising of the sun in the case of the Dawn Prayer, the passing by the sun of its meridian in the case of the two 'Īd Prayers, and the start of the time for the Late Afternoon Prayer in the case of the Friday Assembly Prayer. [32] The falling down of a bandage because the injury is already healed. [33] The removal of the excuse of a devotee who has an excuse.

[34] Incurring the state of minor legal impurity deliberately or through the action of a man other than the devotee. [35] Faintness. [36] Insanity. [37] Incurring the state of major legal impurity as a result of looking at an object of sex or as a result of emission in sleep. [38] The devotee's standing opposite to a woman who excites sexual desire, in an absolute ritual prayer which is common to both when doing the *taḥrīma*, i.e. when saying *Allāhu akbar* for starting the prayer, in the same place without any wall or veil, and the imām has made the intention of leading her ritual prayer.

[39] Uncovering of the private parts of a devotee who has incurred the state of minor legal impurity, even though this uncovering is compelled by the need of the removal of this impurity, e.g. a female devotee's uncovering the forearms for making ablution. [40] Reading the Qur'ān by a devotee who has already incurred minor legal impurity, when going to make ablution anew or when returning from it. [41] His halting, when going to the place of ablution or returning from it, for the measure of time in which he could perform one pillar of the ritual prayer; this halting is made in the state of wakefulness and without any excuse such as crowd of people. [42] His passing beyond the nearby water for something other than ablution. [43] The devotee's going out of the mosque, imagining that he has incurred the minor legal impurity. [44] Crossing the lines of the devotees in a place other than the mosque, imagining that the minor legal impurity has taken place, but really it has not taken place. [45] Moving from the devotee's own place, imagining that he is not in ablution, or that the duration of his wiping over his boots, bandage, etc. is ended, or that unperformed ritual prayers are due

on his responsibility, or that there is filth on his body or cloth, even although, in all these cases, he has not come out of the mosque or the house in which he is praying. Moving from his own place in these cases is taken as abandonment of the ritual prayer and not as its correction. It is better to perform the ritual prayer anew in all these cases — better because this will keep the devotee from being an object of legal controversy.

[46] The devotee's assisting another devotee, who is not his imām, in reading Qur'ānic verses. [His assisting his own imām, however, is 'permissible']. [47] To say *Allāhu akbar* with the intention of passing to a ritual prayer other than that which the devotee is performing. [An example of this is: a devotee performing a ritual prayer *alone* has intended to perform it by *following* the imām, and vice versa.] In all these cases, the ritual prayer is nullified provided the accidental things mentioned in them happen *before* that measure of the last sitting in which the Witnessing can be read.

[48] Prolongation of the voice when pronouncing the first letter of *Allāhu akbar*. [49] Reading from the *muṣḥaf* [i.e. the Qur'ān] any verse which was not memorized. [50-51] Performing a pillar of the ritual prayer, e.g. bowing, or passing that measure of time in which it can be performed, in the state of uncovering the private parts of the devotee, or in the state of his being in such filth as bars the validity of ritual prayer. [52] The follower's performance of a pillar of a ritual prayer before its performance by the imām. [An example of this is that the follower has bowed and raised the head from bowing but the imām has not yet bowed, and he did not repeat the bowing with the imām or after him alone.] [53] Obedience to the imām in his prostration for forgetfulness (*sujūd as-sahw*); this is for a *masbūq*, i.e. one who alone is performing that part of the ritual prayer which he failed to perform following the imām because he came late. [54] Not to repeat the last sitting after making the prostration of the ritual prayer which the devotee has remembered after the sitting. [55] Not to repeat a pillar of a ritual prayer which the devotee has performed in the state of sleeping.

[56-57] A loud burst of laughter of the imām of the *masbūq* (i.e. one who is performing that part of the ritual prayer which he failed to perform with the imām because he came late), even though this laughter is not deliberate; and his deliberately incurring the state of minor legal impurity provided these two occur after that measure of the last sitting in which one can read the Witnessing. [58-61] Salutation at the end of the second *rak'a* of that ritual prayer which

consists of more than two *rak'as*, wrongly imagining that he is on a journey [and hence he has to perform only two *rak'as* of this kind of ritual prayer], or that this ritual prayer is the Friday Assembly Prayer [which is of two *rak'as*], or that it is the Tarāwīḥ Prayer whereas in reality it is the Evening Prayer, or because he is a new Muslim and so he thought that ritual prayer consisted of only two *rak'as*.

ACTS WHICH DO NOT CORRUPT A RITUAL PRAYER

Ritual prayer is not corrupted in the following cases: [1] A person engaged in a ritual prayer has looked at something written and understood it. [It is all the same whether the thing is a part of the Qur'ān or anything else, and whether he has intended to understand it or not. Although looking at a written thing does not corrupt a ritual prayer, it is contrary to the etiquette of such prayer.] [2] The devotee has eaten that which is between his teeth and which is less than the measure of a pea; in eating it he has not resorted to too much action. [3] Someone, whether a man or a woman or a dog or an ass, has passed through the place of the devotee's prostration. [If the one passing is a human being and he passes deliberately, he has committed a sin thereby. The Prophet said:

> If a person passing in front of another person engaged in a ritual prayer, knew the sin he committed thereby, he would have preferred to wait [even] for forty [years] to pass in front of the man engaged in the ritual prayer." [98]

[4] A man engaged in a ritual prayer has looked, with excitement, at the genitals of his divorced wife or of any woman who is a stranger. [If, however, he has kissed her or touched her, his ritual prayer is corrupted by these acts . If she is performing a ritual prayer and he has kissed even though without excitement, her ritual prayer is nullified. If he is engaged in ritual prayer and she has kissed him and he is not in excitement towards her, his ritual prayer is not corrupted.]

ACTS LEGALLY 'DISLIKED' IN A RITUAL PRAYER

It is 'disliked' by the law that one engaged in a ritual prayer should perform any of the following seventy-two acts:

[1] Leaving undone a 'required' act or a sunna act of a ritual prayer deliberately. Examples of this are: to play with one's clothes

[98] Al-Bukhārī, *Ṣaḥīḥ*, Ṣalā, 101; Muslim, *Ṣaḥīḥ*, Ṣalā, 261; at-Tirmidhī, *Sunan*, Ṣalā, 134; an-Nasā'ī, *Sunan*, Qibla, 8. Despite this great sin, people are often seen to pass in front of a devotee engaged in a ritual prayer in the mosque.

or body. [This playing opposes humility towards God which is the spirit of ritual prayer. This humility is emphasized in the Qur'ān, "Successful are indeed the believers who are humble towards God in their ritual prayers."[99] [2] Removal of pebbles or similar things from the place of prostration. To do this once for prostration, however, is not 'disliked' by the law. [3] Cracking the fingers even though once. [4] Entangling the fingers. [5] Putting the hands round the waist. [6] Looking to either side. [7] Sitting in such a state that the hips are put on the ground and the knees are raised up. This is like the sitting of a dog. [8-9] Spreading out the forearms and tucking up the sleeves from them.

[10] Wearing trousers only despite the ability to wear a shirt. [It is 'praiseworthy' for a devotee to wear three pieces of cloth — for a man: trousers, shirt and cap or turban; for a woman: a long shirt, a veil and a garment wrapping her entire body.] [11] Replying to the salutation of someone by indication. [12] Sitting cross-legged without an excuse. [13] Twisting the hair of a male devotee, i.e. to tie it on the head. [14] Binding the head with a towel or a turban, leaving its middle part exposed. [15] Lifting up the clothes from the front or from behind when making prostration. [16] Letting down of a cloth proudly or neglectfully. It means to put a cloth on the head and the shoulders or on the shoulders only, and then to let its sides go down without being joined together.] [17] To wrap oneself with a cloth in such a way that there is no hole through which the hands can be brought out. [18] Wearing a cloth by bringing it from below the right armpit and putting its both sides on the left shoulder, or vice versa. [Covering the shoulders is 'praiseworthy' in a ritual prayer, and hence their uncovering without any need is 'disliked' by the law.]

[19] Reading Qur'ānic verses in a state other than that of standing. [20] Prolongation of the first *rak'a* of every two *rak'as* of a 'supererogatory' ritual prayer. [21] Making the second *rak'a* longer than the first *rak'a* in all ritual prayers, 'supererogatory' and 'obligatory'. [22] Repetition of a sūra in one *rak'a* of an 'obligatory' ritual prayer. [Likewise is its repetition in both *rak'as* of this prayer, if the devotee is able to read another sūra from memory, and if the repetition is deliberate.] [23] In a *rak'a* to read a sūra which precedes that sūra which is read in the preceding *rak'a*. [An example of this is: to read in the first *rak'a* the Sūra of Sincerity[100] and in the

[99] Qur'ān 23:1.

[100] This is the one hundred and twelfth sūra of the Qur'ān. It consists of four short verses.

second *rak'a* the Sūra of Abū Lahb.][101] [24] In two *rak'as* to read two sūras leaving out a sūra between them.

[25] To smell any fragrant thing deliberately. [26-27] Fanning oneself with a cloth or with a fan once or twice. [28-29] Turning away the fingers and the toes from the direction of the Ka'ba in the state of prostration and others. [30] Failing to put the hands on the knees in bowing, [on the thighs in the state of sitting between two prostrations and in the state of reading the Witnessing. Likewise, it is 'disliked' by the law to leave undone the putting of the right hand on the left in the state of standing.] [31] Yawning. [It should be repressed as far as possible. The Prophet said,

> "God certainly likes the sneezer and dislikes the yawner. So when one of you yawns let him check it as far as he can and not say 'hā hā', for assuredly that is owing to the influence on him of Satan who laughs at him."][102]

[32] Closing the eyes. [However, if the eyes are closed in order to aid humility towards God and concentration of the ritual prayer, it is not 'disliked' by the law; rather it is better than keeping the eyes open.] [33] Lifting the eyes towards the sky.[103] [34] Spreading the arms because this is a sign of laziness. [35] Small degree of that action which opposes ritual prayer. [36] Catching a louse and killing it without necessity. [37-38] Covering the nose or the mouth. [39] Putting in the mouth anything which does not melt and which prevents the reading, easily, of Qur'ānic verses which is sunna. [40-41] Prostrating on the folds of the turban around the head or on the picture of a being possessing life, i.e. man or lower animal. [42] Prostrating by using the forehead only when there is no excuse in the nose. [43-48] Performing ritual prayer along a path, in a bath-room, in a privy, in a graveyard, on another man's land without his consent, and in a place near to filth.

[49-52] Performance of ritual prayer by checking the tendency to urinate or to excrete or to pass air through the anus, or by being with filth which is not liquid. If, however, there is fear of exhaustion of time for the ritual prayer or fear of missing the congregation for the prayer, it is not 'disliked' to perform the prayer in any of these conditions. But when the fears are absent, it is 'praiseworthy' first to relieve oneself and to remove the filth, and then to perform the ritual prayer.

101 This is the Qur'ānic sūra No. 111. It consists of five short verses.

102 At-Tirmidhī, *Sunan*, Adab, 8. See also al-Bukhārī, *Ṣaḥīḥ*, Adab, 125, 128.

103 Al-Bukhārī, *Ṣaḥīḥ*, Adhān, 92; an-Nasā'ī, *Sunan*, Sahw, 9.

[53] Performing ritual prayer wearing clothes for daily use which are not always free from dirt. [54] Performing ritual prayer by exposing the devotee's head. Exposing the head for self-humiliation and self-submission to God, however, is not 'disliked' by the law. [55-57] Performance of ritual prayer when food, to which the devotee is inclined, is already made present, when anything diverting mental concentration on the prayer is present, and when any such thing as inpairs humility towards God, e.g. game, is present. [The Prophet said:

> "There is no ritual prayer in the presence of food, or when one is affected by the tendency to urinate or excrete."[104] "If the supper is made present in front of anyone of you and the call (*iqāma*) to the actual start of the Evening Prayer in congregation is also made, then start with the supper and do not make haste until its completion."[105]

[58-59] Enumerating, with the hand, the Qur'ānic verses or the praises of God read in ritual prayer. [Making signs with the finger-tips which are not moved from their places, and enumerating mentally are, of course, not 'disliked' by the law. To enumerate them by using the tongue corrupts the ritual prayer in the opinion of all jurists.]

[60] The imām's standing entirely inside the *miḥrāb*, i.e. the place of the mosque reserved for him. [His standing outside the *miḥrāb* but prostrating inside it, however, is not 'disliked' by the law. In the case of a great crowd, his standing entirely inside the *miḥrāb* is also not 'disliked'.] [61-62] The imām's standing alone on a place of the measure of one cubit high or on a piece of land. [If, however, he stands alone with at least one follower, it is not 'dislike' by the law.] [63] Standing behind a line in which exists a gap.

[64] Performance of ritual prayer by wearing a cloth in which is a photo of a being possessing life, i.e. man or a lower animal. [65-68] Existence of a photo of a man or animal above the devotee's head, or below him, or in front of him, or opposite to him. It is, however, not 'disliked' if the photo is so small that it is visible to a standing man only after minute observation, or big but its head is cut off, or is of that which has no soul, e.g. a tree. [69-71] Existence, just in front of the devotee, of a light, or a fire-pot containing burning coal, or people asleep. [70] Wiping the forehead to remove dust which does not disturb the devotee. If, however, it disturbs him, its wiping is not

104 Muslim, *Ṣaḥīḥ*, Masājid, 67; Abū Dāwūd, *Sunan*, Ṭahāra, 43.

105 Al-Bukhārī, *Ṣaḥīḥ*, Adhān, 42; Muslim, *Ṣaḥīḥ*, Masājid, 64-66.

'disliked' by the law. The same is true of wiping sweat.

[71] Fixing a Qur'ānic sūra, other than the Opening Sūra, so that no other sūra is read in the ritual prayer. However, if a sūra is easy for the devotee to read or was read by the Prophet, its fixation is not 'disliked' by the law. [72] Not to place anything as a barrier (*sutra*) when performing a ritual prayer in a place where someone is likely to pass in front of the devotee. This is 'disliked' by the law because this leads those who pass, to commit sins. The Prophet said:

> "When one of you performs a ritual prayer, let him perform it placing a thing as a barrier (*sutra*) in front of him, and he should not allow anyone to pass in front of him."[106]

SETTING UP OF A BARRIER AND REPELLING ONE PASSING IN FRONT OF THE DEVOTEE

Should a man intending to perform a ritual prayer imagine that someone might pass in front of his ritual prayer, it is 'praiseworthy' for him to implant in front of him a barrier-like thing the length of which is a cubit or more and thickness of which is at least like that of a finger. It is sunna that he stands near to it, that he places it at the position of his eye-brows in prostrating, and that it should not require support.

If the intending devotee does not find anything to set up, he should draw a line which will be visible to one passing in front of him. The line is to be drawn lengthwise or, as the jurists also said, breadthwise like the new moon.

It is 'praiseworthy', whether or not anything is set up as a barrier, not to drive away one passing in front of the devotee, because calmness is important for ritual prayer and it is lost in driving away. It is left to his choice to drive one away with an indication of the head or the eyes or other bodily organs, or with the utterance of a glorification of God. To combine both is 'disliked' by the law. A male devotee will drive one away by uttering a glorification of God or a Qur'ānic verse loudly. A female devotee will drive one away by indication or by clapping the back side of the fingers of her right hand on the backside of her left palm; she will not raise her voice by uttering glorification of God, for this may create disturbance. Physical violence will not be done to one passing in front of the devotee.

ACTS NOT LEGALLY 'DISLIKED' FOR A DEVOTEE

[106] Al-Bukhārī, *Ṣaḥīḥ*, Ṣalā, 90; Abū Dāwūd, *Sunan*, Ṣalā, 106, 107, 109; at-Tirmidhī, *Sunan*, Mawāqīt, 133; an-Nasā'ī, *Sunan*, Qibla, 5; Ibn Māja, *Sunan*, Iqāma, 39.

The law does not 'dislike' that a person engaged in a ritual prayer should tie his waist; should gird himself with a sword or a similar thing provided he is not distracted by its movement; should direct his attention to a case of the Qur'ān, or to a hanging sword, or to the back of a sitting person who is talking, or to a burning candle or a lamp — this is the correct view —; should prostrate on a bed on which are photos of man or the lower animal, if prostration is not made exactly on the photos; should kill a snake or a scorpion the harm of which is feared, even though killing of them requires several blows as well as turning his face from the direction of the Ka'ba.

The devotee is 'permitted' by the law to shake his cloth lest it might cleave to his body when he bows, and to protect it from soil, to wipe his forehead in order to remove dust or grass on completion of the ritual prayer or even before its completion, provided dust or grass disturbs him and lessens his concentration on the ritual prayer, and to look to the right side or to the left with the corner of the eyes without turning the face. [It is, however, better not to look with the corner of the eyes, because this looking is contrary to the good manner of ritual prayer which consists in looking at the place of prostration.]

Likewise, it is 'permissible' to perform ritual prayer on a bed, on a carpet, and on bricks. The best is to perform it on the ground without putting anything on it, or on the things it grows, e.g. grass and straw. Use of grass carpets and straw mats is better than the use of other beds, because the former is nearer to humility needed very much in ritual prayer.

A person is 'permitted' by the law to repeat a particular Qur'ānic sūra in two *rak'as* of a 'supererogatory' ritual prayer.

ACTS 'REQUIRING' THE NULLIFICATION OF A RITUAL PRAYER AND ACTS 'PERMITTING' IT

A devotee is 'required' to nullify his ritual prayer, even though it is an 'obligatory' one, when a heart-broken person appeals for help in his distress, but not when one of his parents calls him in the usual manner, i.e. not being in distress.

A devotee is 'permitted' to nullify his ritual prayer, even though it is 'obligatory', in order to prevent the stealing of a thing worth a silver coin even though it is another man's property, to safeguard goats and the like against a wolf or other ferocious animals, and to save a blind man from falling into a well or a hole or some similar thing. A midwife can nullify her ritual prayer if she fears that her engagement in it may cause the death of the child in birth; for the same fear she is 'permitted' to delay ritual prayer, if she has not yet started it. Likewise, a traveller is 'permitted' to delay his ritual prayer when there is fear of thieves or robbers.

A Muslim who out of laziness deliberately does not perform ritual prayer, will be beaten severely until he bleeds, and after this will be put in prison where admonition, threatening and beating will be continued until he starts its performance or dies in prison. This is his this-worldly punishment. His punishment in the Hereafter is more severe and lasting.[107] In the same way, will be treated a Muslim who does not observe the fasting of the lunar month Ramaḍān.[108] A Muslim will be killed only when he denies ritual prayer or fasting, or neglects any one of these to such an extent that it approaches apostasy.

THE ODD PRAYER (*ṢALĀT AL-WITR*)

كان رسول الله صلى الله عليه وسلم يوتر بعد العشاء ثلاث ركعات.

The Messenger of God (may God bless and greet him!) used to perform the Odd Prayer in three *rak'as* after the Evening Prayer.

The Odd Prayer (*ṣalāt al-witr*) is 'required'. It consists of three *rak'as* with one salutation. In each of these *rak'as*, it is necessary to read the Opening Sūra and another sūra. At the end of the first two *rak'as*, the devotee is required to sit and to read the Witnessing only. In the beginning of the third *rak'a*, he will not read that prayer formula with which a ritual prayer is started, because the third *rak'a* is not the beginning of a new ritual prayer.

On completing the reading of a Qur'ānic sūra in the third *rak'a*, the devotee will raise his hands opposite to his ears and say *Allāhu akbar* (God is the greatest), and then read the *Qunūt* by standing and putting the right hand on the left. The *Qunūt* will be read before the bowing, and will not be read in any ritual prayer other than the Odd Prayer. The *Qunūt* is the formula prayer to be read in the Odd Prayer. It is as follows:

اللهم انا نستعينك ونستهديك ونستغفرك ونتوب اليك ونوءمن بك ونتوكل عليك ونثنى عليك الخير كله. نشكرك ولانكفرك ونخلع ونترك من يفجرك. اللهم اياك نعبد ولك نصلى ونسجد واليك نسعى ونحفد ونرجو رحمتك ونخشى عذابك ان عذابك الجد بالكفار ملحق. وصلى الله على النبى واله وسلم.

107 Qur'ān 20:127.

108 At-Tirmidhī, *Sunan*; Ibn Māja, *Sunan* — quoted by al-Ghazālī in his *Iḥyā'*, I, 195.

(Allāhumma, innā nasta'īnuka wa nastahdīka, wa nastaghfiruka wa natūbu ilayka, wa nu'minu bi-ka wa natawakkalu 'alayka, wa nuthnī 'alayka l-khayra kullahu. Nashkuruka wa lā nakfuruka, wa nakhla'u wa natruku man yafjuruka. Allāhumma, iyyāka na'budu, wa laka nuṣallī wa nasjudu, wa ilayka nas'ā wa naḥfidu, wa narjū raḥmataka wa nakhshā 'adhābaka, inna 'adhābaka l-jidda bi-l-kuffāri mulḥiqun. Wa ṣallā Allāhu 'alā n-nabiyyi, wa ālihi wa sallama.)

(God, we pray to You for help, and we pray to You for guidance; we pray to You for forgiveness, and we turn to You in repentance; we believe in You, and we have put trust in You. We praise You for all forms of good You have bestowed on us, and we are grateful to You and not ungrateful to You; we throw away and abandon him who commits unlawful actions.

God, You alone we worship; for You alone we perform ritual prayer, and for You alone we make prostration; to You alone is directed our spiritual endeavour, and to You alone we hastily come through devotional acts; we hope for Your mercy, and we fear Your punishment; surely Your serious punishment will meet the infidels.

May God bless the Prophet and the members of his family, and greet them!)

In the case of performance of the Odd Prayer in congregation in the month Ramaḍān, the follower will read the *Qunūt* like the imām. Both will read it secretly. On completing the reading of the *Qunūt*, when the imām starts the reading of a prayer formula given below, the follower will immitate him by reading it with him. This is the view of the jurist Abū Yūsuf. The jurist Muḥammad, however, maintains that the follower will not imitate him but will only say *āmīn*. This prayer formula is:

اللهم اهدنا بفضلك فيمن هديت وعافنا فيمن عافيت
وتولنا فيمن توليت وبارك لنا فيما اعطيت وقنا شرما
قضيت. انك تقضى ولايقضى عليك. انه لايزل من واليت
ولايعز من عاديت. تباركت ربنا وتعاليت. و صلى الله على
سيدنا محمد واله وصحبه وسلم.

(Allāhumma, ahdinā bi-faḍlika fīman hadayta, wa 'āfinā fīman 'āfayta, wa tawallanā fīman tawallayta, wa bārik lanā

fīmān a'ṭayta, wa qinā sharra mā qaḍaytahu. Innaka taqḍī wa la yuqḍā 'alyka. Innahu lā yadhillu man wālayta, wa lā ya'izzu man 'ādayta. Tabārakta rabbanā wa ta'ālayta. Wa ṣallā Allāhu 'alā sayyidinā Muḥammadin, wa ālihi, wa ṣaḥbihi, wa sallama.)

(God, through Your grace guide us with those whom You have guided, keep us safe with those whom You have kept safe, take care of us with those whom You have taken care of, bestow blessings for us on whatever You have given us, and save us from the evil of what You have ordained. Surely You can decree [whatever You like], but no one can decree against You. Surely one whom You have taken care of cannot be humiliated by anyone, and one whom You consider an enemy cannot be respected by anyone.[109] Lord, You are blessed and You are exalted. May God bless and greet our prince Muḥammad, the members of his family and his companions!)

A devotee who cannot read the *Qunūt* correctly, should read [1] the prayer formula *'Allāhumma, aghfir lī'* (اللهم اغفرلى: God, forgive me) three times, or [2] the prayer formula *'Rabbanā ātinā fī d-dunyā ḥasanatan, wa fī l-ākhirati ḥasanatan, wa qinā 'adhāba n-nārī'*[110] (ربنااتنا فى الدنيا حسنة، و فى الاخرة حسنة، و قناعذاب النار): Lord, grant us good in this world and good in the Hereafter, and save us from the punishment of Hell), or [3] the prayer *'yā rabbi, yā rabbi, yā rabbi'*(يارب، يارب، يارب: O Lord, O Lord, O Lord).

If a devotee follows the imām who is reading the *Qunūt* in the Dawn Prayer, he will remain standing but silent letting his hands hang loose by his sides during the imām's reading of the *Qunūt*.

A devotee who has forgotten to read the *Qunūt* in the third *rak'a* of the Odd Prayer and has remembered it when he is bowing or when rising from it, will not read the *Qunūt*; [as compensation for it he will make the prostration for forgetfulness]. Should he read it after rising from bowing, no repetition of the bowing is necessary; however, he will perform the prostration for forgetfulness, because the *Qunūt* is moved from its original place.

If the imām has bowed before the completion of the *Qunūt* by the follower, or before the start of it by the follower who fears that if he reads the *Qunūt* he will miss the bowing with the imām, he will not read the *Qunūt* but will obey the imām.

109 Cf. Qur'ān 22:18.

110 Qur'ān 2:201.

If the imām has not read the *Qunūt*, the follower will read it provided he can join the imām in the bowing after completing it. If he cannot join the imām, he will neglect the *Qunūt* and imitate the imām.

A devotee who comes late and finds the imām in the bowing of the third *rak'a* of the Odd Prayer, will legally be deemed to have joined in the *Qunūt*. So he will not read it when performing alone that part of his prayer which he missed with the imām.

It is 'praiseworthy' to perform the Odd Prayer in congregation in the month Ramaḍān only. Performance of the Odd Prayer in congregation in Ramaḍān [in the first part of the night] is more excellent than one's performance of it alone in the last part of the night. This view is held by Qāḍīkhān[111] who considers it the correct opinion. A contrary view is put forward by others as the correct view. [A person who has performed the Odd Prayer before sleep and then after sleep performed the Tahajjud Prayer,[112] will not repeat the Odd Prayer.]

'SUPEREROGATORY' RITUAL PRAYERS (*NAWĀFIL*)

It is the 'emphasized sunna' to perform two *rak'as* of ritual prayer before the 'obligatory' *rak'as* of the Dawn Prayer;[113] two *rak'as* after the 'obligatory' *rak'as* of the Noon Prayer, of the Sunset Prayer, and of the Evening Prayer; four *rak'as* before the 'obligatory' *rak'as* of the Noon Prayer, and of the Friday Assembly Prayer; and four *rak'as* after the 'obligatory' *rak'as* of the Friday Assembly Prayer; the four *rak'as* should be performed with one salutation. [The Prophet said:

> "God builds a house in Paradise for every Muslim who performs twelve *rak'as* of ritual prayer which are sunna, not obligatory, every day."][114]

It is 'praiseworthy' to perform four *rak'as* before the 'obligatory'

111 Qāḍīkhān (d. 592 A.H./1196 A.D.) was one of the most important compilers of Ḥanafī *fatāwā* or legal decisions. His compilation is known as *al-Khāniya*.

112 Tahajjud Prayer is an 'emphasized sunna' ritual prayer and a means of attaining nearness to God. The time for its performance is after the middle part of the night which is best suited for concentration of the mind and for communion with God.

113 Concerning these two *rak'as* the Prophet said, "The two sunna *rak'as* of the Dawn Prayer are better than the world and all that is in it" (Muslim, *Ṣaḥīḥ*, Musāfirīn, 96, 97; at-Tirmidhī, *Sunan*, Ṣalā, 190). Despite this, people, especially in cold countries, remain in bed neglecting the performance of the Dawn Prayer.

114 Muslim, *Ṣaḥīḥ*, Musāfirīn, 102, 103. See also Abū Dāwūd, *Sunan*, Taṭawwu', 1.

rak'as of the Late Afternoon Prayer and before and after the 'obligatory' *rak'as* of the Evening Prayer; and six *rak'as* after the 'obligatory' *rak'as* of the Sunset Prayer. [These six *rak'as* should be performed in three salutations and they are called the ritual prayer of those who turn to God very often (*ṣalāt al-awwābīn*). The Prophet said,

> "One who performs six *rak'as* of ritual prayer after the Sunset Prayer, is recorded in those who turn to God very often (*al-awwābūn*)"[115] Then he recited God's words, "Surely God forgives those who turn to Him very often."][116]

In the first sitting of the four 'emphasized sunna' *rak'as*, the devotee will read only the Witnessing. In the beginning of the third *rak'a*, the devotee will not read that supplication which is read for starting a ritual prayer. However, it will be read at the start of the third *rak'a* of a 'praiseworthy', not 'emphasized sunna', ritual prayer.

A person has performed 'supererogatory' ritual prayer of more than two *rak'as* [e.g. four], and sat only at the end of it. This is correct, for these 'supererogatory' *rak'as* have become one ritual prayer, and in a ritual prayer it is the sitting at the end of the whole prayer, and not the sitting at the end of the first two *rak'as*, which is 'obligatory'. [However, because the first sitting which is 'required' is omitted, its omission will be made good by the prostration for forgetfulness.]

It is 'disliked' by the law that one performs more than four 'supererogatory' *rak'as* with one salutation at daytime, and more than eight *rak'as* with one salutation at night. The most excellent at both times is four *rak'as*; this is the view of the Imām Abū Ḥanīfa.[117] According to Abū Yūsuf and Muḥammad, however, the most excellent at night is to perform two *rak'as* with one salutation, and at daytime four *rak'as* with one salutation as is the view of Abū Ḥanīfa; it is on the views of Abū Yūsuf and Muḥammad that the legal decision has been given.

Ritual prayer at night, especially in the last third of it, is more excellent than the ritual prayer at daytime. Prolongation of standing in ritual prayer, reading the Qur'ān, whether at daytime or at night, is more 'praiseworthy' than performing more *rak'as* and thus prostrating more. [The Prophet said,

115 At-Tirmidhī, *Sunan*, Mawāqīt, 204.

116 Qur'ān 17:25.

117 For an account of Abū Ḥanīfa see al-Ghazālī, *Iḥyā'*, I, 28.

"The best ritual prayer is that in which the state of standing, in which the Qur'ān is read, is prolonged."][118]

RITUAL PRAYER FOR GREETING THE MOSQUE, RITUAL PRAYER FOLLOWING SUNRISE, AND KEEPING VIGIL AT NIGHT

قال رسول الله صلى الله عليه وسلم: اذا دخل احدكم المسجد فليركع ركعتين قبل ان يجلس.

The Messenger of God (may God bless and greet him!) said, "When one of you enters a mosque let him perform two *rak'as* of ritual prayer before he sits."[119]

انه صلى الله عليه وسلم كان يصلي الضحى اربعا ويزيد ماشاء الله.

"The Prophet (may God bless and greet him!) used to perform the Ritual Prayer after Sunrise as consisting of four *rak'as*. [Sometimes] he increased them to as many *rak'as* as God wished."[120]

Greeting the mosque with the performance of two *rak'as* of ritual prayer just on entering the mosque and before sitting down, is 'emphasized sunna', if the time is not that in which ritual prayer is 'disliked' by the law. Performance of an 'obligatory' ritual prayer, or performance of any other ritual prayer just on entering the mosque, without making the intention of greeting the mosque, fills the place of the two sunna *rak'as* of greeting the mosque.[121]

It is 'praiseworthy' to perform two *rak'as* following ablution, before the parts washed in it have become dry.

It is also 'praiseworthy' to perform four *rak'as* or more when the sun is quite up in the morning. [From this time until before the sun passes its meridian, this ritual prayer can be performed. This prayer consists of from four to twelve *rak'as*.]

Likewise it is 'praiseworthy' to perform 'supererogatory' ritual

118 Muslim, *Ṣaḥīḥ*, Musāfirīn, 164, 165; at-Tirmidhī, *Sunan*, Ṣalā, 168; an-Nasā'ī, *Sunan*, Zakā, 49; Ibn Māja, *Sunan*, Iqāma, 200.

119 Al-Bukhārī, *Ṣaḥīḥ*, Ṣalā, 60, Tahajjud, 25; Muslim *Ṣaḥīḥ*, Musāfirīn, 68-70.

120 Muslim *Ṣaḥīḥ*, Musāfirīn, 79.

121 This is because the purpose of the Prayer of Greeting the Mosque is that the start of entering into the mosque should not be devoid of a devotional act special to the mosque, and this purpose is served by any ritual prayer other than the Prayer of Greeting.

It is 'disliked' by the law to enter into the mosque without ablution. If one without ablution enters, one should read this formula four times: glorified is God; praise to God! there is no god but God; God is the greatest (سبحان الله والحمد لله ولا اله الا الله والله اكبر : *subḥāna Allāhi; wa l-ḥamdu li-Allāhi; wa lā ilāha illā Allāhu; wa Allāhu akbar*). The reading of this formula four times will be equal to the Prayer of Greeting the Mosque.

prayer at night, especially in the last third part of it. [The Prophet said,

> "You should perform the 'supererogatory' ritual prayer of the night, for it was habitually performed by those who have passed before you, is a good work drawing you to your Lord, is an atonement for sins committed, and keeps you from the commission of further sins."] [122]

Ritual prayer seeking guidance of God (*ṣalāt al-istikhāra*) on any matter is also 'praiseworthy'. [The Prophet used to teach this ritual prayer to his companions in all affairs as emphatically as he used to teach them the Qur'ānic sūras. [123] He taught its methods as follows. When a person intends to do an important thing, he should make ablution, perform two *rak'as* of 'supererogatory' ritual prayer and then read the prayer formula:

> God, I seek Your guidance on my affair through Your knowledge, I seek ability from You through Your ability, and I pray to You for Your great bounty; for You are able and I am unable, You know and I do not know, and You have the fullest knowledge of the unseen. God, should You know that this thing which I have intended to do is good for me in respect of my religion and my livelihood, and in respect of its final consequence, then decree it for me, facilitate it for me and then bestow blessings upon it for me. But should You know that this thing which I have intended to do is bad for me in respect of my religion and my livelihood, and in respect of its final consequence, then turn it away from me and turn me away from it, decree for me the good wherever it may be, and then confer Your pleasure on it. [124]

(اللهم انى استخيرك بعلمك، واستقدرك بقدرتك، واسئلك من فضلك العظيم؛ فانك تقدر ولااقدر، وتعلم ولااعلم، وانت علام الغيوب. اللهم، ان كنت تعلم ان هذا الامر خير لى فى دينى ومعاشى وعاقبة امرى، فاقدره لى ويسره لى، ثم بارك لى فيه. وان كنت تعلم ان هذا الامر شر لى فى ديني ومعاشى وعاقبة امرى، فاصرفه عنى واصرفنى عنه، واقدر لى الخير حيث كان، ثم رضى به.)

(*Allāhuma, innī astakhīruka bi-'ilmika, wa astaqdiruka*

[122] At-Tirmidhī, *Sunan*, Da'wāt, 101.

[123] Al-Bukhārī, *Ṣaḥīḥ*, Tahajjud, 25, Da'wāt, 49, Tawḥīd, 10.

[124] *Ibid*.

> *bi-qudratika, wa as'aluka min faḍlika l'aẓīmi; fa-innaka ta'lamu wa lā a'lamu, wa taqdiru wa la aqdiru, wa anta 'allāmu l-ghuyūbi. Allāhumma, in kunta ta' lamu anna hādha l-amra khayrun lī fī dīnī wa ma'āshī wa 'āqibati amrī, fa-qdirhu lī wa yassirhu lī, thumma bārik lī fīhi. Wa in kunta ta'lamu anna hādha l-amra sharrun lī fī dīnī wa ma'āshī wa 'āqibati amrī, faṣrifhu 'annī wa ṣrifnī 'ānhu, wa qdir lī l-khayra ḥaythu kāna, thumma raḍī bihi*).

This ritual prayer seeking the guidance of God should be performed for seven days or nights in the manner just described. As a result of this, the mind becomes inclined to the intended work or averse from it. Accordingly, the man should go ahead with the work or stop it. This concerns acts the goodness or badness of which is not known. As for the pilgrimage to Mecca and other acts which are obviously good, ritual prayer seeking the guidance of God on them should be made in order to determine their appropriate time, not to determine whether or not they are good in themselves.]

Ritual prayer for the fulfilment of a need (*ṣalāt al-ḥāja*) is also 'praiseworthy'. [The Prophet taught its procedure as follows.[125] A person who has a religious or secular need from God or from a human being, should make ablution in the best manner, then perform two *rak'as* of ritual prayer, then praise God and invoke blessings upon the Prophet, and then read the formula prayer:

> There is no god but God, the Forebearing, the Noble. Glorified is the Lord of the mighty throne! Praise be to God, the Lord of all the worlds!
>
> I pray to You for momentous acts of Your mercy, for constancy of Your forgiveness, for taking as prey every form of piety, and for safety from every sin. Do not leave any sin of mine unforgiven, any anxiety of mine undispelled and any need of mine in which lies Your pleasure unfulfilled, O Most Merciful of those who show mercy.
>
> (لا اله الا الله الحليم الكريم. سبحان ربى العرش العظيم. الحمد لله ربالعالمين. اسئلك موجبات رحمتك وعزائم مغفرتك والغنيمة من كل بر والسلامة من كل اثم. لاتدع لى ذنبا الا غفرته ولاهما الا فرجته ولا حاجة لك فيها رضا الا قضيتها يا ارحم الراحمين)

(*Lā illāha illā Allāhu l-ḥalīmu l-karīmu. Subḥāna rabbī*

[125] At-Tirmidhī, *Sunan*, Witr, 17; Ibn Māja, *Sunan*, Iqāma, 189.

l-'arshi l-'aẓīmi. Al-ḥamdu li-Allāhi rabbi l-'ālamīna. As'-aluka mūjibāti raḥmatika, wa'azā'ima maghfiratika, wa l-ghanīmata min kulli birrin, wa s-salāmata min kulli ithmin. Lā tada' lī dhanban illā ghafartahu, wa lā hamman illā farrajtahu, wa lā ḥājatan laka fīhā riḍan illā qaḍaytahā, yā arḥama r-rāḥimīna).

On reading this prayer formula, the person will pray to God for the fulfilment of his need which may be the removal of something which has already happened or which will happen, or the achievement of something.]

It is 'praiseworthy' to keep vigil during the last ten nights of Ramaḍān. [In these night the Prophet used to keep vigil himself and to encourage the members of his family to do the same.][126]

Keeping vigil during the night of the two 'Īds is 'praiseworthy'. Prayer for forgiveness, with full concentration of the mind and with humility and submission to God during the nights of the two 'Īds, is 'praiseworthy'; prayer in them is received by God .

Keeping vigil in the night of the tenth of the lunar month Dhū l-Ḥijja and in the nights adjacent to it is also 'praiseworthy'.

It is also 'praiseworthy' to keep vigil during the night of the fifteenth day of the lunar month Sha'bān. [In this night a man's sustenance and other things are allotted by God for one year, and his sins committed in the past one year are forgiven provided he can utilize the night properly. It is one of those nights in which prayer is received by God. Keeping vigil means to devote the greater part of the night to different forms of devotional acts, e.g. 'supererogatory' ritual prayer, Qur'ān-reading, glorification of God, and invoking blessings upon the Prophet.]

The law 'dislikes' that people should assemble in the mosque or in other places for keeping vigil during the nights mentioned above — 'dislikes' because this was not done by the Prophet or his companions.

'SUPEREROGATORY' RITUAL PRAYER BY ONE SITTING OR RIDING

It is 'permissible' to perform a 'supererogatory' ritual prayer, including an 'emphasized sunna' ritual prayer, while sitting despite one's ability to perform it by standing. Performance of it sitting, however, earns half the merit of its performance standing, except if it is for an excuse in which case full merit is obtained. A man

126 Al-Bukhārī, *Ṣaḥīḥ*, Laylat al-Qadr, 5.

performing a ritual prayer sitting should sit in the manner of sitting of one who is reading the Witnessing. On this has been given legal decision.

It is 'permissible' to complete a 'supererogatory' ritual prayer sitting after starting it by standing. This is 'not disliked' by the law; this is the most correct view.

A rider will perform 'supererogatory' ritual prayer on the back of his animal or on his vehicle, by indicating in whatever direction his animal or vehicle faces. If he descends, but not if he ascends, he will build the remaining part of the ritual prayer on the part already performed, even though this prayer is an 'emphasized supererogatory' ritual prayer, e.g. the two 'emphasized sunna' *rak'as* of the Dawn Prayer. Abū Ḥanīfa, however, maintains that the rider must descend if the 'emphasized supererogatory' ritual prayer is the two 'supererogatory' *rak'as* of the Dawn Prayer, since these are more emphasized than others.

It is 'permissible' without being 'disliked' by the law for a person engaged in a 'supererogatory' ritual prayer to lean against a thing, e.g. wall, if he is tired; leaning without an excuse is 'disliked' by the law, because this is against the etiquette of ritual prayer.

Filth on an animal or in a vehicle is not a bar to the validity of ritual prayer on the animal or on the vehicle, even though the filth is on the saddle or its stirrup — this is the most correct legal opinion.

Performance of a ritual prayer in the state of one's walking is not valid. All jurists have agreed on this view.

'OBLIGATORY' AND 'REQUIRED' RITUAL PRAYERS BY ONE RIDING OR IN A VEHICLE

It is not correct to perform, without necessity, on the back of an animal or in a vehicle [1] any 'obligatory' ritual prayer, [2] any 'required' ritual prayer, e.g. the Odd Prayer, the 'Īd Prayers, those ritual prayers which one has promised to God by a vow, and a ritual prayer which is the re-fulfilment of that which was started as a 'supererogatory' ritual prayer but was then nullified by the agent before its completion, [3] ritual prayer over the bier, and [4] a prostration due to a Qur'ānic verse which is recited in the state of the reciter's being on the ground. All these, however, are correct in necessity such as [1] fear, if he descends, of a thief for himself or for the animal or for the vehicle or for the clothes, [2] fear of a ferocious animal for himself or for the animal, [3] the place being muddy, [4] inability to control the animal or the vehicle, and [5] absence of someone to help him in mounting again after descending for the performance of ritual prayer on the ground.

A ritual prayer in a litter on the back of an animal is to be considered as a ritual prayer on its back; it is all the same whether the animal is moving or standing still. If the animal is kept still, and a piece of wood or a similar thing is placed under the litter so that through it the litter touches the ground, then the litter has occupied the place of the ground and consequently it is correct for a person to perform 'obligatory' ritual prayer in it by standing, not by sitting.

RITUAL PRAYER IN A BOAT

According to Imām Abū Ḥanīfa performance of an 'obligatory' ritual prayer inside a sailing boat by sitting and by bowing and prostrating is correct even though there is no excuse, and even though coming out from the boat to the land is possible. However, if possible, to perform it inside the boat by standing, or to come out of the boat is better. Imām Abū Yūsuf and Imām Muḥammad held the view that 'obligatory' ritual prayer inside a boat by sitting is not correct, except when there is an excuse. Examples of excuses are giddiness of the head and inability to come out of the boat. Performance of a ritual prayer inside a boat by indication is not correct for one able to make bowing and prostration. This is the unanimous view of all jurists.

A boat tied in the midst of a sea and moved much by the wind is to be treated like a sailing boat. If it is not moved much it is to be considered like a boat still at the shore; this is the most correct view. The legal ruling on a boat tied to the shore is that the performance of ritual prayer in it by sitting is not correct if one is able to perform it by standing. This view is the consensus of the Muslims. If one performs ritual prayer in it by standing, and the boat is in such a position that part of it is on the ground, one's ritual prayer is correct; but it is not correct if part of the boat is not on the ground, except if it is not possible to come out of the boat.

When starting a ritual prayer inside a sailing boat, the devotee will face the direction of the Ka'ba because he is able to do so, but whenever the boat moves from this direction to another, he will turn himself to the Ka'ba in the midst of his ritual prayer so that he completes it facing the direction of the Ka'ba. In the case of failure to face the direction of the Ka'ba, ritual prayer is not correct in the opinion of all jurists.

TARĀWĪḤ PRAYER

Tarāwīḥ Prayer performed after the Evening Prayer in the lunar month Ramaḍān is an 'emphasized sunna' for both men and women. To perform this ritual prayer in congregation is 'collective sunna,' so that its performance by some people of a locality in congregation while by others alone is correct.

The time for Tarāwīḥ Prayer starts from after the Evening Prayer and continues until the day break. It is correct to perform the Odd Prayer before or after the Tarāwīḥ Prayer, but to perform it after the Tarāwīḥ Prayer is better. It is 'praiseworthy' to delay the Tarāwīḥ Prayer to one-third of the night or to half of the night. To delay it even after the half of the night is not 'disliked' by the law — this is the correct view.

Tarāwīḥ Prayer consists of twenty *rak'as* with ten salutations, each salutation being at the end of every two *rak'as*. It is 'praiseworthy' to sit on completion of every four *rak'as* for as much time as was required for the performance of the four *rak'as*. So also is to sit between the completion of the last four *rak'as* and the start of the Odd Prayer.

It is sunna to complete the reading of the Qur'ān once in the Tarāwīḥ Prayer throughout the month Ramaḍān — this is the correct view. Should the effort to complete the Qur'ān once in the month make people tired and disgusted, that measure of the Qur'ān should be readwhich would not cause their aversion. Reading of the formula of invoking blessings upon the Prophet should not be neglected any time when the Witnessing is read in this ritual prayer, even though this makes people tired, for this is 'emphasized sunna'. Likewise, the reading of the formula of praise of God (*thanā'*) at the start of every two *rak'as*, and the reading of the formulae of glorification of God in bowing and prostration should not be neglected, because these too are 'emphasized sunna'. However, the imām can, if people feel tired, neglect the reading of that supplication which is read just before salutation.

If one fails to perform the Tarāwīḥ Prayer alone or in congregation in due time, there is no provision for its performance at a later time.

RITUAL PRAYER INSIDE THE HOLY KA'BA

Ritual Prayer, whether 'obligatory' or 'supererogatory', is correct inside the Holy Ka'ba and, likewise, above it, even though nothing is placed as a barrier (*sutra*) in front of the devotee; however, ritual prayer above the Ka'ba is 'disliked' by the law because to ascend to the roof of the Ka'ba is contrary to etiquette.

When performing ritual prayer in congregation inside the Ka'ba or above it, if a person has his back to a direction other than the face of his imām, his following the imām is to be considered correct. If, however, he has his back to the face of the imām, his ritual prayer is not correct. A person's following the imām is correct if he is outside the Ka'ba, and the imām is inside, and the door of the Ka'ba is open.

If, in a ritual prayer in congregation outside the Ka'ba, the people have stood encircling the Ka'ba and their imām is outside the Ka'ba, their following the imām is correct, except in the case of him who is closer to the Ka 'ba than the imām and is facing the same direction as the imām. [If, however, one is closer to the Ka'ba than the imām but not facing the same direction as the imām, one's following the imām is to be considered correct.]

RITUAL PRAYER BY A TRAVELLER

واذا ضربتم فى الارض فليس عليكم ان تقصروا من الصلاة.
— قران ٤:١٠١

When you journey in the land it will be no sin on you to shorten ritual prayer. — Qur'ān 4:101

Definition of Travel

The smallest journey by which legal rules are changed is of a distance which can be traversed in the three shortest days of the year by moderate speed of travel at daytime with necessary rest. Moderate speed on land is travelling by camel or man's going on foot; in the hills it is that mode of going which befits it; and on the sea it is by the medium of a moderate wind. [The jurists have calculated the distance mentioned here in terms of mileage and have found it to be of forty-eight miles. So on traversing the distance of forty-eight miles by whatever means of transportation it may be, a person is legally considered a traveller for whom legal rules on certain matters become different from those for a stationary man (*muqīm*).]

The traveller will shorten only the 'obligatory' ritual prayer consisting of four *rak'as*. [Concerning the sunna *rak'as* the rule is that if the traveller has stopped somewhere and feels safe, he will perform them in full; but if he is in movement or does not feel safe, he will not perform them at all.] The traveller will start shortening the 'obligatory' four *rak'as* of ritual prayer after he, having made the intention of travel even though his travel is sinful, has passed by the houses of the place of his stay and has also passed by the courtyard attached to its place. If the courtyard is separated by a seed-sowing field or by an empty space of the measure of around four hundred steps, the passing of it by the traveller is not a stipulation for allowing him to shorten the ritual prayer. The courtyard is defined as a place prepared for ensuring the facilities of the town, such as the race course and burial of the dead.

Stipulations for the Validity of Intention of Travel

There are three stipulations for the validity of intention of travel. They are as follows:

[1] Independence in respect of making judgement, e.g. the husband has this independence but not his wife for she is dependent on him. [2] Maturity. [3] That the duration of traversing the distance of travel [by walking] is not less than three days, i.e. not less than forty-eight miles. From these three stipulations it is found that ritual prayer will not be shortened by a traveller who [1] has not yet passed by the habitations of the place of his stay, or [2] has passed by them but is a child, or [3] is dependent upon a person who has not made the intention of travel, e.g. a wife accompanying her husband and a soldier accompanying his commander, or [4] has intended to traverse a distance of *less* than three days, i.e. less than forty-eight miles. In regard to travel and 'station' what is to be considered is the intention of the one on whom the other is dependent and not the intention of the dependent, in the case where the intention of the former is known. [Thus on a journey, if a wife is accompanying her husband or a soldier his commander, it is the intention of the husband and the commander which is to be considered, so that if their intention of travel is correct their dependents will shorten the ritual prayer consisting of four *rak'as*.]

According to the Ḥanafī school of jurisprudence,[127] the shortening of four obligatory *rak'as* of a ritual prayer is a necessity, not an option. For this reason the Ḥanafī jurists maintain that if a devotee [did not shorten but] has completed the four *rak'as* and, at the end of the first two *rak'as* of them, sat for the length of time in which the Witnessing can be read, his ritual prayer is correct but 'disliked' by the law. If, however, he did not sit at the end of the first two *rak'as*, his ritual prayer is not correct, except if he made the intention of being stationary when he stood up to start the third *rak'a*.

[127] There are four schools of Islamic religious law — Ḥanafī, Shāfi'ī, Mālikī, and Ḥanbalī. These schools do not differ on fundamentals; they differ only on minor points, and this is because of their differences in understanding the texts of the Qur'ān and prophetic tradition which constitute the basis of their laws.

A person recognized by the law as a traveller, will continue shortening the ritual prayer of four *rak'as* until he re-enters his home town, or until he makes the intention of staying at another town or a village for at least half a month. If he intends to stay there for less than half a month, or if he did not make the intention [of staying for any particular length of time and remained in that state even for several years [but there was the possibility of his leaving that town or village at any time] — in all these cases he will shorten the ritual prayer.

Making the intention of being stationary in two towns without fixing the passing of time in any one of them is not legally correct. Making the intention of being stationary in a desert is also not correct for those who are not dwellers in a tent of wool or camel's hair. Likewise, it is not legally correct for a Muslim army to make the intention of being stationary in an enemy's land, or in a Muslim country while beseiging the rebels, even though victory for the Muslim army is obvious, because in both cases the duration of the stay of the army is uncertain.

In a ritual prayer in congregation performed in its due time, if a traveller follows a stationary imām his ritual prayer is correct and he will complete all four *rak'as*, [as does the imām, and will not reduce them to two *rak'as* on the ground that he is a traveller]; however, if this ritual prayer is performed after the due time (*qaḍā'*), the traveller's ritual prayer is not correct. Should the case be the opposite, i.e. a stationary man follows a traveller, the following of the stationary man is correct, whether this ritual prayer is performed in its due time or after it. In this opposite case, it is 'praiseworthy' that the imām, after salutation on completion of the first two *rak'as*, should say to the followers, "you complete four *rak'as*, I am a traveller." He should say this to them before starting the ritual prayer. In that *rak'a* (or those *rak'as*) which the follower, a stationary man, performs after the imām, a traveller, has completed his ritual prayer, the follower will not read Qur'ānic verse [after reading the Opening Sūra] — this is the most correct view.

The reduced *rak'as*, i.e. two *rak'as*, of the travelling time which were not performed at that time but are being performed later (*qaḍā'*) in the stationary time, will have to be performed as two *rak'as*. Likewise, the unreduced four *rak'as* of the stationary time which were not performed at that time but are being performed later at the travelling time, will have to be performed as four *rak'as*, [because the performance at a later time is like the performance at the proper time].

In maintaining that an 'obligatory' ritual prayer consisting of four [or three] ***rak'as*** must be performed in full in the stationary time and as two ***rak'as*** in the travelling time, what is considered is the last part of the time of this ritual prayer. [Thus in the last part, if a person is a traveller he will perform two *rak'as*, and if he is stationary he will perform four *rak'as*.]

A person's original dwelling house is nullified by the making by him of a dwelling house like it, [and not by the making of a dwelling house of station or by his travel]. His dwelling house of station is nullified by one like it, by a journey made after it, and by his return to his original dwelling house. The original dwelling house is defined as that wherein one is born, or married, or does not marry and was not born but in which one has intended to live and not to emigrate from it. The dwelling house of station is defined as a place where one has intended to reside for half a month or more. Consideration is not given by the doctors of law to the dwelling house of halting, which is the place where one has intended to stay for less than half a month.

RITUAL PRAYER BY A SICK MAN

When it is impossible for a sick man to stand completely, or when it is only difficult for him to do so because of a severe pain, or when he fears that his standing may aggravate his sickness or may cause delay in his recovery, he will perform ritual prayer by sitting and with bowing and prostration. He is allowed by the law to sit in any way easy for him — this is the most correct view. Should he be able to stand partially, he will stand as far as possible.

If it is impossible for a sick man to bow and to prostrate [but possible to sit even though leaning against something] he will perform ritual prayer by sitting and indicating with his head for bowing and prostration; his indication with the head for prostration will be lower than that for bowing. If the indication for prostration is not made lower than the indication for bowing, the ritual prayer is not correct. Nothing, e.g. stone and wood, will be raised up to his face in order that he might prostrate on it. If anything is raised up and he has also lowered his head in order to make the lowering for prostration more than the lowering of it for bowing, his ritual prayer is correct. But if the lowering of the head for prostration is not more than its lowering for bowing, the ritual prayer is not correct [because the 'obligatory' act of indication for prostration is not performed].

If it is difficult to sit [even though leaning or supporting himself by a wall or other thing], the sick man will perform ritual prayer by lying on his back or on his side [preferably the right side], and by indicating [with the head]; to lie down on the back is better than lying down on the right side. He will put a pillow under his head in order that his face may be towards the direction of the Ka'ba and not towards the sky, [and in order to be able to indicate correctly with the head for bowing and prostrating]. He should raise his knees, if possible, so that they may not be spread out in the direction of the Ka'ba, [for this spreading out is 'disliked' by the law in the case of one able to avoid it .

Should the indication with the head for bowing and prostration be impossible for the sick man, ritual prayer will be postponed so long as he understands the address made to him by others; it is mentioned in *The Guidance* (*al-Hidāya*)[128] that this is the correct view. The author of *The Guidance* has, however, resolved in *at-Tajnīs wa l-Mazīd* that ritual prayers need not be performed later (*qaḍā'*), if the sick man's inability to indicate with the head for bowing and prostration persists for more than five times of ritual prayer, even though he understands the address made to him by others during these times. Qāḍīkhān considers this view as correct, and the same opinion is expressed in *al-Muḥīṭ*. Shaykh al-Islām Khawāhir Zādeh[129] and Fakhr al Islām as-Sarakhsī[130] have also chosen this view. It is said in *aẓ-Ẓahīriyya* that on this view legal decision has been given. In *al-Khulāṣa* this view is considered the chosen view. In *al-Yanābi'* and *al-Badā'i'*[131] it is called the correct view. Al-Walwālijī firmly held this view.

The sick man who is unable to indicate with his head for bowing and prostration, is 'not allowed' by the law to indicate with his eyes or the mind or the eyebrows. [The reason is that prostration is

[128] The books on Islamic religious law written by the Ḥanafī jurists of the older period were ousted by the works and commentaries produced by the later jurists of the same school. ***The Hidāya*** **(guidance) of al-Marghinānī**(d. 593 A.H./1197 A.D.) is one of the most important of these later works. Several commentaries are written on it.

[129] Shaykh Zāde's *Majma' al-Anhur* is a very popular commentary on the *Multaqā al-Abḥur* of Ibrāhīm al-Ḥalabī (d. 956 A.H./1549 A.D.) which became an authoritative handbook on the Ḥanafī law in the Ottoman Empire. Shaykh Zāde died in 1078 A.H./1667 A.D.

[130] Fakhr al-Islām as-Sarakhsī (d. 483 A.H./1090 A.D.) was one of the older jurists of the Ḥanafī school of Islamic religious law. His *Mabsūṭ*, a commentary on the *Kāfī* of al-Ḥākim ash-Shahīd (d. 334 A.H./945 A.D.), is a comprehensive work on Ḥanafī law. He arranged the subject-matter within each chapter in a logical and systematic way.

[131] *Badā'i' aṣ-Ṣanā'i'* was written by al-Kāsānī (d. 587 A.H./1191 A.D.) It is one of the older works on Ḥanafī law and deals with problems by arranging them in a strictly systematic way.

related to the head and not to these parts of the body.]

A sick man able to stand but unable to bow and to prostrate will perform ritual prayer, not by standing, but by sitting and indicating with the head for bowing and prostration. [If one is unable to prostrate but able to bow, the requirement of bowing ceases to be one's responsibility.]

A person [who has started a ritual prayer as a healthy man but] is afflicted with a disease in course of the ritual prayer, will complete it in a way possible for him, even if only by indication with the head — this is the well-known view.

A sick man who has started the performance of a ritual prayer by sitting and by bowing and prostrating, and who then recovers his health during the ritual prayer, will build (*binā'*) the remaining part on the part already performed. But a sick man is 'not allowed' to build if, after performing some part of the ritual prayer by indicating, he has become able to bow and to prostrate even if only by sitting; [he will perform the ritual prayer anew, from the beginning].

A person who has remained insane or senseless throughout the time of five ritual prayers, will have to perform them later when he recovers his normal state. But if his abnormal state persists for more than this time, he need not perform them later.

FALLING OF RITUAL PRAYER AND FASTING FROM ONE'S RESPONSIBILITY

When a sick man is dying, and he is unable to perform ritual prayer by indication with the head, it is not necessary for him to order his heirs by will to pay ransom (*fidya*) for him, even though the ritual prayer was only a few times, i.e. less than five times. Likewise is the legal rule concerning fasting in the month Ramaḍān — if a traveller or a sick man does not fast and is dying before the former has become 'stationary' and the latter has recovered his health, they are not 'required' to order their heirs to pay ransom for them.

The dying man who did not observe, for an excuse or for no excuse, fasting or ritual prayer in their due times, and had the ability to observe them at a later time but did not do so, and they remain his responsibility until now when he is dying, is 'required' to order his heir by will to pay ransom. So his heir must, on his behalf, pay to poor men half a *sā'* of wheat [or parched barley or flour, or one *sā'* of dried dates or raising or barley], or the price of anyone of these, from the one-third of the wealth the deceased left, as ransom for the fasting of each day or for 'obligatory' ritual prayer of each time including the Odd Prayer. If he did not order his heir by will to pay the ransom but the heir [or any other person] has paid it of his own will, it is 'permissible'. It is not correct that the heir [or any other person] should fast [or perform ritual prayer] on behalf of the deceased man.

If the wealth with which the dying man ordered his heir by will to pay ransom for his unobserved fasting or ritual prayer is not sufficient, the heir will adopt a device: he will first give away this entire wealth to a poor man, so that by this an appropriate part of his unobserved fasting or ritual prayer will be ransomed; then the poor man, after possessing it, will voluntarily give away this wealth to the heir who will seize it and possess it; then the heir will again give it away to the poor man, so that by this an appropriate part of the unobserved fasting or ritual prayer of the deceased will be ransomed; then the poor man will again voluntarily give away the wealth to the heir who, after seizing it, will again give it away to the poor man, so that by this another appropriate part of the unobserved fasting or ritual prayer of the deceased man will be ransomed; this procedure will continue until all fasting or all ritual prayers, which were in his responsibility are redeemed.

It is 'permissible' by the law to give the entire redemption-wealth for several ritual prayers [or for several days of fasting] to a single poor man. This is unlike the redemption-wealth for breaking oath.

PERFORMANCE OF RITUAL PRAYERS AT LATER TIMES (*QAḌĀ'*)

It is necessary for a person to maintain the order between those ritual prayers which he did not perform in their due times in the past but is performing now and that ritual prayer which is of the present time, and between the several ritual prayers of the former category themselves, if their number is less than six. There is, however, no need to maintain this order if any one of the following three things are present:

[1] The 'praiseworthy' part of the time of a ritual prayer is not sufficient to permit that the ritual prayers of the past time which are due and the ritual prayer of the present time can both be performed in it — this is the most correct view. [An example of this is that the 'praiseworthy' part of the time of the Late Afternoon Prayer continues until some change appears in the colour of the sun; a man has come to perform this ritual prayer in this 'praiseworthy' part but finds that if he occupies himself first with the performance of the Noon Prayer which he did not perform at noon, performance of the

Late Afternoon Prayer will fall in the time when some change occurs in the colour of the sun; in this situation, maintenance of order, i.e. to perform the Noon Prayer first and then the Late Afternoon Prayer, ceases to be his responsibility — he will neglect the Noon Prayer.]

[2] Forgetfulness of the ritual prayers which were not performed in their due times in the past. [3] The number of the ritual prayers not performed in their due times in the past has risen to [at least] six excluding the Odd Prayer. The Odd Prayer is not regarded as a ritual prayer by which the necessity of maintaining order ceases to be one's responsibility, even though it must be put in order [with the Evening Prayer, the Dawn Prayer, and so on].

When the number of unperformed ritual prayers of the past has been reduced to less than six by the performance of some of them now, maintenance of order is no longer relevant to them. Nor does it become relevant when one new ritual prayer is left unperformed after [a person forgot about] the old six unperformed ritual prayers [and then remembered them]. These two are the most correct views, and on them have been given legal decisions.

If a devotee performs an 'obligatory' ritual prayer remembering an unperformed ritual prayer of the past time, even though it is the Odd Prayer, the 'obligatory' ritual prayer is conditionally nullified: thus if, after that 'obligatory' ritual prayer, he performs five new ritual prayers remembering in them that unperformed ritual prayer of the past time, [and that unperformed ritual prayer remains due on him on the expiry of the time for the fifth of the five new ritual prayers] — in this case all ritual prayers he has performed are correct; so the five new ritual prayers he has performed remembering the unperformed ritual prayer of the past time, will not be nullified by its performance on the expiry of the time for the fifth of the five new ritual prayers; but if the unperformed ritual prayer of the past time is performed before the expiry of the time for the fifth of the five new ritual prayers, the 'obligatory' quality of all the ritual prayers he performed *before* the performance of this unperformed ritual prayer of the past time remembering it, will be nullified and turned to be 'supererogatory'.

If the unperformed ritual prayers of the past times are many, it is necessary to *fix* each of them when it is performed at a later time. [For example, the devotee will fix by saying: 'I perform the Noon Prayer of 11th July, 1977 that is due on me'.] This is rather difficult. To make the thing easy, he may make the intention of the first Noon

Prayer due on him, or the last Noon Prayer due on him. The same is true when one is observing the unobserved fasting of the month Ramaḍān of the past two years. The necessity of fixing in these cases is one of the two correct legal views on this, the other correct view being the non-necessity of fixing.

A person who has accepted Islam in a non-Muslim country is to be considered as excused [for his non-observance of ritual prayer, fasting and so on], so long as he remains ignorant of the Islamic legal rule, because of lack of opportunity to learn about it in a non-Muslim land. His case is different from that of a Muslim in an Islamic territory.

ATTAINMENT OF AN OBLIGATORY RITUAL PRAYER WITH THE IMĀM

If a person has started the performance of an 'obligatory' or a 'supererogatory' ritual prayer alone and then the 'obligatory' ritual prayer starts in congregation, he will nullify it by saluting at one side and join the congregation, provided he has not yet prostrated for the first *rak'a* of the ritual prayer which he started alone or he has prostrated and that prayer is one not consisting of four *rak'as*. If, however, he has prostrated for the first *rak'a* and that ritual prayer consists of four *rak'as*, e.g. the Noon Prayer, he will add to it the second *rak'a* and, having read the Witnessing at the end of this *rak'a*, will salute at one side so that these two *rak'as* will be a 'supererogatory' ritual prayer for him; and after this he will join the ritual prayer in congregation performing it as an 'obligatory' ritual prayer.

If the person has already performed three *rak'as* of a ritual prayer consisting of four *rak'as*, he will complete the four *rak'as*, and then will join the ritual prayer in congregation performing it as a 'supererogatory' ritual prayer; in the case of Late Afternoon Prayer and the Dawn Prayer, however, he will not join the congregation, because 'supererogatory' ritual prayer after these two ritual prayers is prohibited.

If the person has only stood up for the third *rak'a* of a ritual prayer consisting of four *rak'as* and, before he prostrated for that *rak'a*, the same ritual prayer has started in congregation, he will nullify, by standing and with one salutation, the ritual prayer he was performing alone, and then will join the congregation. This is the most correct view.

If a person starts performing the four sunna *rak'as* of the Friday Assembly Prayer, and at that time the imām comes out to deliver the address; or if the person starts performing the four sunna *rak'as* of the Noon Prayer, and then the congregation for the 'obligatory' *rak'as* of this same ritual prayer starts — then he will salute, [after the sitting] at the end of the first two *rak'as*, and then join the congregation; this is the most reasonable view; then on completing the 'obligatory' *rak'as* [in congregation), he will re-perform those four sunna *rak'as* [along with the order sunna *rak'as* to be performed after the Friday Assembly Prayer and the Noon Prayer].

A person who has arrived when the imām is leading an 'obligatory' ritual prayer, will follow the imām — he should not be kept from following the imām by his performance of sunna *rak'as* before the 'obligatory' *rak'as*, except in the Dawn Prayer in which case he will first perform the two sunna *rak'as* of the Dawn Prayer at a place in the mosque far from the lines of the congregation, if he be sure that, after the performance of these two sunna *rak'as* alone, he will not miss the congregation; but if he is not sure of this, he will neglect these two sunna *rak'as* and join the congregation.

If the two sunna *rak'as* of the Dawn Prayer were not performed before the 'obligatory' *rak'as* of it, there is no provision for their performance later, except if they were not performed together with 'obligatory' *rak'as* of it [in which case they can be performed later until the sun passes its meridian. The unperformed sunna *rak'as* of the Dawn Prayer cannot be performed later before the sunrise and after the sun passes its meridian]. If the four sunna *rak'as* were not performed before the 'obligatory' *rak'as* of the Noon Prayer, they will be performed later, before the two sunna *rak'as* of the same ritual prayer.

One who has taken part in only one *rak'a* or two of the 'obligatory' *rak'as* of the Noon Prayer in congregation, is not considered to have taken part in the congregation; but he has obtained the reward of the congregation; [if he obtains only the last sitting of the four *rak'as* in congregation, then also he is to be regarded as having obtained the reward of the congregation]. There is disagreement of opinion concerning him who has obtained three *rak'as* of a ritual prayer consisting of four *rak'as*, [or two *rak'as* of a ritual prayer which consists of three *rak'as*].

The 'supererogatory' *rak'as* will be performed before the 'obligatory' ones provided the devotee feels secure that the time will not be exhausted or that he will not miss the congregation. If, however, he is not sure of these no 'supererogatory' ritual prayer will be performed before the 'obligatory' ones.

A person who finds his imām in the bowing of a *rak'a*, says *Allāhu akbar* (الله اكبر) and remains standing till the imām raises his head from the bowing or does not remain standing but leans and, before making the bowing, the imām raises his head from the bowing — has not obtained that *rak'a*. [If a man finds the imām in prostration he is required to join him in it, falling prostrated, even though he has not obtained the *rak'a* with the imām thereby; if he has bowed alone and then joined the imām in any of the two prostrations, his ritual prayer is not nullified thereby and he has not taken part in the *rak'a*; if he has joined him only in the second *rak'a*, this has nullified his ritual prayer.]

If the follower bows before the imām's bowing and his bowing is after the imām's reading that much of the Qur'ān which validates a ritual prayer, i.e. a single verse, and then his imām joins him in bowing, the bowing of the follower is correct [but 'disliked' by the law]. If, however, the imām does not join him in bowing, the follower's bowing is not correct. [A follower prostrates before the imām prostrates; if this is after the imām's rising from the bowing and if he then joins the follower in the prostration, this is correct; but if that is before the imām's rising from the bowing, this is not correct.]

It is 'disliked' by the law that a person should leave the mosque in which call to a ritual prayer (*adhān*) is already performed. However, one who establishes another congregation elsewhere, e.g. the imām or the *mu'adhdhin* of another mosque, is allowed to leave without performing the ritual prayer there. Leaving the mosque after performing a ritual prayer alone is not 'disliked', except when the congregation for it has started before one's leaving the mosque in the case of the Noon Prayer and the Evening Prayer; in these two prayers he will follow the imām performing thereby a 'supererogatory' ritual prayer. [It is 'disliked' for a man to remain seated in the mosque without following the imām, except in the case of the Dawn Prayer, the Late Afternoon Prayer and the Sunset Prayer.]

After performing a ritual prayer, one should not perform a ritual prayer resembling it [with the purpose of obtaining more reward].

PROSTRATION FOR FORGETFULNESS

It is 'necessary' to perform two prostrations together with reading the Witnessing and saluting once, as an amendment for the failure to perform a 'required' act of a ritual prayer forgetfully, even though the failure has happened repeatedly in the same ritual prayer.

Leaving undone a 'required' act of a ritual prayer deliberately is a sin. In order to make good the imperfection of the ritual prayer caused by this deliberate action, it is 'necessary' to repeat the ritual prayer; [prostration for forgetfulness is not sufficient for it]. However, there are three cases in which, according to some jurists, deliberate leaving undone may be amended by prostration for forgetfulness. These cases are: to leave undone the first sitting in a ritual prayer deliberately, to delay a prostration of the first *rak'a* to the end of the ritual prayer deliberately, and to reflect inside the ritual prayer deliberately so that it has kept the devotee from performing one of its pillars.

It is sunna to perform the prostration for forgetfulness after salutation. To salute once to the right side is sufficient; this is the most correct view. To perform the prostration for forgetfulness before the salutation is 'slightly disliked' by the law.

Prostration for forgetfulness ceases to be a devotee's responsibility [a] if the sun has risen just after the salutation, in the case of the Dawn prayer, [b] if the salutation is made just before the colour of the sun has changed, in the case of the Late Afternoon Prayer, and [c] if just after the salutation there happens any such thing as bars building (*binā'*) on the part of the ritual prayer already performed. [An example of such a thing is to cause the state of minor legal impurity deliberately.]

In a ritual prayer in congregation, the follower will perform the prostration for forgetfulness [together with the imām], because of the forgetfulness of his imām and not because of his own forgetfulness. The person who joins the imām, not from the beginning of the ritual prayer, but later (*masbūq*), will perform the prostration for forgetfulness together with his imam, and then will stand up for the performance of the *rak'a* or *rak'as* he missed in the beginning. If he forgets to do any 'required' deed in the part of the ritual prayer he is now performing alone, he will perform the prostration for forgetfulness for this forgetfulness also; [the prostration he made with the imām is not sufficient]. The *lāḥiq*, i.e. a person who joined the imām in the beginning of the ritual prayer but is separated from it later by an excuse such as sleep or inattention or nullity of ablution, will not perform the prostration for forgetfulness because of his own forgetfulness.

The imām will not perform the prostration for forgetfulness in the case of the Friday Assembly Prayer and the 'Īd Prayers. [This is for the avoidance of disturbance that might happen in large congregation for these ritual prayers, if the prostration for forgetfulness be made.]

A devotee, whether the imām or one who is performing a ritual prayer alone, who has forgotten to do the first sitting in an 'obligatory' ritual prayer, even though it is the Odd Prayer, is required to return to do the sitting so long as he has not stood up straight — this is the most correct view. But if he be a follower of the imām, his case is like that of one who is performing a 'supererogatory' ritual prayer — he must return to perform the sitting even though he has completely stood up. If a person who has forgotten to perform the first sitting and has stood up to such an extent as is closer to the state of standing than the state of sitting, and who then has returned to perform the sitting, will make the prostration for forgetfulness because he has failed to perform a 'required' act. But if he has stood up only to such an extent as is closer to the state of sitting, he is not required to make the prostration for forgetfulness — this is the most correct view. If the person who has forgotten to do the first sitting, returns to make it after he has stood up completely, there is disagreement among the jurists as to whether or not his ritual prayer will be null and void; [the view to which they are more inclined is that it will not be null].

The person who has forgotten to do the last sitting in a ritual prayer and has stood up, will return to perform this sitting so long as he has not prostrated and will make the prostration for forgetfulness, on the ground that he has delayed the 'obligatory' act of the last sitting. But if he does not return until he prostrates for one more *rak'a*, his 'obligatory' ritual prayer will turn to be a 'supererogatory' one, and he will add a sixth *rak'a*, if he likes, even though his ritual prayer is the Late Afternoon Prayer, but a fourth *rak'a* in the case of the Dawn Prayer — addition of a *rak'a* to these two ritual prayers is not 'disliked' by the law — and he will not make the prostration for forgetfulness; this is the most correct view.

A person who has done the last sitting in a ritual prayer, then has stood up, has read Qur'ānic sūras and bowed, will come back to the last sitting and salute without having repeated the reading of the Witnessing in it. But if, after standing up, he has [not only bowed but also] prostrated, the 'obligatory' nature of his ritual prayer will not be nullified by this; he will add to this additional *rak'a* one more *rak'a* so that these two addition *rak'as* taken together may be a 'supererogatory' ritual prayer for him, and he will make the prostration for forgetfulness because he delayed the salutation by the addition of two *rak'as*.

A person who has performed the prostration for forgetfulness in a 'supererogatory' ritual prayer consisting of two *rak'as*, is not allowed by the law to build (*binā'*) on it two more *rak'as* as a 'praiseworthy' act, because this building will nullify his prostration for forgetfulness. If, however, he builds them this will be correct, but he will have to repeat the prostration for forgetfulness.

If a person on whom the prostration for forgetfulness is due, has saluted and just at that time another person has become his follower, this is correct provided the former person has prostrated for forgetfulness after saluting. But if he has not prostrated, his follower's following him is not valid.

An individual can perform the prostration for forgetfulness, even though he has saluted deliberately in order to withdraw from the ritual prayer, so long as he has not turned away from the direction of the Ka'ba or not spoken.

If a person performing an obligatory ritual prayer consisting of four *rak'as* or three *rak'as*, is in confusion as to whether or not he has completed all *rak'as* and has saluted, and immediately after this he has realized that he has performed only two *rak'as*, in this case he will complete his ritual prayer by performing the *rak'as* he has failed to perform and will make the prostration for forgetfulness. If, in the state of confusion, his thinking in order to determine whether or not he has completed all *rak'as* of his ritual prayer has been prolonged and he did not salute until he has become sure, in this case he is 'required' to make the prostration for forgetfulness, should the time of his thinking be more than that measure of time in which a pillar of a ritual prayer can be performed; but if the time of his thinking be less than this, he need not make the prostration for forgetfulness.

DOUBT IN RITUAL PRAYER

Ritual prayer is nullified if the devotee has doubt concerning the number of *rak'as* he has performed, provided this doubt has come to his mind before the completion of this ritual prayer, and provided this doubt has occurred to him for the first time in his life or it is not habitual to him.

If the doubt concerning the number of *rak'as* the devotee has performed occurs to him after his salutation, [or after his sitting for that measure of time in which one can read the Witnessing but before the salutation], no consideration is to be given to his doubt, except if he has become sure that he left undone something and so he must do it. [If, after salutation, an upright man informs him that he has left one *rak'a* unperformed, whereas the devotee himself feels that he has completed all *rak'as*, no regard is to be given to the information of the upright man. But if two upright men inform him, he should not consider his own doubt, but accept their information. If the imām and his followers disagree on the number of *rak'as* performed, or on any other act in a ritual prayer, their opinion will not be accepted; if some followers share his opinion but others are against it, it is his opinion that will be accepted.]

If doubt occurred to the devotee more than one time before the present doubt, he will think much and accept that view which predominates in his thought. If no view predominates in his thought, he will accept that opinion which is in favour of performance of a less number of *rak'as*, and he will sit and read the Witnessing after every *rak'a* which he imagines to be the last *rak'a* of his ritual prayer, [so that he may not leave undone the 'obligatory' act of sitting].

PROSTRATION CAUSED BY RECITATION OF CERTAIN QUR'ĀNIC VERSES

[The stipulations for prostration caused by a reading of certain Qur'ānic verses are: cleanliness from the state of minor legal impurity and physical defilment, facing the direction of the Ka'ba, and covering the private parts. The pillar of this prostration is to put the forehead on the ground. Its special characteristic is that one is 'required' to perform it immediately, if one recites the appropriate Qur'ānic verses inside a ritual prayer, but later if one recited them outside a ritual prayer.]

The reason for prostration caused by certain Qur'ānic verses is their recitation in the case of the reciter, and their being heard in the case of the hearer — this is the correct view. [Therefore, a deaf man who has recited an appropriate verse but has not heard it, is 'required' to perform the prostration.]

Prostration caused by recitation of certain Qur'ānic verses is such a 'required' act that its performance can be delayed to a later time, if it has become 'required' of one because of one's recitation of them outside a ritual prayer; however, to delay it is 'slightly disliked' by the law. But if they are recited inside a ritual prayer, prostration for their recitation must be made immediately.

Prostration is 'required' if he recites a Qur'ānic verse requiring prostration, even though he recites it in Persian or in any other language; it is all the same whether or not he understands its meaning.

Recitation of a letter of the word '*sajda*' (prostration) together with a word which precedes or follows the letter and which is from the verse requiring prostration, is to be considered as recitation of the entire verse — this is the correct view.

The verses the reading of which requires prostration are fourteen in number. They are in the following sūras: [1] the Heights (*al-A'rāf*), [2] the Thunder (*ar-Ra'd*), [3] the Bee (*an-Naḥl*), [4] the Night Journey (*al-Isrā'*), [5] Mary (*Maryam*), [6] the Pilgrimage (*al-Ḥajj*), [7] the Criterion (*al-Furqān*), [8] the Ant (*an-Naml*), [9] Prostration (*as-Sajda*), [10] *Ṣād*, [11] *Ḥā Mīm as-Sajda*, [12] the Star (*an-Najm*), [13] the Rending (*al-Inshiqāq*), and [14] the Blood-Clot (*al-'Alaq*).[132]

Prostration is 'required' of him who has heard a verse of prostrating, even though he did not intend to hear it. A menstruating woman and a woman with childbirth bleeding are exceptions — prostration is not 'required' of them if they recite a verse of prostration or hear it from others, [but one who hears a verse from them is required to prostrate. If a man who is in the state of major legal impurity, recites a verse of prostration or hears it from others he must prostrate; likewise, one hearing it from him is also 'required' to prostrate. If one hears a verse of prostration from an infidel or a boy whose power of discrimination has already started functioning, one is 'required' to prostrate].

The imām of ritual prayer and his follower will not prostrate if they hear a Qur'ānic verse of prostration from a follower of this imām or from the follower of another imām. [But if one who is not engaged in a ritual prayer hears it from a follower of an imām one must prostrate.]

If the imām and his followers hear a Qur'ānic verse of prostration from one who is not the follower of any imām, they will prostrate after the completion of their ritual prayer. Should they prostrate in it, this will not do but their ritual prayer will not be corrupted.

Prostration is 'required' if one hears a Qur'ānic verse of prostration rendered into Persian, provided one understands its meaning — this is the reliable view.

There is disagreement of opinion among the jurists on the question whether prostration is 'required' of one who hears a Qur'ānic verse of prostration from a sleeping man or from an insane person. Prostration is not necessary for him who hears it from a pet bird reciting it.

In a ritual prayer, prostration caused by Qur'ān-reading is to be

132 The numbers of the relevant verses occuring in these sūras are as follows: 7:206, 13:15, 16:49, 17:107, 19:58, 22:18, 25:60, 27:25, 32:15, 38:34, 41:37, 55:62, 84:21, 96:19.

performed through a bowing, or through a prostration, other than the bowing or the prostration of the ritual prayer. The bowing of the ritual prayer will do instead of prostration caused by Qur'ān-reading provided the intention for this is made when bowing. The prostration of the ritual prayer will do even though when making it the intention for prostration caused by Qur'ān-reading is not made, provided the immediacy of the recitation of the verse of prostration is not broken by the recitation of more than two verses after the verse of prostration.

If a person has heard a Qur'ānic verse requiring prostration from an imām, and he has not become his follower in that ritual prayer at all or has become his follower in a *rak'a* other than that in which the verse was recited, [and the imām makes prostration for recitation], the person will prostrate outside that ritual prayer. If the person becomes a follower of the imām before the imām's prostrating for recitation of the verse, he will prostrate with the imām. If the person becomes a follower of the imām after the imām's prostrating in that *rak'a* in which the verse is recited, the person is deemed to have taken part in the prostration [by virtue of his obtaining that *rak'a*]; so he will not perform this prostration at all.

The prostration caused by Qur'ān-reading which became 'required' of one in a ritual prayer but which was not performed in it, cannot be performed later (*qaḍā'*) outside that ritual prayer.

A person recites a Qur'ānic verse of prostration outside a ritual prayer and prostrates for this; then he starts a ritual prayer and repeats the recitation of the verse; in this case he will make another prostration. If, however, he does not make prostration first when he recites or hears the verse outside the ritual prayer, one prostration, i.e. his prostration for the recitation of the same verse inside the ritual prayer, will suffice. He is like one who repeatedly reads one Qur'ānic verse of prostration in one and the same sitting — one prostration only will suffice this man. But if this man repeats the same verse in two sittings, one prostration will not be sufficient. A person's sitting changes by his moving from it to a distance of at least three steps, by moving from one branch of a tree to another, or by swimming in the case of a river and big well — this is the most correct view. The sitting of reciting or hearing a verse necessitating prostration does not change by one's moving from one corner to another in the case of a small house and of a mosque even though it is big; nor does it change if a boat which was still sails; nor does it change by the performance of one *rak'a* of ritual prayer or two, by drinking anything or eating two morsels of food, by walking two steps, by leaning against something or sitting or standing or ascending or descending to the place of the recitation of the verse requiring prostration, or by the movement of one's riding animal or vehicle while one is engaged in a ritual prayer.

The hearer of a Qur'ānic verse requiring prostration must prostrate repeatedly if his sitting changes, even though the reciter's sitting does not; if the case be the opposite, i.e. the reciter's sitting changes but the hearer's sitting remains the same, the hearer will not prostrate repeatedly — this is the most correct view.

It is 'disliked' by the law that one should read a Qur'ānic sūra leaving aside the verse of prostration that may be in it. The opposite of this is not disliked; it is however, 'praiseworthy' to add one verse or more to the verse of prostration.

It is 'praiseworthy' to read a Qur'ānic verse necessitating prostration with a low voice in the presence of one who is not prepared to hear it.

Likewise, it is 'praiseworthy' that one who has recited a verse of prostration by sitting should stand up and then prostrate for it. The hearer of a verse of prostration should not lift his head from the prostration before its reciter lifts his head. The reciter will be ordered to precede the hearer in prostration; nor will the hearers be commanded to make lines, so that they will prostrate wherever they may be and in whatever state they may be.

The stipulations for the validity of a prostration due to reading the Qur'ānic verses of prostration are identical with those for a ritual prayer, except with regard to the saying of *Allāhu akbar* at the start of a ritual prayer — this *Allāhu akbar* is not a stipulation for the prostration due to Qur'ān-reading.

The method of prostration due to a Qur'ānic verse is: to perform one prostration between saying *Allāhu akbar* twice — once when falling prostrate and once when lifting up the head from prostration. Saying *Allāhu akbar* twice is sunna. There is no lifting of the hands or reading of the Witnessing or salutation in the prostration due to Qur'ān-reading.

PROSTRATION FOR EXPRESSING GRATITUDE TO GOD

Prostration expressing gratitude to God for any good achieved is legally 'disliked', according to the Imām Abū Ḥanīfa. Imām Abū Yūsuf and Imām Muḥammad, have, however, maintained that this prostration is a good work for which reward will be granted by God. [As a proof of this view, they have cited the prophetic tradition:

"The Prophet (may God bless him and greet him!) used to fall prostrate when anything pleasing him happened to him, or when any good news was conveyed to him."][133]

The method of prostration expressing gratitude to God is like the method of prostration due to recitation of a Qur'ānic verse of prostration; [the stipulations for both kinds of prostration are also identical].

AN EFFECTIVE MEASURE AGAINST EVERY SERIOUS MISFORTUNE

Shaykh an-Nasafī said in his book, *The Sufficient* (*al-Kāfī*), "If an individual recites all the Qur'ānic verses of prostration, in one sitting, prostrates once after the reading of every one of them, [and then prays to God that the misfortune which has already visited him or is likely to visit him, be warded off through the effect of this good work and through the mercy of God], then God will be sufficient for him in his misfortune."

THE FRIDAY ASSEMBLY PRAYER

يا ايهاالذين امنوا اذا نودى للصلواة من يوم الجمعةِ فاسعوا الى ذكر اللهِ وذروا البيع. ذلكم خير لكم ان كنتم تعلمون.
— قران ٦٢:٩

O you who believe, when the call is made for the Assembly Prayer on Friday, hasten to the remembrance of God and leave off all business. That is better for you, did you but know. When the Assembly Prayer is finished then disperse in the land and seek of God's grace, and remember God much that you may prosper.— Qur'ān 62:9

قال رسول اللهِ صلى الله عليه وسلم: من ترك الجمعة ثلاثا من غير عذرٍ طبع الله على قلبه.

The Messenger of God (may God bless and greet him!) said, "God puts a seal on the mind of him who leaves the Friday Assembly Prayer unperformed three times successively without any real excuse.[134]

Stipulations for the Friday Assembly Prayer

The Friday Assembly Prayer is 'obligatory' upon every individual who fulfils all of the following seven stipulations: [1] To be male. [2] To be a free man, not a slave. [3] To be a stationary man (*muqīm*) in a town or in a place which is included in the definition of one's being

---

[133] Ibn Māja, *Sunan*, Iqāma, 192.
[134] Muslim, *Ṣaḥīḥ*, Masājid, 254; at-Tirmidhī, *Sunan*, Jumu'a, 7; Abū Dāwūd, *Sunan*, Ṣalā, 203; Ibn Māja, *Sunan*, Iqāma, 93.

stationary in a town, e.g. the race course of the town and the courtyard adjacent to the town — this is the most correct view. [4] To be healthy. [5] To be safe from an oppressor. [6] Soundness of the eyes. [7] Soundness of the legs.

A man who fulfils all these seven stipulations is obliged to perform the Friday Assembly Prayer. His performance of this ritual prayer, however, is valid if it fulfils the following six stipulations. [1] Performance of the Friday Assembly Prayer in a town or in its courtyard. [2] It is supported by the ruler or his deputy. [3] It is performed in the time of the Noon Prayer. So its performance is not correct before this time; it is nullified with the expiry of the time for the Noon Prayer. [4] Addresses are given before the start of the two 'obligatory' *rak'as* of the Friday Assembly Prayer, for the purpose of this ritual prayer, and in the time of it. At least one man must be present for hearing the addresses, and he must be one of those by whom the Friday Assembly Prayer may be performed — this is the correct view. [5] A general permission is granted to all who wish to attend this ritual prayer. [6] A congregation is held for the Friday Assembly Prayer. The congregation must be of at least three men, excluding the imām, even though they are slaves or travellers or sick men. It is a stipulation for the validity of Friday Assembly Prayer that they perform it behind the imām at least until he makes the first prostration — if they nullify their ritual prayer after this prostration by the imām, he will complete this ritual prayer as the Friday Assembly Prayer; but if they nullify it before his prostration his Friday Assembly prayer is invalid. This ritual prayer is not correct if a woman or a child forms this congregation together with two adult men. It is 'permissible' for a sick man or a traveller to lead the Friday Assembly Prayer.

The law defines a town as a place where there are a muftī, a ruler and a judge passing rulings on cases and inflicting penalties, and, moreover, this place is such that its buildings are equal to the buildings of Mina. If the judge or the ruler acts as a muftī, in addition to his own respective function, a third man as a muftī, is not required. During the season of pilgrimage to Mecca, the caliph and the ruler of the Hijaz [but not the leader of the pilgrimage] are 'permitted' by the law to hold the Friday Assembly Prayer at Mina.

It is correct to limit the addresses delivered before the 'obligatory' two *rak'as* of the Friday Assembly Prayer to the utterance of the formula of glorification of God once or praise of God once or oneness of God once or magnification of God once. To utter them only once is, however, 'disliked' by the law. [The addresser should follow what is sunna in the addresses.]

Sunna Acts in the Addresses of Friday Assembly Prayer

Eighteen things are sunna in the addresses given before the start of the two 'obligatory' *rak'as* of the Friday Assembly Prayer. They are as follows:

[1] Ritual cleanliness of the addresser. [2] Covering his private parts. [3-5] His sitting on the pulpit before starting the first address. When he thus sits, performance of *adhān* (call to ritual prayer) in front of him. After the addresses are over, performance of *iqāma* (call to the actual start of a ritual prayer) in front of him. [6] The state of standing when delivering both the addresses of the Friday Assembly Prayer. [To deliver both addresses or one of them by sitting is 'disliked' by the law.] [7] The addresser's state of standing in such a way that a sword lies at his left side; this should be in all countries which the Muslims once captured by force — in the case of the countries conquered through peace, it is not sunna that a sword should exist near the imām. [8] The people's facing towards the addresser.

[9] Starting the first address by praising God, by uttering the two sentences of testimony,[135] and by reading the formula of invoking blessings upon the Prophet.[136]

[10] Admonishing the people through the first address, and reminding them of that which will ensure their salvation. [11] Reading at least one Qur'ānic verse. [12] To deliver two addresses. [13] To sit between the two addresses for a little while. [14] At the start of the second address, to repeat the praise of God and invoke blessings upon the Prophet. [15] In this address, prayer for the good of all male and female believers as well as for the forgiveness of their sins.

[16] The people's listening to the addresses. [It is sufficient if they try to listen, but do not listen because of a long distance or any other thing.] [17] Making the two addresses as short as the length of a long sūra of the Qur'ān. It is 'disliked' by the law that the addresses are made too long and that any of the above mentioned things is left undone.

'Required' Acts in Preparation for Friday Assembly Prayer

[1] A man is 'required' by the law to proceed to the mosque with some degree of haste when the first *adhān* is performed. [The second

[135]For these sentences see *supra*, p. 33. [136]For this formula see *supra*, p. 104.

adhān is that which is performed for the start of the first address. To proceed to the mosque before the first *adhān* is of course 'praiseworthy.] [2] He is also 'required' to abandon trafficking [or any other act which bars him from proceeding towards the mosque or which impairs this proceeding, such as buying or selling in the state of progress], when the first *adhān* is already performed — this is the correct view.

Disliked Acts in the Friday Assembly Prayer

No ritual prayer of any type whatever and no utterances are 'permissible' from the time, when the imām comes out to ascend to the pulpit for delivering the addresses of the Friday Assembly Prayer, until the time when he completes the two 'obligatory' *rak'as* of it. The law 'dislikes' that a man, present when the imām is making an address, should eat or drink or do any vain thing or look around. He should not reply if someone salutes him; nor should he reply to someone's sneezing, by saying *yarḥamuka Allāhu* (may God have mercy upon you!), [because these will keep him from listening to the addresses]. The addresser should not salute the people when he has ascended to the pulpit.

It is 'disliked' by the law that a man should leave the town, without performing the Friday Assembly Prayer, after the first *adhān* is performed. [To leave the town before the sun has passed its meridian or after the performance of this ritual prayer is of course not 'disliked'.]

If a person on whom the Friday Assembly Prayer is not 'obligatory', [e.g. a sick man or a traveller or a blind man or a lame man or a woman], has performed it, he need not perform the Noon Prayer. [Even though the Friday Assembly Prayer is not 'obligatory' upon these people, it is better for them, except the woman, to perform it, if possible, rather than the Noon Prayer.]

Performance of the Noon Prayer before the Friday Assembly Prayer is 'unlawful' for a man who has no excuse [preventing him from attending the Friday Assembly Prayer]. If, after this performance, he proceeds towards the mosque to perform the Friday Assembly Prayer, and the imām was engaged in it when he has just left his house, his Noon Prayer which he has already performed is invalid, even though he could not join the Friday Assembly Prayer for which he has proceeded.

The law 'dislikes' that an excused man, [e.g. a sick man or a traveller], and an imprisoned man should perform the Noon Prayer *in congregation* in a town on Friday. [It is 'praiseworthy' for these people to perform the Noon Prayer *individually after* the Friday Assembly Prayer has already been performed by others. To perform it individually *before* the Friday Assembly Prayer is 'disliked' by the law.]

The man who has joined the Friday Assembly Prayer when the imām is reading the last Witnessing or making the prostrations due to forgetfulness, will complete the remaining part of this ritual prayer as the Friday Assembly Prayer, not as the Noon prayer.

'Īd PRAYERS

Stipulations for 'Īd Prayers

The two 'Īd Prayers — i.e. the ritual prayer of 'Īd al-Fiṭr (the Festival Day on the expiry of the lunar month Ramaḍān) and the ritual prayer of 'Īd al-Aḍḥā (the Festival Day of the Sacrifice of Animals) — are 'required' of every such one as is 'required' to perform the Friday Assembly Prayer. The stipulations which make the 'Īd Prayers 'required' of a man and the stipulations which make their performance valid are the same as those for the Friday Assembly Prayer, as described in the preceding section, except the stipulation concerning the address in the Friday Assembly Prayer. Thus 'Īd Prayers are valid without an address in them; however, it is bad to perform them without an address as it is bad to deliver an address *before* the 'Īd Prayers — bad because these are contrary to what the Prophet did.

'Praiseworthy' Acts on the Day of 'Īd al-Fiṭr

It is 'praiseworthy' to perform thirteen acts on the day of 'Īd al-Fiṭr (the Festival Day on the expiry of the lunar month Ramaḍān). These acts are as follows:

[1-3] Eating any sweet thing before going to perform the ritual prayer of 'Īd al-Fiṭr. It is 'praiseworthy' that one should eat dates and that they should be of an odd number. [The Prophet used to do this.][137]

[4-7] To bathe, to use the tooth-stick for cleaning the mouth, to apply scented oil or perfume to the body, and to wear the best of all clothes one possesses.

[8] To pay, before going to perform the 'Īd Prayer, the 'obligatory' alms of 'Īd al-Fiṭr (*ṣadaqat al-fiṭr*) if these alms are 'obligatory' on the individual, to express joy and gladness, and to pay 'supereroga-

137 Al-Bukhārī, *Ṣaḥīḥ*, 'Īdayn, 4.

tory' alms according to one's ability.

[9-10] Waking from sleep very early in the morning. Hastening to the place of performance of the 'Īd Prayer, [so that one might obtain the excellence of going there early and of performance of this ritual prayer in the first line]. [11] Performance of the Dawn Prayer in the mosque of one's own locality.

[12] After doing all that is mentioned above, to proceed to the place of the 'Īd Prayer on foot, if possible, and constantly saying *Allāhu akbar*(الله أكبر: God is the greatest) with low voice. Saying of this will be stopped when one reaches the place of the 'Īd Prayer. This is to be found in one legal report. In another report it is mentioned that the saying of this formula will be stopped when the 'Īd Prayer starts. [13] To return from the place of the 'Īd Prayer by a path different from the one by which one went to the place of the 'Īd Prayer.

The law 'dislikes' that one should perform 'supererogatory' ritual prayer in the place of the 'Īd Prayer or at home *before* the performance of the 'Īd Prayer, and in the place of the 'Īd Prayer *after* it. This view is adopted by the majority of the jurists.

Time and Methods of the 'Īd Prayer

The time for the 'Īd Prayers starts from the time when the sun has risen high up the measure of one spear or two, and continues to just before the sun passes its meridian.

The methods of the two 'Īd Prayers are as follows. [1] First to make the intention of the 'Īd Prayers. [Intention is to be produced in the devotee's mind. He should also utter the formula of intention thus: 'I Perform the 'Īd Prayer in order to please God as the imām'. This formula is for the imām. The follower will only replace the expression 'as the imām' by the expression 'as a follower'.] [2] After this, to say *Allāhu akbar* for starting the 'Īd Prayer. [3] Then to read the formula of praising God.[138] [4] Then to say *Allāhu akbar* three times as additional *takbīr*, lifting the hands up when saying each of them. [5] Then to seek the protection of God by reading the formula: *a'ūdhu bi-Allāhi mina sh-shayṭāni r-rajīmi*. [6] Then secretly to say: *bi-smi Allāhi r-raḥmāni r-raḥīmi.* [7] Then the imām will read the Opening Sūra of the Qur'ān. [8] Then to add another Qur'ānic sūra to it. It is 'praiseworthy' that this sūra be the one which starts with the verse, "Glorify the name of your Lord, the Most High ...."[139]

[138] See *supra*, p. 101.

[139] This is the eighty-seventh sūra of the Qur'ān. It consists of fifteen verses.

[9] Then the imam will bow, and the followers will imitate him. [10] Then, after the prostration of the first *rak'a,* when the imām will stand up for the second *rak'a*, he will start with the reading of *bi-smi Allāhi r-raḥmāni r-raḥīmi*, then of the opening Sūra of the Qur'ān, and then of another Qur'ānic sūra; it is 'praiseworthy' that this additional sūra be the one starting with the verse, "Has the news of the overspreading calamity reached you?"[140] [11] Then both the imām and the followers will say *Allāhu akbar* three times as additional *takbīr*, lifting the hands every time, as is done in the first *rak'a*. This, i.e. saying of *Allāhu akbar* three times *after* reading the Qur'ānic sūra, is better than saying this *before* reading it in the second *rak'a*. It is, however, 'permissible' to say *Allāhu akbar* three times *before* reading the sūra in the second *rak'a*.

[12] On completion of the 'Īd Prayer the imām will deliver two addresses through which he will instruct the people concerning the 'obligatory' alms of the 'Īd al-Fiṭr. [He will sit between the addresses for a while. He will also magnify God in them. He will start them with magnification of God by saying *Allāhu akbar*. The people will magnify God along with the imām; they will also secretly read the formula of invoking blessings upon the Prophet; this formula is cited in a previous section].[141]

The man who has missed the performance of the 'Īd Prayer with the imām, will not perform it later. [If he likes he will go back from the place of 'Īd Prayer or if he likes he can perform here four *rak'as* of 'supererogatory' ritual prayer which will be the Supererogatory Ritual Prayer after Sunrise (*ṣalāt-aḍ-ḍuḥā.*]

The ritual prayer for 'Īd al-Fiṭr can be delayed only to the next day for an excuse. [In the absence of any legitimate excuse this ritual prayer is not correct the next day].

The legal rulings concerning the ritual prayer of 'Īd al-Aḍḥā (the Festival Day of the Sacrifice of Animals) are similar to those concerning the ritual prayer of 'Īd al-Fiṭr, except that in the former ritual prayer it is 'praiseworthy' to delay eating anything until after the ritual prayer and to say *Allāhu akbar* loudly on the road when going to the place of 'Īd Prayer. There are two other differences: one is to instruct, through the addresses, the people concerning the sacrifice of animals and concerning the saying of *Allāhu akbar* on the Days of Drying the Meat (*Ayyām at-Tashrīq*), [i.e. the eleventh, twelfth and the thirteenth of the lunar month Dhū l-Ḥijja]. The other difference is that the ritual prayer of 'Īd al-Aḍḥā can be

[140] This is the eighty-eighth Qur'ānic sūra consisting of twenty-six short verses.

[141] See *supra*, p. 104.

delayed for three days for an excuse. [If there is no excuse this delay is 'disliked' by the law.]

It is 'required'[142] to say *Allāhu akbar* on the Days of Drying the Meat once immediately after every 'obligatory' ritual prayer performed in 'praiseworthy' congregation, from the Dawn Prayer of the Day of 'Arafa, i.e. the ninth of Dhū l-Ḥijja, up to the Late Afternoon Prayer of the Day of 'Īd al-Aḍḥā, i.e. the tenth of Dhū l-Ḥijja. [This means that *Allāhu akbar* is to be said after eight 'obligatory' ritual prayers performed in congregation.] So it is 'required' of an imām who is 'stationary' in a place defined by law as a town; [it is not 'required' of an imām who is a traveller or who is 'stationary' in a place legally considered as a village]. It is also 'required' of the person who follows the imām who is a 'stationary' person, even though this person is a traveller or a woman; [a woman will say *Allāhu akbar* with a low voice, but a man with a loud voice. A pilgrim in *iḥrām* will read *Allāhu akbar* first and then the formula of *talbiya*. For the reading of this *Allāhu akbar* it is not necessary that the devotee should be in the state of ritual cleanliness]. All this is the view of the Imām Abū Ḥanīfa. Imām Abū Yūsuf and the Imām Muḥammad maintain that saying of *Allāhu akbar* is 'required', immediately after every 'obligatory' ritual prayer, of anyone who has performed it even though being alone or a traveller or in a place considered by the law as a village, from the Dawn Prayer of the Day of 'Arafa up to the Late Afternoon Prayer of the fifth day from the Day of 'Arafa, i.e. to the end of the Days of Drying the Meat. On this view has been the practice of the Muslims, and on this has been given the legal decision.

There is no sin in saying *Allāhu akbar* at the end of the two 'Īd Prayers, in the market place, and in similar places. This *Allāhu akbar* in its complete form is:

الله اكبرۦ الله اكبر.
لا اله الا الله.
والله اكبرۦ والله اكبر.
ولله الحمد.

(*Allāhu akbar, Allāhu akbar. Lā ilāha illā Allāhu. Wa Allāhu akbar, wa Allāhu akbar. Wa li-Allāhi l-ḥamdu.*)
(God is the greatest, God is the greatest. There is no god but God. God is the greatest, God is the greatest. To God belong all types of perfect praise).

142 Qur'ān 2:203.

RITUAL PRAYERS FOR REMOVAL OF FEAR AND ECLIPSE OF THE SUN AND THE MOON

قال النبى صلى الله عليه وسلم: ان الشمس والقمر ايتان من ايات الله... فاذا رائيتم ذلك فافزعوا الى ذكر الله والصلواة.

The Prophet (may God bless him and greet him!) said, "The sun and the moon are certainly two signs of God ... When you see them eclipsed, flee to remembrance of God and to ritual prayer."[143]

For the removal of an eclipse of the sun it is sunna to perform two *rak'as* of ritual prayer in the manner of a 'supererogatory' ritual prayer, but following the imām of the Friday Assembly Prayer, or by following one who is instructed by the ruler to lead this special ritual prayer. Either of these two will lead this ritual prayer without *adhān* (i.e. call to ritual prayer), without *iqāma* (i.e. call to the actual *start* of a ritual prayer), without loudly reading Qur'ānic verses, and without delivering any address. Rather people will be summoned to this special ritual prayer by shouting: 'Ritual prayer for an eclipse of the sun is starting in congregation' (الصلوة جامعة: *aṣ-ṣalātu jāmi'atun*).

It is sunna to prolong the two *rak'as* of this ritual prayer, as well as the bowing and the prostrations made in them. On completing these *rak'as*, the imām will pray to God for the removal of the eclipse, by sitting and facing the direction of the Holy Ka'ba if he likes, or by standing and facing the people present, and this latter is better. [He will not ascend to the pulpit for praying.] When he prays, the people will say: *āmīn*. In this state of praying they will persist until the sun is fully bright.

Should the imām be not present, people will perform this special ritual prayer individually [at home], like the ritual prayer for removal of an eclipse of the moon [which is performed individually], and like the ritual prayer for the removal of terrible darkness at daytime, of a strong gusty wind, and of frightening and fearful calamities, such as earthquakes, thunderbolts, constant rainfalls, serious diseases, and the attack of enemies.

RITUAL PRAYER FOR RAIN

At the time of drought when people are in severe need of water for themselves, for their cattle and for their harvest, there is a ritual prayer for rain. It is to be performed, not in congregation, but

143 Al-Bukhārī, *Ṣaḥīḥ*, Kusūf, 2, 6, 9, 15, 17; Muslim, *Ṣaḥīḥ*, Kusūf, 1ff., 10; an-Nasā'ī, *Sunan*, Kusūf, 1; Ibn Māja, *Sunan*, Iqāma, 152.

individually; [its performance in congregation, however, is 'permissible', though not sunna. It consists of two *rak'as*. There is neither *adhān* nor *iqāma* for prayer for rain. If this ritual prayer is performed in congregation the imām will read Qur'ānic sūras in it in a loud voice]. Part of this ritual prayer consists in seeking forgiveness of sin from God.[144]

In the case of ritual prayer for rain it is 'praiseworthy' that people should come out of their houses for three consecutive days, on foot, wearing old but washed, unpatched clothes or patched clothes, being extremely lowly, humble and submissive towards God, with downcast heads, and having given alms every day before coming out of their houses for this ritual prayer. It is 'praiseworthy' to bring out the domestic animals together with their calves, and very old people as well as children, since the severe need of these and their prayers may easily bring down divine mercy in the form of rain.

People will come out from their houses to an open field for the ritual prayer for rain. In the holy cities of Mecca and Jerusalem, however, people will assemble in the Sacred Mosque (*al-Masjid al-Ḥarām*) and the Dome of the Rock (*al-Masjid al-Aqṣā*) respectively because divine mercy descends in these mosques more than in other places.[145] The people of Medina should assemble in the Mosque of the Prophet, [since in Medina this is the best place for appeal to God for mercy. Domestic animals will be kept near the door of the mosque].

The method of supplication to God for rain is: the imām will supplicate, by standing, facing the direction of the Ka'ba, and raising the hands; the people will be in the condition of sitting, facing the direction of the Ka'ba, and saying *āmīn* at his supplication. This supplication formula is as follows:

اللهم، اسقنا غيثا مغيثا هنيئا مريئا غدقا عاجلا غير رائث، مجللا سحا طبقا دائما.

(*Allāhumma, asqinā ghaythan mughīthan, hanī'an marī'an ghadaqan, 'ājilan ghayra rā'ithin, mujallilan saḥḥan ṭabaqan dā'iman.*)

Other formulae of supplication resembling this should also be read secretly or loudly. There is no provision for such a thing as turning away of the mantle in a prayer for rain.[146] [Sometimes people do this

144 Qur'ān 11:52.

145 The Sacred Mosque is mentioned in the Qur'ān several times (2:144, 149, 150, 191, 196, 217, 5:2, 97, 8:34, 9:7, 19, 28, 17:1). The precincts of the mosque in Jerusalem are blessed by God; see Qur'ān 17:1.

146 Cf. al-Ghazālī, *Iḥyā'*, I, 204.

as a good sign for rain.] Non-Muslims who are granted protection in a Muslim state, need not attend the ritual prayer for rain.

RITUAL PRAYER IN FEAR

Performance of ritual prayer in a special manner is 'permissible' when an enemy is present and when there is fear of drowning or of burning.

If, at the time of fear, people are in dispute with one another concerning the performance of a ritual prayer behind one imām, they will be divided into two groups. One group will stand in front of the enemy as protection. The imām, together with the other group, will perform one *rak'a* of that ritual prayer which consists of two *rak'as*, or two *rak'as* of that ritual prayer which consists of four *rak'as*, or two *rak'as* of the Sunset Prayer. Then this group will go, on foot, to the enemy. The other group which stood as protection, will come and start the ritual prayer with the imām, and the imām will perform with them the remaining *rak'a* or *rak'as* and will salute alone thereby himself completing the ritual prayer. This group will go, on foot, to the enemy. Then the other group will come, complete its ritual prayer without reading Qur'ānic sūras in this part of it and will salute, and it will go to the enemy. Then the other group will come, if it wants, and complete what remains of the ritual prayer, reading Qur'ānic sūras in this part of it.

If the fear of the enemy is very strong, people will perform ritual prayer while riding, [though their riding animals or their vehicles are moving], individually and with indication of the head, facing whatever direction possible.

Ritual prayer in fear is 'not permissible' if the enemy is not present. It is 'praiseworthy' to carry weapons when one is engaged in a ritual prayer, if there is fear of attack by an enemy.

If, at the time of fear, people do not dispute with one another concerning the performance of a ritual prayer behind one imām, the best course of action is that one group performs the ritual prayer *completely* behind one imām, and the other group then comes and performs the ritual prayer *completely* behind another imām. This is like performance of a ritual prayer during times of safety.

LEGAL RULES CONCERNING FUNERALS

قال رسول اللهم صلى الله عليه وسلم: من كان اخر كلامه لا اله الا اللهم دخل الجنة.

The Messenger of God (may God bless and greet him!) said, "One whose last words [at death] are: 'there is no god but God', will enter Paradise." [147]

Duties towards a Dying Man. Preparing the Dead for Burial

It is sunna to keep the dying man on his right side. To keep him on his back is 'permissible' by the law; however, his head should be raised up a little [so that his face may be towards the direction of the Ka'ba and not towards the sky]. It is sunna indirectly to teach him about the oneness of God and the prophethood of Muḥammad. This is by mentioning near him the two sentences of testimony. Mention of the two sentences near him should be made without much repetition, [since too much repetition may annoy him at the most difficult hour of death]. For the same reason he should not be *ordered* to utter these sentences of testimony.

Teaching the sentences of testimony to a deceased person after his dead body is put in the grave [and after burial is completed] has its source in the Sharī'a. [The procedure of this teaching is as follows. When burial is completed, one will come very close to the grave and instruct him three times, "O so-and-so, say: there is no god but God." Then he will again instruct, "O so-and-so, say: my Lord is God, my religion is Islam, and my prophet is Muḥammad; God, through the Means of Your chosen friend, i.e. the prophet Muḥammad, I pray to You that You show mercy to me by granting my death in Islam and in faith and that You permit Your prophet to intercede to You for us."] [148] Some authorities, the Mu'tazilas among them, maintain that the sentences of testimony will not be taught after the burial. Others say that the buried person will neither be ordered to utter the sentences of testimony nor be prohibited from this. [This middle course may be effected by instructing him, "O so-and-so, remember the religion in which you believed in your life of the world, by testifying that there is no god but God and that Muḥammad is His servant and messenger."] [149]

When a person is dying it is 'praiseworthy' that his relatives and neighbours should be near him [in order to give him water for quenching his thirst, to mention to him the unlimited mercy of God, and to create in his mind a good idea about God, for God forgives him who dies with the hope of forgiveness of God through His mercy]. [150] They should also read the Sūra Yā Sīn. [151] Some later authorities on Islamic jurisprudence have said that it is good to read

147 Al-Bukhārī, *Ṣaḥīḥ*, Janā'iz, 1.

148 Ash-Shurubalālī, *Marāqī*, p. 223.

149 *Ibid.*, p. 222.

150 Muslim, *Ṣaḥīḥ*, Janna, 81f.; abū Dāwūd, *Sunan*, Janā'iz, 13; Ibn Māja, *Sunan*, Zuhd, 14.

151 See *infra*, n. 180.

the Sūra of Thunderbolt (*ar-Ra'd*)[152] [because the reading of this sūra facilitates the soul's departing from the body]. Authorities have differed as to whether or not menstruating women and women with childbirth bleeding should be allowed to be near the dying man.

After death the beard of the dead will be tied, and his eyes closed. The person who will close his eyes will read the formula prayer:

> In the name of God and on the religion of the Messenger of God (may God bless him and greet him!). God, make his [immediate] affair easy for him, facilitate for him that which is after this affair, make him happy by granting him encounter with You, and make that which comes out towards him better than that which comes out from him.
> (بسم الله وعلى ملة رسول الله صلى الله عليه وسلم. اللهم يسر عليه امره وسهل عليه مابعده واسعده بلقائك واجعل ما خرج اليه خيرا مما خرج عنه).
> (*Bi-smillāhi, wa 'alā millati rasūli Allāhi, ṣallā Allāhu 'alayhi wa sallama. Allāhumma, yassir 'alayhi amrahu, wa sahhil 'alayhi mā ba'dahu, wa as'adhu bi-liqā' ika; wa aj'al mā kharaja ilayhi khayran mimmā kharaja 'anhu*).

[Then his body will be covered with a long piece of cloth]. A piece of iron should be put on his belly, so that it may not swell; [there is some property in the iron which prevents swelling of the belly]. His hands will be kept by his both sides; it is 'not permissible' to keep them on his chest. It is 'disliked' by the law that the Qur'ān should be read near him until he is washed. It is 'praiseworthy' to inform people of his death so that the number of those who will perform ritual prayer over him may increase. The preparation for his burial will be hastened. Thus soon after his death he will be put on a bedstead fumigated an odd number of times, [i.e. thrice or five times], and his position may be in any way it happens — this is the most correct view. His private parts will be covered. Then his cloth will be taken off [and the private parts will be washed using a rag]. After this others will make his ablution; this is the correct view; if, however, he is a child unable to understand what ritual prayer means, ablution need not be made for him. In ablution gargling and blowing out of the nose will not be made [because these are difficult — his mouth and nose will only be wiped with a rag wetted with water]. If, however, he is in the state of major legal impurity, [or if she is a menstruating woman or a woman with childbirth bleeding],

152 This is the thirteenth Qur'ānic sūra consisting of forty-three verses.

washing of the mouth and the nostril is 'necessary', even though it is difficult.

On completion of ablution, boiled water mixed with potash or leaves of lote-tree will be poured on his body; if these are not available, pure water which is slightly hot will be sufficient. The hair of his head and beard will be washed with water mixed with khiṭmī, a kind of fragrant herb which cleanses like soap; [if this herb is not available, soap is sufficient]. After this he will be reclined on his left side, and his right side will be washed until the water reaches that part of his body which touches the bedstead. Then he will be put on his right side, and the left side of his body will be washed in the same way; [thus the water will have reached his whole body]. Then his body will be seated a little leaning against something, and his belly will be wiped gently; anything which comes out of it will be washed away — repetition of the washing of the entire body [or of ablution] is not necessary. Then the wetness of the body will be absorbed with a piece of cloth. Then a shirt will be put on him, and then the clothes of the shroud will be spread out. Perfume will be applied to his beard and the head, and camphor to all his bodily parts with which one prostrates in a ritual prayer, [i.e. the forehead, the nose, the hands, the knees, and the feet]. In the clear legal reports there is no mention of the use of cotton in washing a dead body. His nose hair will not be trimmed; and the hair of his head will not be cut. Nor will his hair and beard be combed.

A woman can wash the dead body of her husband but not vice versa. If a woman is not found to wash the dead body of a woman, her husband will purify it through ablution with clean sand. If a woman dies with men, they will purify her body through ablution with clean sand; similarly, if a man dies with women, they will purify his body through ablution with clean sand; the man effecting this purification of the dead body of a woman will, [because he is a stranger for her], wrap his hand with a rag [in order that his naked hand may not touch her body]; if a man who has blood relationship with the deceased woman and who is not legally allowed to marry her during her lifetime, is found, he will purify her dead body through ablution with clean sand without using a rag, [because he is 'permitted' by the law to touch her bodily parts wiped in ablution with clean sand]; likewise, the dead body of a hermaphrodite will be purified through ablution with clean sand — this is mentioned in a clear legal report.

It is 'permissible' for both man and woman to wash such boys and girls as have not attained the age of sex, [because their bodily parts do not fall under the legal ruling concerning the private parts. There is no sin in kissing the dead body out of love or for blessings].

It is the duty of the husband to prepare his deceased wife for burial, even though he is in financial difficulty; this is the most correct view, [and on this has been given legal decision]. The cost of the shroud of a deceased person who has left behind no wealth, will be paid by his relative who was legally 'required' to maintain him or her in his or her lifetime. In the absence of such a relative, the expenditure will be born by the state treasury. If the treasury refuses to bear the expenditure because of inability or injustice, the individuals will bear it. An individual unable to buy the shroud and to arrange the burial of a deceased person, will seek assistance from others.

Shrouding a dead body is something 'obligatory'. In respect of the number of pieces of cloth to be used, a shroud is of three kinds, namely, sunna, sufficient, and essential. The sunna shroud for a man is [1] a shirt [covering the body from the base of the neck to the feet], [2] a waist-wrapper [which is so long as to reach the feet], and [3] a wrapper [which is longer than the body and with which the entire body can be wrapped, and even after this its both extremes, upper and lower, can be tied]. The quality of these pieces of cloth should be equal to that of the dress he used to wear in his lifetime [on the occasion of the Friday Assembly Prayer and 'Īd Prayers]. The sufficient shroud for a man is one consisting of [1] the waist-wrapper and [2] the wrapper. White cotton cloth is preferable to other cloth. [Old cloth but washed and new cloth are same in merit.] The waist-wrapper and the wrapper will both be so long as to cover the body from the lock of the hair of the head to the feet [and even more]. The shirt will have no sleeve, no rolling down and no pocket. Nor will its sides be hemmed. A turban is 'disliked' by the law — this is the correct view. [The procedure of putting on the shroud is that the wrapper will be spread out first, then the waist-wrapper over it; then the body wearing the shirt will be put on the waist-wrapper]; then the waist-wrapper will be wrapped from the left side and then from the right side; [then the wrapper will be wrapped in the same way]. The shroud will be tied if it is feared that it may be spread out.

In the sunna shroud for a woman, two pieces of cloth will be added [to those used for a man]. These two are: [1] a veil for her face [and head], and [2] a rag [the breadth of which is equal to that between the breast and the navel and] which is for tying her breasts.

In the case of the sufficient shroud for a woman, only a veil for her face will be added to the two pieces used for a man's sufficient shroud. Her hair will be made two plaits which will be put on her chest over her shirt. Then the veil will be put [on her head and face and] on the shirt; so it will be under the wrapper. Then the rag will be tied over the wrapper in order that the pieces of cloth may not spread out.

The shroud, whether of man or woman, will be fumigated an odd number of times before the dead body is inserted into it. The essential shroud for a man or a woman is that which is available.

Ritual Prayer over a Bier

Ritual prayer over a deceased person is a collective obligation, i.e. it is obligatory upon every individual of the society but if a single individual performs it its obligation ceases to be the responsibility of all others.

The pillars of the ritual prayer over a deceased person are: the saying of *Allāhu akbar*, and standing.

There are six stipulations for the validity of ritual prayer over the bier. They are as follows: [1] The deceased person is a Muslim. [2] He is clean, [and the place where he is put for the prayer is also clean]. [3] He is in front of the people who are praying for him. [4] He is present fully, or the greater part of his body or at least half of it together with the head is present. [5] The people performing ritual prayer for him are neither riding nor sitting without an excuse. [This is because standing is a pillar for this prayer; so it cannot be neglected without an excuse.] [6] The deceased person should be placed on the ground. If he be on the back of an animal or on a vehicle or in people's hands, the ritual prayer is not valid according to the chosen view, except in the case of the existence of an excuse.

The sunna acts in the ritual prayer over a deceased person are four in number. They are as follows. [1] The standing of the imām (i.e. one who leads a ritual prayer) opposite the chest of the deceased person, whether male or female. [This is because the chest is the bodily part inside which his soul as well as the light of the faith existed.] [2] Reading the formula of praise of God (*thanā'*), following the saying of *Allāhu akbar* for the first time in this ritual prayer.[153] [3] Reading the formula of invoking blessings upon the Prophet, following the saying of *Allāhu akbar* for the second time.[154] [4] To supplicate to God for the dead, following the reading of *Allāhu akbar* for the third time. This supplication should not

[153] for this formula see *supra*, p. 101. [154] This formula is cited *supra*, p. 104.

concern anything [other than affairs of the Hereafter]. Reading of that supplication formula which is transmitted from the Prophet is better, because in this case the chance of the acceptance of supplication by God is greater. This supplication formula, as memorized by 'Awf ibn Mālik [155] when he performed the ritual prayer over a bier along with the Prophet, is:

> God, forgive him, have mercy upon him and pardon him. Give him generous hospitality and widen his grave. Wash him with water, snow and hail, and cleanse him from sins as white cloth is cleansed from dirt. Grant him a house better than his house in this world, a family better than his family in this life, and a wife better than his wife left behind. Allow him to enter into Paradise, and protect him from chastisement of the grave and punishment of Hell. [156]
>
> (اللهم، اغفرله وارحمه. وعافه واعفعنه. واكرم نزله، ووسع مدخله. واغسله بالماء والثلج والبرد. ونقه من الخطايا، كما ينقى الثوب الابيض من الدنس، وابدله دارا خيرا من داره، واهلا خيرا من اهله، وزوجا خيرا من زوجه. وادخله الجنة، واعذه من عذاب القبر وعذاب النار)
>
> (*Allāhumma, aghfir lahu wa arḥamhu. Wa 'āfih wa a'fu 'anhu. Wa akrim nuzalahu, wa wassi' madkhalahu. Wa aghsilhu bi-l-mā'i wa th-thalji wa.l-baradi. Wa naqqihu min al-khaṭāyā, kamā yunaqqa th-thawbu l-abyaḍu min ad-danasi. Wa abdilhu dāran khayran min dārihi, wa ahlan khayran min ahlihi, wa zawjan khayran min zawjihi. Wa-dkhilhu l-jannata, wa a'idhhu min 'adhābi l-qabri wa 'adhābi n-nāri*)

It is required to salute after saying *Allāhu akbar* for the fourth time. No formula prayer will be read after this; this view is to be found in clear legal report. [The prayer formula mentioned above will be read secretly, but *Allāhu akbar* loudly.] The hands will not be lifted up otherwise than in saying *Allāhu akbar* for the first time. If the imām

155 'Awf ibn Mālik was one of the companions of the Prophet. For his biography see Ibn 'Abd al-Barr, *al-Istī'āb*, Egypt, 1960, III, 1226.

156 Muslim, *Ṣaḥīḥ*, Janā'iz, 85f.; at-Tirmidhī, *Sunan*, Janā'iz, 38; an-Nasā'ī, *Sunan*, Ṭahāra, 49; Ibn Māja, *Sunan*, Janā'iz, 23. 'Awf ibn Mālik who had memorized this formula prayer from the Prophet and later narrated it, said that, when he had heard the Prophet pray over the bier by reading this prayer formula, he had wished that he could be that bier. This is because this prayer is very comprehensive, and because it was made by one whose prayer was sure to be received by God.

says *Allāhu akbar* a fifth time forgetfully the follower should not imitate him, but should wait for his salutation [so that they may salute together with him]. In the ritual prayer over a deceased person who is insane or a child, one will not pray to God for their forgiveness, [because they have no sin]. Rather in their case one should read the formula of prayer:

> God, make him for us a child sent before; make him a means of reward for us and a treasure; and make him for us an intercessor whose intercession is acceptable to You.
> (اللهم اجعله لنا فرطا. واجعله لنا اجرا وذخرا. واجعله لنا شافعا مشفعا)
> (*Allāhumma, aj'alhu lanā faraṭan. Wa j'alhu lanā ajaran wa dhukhran. Wa j'alhu lanā shāfi'an mushaffa'an*)

[Who will Lead the Ritual Prayer over a Deceased Person]

The person who is most deserving of leading the ritual prayer over a man who has died, is the Muslim ruler of his country. Next to the ruler is his Muslim deputy, then the Muslim judge, [then the Muslim deputy of the judge], then the Muslim leader of the locality of the dead, and then his Muslim guardian who is male and who is obliged to perform the religious duties.[157] [A woman, a minor, and one possessing very little degree of intellect have no right to lead this ritual prayer. The father of the deceased has preference over his son. If the deceased person has no guardian, his wife or, if he has no wife, his neighbours will occupy the place of his guardian.] He who has priority to lead the ritual prayer over a bier, has the right to permit another person to lead it. If another person has led it without his permission [and he did not follow that person], he can repeat it, if he likes. However, those who performed this prayer following that person, will not repeat it. The man who has priority to lead this ritual prayer by virtue of his guardianship, is more deserving than one whom the deceased ordered by way of a will to lead the prayer over him, [for his order by a will is nullified in this case] — this is the view on which legal decision has been given. If a man over whom ritual prayer is not performed is buried, it will be performed on his grave, even though he was not washed, so long as he is not swollen inside the grave.

[In a ritual prayer over the bier, if only seven persons are present one of them will go ahead as the imām, three will stand behind him,

157 A person is obliged to perform the religious duties if he is neither insane nor minor.

two will make the second line, and one will stand in the third. This making of three lines is necessary because there is a Tradition:

> "One over whom three lines of devotees pray, is forgiven by God. The best of these lines is the last one, because the prayer of the devotees standing in this line is most likely to be accepted because of their humility."] [158]

When several biers are assembled, it is better to perform ritual prayer over each of them individually. The best of them will precede, then the second best, and so on. If all biers are assembled and the ritual prayer is performed over all of them at once, this is correct; they will be put in a long line from that side which is closer to the direction of the Ka'ba, in such a way that the chest of each of them will be in front of the imām, [being opposite to him]. In putting them thus, their order should be maintained: men should be put from that side which is adjacent to the imām; after them children, then the hermaphrodites, and lastly women. If all are buried in one grave for a necessity, they will be put in it in an opposite order.

A person who has arrived late and has found the imām between the saying of two *Allāhu akbars*, will wait for the imām's saying of *Allāhu akbar*; when the imām says *Allāhu akbar*, he will start the ritual prayer with the imām and will agree with him in his supplication; then, before the bier is lifted up from the ground, he will perform that part of the ritual prayer which he missed in the beginning. The man who has arrived when the imām has said *Allāhu akbar* at the start of this ritual prayer, will not wait for his saying *Allāhu akbar* a second time, but will say *Allāhu akbar* and thus start the ritual prayer; he is considered to have performed the whole ritual prayer with the imām, and consequently will salute along with him. The man who has arrived after the imām's saying of *Allāhu akbar* for the fourth time but before salutation, has missed the ritual prayer in its entirety; this is the correct view.

It is 'slightly disliked' by the law that the ritual prayer over a bier should be performed in a mosque in which the ritual prayer which a Muslim performs five times daily is performed in congregation. This is when the bier is inside the mosque, or outside it but some of the people present are inside the mosque.

A baby in whom the sign of life, e.g. movement or crying, was seen or heard when coming out of his mother's womb but who died immediately after it, will be given a name and will be washed, and ritual prayer will be performed over him. But if no sign of life was

[158] At-Tirmidhī, *Sunan*, Janā'iz, 40; Abū Dāwūd, *Sunan*, Janā'iz, 39.

apparent, he will be washed and then will be put in a rag and buried; ritual prayer will not be performed over him.

A child who is taken as a prisoner with one of his parents [from an enemy's land] and who has died, will be washed, put in a rag and buried; no ritual prayer will be performed over him. But this child will be buried like a Muslim, should one of his parents accept Islam, or should he himself, who can understand what Islam means, accept Islam, or should none of his parents be taken as a captive with him.

If an infidel dies and [has no guardian who is infidel but] has a Muslim relative, this relative will wash him [not like washing the dead body of a Muslim but] like washing a filthy piece of cloth, then wrap him in a rag and throw him inside a ditch or hand him over to the people of his faith.

Ritual prayer over a bier will not be performed over one who rebels against a just Muslim government (*bāghī*) [even though he be a Muslim, or over a highwayman if they are killed in the condition of fighting; [nor will they be washed; however, if they are killed after the Muslim ruler achieves control over them, they will be washed and ritual prayer will be performed over them].

Likewise, ritual prayer over the bier will not be performed over one who has killed another by strangling, over one who mischievously goes round the town at night with a weapon if he is killed in that state, and over one who is killed in an affray; all these people will of course be washed.

A Muslim who has killed himself deliberately will be washed, and ritual prayer will be performed over him [because he is a believer, even though a sinner. If he has killed himself by mistake or by being unable to tolerate physical pain, then also he will be washed, and ritual prayer will be performed over him].

Ritual prayer over the bier will not be performed over one who has killed anyone of his parents deliberately [and unjustly].

Bearing of a Bier to the Graveyard and its Burial

It is sunna that four men bear the bier to the graveyard. [To bring the bier by putting it on the back of a riding animal or on a vehicle without an excuse is 'disliked' by the law. The bier of a child will be carried by one man with his hands, but the carrier will be changed four times.] When bearing the bier of an adult, every one of the four bearers should bear it forty steps in total, starting from the frontal right corner of the bedstead in which the dead body is put; so he will put this corner on his shoulder, the right side of the bier being at his left side. Then he will put the rear frontal corner of the bier on his right shoulder. Then he will complete the bearing of the left side of the bier by putting it on his left shoulder. Thus by bearing every corner he will have walked ten steps; [so the total steps will be forty in number]. It is 'praiseworthy' that the bearers should walk hastily, but not so hastily as to put the dead body on the bedstead in trouble.

People's walking behind the bier is better than their walking in front of it, just as an 'obligatory' ritual prayer is more excellent than a 'supererogatory' ritual prayer. [There is no sin in following a bier by riding or by being on a vehicle.] To praise God and to recite Qur'ānic verses loudly, and to sit before the bier is put inside the grave are 'disliked' by the law. [What is necessary is silence. To follow the bier by a woman is 'disliked'. There is no sin in weeping for the dead silently; weeping with a loud voice is 'disliked'.]

The grave will be dug to the measure of half the length of a man's body, or to the measure of the length of a man up to his chest. To dig it more is better. The *laḥad* form of grave should be prepared, not its *shaqq* form. In a *laḥad* grave a ditch is made in the bottom of the grave on that side of it which is towards the direction of the Ka'ba; in this ditch the dead body is put. In a *shaqq* grave a ditch is made in the depth of the grave, but at its middle and not at the side as in the *laḥad* grave; in this ditch the dead body is put. The *shaqq* form of grave should be prepared only if the soil is soft. [No casket containing the dead body even though it is made of iron should be put in the grave.]

The dead body will be inserted into the grave from the direction of the Ka'ba and those who will insert it should say:

> In the name of God [we put you in the grave], and on the religion of the Messenger of God (may God bless him and greet him!) we submit you.
> (بسم الله، وعلى ملة رسول الله، صلى الله عليه وسلم)
> (*Bismi Allāhi, wa 'alā millati rasūli Allāhi, ṣallā Allāhu 'alayhi wa sallama*.)

The dead body will be put in the grave, facing the direction of the Holy Ka'ba and on its right side. The knots of the shroud will be untied. Raw bricks and pieces of bamboos will be put straight at the side of the *laḥad*; to put baked bricks and pieces of wood is 'disliked' by the law, if raw bricks and pieces of bamboos are available. It is 'praiseworthy' to cover the grave of a woman [until raw bricks or pieces of bamboos are placed by the side of the *laḥad*]. The grave of a man should not be covered [unless there is necessity, e.g. rain and excessive heat]. Soil will be poured into the grave. The outward side of the grave will be shaped like the back of a camel; it will not be square-shaped.

To build on the grave for adornment is 'unlawful'. To build on it after burial in order to strengthen it is 'disliked'; [however, building is 'permissible' if it is before the burial]. Likewise, it is 'permissible' to write something on a piece of stone and to put it on the grave in order that the sign of the grave may exist and that the grave may not be desecrated.

The law 'dislikes' that one should be buried inside a house, for burial inside a house is special to prophets. [A Muslim should be buried in the graveyard for Muslims.] There is no sin in burying more than one dead body in one grave if there is necessity. In such a case, all the dead bodies will be prevented by soil from touching each other. [If a dead body buried long ago has became dust, it is 'permissible to bury another dead body in his grave; but it is 'not permissible' to break his bones or to shift them to another place.]

One who has died in a boat and is far from the land and there is fear for him, will be washed and shrouded; then the ritual prayer for the bier will be performed over him, and then he will be thrown into the sea.

It is 'praiseworthy' to bury the dead body of a person in the locality of his death or murder. There is no sin in transferring it, before burial, to a distance of one mile or two. To transfer it to a distance more than this is 'disliked' by the law. All Ḥanafī jurists have agreed that it is 'not permissible' to transfer it after burial, except if the land of its burial is an usurped land or if the land is taken away through the right of neighbourhood.

If the dead body of a man is buried in a grave dug for another, someone will be responsible for the price of digging, but the dead body will not be taken out of it. [The price will be paid from the property the dead left behind. If no property is left it will be paid by the Muslims. There is no sin in one's preparing a grave for oneself before one's death; rather one will be rewarded for it by God.]

The grave can be ransacked if such a thing as a piece of cloth or a silver coin dropped in it, or if the shroud of the man buried was taken by force from someone who demands its return, or if any valuable thing remained with the dead. The grave, however, will not be ransacked if the dead body was put in the grave facing a direction other than that of the Ka'ba or on its left side.

[It is 'praiseworthy' that the dead man's neighbours and relatives prepare food for the members of his aggrieved family and entertain them a day and a night.[159] It is also 'praiseworthy' to express sorrow and sympathy towards them.

Visiting the Graves

According to the most correct view, it is 'praiseworthy' for both men and women to visit the graves of those who have died. The state of standing when visiting the graves and when praying for their inmates is sunna. Likewise, it is sunna to salute them on arrival, by reading the formula:

> May peace be upon you, O the group of the believers. Surely, if God pleases, we are joining you. I pray to God for the good of me and you.
>
> (السلام عليكم دار قوم مومنين. وانا ان شاءالله بكم لاحقون. اسأل الله لى ولكم العافية).
>
> (*As-salāmu 'alaykum, dāra qawmin mu'minīna. Wa innā, in shā' Allāhu, bikum lāḥiqūna. As'alu Allāha lī wa lakum al-'āfiyata.*)

It is 'praiseworthy' to read the Sūra Yā Sīn,[160] standing by the side of the grave. It is to be found in Tradition that if a person enters into the graveyard, reads this sūra and offers its reward to the dead, God makes the punishment light for those buried in it for that day, and he obtains the reward of acts equal to the number of them.

Sitting on a grave in order to read part of the Qur'ān is 'not disliked' by the law. To sit on it for a purpose other than Qur'ān-reading, to walk on it, to sleep on it, to urinate or to excrete on it, and to uproot weeds or trees grown in the graveyard — are all 'disliked' acts. There is, however, no sin in uprooting dry weeds or dry trees.

LEGAL RULES CONCERNING THE MARTYR

> لاتحسبن الذين قتلوا فى سبيل الله امواتا بل احياء عند ربهم يرزقون فريحين بما اتاهم الله من فضله.
> — قران ١٧٠ـ٣:١٦٩
>
> Do not account those who are slain in the cause of God, as dead. Indeed they are living in the presence of their Lord and are provided for. They are jubilant over that which God has bestowed upon them of His bounty. — Qur'ān 3:169-70

159 Abū Dāwūd, *Sunan*, Janā'iz, 26; at-Tirmidhī, *Sunan*, Janā'iz, 21.

160 This is the thirty-sixth sūra of the Qur'ān. It consists of eighty-three verses. The Prophet called it "the heart of the Qur'ān". See Ibn Ḥanbal, *Musnad*, 50:26.

The death of a man killed for whatever reason occurs at the expiry of his predetermined lifetime; it is not that the killer kills him before his predetermined lifetime comes to an end. This is the opinion of the People of Sunna and Jamā'a.

The law defines the martyr as a person [a] who is killed by the people of an enemy's land, or by rebels, or by highwaymen, or by thieves in his house at night or at daytime even though with a heavy thing, or [b] who is found in battle [against the people of an enemy's land, rebels, or highwaymen], and the sign of being killed is present on his body, or [c] who is killed by a Muslim unjustly and voluntarily with a sharp weapon — and in all these cases the person killed is a major Muslim free from menstruation and childbirth bleeding [in the case of a woman] and from the state of major legal impurity and did not live long after the end of the battle.

The martyr will not be washed; he will be shrouded together with his blood and clothes. The ritual prayer over the bier will be performed over him in his unwashed state. Things which are not fit to be used as a shroud, e.g. furred garment and stuffed garment, will be taken away from him if other things fit for being a shroud are available; weapon and coat of mail will also be taken away. If the clothes which are already present on his body are not sufficient for making the sunna form of the shroud, other pieces of clothes will be added to them; but if they are more than this form of a shroud their number will be reduced. It is 'disliked' by the law to take away all clothes with which he was killed.

The martyr will be washed if he is killed in the state of major legal impurity, or being a child or an insane person or a menstruating woman or a woman with childbirth bleeding or if, after the end of battle, he is carried away from the battlefield in the state of being wounded and having the last breath of life and he ate or drank or slept [even though for a little while] or he passed the time of single ritual prayer in such a condition that his power of understanding was not yet lost, or if he is transferred from the battlefield alive not for fear of molestation by horse or other animals, or he ordered his heir by a will to do something concerning this world or the Hereafter, or he sold or bought anything or spoke much; if eating, drinking and so on, are found to have been done by him before the end of the battle, he will not be regarded as having been carried away from the battlefield in the state of being wounded and having the last breath of life.

[A man who is killed in a town, and it is not known whether he is

killed for legal penalty or unjustly, or whether he is killed for legal penalty or in retaliation, will be washed and then the ritual prayer over the bier will be performed over him.]

IV

FASTING

فمن شهد منكم الشهر فليصمه. ـ القران ٢:١٨٥

He who witnesses the month Ramaḍān [being stationary (*muqīm*) and in health] should fast through it. — Qur'ān 2:185

قال رسول الله صلى الله عليه وسلم: من صام ايمانـا واحتسابا غفرله ما تقدم من ذنبه.

The messenger of God (may God bless and greet him!) said, "He who fasts during Ramaḍān with faith and seeking his reward from God will have his past [minor] sins forgiven."[161]

DEFINITION

Fasting consists in abstention, at day time, i.e. from the daybreak to sunset[162] , [1] from allowing, whether deliberately or mistakenly, anything to enter into the stomach or any other part of the body which falls under the same legal judgement as the stomach, and [2] from the gratification of sexual desire with one's wife or anyone else with intention.

STIPULATIONS FOR FASTING

The Ramaḍān fast is made 'necessary' in a general way by the arrival[163] of a part of the lunar month Ramaḍān. The actual observance of fasting on every day of this month is 'necessitated' by the arrival of that day.

When Fasting is 'Obligatory'

The Ramaḍān fast, whether during the month Ramaḍān or later

161 Al-Bukhārī, *Ṣaḥīḥ*, Īmān, 28, Ṣawm, 1; Muslim, *Ṣaḥīḥ*, Musafirīm, 175.

162 The time for fasting has been made fixed so that no one may have a chance of doing excess or slackness. Abstention from eating, drinking and sexual intercourse from daybreak to sunset is considered moderation in the hours of fasting; this moderation is prescribed because it is the proper means to the aim of fasting, which is to reduce the intensity of passions and carnal desires. Abstention for more or less than these hours is not prescribed by Islam, because this would be either unbearable hardship or insufficient means to reduce the violence of carnal desires. This point is elaborated by Shāh Walī Allāh in his *Ḥujjat Allāh al-Bāligha*, ed. as-Sayyid Sābiq, Cairo, n.d., II, 518-20.

163 Qur'ān 2:185.

in case of one's failure to fast during the month for a certain reason, is 'obligatory' upon an individual if he possesses *all* the following four qualifications.

The first qualification is Islam. The second is sanity. The third is physical maturity which has already been defined in a previous section. One who has not yet attained the age of maturity, i.e. a child, is not legally obliged to fast in the month Ramaḍān. The fourth qualification is the knowledge that the Ramaḍān fast is 'required' by the law. One who lacks this knowledge is not under an obligation to fast. This is appropriate to those who have accepted Islam in a non-Muslim country where there is but little opportunity to know about the tenets of Islam.[164] In the case of a person who is brought up in a Muslim territory, the stipulation for him is only his living in such a territory; knowledge that fasting in the month Ramaḍān is 'obligatory' is not a stipulation — his ignorance is not an excuse.

Stipulations for Observance of Fasting

The above qualifications taken together make the Ramaḍān fast 'obligatory' upon a Muslim. The actual observance of this fasting, however, may not be 'required' at that time for certain obstacles. It will be 'required' only if one fulfils the following three stipulations.

[1] Bodily health. An individual on whom the Ramaḍān fast is 'obligatory', is 'required' by the law to fast at that time provided he is in good health. If he is sick he must fast later when he recovers his health.[165] [2] For a woman, freedom from menstruation and childbirth bleeding. A woman on whom the Ramaḍān fast is 'obligatory', will fast in the month Ramaḍān if she is free from any of these two complaints. If she is not free, she must observe fasting later when her menses leave her or her childbirth bleeding period expires.

164 Islam is an universal religion — a religion given by God for all people of the world and for all time until Doomsday. There are people who do not know at all that there is a religion called Islam. Such people are not subject to Islamic religious obligations, and will not be judged by the Islamic standard on the Day of Judgement. This is explicit in the Qur'ān (17:15). Those who know about the existence of Islam are under an obligation to accept it and then to learn at least about its fundamentals. In a non-Muslim country if, despite making efforts to learn about these, they remain ignorant of any basic tenet of Islam because of lack of opportunity to learn about Islam in that country, they are exempted from obligation with respect to that tenet. But where there is an opportunity to learn about Islam, ignorance is no excuse; rather to remain ignorant is a major sin, for it is non-fulfilment of a religious duty. The prophet Muḥammad said, "Pursuit of knowledge [about the fundamentals of Islam] is a binding duty upon every male and female Muslim." See Ibn Māja, *Sunan*, Muqaddama, 17.

165 Qur'ān 2:185.

[3] To be 'stationary'. An individual on whom the Ramaḍān fast is 'obligatory' will observe this fasting in the month Ramadān if he is 'stationary'. If, however, he is on a journey, he may postpone it until he becomes 'stationary'.[166]

Stipulations for the Validity of Fasting

Fasting is legally considered to be observed correctly if the following three stipulations are fulfilled in its observance.

[1] Making of intention for fasting. [This consists, not in the mere verbal utterance of a formula of intention, but in the mental resolve and firm determination to fast. When making this resolve, however, it is better to read the following formula of intention:

> I intend to fast tomorrow, a day of the holy month Ramaḍān, as an 'obligatory' fasting for You, O God. Lord, accept it from us; surely You alone are the All-hearing, the All-knowing.
> (نويت ان اصوم غدا من شهر رمضان المبارك، فرضا لك، يا الله. ربنا تقبل منا؛ انك انت السيمع العليم.)
> (*Nawaytu an aṣūma ghadan min shahri Ramaḍāni l-mubāraki; farḍan laka, yā Allāh. Rabbanā taqabbal minnā; innaka anta s-samī'u l-'alīmu*).]

[2] Freedom from menstruation and childbirth bleeding. A woman, if her fasting on a particular day is to be valid, must be free from any of these two complaints on that day. [3] Freedom from any act which corrupts fasting. These acts will be discussed shortly.

Freeedom from the major legal impurity is not a stipulation for the validity of fasting. Thus should one who is fasting be in the state of this impurity, even though throughout the day, his fasting is legally correct.

THE PILLAR OF FASTING

The pillar of fasting is abstention from the fulfilment of the desire for food, the desire for sexual intercourse and the desire for anything associated with food and sexual intercourse.

The legal judgement concerning the correct observance of the Ramaḍān fast is that by this a religious obligation is discharged in this life, and reward will be obtained in the Hereafter. [This reward will be great and special as God said,

[166] However, if possible, it is better for him to fast when he is on a journey than not to fast. See al-Ghazālī, *Iḥyā*,' I, 233.

> "Every good work is recompensed by the reward of an act greater than it from ten to seven hundred times; fasting is an exception to this, for it is observed for Me and it is I Who will recompense it." [167]

The prophet Muḥammad said,

> "Paradise has a gate called the Rayyān; only those who fast will enter into Paradise through it ...." [168] "A person who fasts has two occasions of joy — one when he breaks his fast, and the other when he will encounter his Lord."] [169]

KINDS OF FASTING

There are six kinds of fasting, namely, 'obligatory', 'required', sunna, 'praiseworthy', 'supererogatory, and 'disliked'.

The 'obligatory' fasting is [a] the Ramaḍān fasting, [170] whether it is observed in the month Ramaḍān or after it in the case of one's failure to observe it in the month for a certain reason, [b] fasting of atonements for commission of legal offences, [171] and [c] the fasting vowed to God. [172] The 'required' fasting is the re-observance of that 'supererogatory' fasting which is made null and void by its agent. [173]

The sunna fasting is the fasting on the tenth day of the lunar month Muḥarram [174] together with the ninth day. The 'praiseworthy' fasting is the fasting on three days of every month. It is

[167] Al-Bukhārī, *Ṣaḥīḥ*, Ṣawm, 2; Muslim, *Ṣaḥīḥ*, Ṣiyām,164f.; Ibn Māja, *Sunan*, Ṣiyām, 1. This is a 'holy Tradition' (*ḥadīth qudsī*). For the meaning of the last part of this Tradition see al-Ghazālī, *Iḥyā*,' I, 231f. The meaning of 'holy Tradition' is discussed by J. Robson, "Ḥadīth Ḳudsī", *EI*², III, 28.

[168] Al-Bukhārī, *Ṣaḥīḥ*, Ṣawm, 9; Muslim, *Ṣaḥīḥ*, Ṣiyām, 162, 164f.

[169] Al-Bukhārī, *Ṣaḥīḥ*, Ṣawm, 4f.; Muslim, *Ṣaḥīḥ*, Ṣiyām, 1f., 166. The reward of fasting as mentioned in these and other prophetic traditions cannot be obtained by one whose fast is lifeless, who fasts out of habit or for fear of social disapproval. God accepts only that fast which is observed in the spirit of faith (*īmān*) and with trust in reward from Him. See al-Bukhārī, *Ṣaḥīḥ*, Īmān, 28, Ṣawm, 1; Muslim, *Ṣaḥīḥ*, Musāfirīn, 175.

[170] Qur'ān 2:183, 185.

[171] Qur'ān 5:89, 2:196, 58:4.

[172] Vows made to God may be of various forms. One of them is the vow of fasting. A Muslim must fulfil the vow he makes to God. Not only in Islam, but also in previous revealed religions, fulfilment of vows is stressed; see Qur'ān 22:29, 19:26, 20:270, 2:35.

[173] Qur'ān 47:33.

[174] This fast is important. On his migration to Medina, the Prophet observed this fast and commanded his companions to do the same. But next year when the Ramaḍān fast was prescribed, he neither enjoined it nor prohibited it; thus it remained as a sunna fast. For more information on this fast see al-Bukhārī, *Ṣaḥīḥ*, Ṣawm, 1, 69; Muslim, *Ṣaḥīḥ*, Ṣiyām, 144, 116, 164, 125.

'commendable' that these days are the days of the bright nights (*al-ayyām al-bīḍ*) i.e. the thirteenth, the fourteenth and the fifteenth of a month of the lunar year.[175] 'Praiseworthy' fasting also includes: [a] fasting on Monday, Thursday and Friday,[176] [b] fasting on six days of the lunar month Shawwāl — some authorities have maintained that the most excellent is to fast these days consecutively, while others are in favour of their separate observance —, and [c] any other fasting the seeking of, and reward for, which are established by the sunna,[177] e.g. the fasting of the prophet David. The fasting of David consists in fasting every alternate day; it is the best of all types of 'praiseworthy' fastings; it is the most liked of them to God.[178] The 'supererogatory' fasting is all fastings other than those mentioned above, so long as they are not established to be 'disliked' fastings.

The 'disliked' fasting is of two kinds: 'slightly disliked' and so 'gravely disliked' that it is almost 'forbidden'. An example of the former is the fasting on the tenth of the month Muḥarram alone, without joining it with the ninth. The latter is the fasting on the Festival Day on the expiry of the month Ramaḍān (*'Īd al-Fiṭr*), on

[175] Cf. al-Bukhārī, *Ṣaḥīḥ*, Ṣawm, 60; at-Tirmidhī, *Sunan*, Ṣawm, 54.

[176] In Islam these are the excellent days of the week. The reward of fasting and doing deeds on these days is multiplied. See al-Ghazālī, *Iḥyā'*, I, 237.

[177] A few of these fasts may be mentioned here. (1)1 Fasting on the day of 'Arafa, i.e. the ninth day of the lunar month Dhū l-Ḥijja. (2) Fasting on the first nine days of Dhū l-Ḥijja. (3) Fasting on the first ten days of the month Muḥarram. (4) Fasting in sacred months, i.e. Dhū l-Qa'da, Dhū l-Ḥijja, Muḥarram and Rajab. (5) Fasting in the month Sha'bān. The Prophet used to fast in this month so frequently that people imagined that he was observing the Ramaḍān fast (al-Bukhārī, *Ṣaḥīḥ*, Ṣawm, 52; Muslim, *Ṣaḥīḥ*, Ṣiyām, 176f.). He also said: besides the month Ramaḍān the most excellent month for fasting is the month Muḥarram (Muslim, *Ṣaḥīḥ*, Ṣiyām, 202, 302; an-Nasā'i, *Sunan*, Qiyām al-layl, 6). Concerning the first ten days of Dhū l-Ḥijja he said, "No good works are more excellent or more liked by God than those performed in the first ten days of Dhū l-Ḥijja. Surely the fast on one of these days is equal to the fast of one whole year ...." See at-Tirmidhī,, *Sunan*, Ṣawm, 52. For an account of 'supererogatory' fasts see al-Ghazālī, *Iḥyā'*, I, 237f.; Walī Allāh, *Ḥujja*, II, 521, 532f.

[178] A reason for this is that this fast is most difficult for the carnal soul to observe and is most effective in subjugating it. Another reason is that through this fast both patience and gratitude to God are exercised — patience on the day of fasting and gratitude the next day when one eats and drinks. Exercise of these two virtues was considered by the Prophet as very important. (at-Tirmidhī, *Sunan*, Zuhd, 35). Concerning the fast of the prophet David, the prophet Muḥammad said, "The best type of fast is that of my brother, David; he used to fast one day and omit the other day" (al-Bukhārī, *Ṣaḥīḥ*, Isti'dhān, 38, Ṣawm, 56, 58f.; Muslim, *Ṣaḥīḥ*, Ṣiyām, 181f., 186, 189). The prophet Muḥammad further said, "Fast on alternate day ... there is no fasting more excellent than this." See al-Bukhārī, *Ṣaḥīḥ*, Anbiyā', 37.

the Festival Day of the Sacrifice of Animals (*'Īd al-Aḍḥā*), and on the Days of Drying the Meat (*Ayyām at-Tashrīq*), i.e. the three days following the Festival Day of the Sacrifice.

It is 'disliked' by the law to fast on Friday alone,[179] on Saturday alone, on New Year's day, and on the day of autumnal equinox. There is of course no harm in fasting if these two last mentioned days happen to be on the days of one's habitual fasting. It is also 'disliked' to fast without break even though for only two days. In this kind of fasting, one does not break the fast after the sunset at all, so that this fasting is joined with the fasting of the next day. Fasting every day for a long time is also 'disliked' by the law.[180]

MAKING THE INTENTION OF FASTING

The making of the intention for every day of fasting is necessary. [a] There are certain kinds of fasting in which it is not a stipulation that the intention should be made *fixing* the kind of fasting to be observed and that the intention should be made at *night*. These kinds of fasting are: [1] the Ramaḍān fast observed in the month Ramaḍān, [2] that fasting which one has promised to God to observe as a vow at a fixed time, and [3] 'supererogatory' fasting. These three kinds of fasting are valid if the intentions for them are made any time from the daybreak to the time when the sun is about to be on the meridian. This is the most correct view. Likewise, they are correct if one has made for them a general intention, without specifying the kind of fasting to be observed, or if the intention made is for 'supererogatory' fasting, even though one is on a journey or is sick. This is the most correct legal opinion.

Observance of a Ramaḍān fast in the month Ramaḍān with the intention of another 'required' fasting is valid for one who is in health and who is 'stationary', but not for one on a journey — in the case of a person on a journey his fasting of Ramaḍān will turn to be that 'required' fasting for which he has made the intention. A sick

179 One who fasts on Friday should also fast on Thursday or Saturday. Similar is the case with fast on Saturday. See al-Bukhārī, *Ṣaḥīḥ*, Ṣawm, 64; Abū Dāwūd, *Sunan*, Ṣawm, 52.

180 This sort of fast is 'disliked' by the law because its observance is so difficult that it contradicts the easy nature of Islamic religion. It introduces to Islam extremism and excess in devotional acts, which are opposed to God's desire: "God desires ease for you; He does not desire hardship for you" (Qur'ān 2:185). "God has not laid upon you any hardship" (Qur'ān 22:78). See Walī Allāh, *Ḥujja*, II, 39; al-Ghazālī, *Iḥyā'*, I, 238. The prophet Muḥammad strictly prohibited this type of fast. See al-Bukhārī, *Ṣaḥīḥ*, Ṣawm, 56f., 49; at-Tirmidhī, *Sunan*, Ṣawm, 56; Muslim, *Ṣaḥīḥ*, Ṣiyām, 186, 196.

man fasting in the month Ramaḍān with the intention of another 'required' fasting is a subject of controversy as to whether his fasting will be considered as a Ramaḍān fast or as the 'required' fasting for which he has made the intention.

A fasting vowed to God to observe at a fixed time is not correct if it is observed with the intention of another 'required' fasting. Rather it will turn into that 'required' fasting which is intended.

[b] There are certain kinds of fasting in which it is a stipulation that the intention which needs to be made should specify the kind of fasting to be observed and should be made at night.[181] These kinds of fasting are: [1] the Ramaḍān fast if observed after the month Ramaḍān, in case of one's failure to observe during the month for a certain reason, [2] re-observance of that 'supererogatory' fasting which one has made null and void, [3] fasting of all forms of atonement, and [4] the fasting vowed to God in a general way, without fixing its time, e.g. one's statement, "If God heals my disease I must fast a day," and he is then healed.

THE SIGHT OF THE NEW MOON FOR FASTING AND FOR FESTIVAL DAYS. FASTING ON DAYS DOUBTFUL TO BE DAYS OF RAMAḌĀN

The start of the month Ramaḍān is established by the sight, i.e. knowledge,[182] of the new moon of this month or, if the new moon is not visible because of clouds, by the enumeration of thirty days of the month Sha'bān, the lunar month preceding the month Ramaḍān. The day of doubt as to whether it is a day of Ramaḍān or not, is the day which follows the twenty-ninth day of the month Sha'bān and concerning which there is an equal degree of knowledge and ignorance that the new moon has risen but is concealed behind the cloud.

On the day of doubt it is 'disliked' by the law to observe any kind of fasting except the 'supererogatory' one which is irrevocably decided as such, without reciprocation between it and another kind of fasting. If a person observed, on the day of doubt, a decidedly 'supererogatory' fasting and then it became plain to him that that day was really the day of Ramaḍān, his 'supererogatory' fasting

181 If after making the intention at night, one eats something and this eating is before the daybreak, one need not repeat the intention. If a menstruating woman makes the intention at night and then her menses leave her before the daybreak and she starts fasting, her fast is valid with that intention. See al-Ghazālī, *Iḥyā'*, I, 232.

182 Al-Ghazālī, *Iḥyā'*, I, 232 where he says, "By sight we mean knowledge [that the new moon has risen in the sky]."

would do instead of Ramaḍān. Fasting on the day of doubt is not correct at all if one observes it regarding it as a fasting should the day be really a day of Ramaḍān and not a fasting should the day be otherwise. It is 'disliked' to fast the last one day or two of the month Sha'bān; to fast more than this is not 'disliked'. On the day of doubt, the muftī will first order the general people to fast, and then, when the time for making the intention which is until the midday has elapsed but still it is not clear whether or not the day is really of Ramaḍān, he will ask them to break the fast. The muftī himself, the magistrate, and the elite will fast as a 'supererogatory' act; these are able to control themselves against reciprocity in intention and against considering the fasting as 'obligatory'.

Anyone who alone has seen the new moon of the month of fasting or of the following month, i.e. Shawwāl, but his claim to have seen it is rejected by the magistrate, must fast himself [on what he considers to be the first day of Ramaḍān or the first day of Shawwāl]. He is 'not permitted' by the law to nullify his fast even though he is absolutely sure that [the month Ramaḍān has already expired and] the new moon for Shawwāl [which he saw himself] has risen. If he nullifies the fasting on these two days, he will have to re-observe them on other days, but no atonement is necessary for this nullification, even though this nullification has occurred prior to the magistrate's rejection of his claim. This is the correct legal view.

If in the sky there is cloud or smoke or some similar thing which has made difficult the sight of the new moon for the *start* of fasting, the information of an upright man or of a man whose uprightness is unknown to the effect that he has seen the moon, will be accepted — this is the correct view —, even though someone has witnessed against his testimony, even if this someone is a woman or one repented after having been penalized for false accusation. It is not a stipulation that the upright man or the man whose uprightness is unknown should emphasize his information by using such words as 'I bear witness' and 'I make a strong claim'.

In the case of the new moon for *stopping* the Ramaḍān fast, however, if there is an obstacle in the sky, it is a stipulation that two free, not slave, men or one free man and two free women should inform that they have seen the new moon and that when informing they use the words 'bear witness'; [183] it is not a stipulation to emphasize the information by the use of the word 'claim'.

If in the sky there is no obstacle to the sight of the new moon, it is

[183] All this should be done as a precaution against missing such a major devotional act as fasting. See al-Ghazālī, *Iḥyā'*, I, 232.

'necessary that a group of people sees the new moon for the start of fasting as well as the new moon for the end of it. The number of the group will be determined by the imām of the place; this is the most correct view.

If, after completing thirty days of fasting which started in reliance on the witness of one upright man that he saw the new moon for the start of the fasting, no new moon for the end of fasting is seen and the sky is clear, then it is 'not lawful' to stop fasting. If, however, the thirty days of fasting completed were started on the basis of the witnesses of two upright men, in this case there is a controversy. There is no controversy over the 'lawfulness' of ending fasting if, on completion of thirty days of fasting, no new moon is sighted and the sky is cloudy, even though those thirty days were started relying on the witness of one upright man.

The legal judgements concerning the sight of the new moon for the Festival of the Sacrifice of Animals are like those which concern the sight of the new moon for the end of the Ramaḍān fast.

For the establishment of the sight of all other new moons the stipulation is that the witness should be borne by two upright men, or by one free man and two free women who have not been penalized for false accusation.

When the rising of the new moon in the celestial zone of a country is proved, all men of that country must accept it. On this has been given legal decision, and this is what is held by most of the doctors of Islamic religious law.[184]

No consideration is to be given to the sight of the new moon at daytime, whether before the sun passed its meridian or after it. Such a moon is for the coming night. This is the view adopted by all.

ACTS WHICH DO NOT CORRUPT FASTING

There are twenty-three acts which do not corrupt fasting. They are as follows: [1-3] Eating, drinking or having sexual intercourse forgetfully. The person doing these forgetfully should be reminded of his fast by those who see him doing these, if the person has the capacity to continue his fast — not to remind him is an act 'disliked' by the law. If, however, he lacks capacity to continue his fast, it is

[184] Al-Ghazālī, however, says, "If the new moon [of the month Ramaḍān] is seen in one town but is not seen in another, and the distance between the two is less than two day's journey, the people of both towns are required to fast; but if the distance is more than two days' journey, every town will have its own legal ruling and the necessity of fasting will not pass from one town to another." See al-Ghazālī, *Iḥyā'*, I, 232.

better not to remind him. [4] Occurrence of emission as a result of a fasting man's looking with excitment at an object of sex or his thought about sex, even though his look and thought have been prolonged. [5] Application of oil to the body of the person fasting. [6] Application of collirium to the eye, even though it went down to the throat where its taste is felt. [7] cupping. [8] Backbiting of someone.[185] [9] Making the intention to nullify the fast but not actually nullifying it. [10] Entering of smoke into the throat without its being the result of one's own action. [11-12] Entering of dust — even though the dust of flour mill — or a fly into the throat. [13] Feeling, in the state of remembering the fast, the taste of medicine applied to the throat. [14] To be in the state of major legal impurity in the morning, and even to pass the whole day in that state. [15-16] Pouring of water or oil on the opening of the penis or a woman's genitalia. [17] Entering of water into the ear as a result of diving in a river, pond, and so on. [18] Poking into the ear with a woodstick or some similar thing and the coming out of dirt as a result of it; the inserting of it repeatedly into the ear. [19] The coming of mucus into the nose, allowing it to go into the throat deliberately and the swallowing of it. Phlegm should be thrown out so that fasting may not be corrupted according to the opinion of Imām Shāfi'ī.[186] [20] Vomiting which could not be checked, and its recurring of itself, without being caused by an action on the part of the fasting person. Fasting is not corrupted by such vomiting even though it has filled the mouth. This is the correct view. [21] Vomiting less than the fill of the mouth as a result of exciting oneself. This is the correct view. Repetition of this also will not corrupt fasting, according to the correct opinion. [22] Eating of that which is between the two teeth and it is less than the measure of a pea. [23] Chewing of a thing like sesame from the exterior part of the

[185] There is a controversy as to whether or not backbiting corrupts a fast. Sufyān ath-Thawrī maintains that it does corrupt. Bishr ibn Ḥārith has transmitted this from him. Layth ibn Abī Sulaym (d. between 754 A.D. and 760 A.D./136 A.H. and 143 A.H.; cf. Ibn Sa'd, *Ṭabaqāt*, VI, 243-44; Ibn al-'Imād, *Shadharāt adh-Dhahab*, I, 207, 212) has narrated from Mujāhid who said: two things corrupt a fast — backbiting and falsehood. Al-Ghazālī holds the same view. A fasting man should safeguard his tongue against unnecessary talk, falsehood, backbiting, calumny, quarrel, and so on. The Prophet said, "Fasting is like a shield; so whenever one of you fasts let him not speak obscenely or act foolishly; if anyone attacks him or rebukes him he should say: I am fasting, I am fasting, [so I cannot reply to you] " (al-Bukhārī, *Ṣaḥīḥ*, Ṣawm, 2; Muslim, *Ṣaḥīḥ*, Ṣiyām, 162f.). A fasting man should speak little and be occupied with rememberance of God and recitation of the Qur'ān.

[186] For an account of Imām Shāfi'ī see al-Ghazālī, *Iḥyā'*, I, 24-27.

mouth until it is reduced to nothing, and no taste of it is felt inside the throat.

ACTS WHICH CORRUPT FASTING AND 'REQUIRE' BOTH ATONEMENT AND RE-OBSERVANCE

There are twenty-two acts which, if a fasting individual performs any of them willingly and without being compelled, corrupt his fasting and require atonement for it as well as the re-observance of it on another day. These acts are the following.

[1] Sexual intercourse whether done in the genitals or in the anus. It corrupts the fasting of the doer as well as the fasting of the person with whom it is done. [2-3] Eating or drinking something. It is all the same whether the thing eaten or drunk is considered food or medicine. [4] The swallowing up of rain that has entered into the mouth. [5] The eating of raw meat except when it is maggoty. [6] The eating of fat according to the view of the jurist Abū l-Layth. [7] The eating of cured meat. This is the view agreed upon by all jurists. [8] The eating of corn and crunching it dry. However, the chewing of a grain of wheat until it is reduced to nothing does not corrupt fasting. [9] The swallowing up of a sesame seed or the like from the exterior part of the mouth. [10] The eating of Armenian clay absolutely. [11] The eating, like a child, of any other clay if the habit of eating it is formed. [12] The eating of a little salt. [13-14] The swallowing of saliva of one's wife or one's friend, but not of others. [15-19] The deliberate eating of anything after backbiting or cupping, or after touching or kissing someone with excitement as a result of which no emission has occurred, or after the application of oil to one's moustache, imagining, in all these cases, that the fasting has already been corrupted by these acts. However, deliberate eating, after a jurist has passed legal opinion that these acts have already corrupted the fast, is not harmful to the fast. Likewise, deliberate eating by the fasting man, after coming across a prophetic tradition which apparently says that these acts corrupt fasting but he did not know the deep interpretation of the Tradition by the jurists, does not corrupt fasting. [20] But if he knows the interpretation, atonement is 'required' of him for eating deliberately and thus corrupting the fast. [21] Atonement is 'required' of a fasting woman who unwillingly obeys a man in sexual activity.

ATONEMENT FOR CORRUPTION OF FASTING. WHAT DROPS ATONEMENT FROM RESPONSIBILITY

[The acts mentioned in the preceding section necessitate atonement as well as re-observance of fasting. In the present section atonement is defined and things related to it are described. There are certain cases where atonement is not necessary; only re-observance is sufficient].

Atonement is not a responsibility in the case of [a] a woman who fails to fast either because of menstruation or because of childbirth bleeding, and [b] an individual who could not fast a day because of such sickness as 'permits' him to nullify his fasting on that day. [In all these cases what is 'necessary' is only the re-observance of fasting.]

Atonement is not a responsibility of a person who has nullified his fasting for difficulty, in a journey, after fasting became 'obligatory' upon him when he was stationary.

Atonement for nullification of a single day of the Ramaḍān fast is the emancipation of a slave even though he or she is not a believer. In the case of inability to emancipate a slave, one has to fast two months consecutively — during these two months there must not be the Festival Day on the expiry of the month Ramaḍān, the Festival Day of the Sacrifice of Animals, and the Days of Drying the Meat, i.e. the eleventh, twelfth and thirteenth of the lunar month Dhū l-Ḥijja. Should one be unable to accomplish this, one has [1] to feed with satiety sixty poor people either one day both in the morning and the evening, or in two mornings only, or in two evenings only, or one day both in the evening and before the dawn; or [2] to give away to each of the sixty poor people half a *ṣā'* of wheat or flour or gruel of parched barley, or one *ṣā'* of date or barley, or the price of any of these.

One atonement is sufficient for several acts of sexual intercourse done on many days or for several acts of voluntary eating done on many days — even though these days are days of Ramaḍān of two different years — and if no atonement has intervened between these several times of sexual intercourse or between several times of voluntary eating. [This is because atonement is prescribed as a deterrent against these prohibited acts, and this deterrent is achieved if atonement be made once at the end of several of these acts.] But if an atonement has intervened between two acts of sexual intercourse or between two acts of voluntary eating, this one atonement will not be sufficient, because in this case no deterrent has been effected for the sexual intercourse or for the voluntary eating done the second time. For this second time it is necessary to make atonement again.

ACTS WHICH CORRUPT FASTING BUT DO NOT REQUIRE ATONEMENT

The following acts nullify fasting 'requiring' its re-observance but not atonement:

A fasting individual's eating of rice or flour or much of salt at a time or the stone of a fruit or cotton or paper or an uncooked quince or a raw walnut. Swallowing of a pebble or soil.

Taking of an injection or application of medicine to the nostril. Forceful pouring of anything inside the throat — this is the most correct view. Dripping of oil or water in the ear — this is the most correct view. Application of medicine to a wound in the belly or in the head and its reaching inside the belly or the brain. Entering of rain or snow into the throat and not swallowing it by one's own action — this is the most correct view. Nullifying the fast mistakenly by the slipping of water for rinsing the mouth into the throat. Nullifying the fast under compulsion even though the nullification is made by sexual intercourse. A woman's doing sexual intercourse under compulsion. Nullifying of fast by a woman, whether a female servant or a wife, for fear of falling ill, and thus of being unable to serve others.

Pouring of water into the stomach when one is asleep. Eating of anything deliberately after eating something forgetfully, even though one knows the Tradition concerning it[187] — this is the most correct view. To do sexual intercourse first forgetfully and then deliberately. Eating of anything after the making of the intention of fasting at daytime — the intention not being made at night. Being on a journey in the morning and then making the intention of being 'stationary', and then eating anything. Starting of a journey after being 'stationary' in the morning, and then eating something.

Abstention from eating, drinking and sexual gratification neither with the intention of fasting nor with the intention of not-fasting. Taking the last night meal or doing sexual intercourse doubting that the day has not yet broken, whereas in reality it has broken. Breaking the fast imagining that the sun has set, whereas really it has not set.[188]

Occurrence of emission as a result of the fasting man's sexual intercourse with a dead person or an animal, or as a result of his use

[187] The prophetic tradition is: "A fasting man who, forgetting his fast, has eaten or drunk anything, should complete his fast." See ash-Shurunbalālī, *Marāqī*, p. 265.

[188] A fasting person should be very careful in deciding about daybreak and sunset. Nothing contrary to fast should be done at these times, except after reflection and careful judgement. See al-Ghazālī, *Iḥyā'*, I, 233.

of the thigh or adoption of any other device or his kissing or touching someone with excitement. Nullifying of a fast other than the Ramaḍān fast observed in the month Ramaḍān. Sexual intercourse with a woman asleep. Dripping of anything into the genitalia of a woman; this is the most correct legal view. Inserting a finger wet with water or oil into the anus or into the inner part of a woman's genitalia. Inserting a piece of cotton or similar thing into the anus or into the interior part of a woman's genitalia to such an extent that it disappeared.

Inserting smoke into the body through one's own action. Exciting one's vomiting even though it is less than the fill of one's mouth. According to the jurist Abū Yūsuf, however, vomiting must be of a mouthful — this is the correct view. Causing the automatic vomiting, which is mouthful, to repeat; this is while remembering fasting. Eating of that which is between one's teeth and which is of the measure of a pea. Making the intention of fasting at daytime after eating or drinking anything forgetfully before renewing the intention at daytime. Being senseless even though throughout the month Ramaḍān; there is, however, no need to reobserve the fasting of that day on which or in the night of which the state of senselessness started. Being mad for a number of days which are less than the whole month Ramaḍān; it is not necessary to re-observe the fasting of this duration because of the mad man's coming to his senses for a night or for a day after the passing of the time for making the intention of fasting of that day — this is the correct view.

FASTING PART OF THE DAY

If a person's fasting is corrupted at sometime on a day of Ramaḍān, he is 'required' by the law to abstain, like a man fasting, from eating, drinking and gratification of sexual desire in the remaining part of the day. The same is also required of [a] a menstruating woman and [b] a woman with childbirth bleeding who both became free from their bleeding after the daybreak, [c] a child who reached the age of maturity at sometime of a day of Ramaḍān, and [d] an infidel who has accepted Islam after the passing of a part of a day of Ramaḍān. All these people, except the last two, will have to observe the fasting of that day after the expiry of the month Ramaḍān.

ACTS 'DISLIKED', ACTS NOT 'DISLIKED', AND ACTS 'PRAISEWORTHY' TO A FASTING INDIVIDUAL

It is 'disliked' by the law that a fasting individual does any of the following seven deeds:

1-2. Tasting anything and chewing it without an excuse. 3. Chewing of chewing gum. 4-5. Kissing and touching anyone with sexual excitement if there is no surety that these will not cause emission or sexual intercourse. 6. Keeping saliva together in the mouth and then swallowing of it. 7. Any such act as is imagined to weaken fasting, e.g. drawing of blood and cupping.

There are nine activities the performance of which by a fasting person is not 'disliked' by the law. They are the following. 1-2. Kissing and touching someone if there is surety, as in the case of an old man who has firm control over himself, that these will not cause emission or sexual intercourse.[189] 3. Application of oil to moustache. 4. Use of collirium in the eye. 5. Cupping. 6. Drawing of blood. 7. Cleaning the teeth by using a tooth-stick in the afternoon — rather this is sunna like the use of the tooth-stick in the morning —, even though the tooth-stick is raw or wet with water. 8. Rinsing of the mouth and snuffing of water for a purpose other than ritual ablution. 9. Washing of the entire body, and wrapping oneself with a wet cloth for cold — a view on which legal decision has been given.

The following acts are 'praiseworthy' to a fasting individual.

1. Taking of a meal in order to strengthen oneself for fasting. 2. Delaying the meal to a time just before the daybreak.[190] 3. Breaking the fast quickly[191] after the sunset if the sky is not cloudy.

ACCIDENTAL CIRCUMSTANCES AND FASTING

The law permits certain people to nullify the Ramaḍān fast or not to

[189] Even though there is surety that as a result of kissing or touching someone seminal emission or sexual intercourse will not occur, it is better not to do these. See al-Ghazālī, *Iḥyā'*, I, 233.

[190] There are extremists who do excess to their carnal soul (*nafs*) either by not taking a meal for fasting at all, or by taking it much earlier than just before the daybreak. This is prohibited since it is against moderation. The Prophet and all his companions used to take a meal in order to find strength for fasting the next day, and they used to delay the taking of the meal; the delay was to such an extent that the time intervening between taking the meal and the daybreak was equal to the time in which one could recite about fifty Qur'ānic verses (cf. al-Bukhārī, *Ṣaḥīḥ*, Ṣawm, 19; an-Nasā'ī, *Sunan*, Ṣiyām, 28, 20). The Prophet commanded, "Take a meal before the daybreak, for there is blessing in it" (al-Bukhārī, *Ṣaḥīḥ*, Ṣawm, 2; Muslim, *Ṣaḥīḥ*, Ṣiyām, 45). He further said: what distinguishes our fasting from that of the people of the Book [i.e. Jews and Christians] is the taking of a meal before the daybreaks. See Muslim, *Ṣaḥīḥ*, Ṣiyām, 46.

[191] There are extremists who, being overcautious, make delay in breaking their fasts even though the sky is not cloudy. The sunna is to break the fast promptly after the sunset. The Prophet said, "People will remain on the side of the good so long as they break their fast promptly." See al-Bukhārī, *Ṣaḥīḥ*, Bad' al-Waḥy, 5; Muslim, *Ṣaḥīḥ*, Faḍā'il, 50.

observe it. They are considered to have excuses. They are the following:

1. A sick person who fears that fasting may aggravate his sickness or delay the healing of his wounds. 2-3. A pregnant woman and a suckling woman who fear that fasting may cause impairing of the intellect or destruction or sickness to themselves or to the child a pregnant woman is bearing or a suckling woman is suckling, whether it is her own child or of another woman. Their fear will be considered genuine should it predominate in their minds and be based on their own experiences or on the information of an experienced upright Muslim physician. 3. One suffering from unbearable thirst, or from such a strong hunger as may destroy one.

A person on a journey is allowed by the law not to fast. However, to fast is better for him provided fasting does not harm him, and provided most of his companions are also fasting and he is paying his own expenses separately. If they are paying jointly or are not fasting, it is better for him not to fast in agreement with the party.

An individual who has an excuse of disease or being on a journey or the like, as mentioned above, and who is dying before his excuse is removed, is not required by the law to order his heirs by will to pay ransom (*fidya*) for the fasting he could not observe. If those who have an excuse have, before death, time in which their excuse is inapplicable, they will observe as many unobserved fasts as are possible to observe in that measure of time in which they remain without excuse by being stationary or by being healthy. [If they do not observe fasts in that time, they must order their heirs by a will to pay ransom for them.]

It is not a stipulation that the observance of fasting on other days after Ramaḍān by those who failed to fast in Ramaḍān with real excuses, be made consecutively. [Thus one who could not fast ten days in Ramaḍān with an excuse may fast these ten days later separately — ten days, for example, in ten months.] If another Ramaḍān has come in before the completion of the observance of the fasting of the previous Ramaḍān, fasting of the new Ramaḍān will be observed first, and no redemption (*fidya*) is needed for delay in the observance of the fasting of the previous Ramaḍān.

A very old man and a very old woman are 'permitted' by the law not to fast in the month Ramaḍān. They must redeem themselves from this by almsgiving of half a *ṣā'* of wheat for every day of fasting. Similar is the case of a person who promised to God by a vow to fast perpetually but who has, after fasting for sometime, become too weak to continue. Such a person will discontinue his fasting and redeem himself by giving away half a *ṣā'* of wheat for each day. In case of his inability to redeem himself because of his poverty, he will seek forgiveness of God and recind his vow.

If the redemption for the break of a compact confirmed by swearing by God or for murder is 'required' of a person but he is unable to redeem by emancipation of a slave and he is also very old, or redemption was 'required' of him long ago when he had the physical strength to redeem by fasting as a substitute of emancipation but he did not fast until he has now become very old — in both cases the law permits him [not to fast for redemption of the break of the compact or of murder and] to redeem the non-observance of this fasting by giving as alms half a *ṣā'* of wheat for every day, because fasting here is a substitute for something else, i.e. the emancipation of a slave.

A person observing 'supererogatory' fasting is 'permitted' by the law to nullify his fast even though he has no excuse for it. Entertainment is obviously an excuse for the guest as well as the host. Therefore, both can nullify their 'supererogatory' fasting for this excuse. A 'supererogatory' fast which is nullified must be observed on another day. If, however, it is on any of the five days — the Festival Day on the expiry of Ramaḍān, the Festival Day of the Sacrifice of Animals, and the Days of Drying the Meat — no observance of it for its nullification is necessary.

ACCOMPLISHMENT OF VOWS

A person who has promised to God any act by a vow must accomplish the act, if it meets three stipulations:

[1] The act is of a category which also comprises legally 'necessary' acts, [2] it is intended by the person vowing it, and [3] it is not itself a legally 'necessary' act. Therefore, one who has promised to God by a vow to perform ritual ablution or prostration due to Qur'ān-recitation or to visit a patient or to perform any legally 'necessary' acts, is not required to do any of these things. The vow of them is not correct.

It is correct to make a vow of solitary devotion in a mosque (*i'tikāf*), of non-obligatory ritual prayers and, of fasting. If these acts are promised by a vow absolutely, or the promise is made dependent upon a certain stipulation and the stipulation is fulfilled, then in either case the accomplishment of the vow is 'necessary'.

It is correct to promise to God by a vow to fast on the Festival Day on the expiry of Ramaḍān, the Festival Day of the Sacrifice of Animals, and the Days of Drying the Meat. Fasting, of course, must be observed, not on these, but on other days. If, however, it is observed on these days, the vow is accomplished thereby, but the man has committed a sin since fasting on these days is 'unlawful'.

In a vow, fixation of time, of place, of type of money and of the identity of a poor man is not binding. Therefore, fasting in the lunar month Rajab will do instead of the vow of fasting in the lunar month Sha'bān; performance of two *rak'as* of ritual prayer in Egypt is sufficient for the vow of their performance in Mecca; giving away of any silver coin will do instead of the vow of giving away of a fixed type of silver coin; almsgiving to the poor man[192] 'Amr is enough for the vow of almsgiving to the poor man Zayd.

Should a vow be suspended on a stipulation, its accomplishment before the occurrence of the stipulation is of no avail. It needs to be accomplished again after the stipulation is fulfilled.

I'TIKĀF — SECLUSION FOR COMPLETE DEVOTION IN A MOSQUE

I'tikāf means staying, with the intention of seclusion for complete devotion, at a mosque in which congregation is actually held for ritual prayers of five times daily. It is not valid in a mosque in which congregation for ritual prayer is not held. A woman will observe i'tikāf in that place in her house which she has fixed for ritual prayer.

I'tikāf is of three kinds: 1. 'Required' i'tikāf. It is the i'tikāf one promises to God to observe as vow at a particular time. 2. 'Emphasized sunna' i'tikāf. It is that i'tikāf which is to be observed during the last ten days of Ramaḍān.[193] 3. 'Praiseworthy' i'tikāf. It

[192] The day one fasts one should also do other forms of good works, especially almsgiving, so that their reward may be multiplied through the blessings of the day of fasting. The prophet Muḥammad was very generous in the month Ramaḍān; he appeared to be faster than the wind in the act of almsgiving. See al-Ghazālī, *Iḥyā'*, I, 233; Ibn Qayyim, *Zād al-Ma'ād*, 2nd ed., Egypt, 1369/1950, I, 154.

In the month Ramaḍān Muslims should vie with one another in almsgiving, rememberance of God, Qur'ān-reading, repentance, and so on. All this will add to the life and spirt of fasting which consist in piety and purity. Concerning a lifeless fast, the Prophet said, "Many a man gets nothing out of his fast except hunger and thirst." See Ibn Māja, *Sunan*, Ṣiyām, 21.

[193] The prophet Muḥammad observed it in every Ramaḍān. It was his custom, upon the arrival of the last ten days of the month Ramaḍān, to roll up his mattress, fasten his mantle around his waist, and, making his family to do the same, continue in his worship until the end of the ten-day period (al-Bukhārī, *Ṣaḥīḥ*, I'tikāf, 17, 14, 1, 6; Muslim, *Ṣaḥīḥ*, I'tikāf, 1-4), since during these ten-days the Night of Decree (*Laylat al-Qadr*) falls. More probably the Night of Decree falls on an odd night; most likely among these is the twenty-first, or the twenty-third, or the twenty-fifth, or the

is the i'tikāf which is observed at a time other than the last ten days of Ramaḍān. Fasting is a stipulation for the validity of the first kind of i'tikāf only. The smallest duration for a 'praiseworthy' i'tikāf is a very small time even though it is by walking through the mosque — a view on which legal decision has been given.

The man observing i'tikāf will not come out of the mosque except [1] for a religious need, such as the performance of the Friday Assembly Prayer, renewal of ablution, and funeral prayer, [2] or for a natural need like relieving himself,[194] [3] or for such necessities as demolition of the mosque, compulsion by an oppressor to come out of the mosque, and fear for his own life or for his belongings from rogues — for these necessities he may come out of this mosque and enter into another at that very moment. If he comes out for a moment without an excuse, the 'required' quality of the i'tikāf will be corrupted and it will come to an end being a 'supererogatory' i'tikāf.

It is correct for a person observing i'tikāf to eat, drink and sleep and to contract for the purchase of anything he needs for himself or for his family, in the mosque. But to make the thing purchased present in the mosque is 'disliked' by the law. Concluding a contract of purchase as a trade is also 'disliked'. Likewise, it is 'disliked' to keep silent about a matter believed to be a good work and to speak except for something good. Sexual intercourse and acts that lead one to it are 'unlawful' to him. I'tikāf is nullified by sexual intercourse and by the occurrence of emission caused by acts leading to sexual intercourse.

The vow of observance of I'tikāf in days requires its observance in the nights of the days as well. Vow of its observance at nights involves days successively, even though succession is not made a stipulation when vowing. Observance of i'tikāf in two nights is necessary for the vow of its observance in two days. Making the intention of observance of i'tikāf in days especially, without nights, is legally correct.

I'tikāf is prescribed by the Qur'ān and the Sunna. If performed sincerely for God, it is one of the noblest acts. Its benefits are:

twenty-seventh. The Night of Decree is more excellent than one thousand months (Qur'ān 97:3-5); the merit of worship in it increases accordingly. See al-Ghazālī, *Iḥyā'*, I, 233.

194 The prophet Muḥammad did not go out of the mosque except for answering the call of nature (al-Bukhārī, *Ṣaḥīḥ*, I'tikāf, 4) and, on his way [from and back to the mosque], he did not inquire about the sick except as he passed by [without stopping]. See Abū Dāwūd, *Sunan*, I'tikāf, 4, Ṣawm, 80.

making the mind free from worldly affairs, submission of oneself to the Master, persistence in devotion to Him in His house [which is the mosque], and fortification of oneself with His stronghold. [195] 'Aṭā' [196] said, "The man observing i'tikāf is like one who repeatedly comes to the door of a great man to have his needs fulfilled. The man observing i'tikāf as it were entreats to God: I shall not leave Your house, i.e. the mosque, until You forgive me." This is the most that a humble man can do to obtain the kindness of his Master, the Strong, the Most Powerful.

[195] Concerning the benefit of i'tikāf Shāh Walī Allāh (*Ḥujja*, II, 534) says; "Since i'tikāf in the mosque is a means of concentration of the mind on God, of purification of the soul, of obtaining free time for devotional acts, of effecting resemblance with the angels [who are in continuous worship of God], and of finding [an opportunity to worship in] the Night of Decree, the Prophet (may God bless him and greet him!) observed i'tikāf in the last ten days of Ramaḍān and made it a sunna for those who are pious among his people." A more elaborate description of the benefit of i'tikāf is given by Ibn Qayyim in his *Zād al-Ma'ād*, I, 170-71.

[196] 'Aṭā' ibn Abī Rabāḥ was a prominent representative of the ancient Meccan school of Islamic religious law. Already in his lifetime his reputation spread far beyond Mecca, and Imām Abū Ḥanīfa states that he was present in his lecture meetings. 'Aṭā' died in 114 or 115 A.H./732 or 733 A.D. at a very old age. For an account of him see Schacht, "'Aṭā' b. Abī Rabāḥ", *EI*², I, 730; Ibn Ḥajar al-'Asqalānī, *Tahdhīb at-Tahdhīb*, VII, Hyderabad, 1326 A.H., 199ff.

V

DIVINE TAX *(ZAKĀ)*

فاقيموا الصلاة واتوا الزكاة واعتصموا بالله. هو مولاكم
فنعم المولى ونعم النصير! ــ القران ٢٢:٧٨

Perform ritual prayer, pay divine tax and hold fast to God. He is your Master. How excellent is the Master and how excellent is the Helper! — Qur'ān 22:78

Divine tax (*zakā*) is that tax which is made 'obligatory' by God [197] and which is to be paid to a particular person or particular persons possessing certain special characteristics. [198] It is not a tax payable to any other individual or for the welfare of any institution which is not a person.

STIPULATIONS FOR, AND RATES OF, DIVINE TAX

Divine tax is 'obligatory' on a free Muslim responsible to fulfil religious obligations and possessed of wealth equivalent to a certain minimum (*niṣāb*), [199] whether this wealth is money or gold or silver or ornaments or utensils of gold or of silver or articles of merchandise of whatever description which equal the value of the certain minimum liable to divine tax. The minimum wealth liable to divine tax must be free from debt and from one's basic necessaries of life, and be such that it increases even if only potentially. [The basic necessities of life are: dwelling houses, articles of clothing, household furniture, cattle kept for immediate use , armour and weapons designed for present use. Books, with respect to scholars, and tools, with respect to handicrafts, are also included in the necessities of life. None of these types of wealth is considered as increasing wealth.]

An individual possessing the qualities mentioned above is 'required' to pay divine tax only if he fulfils the following one stipulation:

Possession of the original minimum (*niṣāb*) liable to divine tax for at least one uninterrupted year. [If at any time during the year the

[197] Qur'ān 22:78. [198] See *infra*, pp. 202ff. [199] See *infra*, pp. 198-201.

individual possesses, not the minimum, but less than this, the year's possession is interrupted, and consequently the obligation of divine tax falls.] [200] As for the produce of the original minimum obtained within the year, it will be added to the same type of wealth, and divine tax will be levied on it, as on the original minimum, on completion of one uninterrupted year for the original minimum. It is all the same whether the produce obtained is by trade, or by inheritance, or by other means.

It is correct to pay divine tax of a certain number of years in advance if the payer possesses the minimum wealth liable to divine tax.

The payment of divine tax is legally considered to be made correctly if the following stipulations are fulfilled when making the payment:

Intention which means that the person paying divine tax should purpose in his mind the payment of divine tax. The intention needs to be made when paying the tax to a beneficiary, or when the payer sets apart the proportion of divine tax from his total wealth for payment at a later convenient time. In this latter case, the intention is found coupled with the payment only in principle, as, for example, where the payer has paid divine tax without any intention, but later made the intention while the divine tax paid is still in the possession of the beneficiary.

It is not a stipulation for the validity of payment of divine tax that the poor man should know that the payment made to him is of divine tax — this is the most correct legal opinion —, so that it is wholly correct if one pays him a sum saying that it is a gift or a loan for him but one has really intended by it the payment of divine tax 'obligatory' upon him.

If a person gives away his whole wealth in charity, without the intention of divine tax, the obligation of divine tax, with respect to him, drops.

Divine tax in respect of loan may be divided into three kinds: strong, moderate and weak. The strong loan is the changing of money and articles of merchandise which the debtor received. He acknowledged this although he possessed nothing, or he disputed the claim of the lender but there was sufficient proof against him. In these cases, divine tax is 'obligatory' upon the lender for all the years passed. Its actual payment will, however, be made later when he recovers from the debtor one-fifth of the minimum for liability of

[200] See Abū Dāwūd, *Sunan*, Zakā, 5.

divine tax (*niṣāb*), i.e. forty dirhams — on which one dirham is due — because the amount less than one-fifth is forgiven, not subject to divine tax. For the recovery of more than forty dirhams also, payment of divine tax is required according to the same reckoning, i.e. one dirham for every forty dirhams and no payment if the amount recovered is less than forty.

The moderate loan is the changing of that which is not for traffic, e.g. the value of wearing cloth, and dwelling house. [This means that these things are sold, and their price is not paid by the buyer until one year has passed.] In this case, divine tax is not required until the lender recovers from the buyer the minimum liable to divine tax (*niṣāb*), i.e. two hundred dirhams. The measure of one uninterrupted year is to be considered from the time when the loan became the responsibility of the buyers.

The weak loan is the changing of that which is not wealth, e.g. dowry, bequest, exchange of the *khul'a* form of divorce,[201] compensation for deliberate murder, indemnity, and cost of labour. In this kind of loan, divine tax is not 'necessary' until the lender receives the minimum liable to divine tax (*niṣāb*) and until one uninterrupted year passed after receiving it.

The above is the view of Imām Abū Ḥanīfa. Imām Abū Yūsuf and Imām Muḥammad maintain that in all three cases of loan mentioned above it is 'necessary' to pay divine tax on whatever amount, small or great, is recovered according to the reckoning.

On the obtaining of an uncertain sort of wealth, it is not 'necessary' to pay divine tax for the years during which it remained uncertain.[202] Examples of such wealth are: usurped property respecting which there is no proof, wealth sunk in the sea, wealth tyrannically confiscated by the government, and a loan given to someone who denied it and there was no proof against him. [On regaining these forms of wealth, their owner is exempted from divine tax on them for the years in which they were uncertain.]

If a person exempts a poor man or any other beneficiary of divine tax from the repayment of the debt, intending that the debt is the payment of divine tax 'obligatory' upon himself, this is not consider-

[201] In this form of divorce an agreement is entered into for the purpose of dissolving a connubial connection, in lieu of a compensation paid by the wife to her husband out of her property. See *Hidāya*, I, 112.

[202] The reason for this is that the cause of the obligation to pay divine tax is the possession of wealth in the state of increase, which cannot be the case but where the owner has an immediate power of management over it. But this does not apply to uncertain wealth or to a traveller who has property at home. See *Hidāya*, I, 3.

ed as payment of divine tax, because delivery does not appear in this case.

It is correct to pay the divine tax on gold and silver (*naqdayn*) by giving to the beneficiaries moveable properties, measurable things and weighable goods, depending on the value of gold or silver. Should the payment be made in kind, i.e. by giving part of the gold or silver itself, what is to be considered is its weight and not price. In the case of money, if an owner should, in lieu of the actual money due, pay the value in other things, it is approved.

[Moveable articles, of whatever description, are subject to divine tax if they are kept with a view to traffic and if, on being appraised, their value amounts to the minimum (*niṣāb*) of gold or silver liable to divine tax. The rate of divine tax in the case of such moveables is: five dirhams on every two hundred dirhams (silver coins) worth of goods.]

The value of moveables will be added to the value of gold or silver. That is to say, if, for instance, the proprieter should have articles estimated at a value of one hundred dirhams and also one hundred dirhams in money, the value of the articles, as above, must be added to the one hundred dirhams, so as that the whole may make the minimum liable to divine tax, i.e. two hundred dirhams; and divine tax is due thereon.

In the same manner, gold is to be added to silver in respect of their value, not quantity. That is to say, both may be resolved into one minimum liable to divine tax (*niṣāb*), not by the respective weight of each, but by a general valuation of both. For example, if a man were possessed of one hundred dirhams in silver, and five *mithqāls* of gold (the value of which would amount to one hundred dirhams), this person would be liable to divine tax.

In the case of moveables, there is no cessation for liability of divine tax in a case where the minimum required for levying divine tax (*niṣāb*) is complete at *both* ends of the year, but is less than it at any time within that period. Thus if a person owns moveable property for trafficking and it is not equivalent to the minimum liable to divine tax, and he has no other form of wealth so as to be added to it in order to complete the moveable property, but at the end of the year the value of his moveable property has risen to the extent of being equal to the minimum — in this case he is not liable to divine tax for this year, because the minimum was not complete at *both* ends of the year.

The minimum liable to divine tax (*niṣāb*) is: for gold twenty *mithqāls*, and for silver two hundred dirhams the weight of every ten of which is equal to the weight of seven *mithqāls*. [No divine tax is due on less than these minimums. The divine tax due upon two hundred dirhams is five dirhams, and on twenty *mithqāls* of gold is one half *mithqāl*. Thus the rate in these forms of wealth is one fortieth of the total wealth.] The rate on an excess above the minimum (*niṣāb*) for gold or the minimum for silver, if the excess reaches at least one-fifth of the minimum, is in proportion to the minimum; [less than one-fifth is not liable to divine tax. Thus in the case of silver, if the excess is forty dirhams, divine tax is due — and it is one dirham; upon the succeeding forty the same divine tax is due, but not on fewer than forty. If the quantity of gold exceeds twenty *mithqāls*, on every four *mithqāls* of such excees is divine tax].

If gold and silver contain some alloy but gold and silver predominate, they are to be accounted as pure gold and silver and the laws of gold and silver apply to them.

No divine tax is levied on jewels and pearls except if one possesses them for trafficking in them. The same is true of all moveables.

If a person possesses measurable things or weighable goods equivalent to the minimum liable to divine tax (*niṣāb*) for *one* year but has not paid the divine tax due on these, and then their value has increased or decreased and now he pays the divine tax in kind — one fourth of one-tenth of them — this is approved by the law. If, however, he now pays the divine tax in value, it is their value on the day of the obligation to pay the divine tax on them that is to be considered; and that day is just the day of the completion of the year; this is the view of Imām Abū Ḥanīfa. Imām Abū Yūsuf and Imām Muḥammad hold the opinion that regard is to be paid to the value on the date of the payment of the divine tax to the beneficiaries.

No bail is necessary for a man who does not pay divine tax when its payment is due and who does not destroy the wealth himself. If, after being possessed by an individual for an uninterrupted year, the whole wealth is destroyed of itself, the divine tax for the year falls. If part of this wealth should be destroyed, the claim of divine tax drops proportionately; the divine tax for the destroyed part of the wealth is forgiven by God. Should the destroyed part not surpass the minimum liable to divine tax, the 'necessity' of payment of divine tax remains as it is.

Divine tax will not be collected by force. Nor will it be collected from the property one leaves behind after death, except if one orders one's heir by will to pay the tax from one's property, in which case it will be collected from one-third of this property. Adoption of a device (*ḥīla*) in order to escape the payment of divine tax is 'permissible' according to the jurist Abū Yūsuf. But this is disliked by the jurist Muḥammad. [203]

PERSONS TO WHOM DIVINE TAX CAN BE PAID

Divine tax can legally be paid to the following categories of Muslims. There is no other beneficiary of this tax. They are specified in a single verse of the Qur'ān. [204]

[1] The poor. He is one possessed of wealth the whole of which amounts to somewhat less than the minimum liable to divine tax (*niṣāb*) or its value, from whatever type of wealth it may be. Such a one is legally considered poor even though he is in sound health and capable of earning wealth. [2] The destitute. He is one who has no wealth whatever. [3] A slave who has made a contract with his master that he will ransom himself by a certain amount of wealth. [4] A debtor whose wealth, after his debt is deducted from it, is less than the minimum liable to divine tax (*niṣāb*) or its value. [5] Those who are striving in the cause of God. They are [a] the warriors who, by poverty, are incapacitated and cut off from taking a part in holy war, and [b] the pilgrims to Mecca who, because of poverty, are incapable of returning home. [6] Wayfarers who have wealth at home but not with them on the journey. They may be paid as much of divine tax as they need to support them in their travel. [7] Those employed in connection with the collection and distribution of divine tax even though they are rich. They may be paid as much out of divine tax as is in proportion to their labour.

203 Abū Yūsuf considered the payment of divine tax from the standpoint of this world. At his time the Islamic state was ruled in accordance with Islamic laws, and the divine tax used to be collected by the state. If a man could carefully devise a method of escaping the payment of divine tax, the political authority could not compel him to pay the tax. The jurist Muḥammad and others, including al-Ghazālī, do not approve of the adoption of a device; they consider the payment of divine tax from the viewpoint of the Hereafter. They say that divine tax is mainly ordained by God in order that the evil quality of miserliness may be removed from man's soul. This quality remains in the mind of a man who escapes the payment through a device. The ruler of this world cannot see this quality existing in the man's soul, but the Ruler of all the rulers (i.e. God) who looks on the soul, sees it and will punish the man on the Day of Judgement. So no one should escape payment throught any device.

204 Qur'ān 9:60 — "Obligatory alms are only for the poor, for the destitute, for those employed in connection with their collection and distribution, for those whose minds are to be reconciled with Islam, for the freeing of slaves, for those burdened with debt, for those striving in the cause of God, and for wayfarers. This is an ordinance from God. God is All-knowing, Wise."

An individual paying divine tax is 'allowed' by the law to pay to all these categories of beneficiaries. He is also 'allowed' to limit his payment to anyone of them, despite the existence of others in his locality.

It is not correct to pay divine tax [1] to an infidel, [2] to a rich man, i.e. one who possesses the minimum wealth liable to divine tax (*niṣāb*) or its value from whatever kind of wealth it may be and which is in excess of his basic needs, [3] to a rich infant, [4] to a person of the family of Hāshim [205] and their freed slaves — the jurist Ṭaḥāwī, however, considers it 'permissible' to pay to the members of Hāshim's family —, [5] to those from whom the payer of divine tax is descended, e.g. his parents, grand-parents, and so on, [6] to those who have descended from him, e.g. his sons and daughters, grandsons, and granddaughters, and so on, [7] to his wife, [8] for the purchase of a shroud for the dead, and [9] in the payment of the payer's own debt.

[If a person employs divine tax on his wealth in the erection of a mosque, his divine tax is not considered as being thereby discharged, because, in the payment of divine tax, it is established as a principle that it should be made over to a person or persons entitled to it; and such delivery does not appear in this case.] [206]

If the payer of divine tax has paid it to a person after due deliberation and thus imagining that he is one of the proper persons to receive divine tax, but later on it has become clear that he is not a really deserving person — in this case divine tax is legally considered to be discharged correctly.

It is 'disliked' by the law to pay as much divine tax to a single poor man as would make him rich, i.e. make him such that he possesses the minimum liable to divine tax (*niṣāb*), after he repays his debt and after he gives each member of his family less than the minimum liable to divine tax. Should the payment of divine tax not elevate him to such a state, this payment is not 'disliked' by the law. It is 'praiseworthy' to pay divine tax to a single poor man to such an extent as may preclude him from the need of begging.

205 Hāshim is the great-grandfather of the Prophet. He gives the name to a Meccan tribe called the tribe of Hāshim. In the context of alms, by the tribe of Hāshim are to be understood the descendants of 'Abbās, Ḥārith and Abū Ṭālib. Descendants of Abū Ṭālib are those who descended from 'Alī, Ja'far and 'Aqīl. They are endowed with some special attributes for which they are considered too exalted to accept divine tax or any alms. This opinion is based on a statement of the Prophet, "Alms for the family of Muḥammad are unlawful, because alms are made of men's filth." See an-Nasā'ī, *Sunan*, Zakā, 98; Muslim, *Ṣaḥīḥ*, Zakā, 167f.; also see *Hidāya*, I, 21.

206. *Hidāya*, I,20.

It is 'disliked' by the law to transfer the wealth of divine tax to a city other than the payer's own. The transfer, however, is 'permissible' if it is made for those who are the relatives of the payer, those who are more needy than the inhabitants of his own city, those who are more pious,[207] and those who are more beneficent to Muslims by imparting useful knowledge.[208]

The best is to pay divine tax [1] first to such a deserving one who is nearest to the payer among all his blood-kindred[209] with whom his or her marriage relationship is not made lawful by Islam, [2] then to his neighbour, [3] then to the people of his locality, [4] then to the people of his own occupation, and finally [5] to the people of his own city. Shaykh Abū Ḥafṣ al-Kabīr said, "The almsgiving of a man is not received by God until he starts it with his needy relatives and meets their needs."

DIVINE TAX OF THE DAY OF 'ĪD AL-FIṬR

فرض رسول اللهم صلى الله عليه وسلم ذكواة الفطر من رمضان.

The Messenger of God (may God bless and greet him!) made it 'obligatory' to pay the divine tax of the Festival Day on the expiry of Ramaḍān.[210]

At the dawn of the day of 'Īd al-Fiṭr (the Festival Day on the expiry

[207] The pious should be given preference over the impious, because payment of divine tax to the pious will be an aid to them in their pious living, and through this aid the payer will be a sharer in their acts of piety. It is for this reason that the Prophet said, "Do not partake except of the food of a pious man, and let no one partake of yours except the pious" (cf. at-Tirmidhī, *Sunan*, Zuhd, 56; Abū Dāwūd, *Sunan*, Adab, 16), "Set your food before the pious and bestow your favours upon the believers." See Ibn al-Mubārak, *al-Birr wa ṣ-Ṣila*.

[208] The learned men who, with good intention, acquire useful knowledge and impart it, need to be given special consideration, because help to them is in effect help to "search after knowledge which is the noblest of all devotional acts (*'ibādāt*) when it is coupled with sound intention." See al-Ghazālī, *Iḥyā'*, I, 219.

[209] When paying divine tax or supererogatory alms, preference should be given to the deserving blood-kindred, for by paying to them the payer does a favour towards them as well as pays the tax. The doing of favour towards them is enjoined in the Qur'ān (33:6, 47:22). 'Alī, the fourth caliph of Islam, said: I had rather give one of my brothers a single dirham than give twenty dirhams in alms to others; I had rather give my brother twenty than give away a hundred in alms to others; I had rather give him a hundred dirhams than emancipate a slave (al-Ghazālī, *Iḥyā*, I, 220). When Abū Ṭalḥa al-Anṣārī (d. 34 A.H./654-55 A.D.) became too much occupied with his garden, he announced his intention to give it away as 'supererogatory' alms, the Prophet advised, "It is better that you give it to your relatives." So he settled the garden on his cousins, Ḥassān Ibn Thābit (d. 54 A.H./674 A.D.) and Abū Qatāda (d. 54 A.H./674 A.D.). See al-Bukhārī, *Ṣaḥīḥ*, Zakā, 45.

[210] Al-Bukhārī, *Ṣaḥīḥ*, Zakā, 70f., 77; Muslim, *Ṣaḥīḥ*, Zakā, 12f., 16.

of the lunar month Ramaḍān), divine tax of that day (*zakāt al-fiṭr*) becomes 'obligatory' upon every free Muslim possessed of the minimum wealth (*niṣāb*) liable to the yearly divine tax or its value, even though it is not possessed for one uninterrupted year, and this wealth or its value is not possessed for trade and is free from debt and from the basic necessities of himself and the members of his family. Basic necessities mean those things which one needs for sufficiency only; they are house, furniture, clothes, horse and other means of transport, weapons, and tools for work.

Such a Muslim as just described is 'required' by the law to pay the divine tax of the day of 'Īd al-Fiṭr [1] for himself and [2] for his small poor children — if these small children are rich, possessed of independent property, this divine tax will be paid out of their wealth. The grandfather is not under an obligation to pay for these small poor children. Another view, however, is that the grandfather takes the place of the father when the latter is absent or poor.

The divine tax of the day of 'Īd al-Fiṭr need not be paid by a Muslim for his mature offspring although they form a part of his family, or for his wife. If, however, he disburses this divine tax on behalf of his wife or adult offspring , without their desire, it is 'lawful', on a principle of benevolence, their consent being by custom understood.[211]

The divine tax of the day of 'Īd al-Fiṭr is half a *ṣā'* of wheat or its flour or gruel of parched barley, or one *ṣā'* of dried date or raisin or barley. A *ṣā'* consists of eighty Iraqi *raṭls*; a *raṭl* is about fourteen ounces. It is 'permissible' to pay the value of these things in cash. This is better when the things needed by the poor are available easily — better because the payment of value in terms of money enables them to meet their needs more quickly. At the time of hardship, however, giving of wheat, barley and such other things as are used as food is better than the payment of value in terms of money.

The time when this divine tax becomes 'obligatory' upon a Muslim is the dawn of the day of 'Īd al-Fiṭr. [That is to say, the arrival of that appointed period is the condition of the obligation of this tax.] Therefore, one who died or became poor on the eve of this period, is not 'required' by the law to pay this divine tax. Nor will it be paid by one who, after this period, became a Muslim or rich or was born.

It is 'praiseworthy' to pay this divine tax before one proceeds towards the place of performance of the ritual prayer for 'Īd al-

[211] *Hidāya*, I, 23.

Fiṭr.[212] Its payment before or after this period is correct. Payment after this period is, however, 'disliked' by the law; yet it must be made, for the obligation continues until it is discharged.

This divine tax payable by one individual should be paid to one poor man. Jurists have disagreed on whether or not it is 'permissible' to divide this divine tax payable by one individual among several poor men. It is correct to pay this divine tax payable by a group of individuals to a single poor man — this is the correct view.

[212] The 'obligatory' alms of 'Īd al-Fiṭr are to be expended in the same way as the divine tax (*zakā*). Thus these alms can only be given to the eight categories of people to whom divine tax can correctly be paid. See al-Ghazālī, *Iḥyā'*, I, 211.

VI
PILGRIMAGE

ولله على الناس حج البيت من استطاع اليه سبيلا؛ ومن كفر فان الله غنى عن العالمين.ـ القران ٣:٩٧

Pilgrimage to the Holy House is a duty laid upon people which they owe to God — those of them who can afford the journey to it. Those who repudiate it should remember that God is certainly independent of all creatures. — Qur'ān 3:97

قال رسول الله، صلى الله عليه وسلم: الحج المبرور ليس له جزاء الا الجنة

The Prophet (may God bless him and greet him!) said, "Paradise is the only reward for a pilgrimage accepted by God." [213]

DEFINITION

Pilgrimage (*ḥajj*) means a visit to Mecca and performance therein of a special type of devotional act during the months of pilgrimage, which are the lunar months Shawwāl, Dhū l-Qa'da, and the first ten days of Dhū l-Ḥijja.

STIPULATIONS FOR THE OBLIGATION OF PILGRIMAGE

Pilgrimage becomes 'obligatory' once in a person's lifetime. If it has become 'obligatory' it needs to be performed immediately; this is the most correct view. Some legal authorities, however, maintain that it can be delayed to a later part of life.

Pilgrimage becomes 'obligatory' upon a person should he fulfil eight stipulations. This is the most correct view. These stipulations are as follows:

[1] Islam. [2] Sanity. Pilgrimage can only be 'obligatory' upon one who is a sane person. [3] Maturity. A person who is a major can be under an obligation in respect of pilgrimage. [4] Freedom. Pilgrimage can be 'obligatory' upon a person who is free, not slave. [5] Pilgrimage can be 'obligatory' only in the time of pilgrimage. [6] A

[213] Al-Bukhārī, *Ṣaḥīḥ*, 'Umra, 1; Muslim, *Ṣaḥīḥ*, Ḥajj, 437; at-Tirmidhī, *Sunan*, 2, 88; an-Nasā'ī, *Sunan*, Ḥajj, 3, 5f,; Ibn Māja, *Sunan*, Manāsik, 3.

person's ability for a moderate degree[214] of maintenance of himself and his family until his return home, although he is in Mecca. [7] Ability regarding transport special to the person, or regarding transport which partly belongs to him by ownership or by hiring, but not by obtaining free of charge or by borrowing; this is for those who are not dwellers in Mecca and who are not living in the neighbourhood of these dwellers, if it is possible for them to walk without any difficulty; otherwise transport is absolutely necessary. The ability regarding transport must be additional [a] to the ability to maintain oneself and one's family until one's return home, [b] to provide one's essential things such as house and its furniture, and the instruments of one's occupation, and [c] to repay debt. [8] For a person who has accepted Islam in a non-Muslim country, it is a stipulation that he knows that pilgrimage is 'obligatory'.

STIPULATIONS REGARDING THE 'NECESSITY' OF PERFORMANCE OF PILGRIMAGE

Even though pilgrimage is 'obligatory' upon a person its actual performance is not 'necessary' for him at a particular time unless he satisfies five stipulations. That these stipulations are five in number is the most correct view. The legal authorities have mentioned these stipulations as follows.

[1] Bodily health. A sick man or woman on whom pilgrimage is 'obligatory' is 'required' to perform it only after he or she recovers his or her bodily health. [2] Absence of all other physical obstacles to one's going on pilgrimage. [3] The way to Mecca must be safe. [4] In the case of a widow or a divorced woman, she must not be in the legal period of retirement assigned to her before she can marry again. [5] In the case of a woman, a man who cannot legally marry her (*muḥarram*), even though this is because of suckling or marriage relationship, must be prepared to accompany her in the pilgrimage in order to take care of her; this man must be a Muslim, trustworthy, sane and major. Or the husband of a woman, if she is married, must be prepared to go with her.

Concerning safety on the way to Mecca as mentioned above what is 'required' by the law is safety for the most part in the land or the sea. This is the view on which the legal decision has been given.

STIPULATIONS FOR THE VALIDITY OF PERFORMANCE OF PILGRIMAGE

Pilgrimage is legally considered to be performed correctly if a person

[214] See *supra*, p. 54.

has performed four things in his pilgrimage. [1] *Iḥrām*. This will be discussed later. [2] Islam. The pilgrim has performed the pilgrimage in the condition of being a Muslim. These two stipulations are meant for the validity of a pilgrimage. In addition to the fulfilment of them, the pilgrim must do the following two things which are the two pillars of pilgrimage. [1] The rite of halting, in the state of a pilgrim's being in *iḥrām*, at 'Arafa for a moment between the passing of the sun its meridian of the ninth of the lunar month Dhū l-Ḥijja and the dawn of the Day of the Sacrifice, i.e. the tenth of Dhū l-Ḥijja, provided the pilgrim, while in the state of *iḥrām*, did not have sexual intercourse before this halting. [2] Performance of the greater part of the Hastening Circumambulation of the Ka'ba (*ṭawāf al-ifāḍa*] in its proper time, i.e. after the dawn of the Day of the Sacrifice of Animals.

'REQUIRED' ACTS IN PILGRIMAGE

The 'required' acts in pilgrimage are the following. [1] To start the rite of *iḥrām* from the *mīqāt*. [*Mīqāt* is the place where a person intending *ḥajj* (the greater pilgrimage) or '*umra* (the lesser pilgrimage) must enter *iḥrām*. There are five such places: [a] Dhat Irq is for pilgrims approaching Mecca from the side of Iraq; [b] Juhfa or Rabigh is for those arriving from the side of Egypt and Syria; [c] Dhu l-Hulayfa, now called Abiar 'Ali, is for pilgrims coming from the direction of Medina; [d] Qarn is for those approaching Mecca from the side of Nejd; and [e] Yalamlam is for those approaching from the direction of the Yemen. Natives of Mecca enter *iḥrām* in Mecca itself.]

[2] Prolongation of the rite of halting at 'Arafa to the time of sunset. [3] The ritual of halting at Muzdalifa [215] in the time from after the appearance of the dawn of the Day of the Sacrifice, i.e. the tenth of Dhū l-Ḥijja, and the sunrise. [4] Casting of pebbles at the Jamras. [5] Slaughtering of an animal in sacrifice by a pilgrim performing the Qirān type of pilgrimage or the Tamattu' type. [6] Shaving of the head or cutting of the hair inside the sacred area of Mecca (*ḥaram*) and in the Days of the Sacrifice, i.e. the tenth, eleventh and twelfth of Dhū l-Ḥijja. [7] Accomplishment of the

[215] Muzdalifa is a sacred spot in the wilderness between 'Arafa and the valley of Mina. On passing the night at Muzdalifa when the pilgrims pass, just before sunrise, by that part of Muzdalifa which is called Nash'ar Ḥarām, they should remember God whole-heartedly; God commanded, "When you return from 'Arafa remember God at Mash'ar Ḥarām, and remember Him as He has guided you" (Qur'ān 2:198).

throwing of pebbles before the shaving, not after it. [8] Sacrifice of an animal by the pilgrim performing the Qirān type of pilgrimage or the Tamattu' type at the time between the throwing of pebbles and the shaving. [9] To make the Visiting Circumambulation of the Ka'ba (*ṭawāf az-ziyāra*) occur in the Days of the Sacrifice.

[10] Performance of the rite of running between Safa and Marwa (*sa'ī*) in the months of pilgrimage and *after* such a circumambulation of the Ka'ba as is reckoned as an act of pilgrimage. [11] Performance of the rite of running on foot, not riding or using any transport. A pilgrim who is unable to walk for illness or old age or any other reason, however, is exempted from the 'requirement' of walking. [12] To start the rite of running from Safa.

[13] Farewell Circumambulation of the Ka'ba (*ṭawāf al-wadā'*). [14] To start every circumambulation of the Ka'ba from the Black Stone (*ḥajar aswad*) and to go to the right side. [15] Circumambulating the Ka'ba on foot. A pilgrim who has an excuse, however, is 'permitted' by the law to circumambulate in any way other than walking. He may hire bearers and a litter and be borne throughout circumambulation. [16] When circumambulating, the pilgrim's being in the state of purification from both minor and major legal impurities, and [17] also covering his private parts.[216] To reduce his pace after doing the greater part of Visiting Circumambulation of the Ka'ba.

[18] Leaving undone of the acts forbidden by the law, such as a male pilgrim's wearing of a sewn cloth and covering of his head and the face, a female pilgrims's covering of her face, sexual intercourse, its discussion and obscene talk, sins, quarrel, killing of an animal, a bird, or any other thing that can be hunted, or hinting at these and suggesting these.

SUNNA ACTS IN PILGRIMAGE

Among the sunna acts in pilgrimage some are the following. [1] Taking of a bath or performance of ritual ablution when the pilgrim

[216] This covering of the private parts is enjoined against the pre-Islamic custom. In ancient, pagan times pilgrims approaching the Holy Ka'ba removed all of their clothing as a sign of humility. Naked, they performed the ritual circumambulation of the Ka'ba, kissed the sacred Black Stone, and otherwise did as we do now. Until the time of the prophet Muḥammad it had been the custom to go naked, in the dark before dawn to the Ka'ba for the rites of absolution. The Prophet disapproved of this nudity (al-Bukhārī, *Ṣaḥīḥ*, Ṣalā, 10; Muslim, *Ṣaḥīḥ*, Ḥajj, 435), God prohibited the nudity of some pagan worship; He commanded (Qur'ān 7:31), "Children of Adam, take your adornment [i.e. use your best clothes] at every time and place of worship." For nudity cf. 2 Samuel 6:20.

intends to enter *iḥrām*; bathing is sunna even though the pilgrim is a menstruating woman or a woman with childbirth bleeding. [2] Wearing of a new, white waist-wrapper and a new white wrapper, use of scent, and performance of two *rak'as* of ritual prayer, when a pilgrim intends to enter *iḥrām*. [3] After taking *iḥrām*, to read the formula of *talbiya* with a loud voice at the end of every ritual prayer, when ascending an elevated place, descending a valley, meeting a pilgrim caravan, and at dawn. [4] Repetition of the *talbiya* whenever the pilgrim starts reading it. [5] After taking *iḥrām*, supplication to God for blessings upon the Prophet, for Paradise and companionship of the pious therein, and for protection from Hell.

[6] Taking of a bath for entering into Mecca. [7] To enter into Mecca through the Bāb al-Mu'allā (the elevated gate) at daytime. [8] To say 'God is the greatest' (الله اكبر: *Allāhu akbar*), and 'there is no god but God' (لا اله الا الله: *lā ilāha illā Allāhu*), when the pilgrim arrives at the place opposite to the Holy House. [9] Supplication to God for anything the pilgrim likes whenever he sees the Holy House for the first time. This supplication is received by God. [10] The Arrival Circumambulation of the Ka'ba (*ṭawāf al-qudūm*) even though it is performed at a time other than the months of pilgrimage. [11] Accomplishment of the Arrival Circumambulation in such a state that the pilgrim brings one extreme of his wrapper from below his armpit and puts it on his left shoulder together with the other extreme. This is called *iḍṭibā'*. [12] To do *raml* in the Arrival Circumambulation, if the rite of running between Safa and Marwa is to be performed after this circumambulation in the months of pilgrimage. The meaning of *raml* will be explained later. [13] When performing the rite of running between Safa and Marwa, a man's passing the distance lying between the two green pillars quickly, but his passing the remaining distance at ease. A woman, however, will pass the entire distance with ease. [14] Performance of as many circumambulations of the Ka'ba as possible.[217] Each circumambulation consists of seven circuits of the Ka'ba. 'Supererogatory' circumambulation is more excellent than a 'supererogatory' ritual prayer for those pilgrims who are not dwellers in Mecca. [15] Address by the leader at Mecca after the Noon Prayer

[217] There are three *ṭawāfs* in a pilgrimage. The first is *ṭawāf al-qudūm* (the Arrival Circumambulation). It is done just on arrival at Mecca. The second is *ṭawāf al-ifāḍa* (the Hastening Circumambulation). Is is performed, after return from 'Arafa in the Days of Drying the Meat (*ayyām at-tashrīq*). The third is *ṭawāf al-wadā'* (the Farewell Circumambulation). This is the last of the ritual circlings of the Ka'ba; it is performed just prior to the pilgrim's departure for his homeland.

on the seventh day of Dhū l-Ḥijja. This is a single address; the person addressing should not sit in course of it; the address is an instruction on the activities of pilgrimage.

[16] To depart from Mecca to Mina after sunrise on the Day of Quenching Thirst (*Yawm at-Tarwiyya*), i.e. the eighth day of Dhū l-Ḥijja, and to pass the night there. Then to depart to 'Arafa after sunrise on the Day of 'Arafa, i.e. the ninth day of Dhū l-Ḥijja. [17] Imām's delivering of two addresses at 'Arafa after the sun passes its meridian but before the performance of the Noon Prayer and the Late Afternoon Prayer combined — a combination to be made in the time of the Noon Prayer. The imām, i.e. the leader of the pilgrimage, should sit for a while between the two addresses. [18] When performing the Noon Prayer and the Late Afternoon Prayer together at 'Arafa and also when performing the Sunset Prayer and the Evening Prayer together at Muzdalifa, the pilgrims's utmost effort in humility and submission towards God, in weeping, and in prayer for the good of this world and the Hereafter for himself, his parents, and his Muslim brethren.

[19] After sunset to depart from 'Arafa with tranquility of mind, to stop at that place of Muzdalifa which is higher than the interior of the valley and which is near the Quzaḥ Hill (*Jabal Quzaḥ*), and to pass the night of the Day of the Sacrifice there. [20] To pass the nights at Mina with all things in the Days of Mina. It is 'disliked' by the law to send them to Mecca while the pilgrim is still in Mina. [21] Keeping Mina at the right side and Mecca at the left when the pilgrim stands for casting pebbles at Jamras. [22] The pilgrim's being in riding condition when throwing pebbles at the Jamra al-'Aqaba in all three days, and on foot when throwing pebbles at the first Jamra, which is near to the Masjid al-Khayf, and the middle Jamra. [23] To stay in the interior of the valley during the days of throwing pebbles. [24] Casting of pebbles at the time between sunrise and the sun passing its meridian on the first day, and between the sun passing its meridian and sunset on the remaining days. It is 'disliked' by the law to throw pebbles, on the first day and the fourth day, at the time between the appearance of dawn and sunrise. Throwing of pebbles in the three nights is 'disliked' by the law, but is correct because every night is counted by the law to be under the following day — except the night which follows the Day of 'Arafa immediately so that it is correct to perform the rite of halting at 'Arafa in that night. These nights are the nights of the 'Īd and the nights of the duration of throwing pebbles at the three Jamras, for

these are counted to be under the days preceding them. The 'permissible' time for throwing pebbles is from after the sun passes its meridian to its setting on the first day of throwing.

[24] For a pilgrim performing the Ifrād type of pilgrimage, it is sunna to offer up an animal in sacrifice. [26] It is also sunna to eat of its flesh, and of the flesh of an animal offered up in sacrifice as a 'supererogatory' act, or offered up in sacrifice for the Tamattu' form of pilgrimage or for the Qirān form.

Of the sunna acts in pilgrimage are also the following. [27] Imām's delivering an address on the Day of the Sacrifice like his first address given at Mecca.[218] Through this address he should instruct the pilgrims on the remaining acts of pilgrimage. This address is the third of the three addresses of pilgrimage. [28] If the pilgrim has intended to leave Mina for Mecca on the twelfth of Dhū l-Ḥijja, it is sunna to leave before the sunset. If, however, he stays at Mina at sunset or after it, no atonement is 'necessary' but he has done a wrong thing. Should he prolong his stay at Mina until the appearance of the dawn of the fourth day, i.e. the thirteenth of Dhū l-Ḥijja, it is 'necessary' for him to throw pebbles at Jamras on that day also.

The following acts are also included in the sunna acts of pilgrimage. [29] After leaving Mina for Mecca, to stop at a place called Muhassab for a while. [30] To face towards the Holy House and to look at it standing. [31] To drink of the water of the well Zamzam, to drink it from the palm, and to pour it on the head and on other parts of the body. The water of Zamzam is useful for any purposes, both of this world and of the other world, for which one drinks it.[219]

Of the sunna acts are also the following. [32] Taking hold of the

218. The addresses delivered in a pilgrimage are three in number. The first is delivered at Mecca, the second at 'Arafa, and the third at Mina.

219 The well of Zamzam is outside the stream of those who perform *ṭawāf*; it stands apart from the Ka'ba, but is within the limits of the marble-and-stone paved area which encompasses the Most Ancient House and indicates the boundaries of the original place of worship. The water of Zamzam is slightly brackish and tepid despite the depth from which it is drawn through pipes. Water from this — discovered to them by the angel Gabriel — quenched the thirst of the prophet Abraham's wife Hajar and his son Ishmael when, mother and child, they were abandoned in this barren, burning valley — before there was a Mecca. The mortar joining the stone of the Ka'ba was mixed with water from this well. Muḥammad the child, Muḥammad the man, and Muḥammad the prophet drank of these ancient waters. It was his habit to drink from Zamzam at the close of his *ṭawāf*, preparing himself for the rite of running between Ṣafa and Marwa.

220 Multazam is one of the places where prayers are accepted by God. The Prophet said that all his prayers at Multazam were received by God. The time for prayer at Multazam is on completion of seven circuits of the Ka'ba.

Multazam, the wall of the Ka'ba lying between the door and the Black Stone. The procedure of clinging to Multazam is: the pilgrim puts his chest and face on it and takes hold of the veil of the Ka'ba for a while, praying to God for whatever he likes.[220] [33] Kissing the threshold of the door of the Ka'ba in full reverence and honour and entering into it with full courtesy and respect. [34] After all these sunna acts of pilgrimage, there remains for the pilgrim only the greatest of all 'supererogatory' good works, i.e. visit to the tomb of the Prophet and to the graves of his companions. So he should intend this visit when going out of Mecca through Bāb Sabīka (the Gate of Sabīka) at ath-Thaniyya as-Suflā.

HOW TO PERFORM THE ACTIVITIES OF PILGRIMAGE ONE AFTER ANOTHER

When a person intends to start the activities of pilgrimage, he will enter the rite of *iḥrām* at the appropriate *mīqāt*. In preparation for *iḥrām*, he will bathe entirely or perform the ritual ablution as if for ritual prayer. To bathe, if possible, is better since through this cleanliness is achieved more — so the menstruating woman and the woman with childbirth bleeding will also bathe if this is not harmful to them. It is 'praiseworthy' to achieve complete cleanliness by trimming the nails, by cutting the moustache, and by removing underarm and pubic hair. This should be done before bathing and making the ritual ablution. It is also 'praiseworthy' to apply oil to the body after bathing and performing ablution, even though the oil is fragrant. Then the pilgrim will wear the garments of *iḥrām* — a man[221] will wear a large waist-wrapper and a large wrapper[222] which are new or, if these are old, washed; it is better that these are new and white. These will be without seam, sewing, knot, button, design and decoration; it is 'disliked' by the law to do any of these things but no atonement is necessary for doing these. The pilgrim then will use scent and perform two *rak'as* of ritual prayer (*ṣalā*). Just on completion of this ritual prayer, he will make the ritual intention (*niyya*) for the pilgrimage by reading the following prayer formula (*du'ā'*):

God, I intend to perform the pilgrimage, [and I am taking

[221] For a woman's garments of *iḥrām* see *infra* p. 225.

[222] Each of these two pieces of cloth should measure approximately two and a half meters in length and one and a half meters in breadth. No other garment is to be worn over these or beneath these, but is 'permissible' to wear a money-pouch or a shoulder sling or a moneybelt; one of these is a requisite, as the *iḥrām* robes should have no pockets.

iḥrām for it]. Make it easy for me, and receive it from me.

(اللهمّ انى اريد الحج. فيسره لى، وتقبله منى)

(Allāhumma, innī urīdu al-ḥajja; fa-yassirhu lī, wa taqabbalhu minnī)

At the end of these two *rak'as* and immediately after reading the above *du'ā'*, you will utter the formula of *talbiya* intending by it the pilgrimage. The *talbiya* is:

لبيك، اللهمّ، لبيك. لاشريك لك، لبيك. ان الحمد والنعمة والملك لك، لا شريك لك.

(Labbayka, Allāhumma, labbayka. Lā sharīka laka, labbayka. Inna l-ḥamda wa n-ni'mata wa l-mulka laka, lā sharīka laka.)

(I am here, God, I am here in Your presence. You have no partner, I am here. Praise, blessings and kingdom surely belong to You, You have no partner).

Do not utter less than these words. Rather add to them the following words. This addition is sunna.

I am here, God, in Your presence; may You be always happy and aided! All good lies in Your hand. I am here; my desire is directed towards You.

(لبيك وسعديك، والخير كله بين يديك. لبيك والرغبى اليك).

(Labbayka wa sa'dayka; wa l-khayru kulluhu bayna yadayka. Labbayka wa r-rughbā ilayka.)

On completion of the utterence of *talbiya* with the intention of pilgrimage, you have taken to *iḥrām*. You are now prohibited from doing certain things. Guard against [a] *rafath* which means sexual intercourse or, according to another interpretation, discussion of sexual intercourse, [b] obscene talk, [c] wickedness, [d] sin, [e] quarrel with companions, servants and others,[223] [f] killing of any hunted animal, bird, etc., of the land, hinting at it and suggesting it,[224] [g] wearing of any sewn cloth,[225] of turban and of boots,[226] [h] covering of the head and the face,[227] [i] touching of scent, and [j] shaving of the head and of hair or any other part of the body. It is 'permissible' to bathe, to enjoy the shade of a tent, litter, and similar

223 Qur'ān 2:197.

224 Qur'ān 5:1-2, 96.

225 For a woman's dress see *infra*, p. 225.

226 Sandals which do not cover the heels and half of the outer part of the feet and which are not sewn in the least, may be worn.

227 This is not applicable to a female pilgrim.

things, and to tie a money-bag at the waist.

Read the formula of *talbiya* very frequently with a loud voice,[228] but not with harmful effort, when you have performed a ritual prayer, ascended to an elevated place, descended to a valley, met a pilgrim caravan, and at day break. In this way proceed.

When you have reached the boundary of Mecca it is 'praiseworthy' to bathe in order to be bodily clean and then to enter into it at daytime through Bāb al-Mu'allā (the Gate at the Elevated Place) so that, when entering Mecca, you will face towards the door of the Holy Ka'ba out of respect for it. It is also 'praiseworthy' to be in the state of uttering the formula of *talbiya* throughout your journey from entering into Mecca to your arrival at Bāb as-Salām (the door of greeting). Through this door you will then enter into the Sacred Mosque (*al-Masjid al-Ḥarām*),[229] with full humility and submission, with the reading of *talbiya*, with consideration of the majesty of the place, with the utterance of 'God is the greatest' (الله اكبر: *Allāhu akbar*), 'There is no god but God'(لا اله الا الله: *lā ilāha illā Allāhu*), and 'God, bless Muḥammad and the family of Muḥammad',(اللهم صل على محمد وعلى ال محمد: *Allāhumma, ṣalli 'alā Muḥammadin wa 'alā āli Muḥammadin*), with compassionate behaviour towards those who are competing with you to enter through this door, with prayer to God for whatever you like — prayer, when seeing the Holy Ka'ba for the first time, is accepted by God.

Then go in front of the sacred Black Stone (*Ḥajar Aswad*), uttering 'God is the greatest' (*Allāhu akbar*) and 'there is no god but God' (*lā ilāha illā Allāhu*), and lifting your hands as you do so at the start of a ritual prayer. Put your hands on the sacred Stone and kiss it without producing any sound. A pilgrim who can only kiss or touch the Stone by giving pain to other pilgrims, should leave the kissing or touching undone. What he should do is to touch the Stone with something and kiss it; or he should only indicate, by lifting the right hand in a gesture of touching, to the Stone from a distance,

228 This does not apply to women; see *infra*, p. 225. *Talbiya* is the most frequently uttered of all formulae prayers of pilgrimage. The origin of *talbiya* is: Ka'ba disappeared after the time of the prophet Noah and the Deluge; at divine command the prophet Abraham and his son Ishmael rebuilt the edifice in order that it might be a place of worship again; on completion of the edifice Abraham climbed up to the top and, by divine command, called to all mankind, summoning them to pilgrimage (Qur'ān 22:26-29). The response to that call is made by each pilgrim through *talbiya*.

229 There are twenty-four doors through which one may enter into the Sacred Mosque. It is, however, 'praiseworthy' to enter tnrough the Bāb as-Salām. From this Bāb (gate) a path goes diagonally to the Ka'ba.

uttering *Allāhu akbar, lā ilāhā illā Allāhu*, 'praise be to God' (الحمد لله: *al-ḥamdu li-Allāhi*), and *Allāhumma, ṣalli 'alā Muḥammadin, wa 'alā āli Muḥammadin*.

After this, circumambulate the Ka'ba[230] starting from your right side of that part of the courtyard which is adjacent to the door of the Ka'ba. Bring the wrapper from below your right armpit and put its both extremes upon your left shoulder. This is called *idṭibā'*. In this state make seven circuits of the Ka'ba, praying during them by using whatever prayer formula you like. Circumambulate from outside the Ḥatīm.[231] Do *raml* in the first three circuits, if you have intended to perform the ceremony of running between Safa and Marwa just after this circumambulation of the Ka 'ba. *Raml* means to walk quickly, shaking the shoulders like a man who fights a duel, swaggering gracefully between two lines of the circumambulators. When doing this, if you are barred by people's rush, stop but whenever you find an opening move quickly. This *raml* is something that should be done; so you will stand until you become able to perform it in the way that is sunna.[232] *Raml* is not like the kissing of the sacred Black Stone, for the latter has a substitute which is to face towards the Stone, but the former has not. In course of circumambulation, you will kiss the Black Stone, if possible, whenever you will pass by it. You will end the circumambulation by touching the Stone, if possible, and by performing two *rak'as* of ritual prayer in the Maqām Ibrāhīm (the standing place of the prophet Abraham[233] or

230 Qur'ān 22:29, 26, 2:125. The weak and the sick of either sex may hire bearers and a litter and be borne through the seven circumambulations.

231 Shielding the lower section of the northernly face of the Ka'ba (i.e. the face between the Iraq corner and the Damascus corner of the Ka'ba) and within the area circled during *ṭawāf*, is a massive stone wall built in the form of a half-circle. This is Ḥatīm. Shoulder high, the wall encloses a place of prayer. This place is Ḥijr, and here, beneath the worn marble floor, are buried seventy of the prophets, among them Ishmael. Here too lies the prophet Ishmael's mother Ḥajar. The prophet Muḥammad was sleeping here in the night of the twenty-seventh of the lunar month Rajab, a year before his flight from Mecca to Medina (*hijra*), when the angel Gabriel descended with the heavenly steed al-Burāq. From this spot, whether in the flesh or in spirit, Muḥammad began his miraculous night journey (*al-isrā'*) to Jerusalem (Qur'ān 17:1) and the ascent (*mi'rāj*) through the seven heavens, to the near presence of God — returning before daybreak; see Muslim, *Ṣaḥīḥ*, Īmān, 259, 263; al-Bukhārī, *Ṣaḥīḥ*, Ḥajj, 76, Manāqib al-Anṣār, 42.

232 A female pilgrim is not to do the *raml*: she will walk at ease throughout the *ṭawāf*. For the origin of *raml* see Muslim, *Ṣaḥīḥ*, Ḥajj, 241; al-Bukhārī *Ṣaḥīḥ*, Ḥajj, 55.

233 Qur'ān 2:125, 3:97. The standing place of the prophet Abraham is a stone on which he stood when building the Ka'ba and which used to go high and low

in any other place of the Sacred Mosque where you find it easy to perform these two *rak'as*. Then return to the Stone and touch and kiss it. The above constitutes the Arrival Circumambulation (*ṭawāf al-qudūm*), which is sunna for those who are not the dwellers in Mecca.

Then you will come out of the Sacred Mosque through Bāb as-Ṣafā and go to the hill Safa.[234] You will mount it to such an extent that by standing over it you can see the Holy House towards the direction of which you will face, uttering *Allāhu akbar, lā ilāha illā Allāhu*, the formula of *talbiya, Allāhumma ṣalli 'alā Muḥammadin wa 'alā āli Muḥammadin*, and other prayers; when reading these prayers you will raise your hands extending towards the sky. Then descending from Safa you will proceed towards the hill Marwa, at a distance of four hundred and five meters, at ease.[235] When you reach about the middle of this distance, run between the two green pillars, a distance of about forty meters. After crossing these pillars walk at ease until you reach Marwa. You will mount to Marwa and will do here the same as you have done on mounting to Safa — you will face towards the Holy House, uttering *Allāhu akbar, lā ilāha illā Allāhu*, the formula of *talbiya, Allāhumma ṣallī 'alā Muḥammadin wa 'alā āli Muḥammadin*, and other prayers, and extending the hands towards the sky. All this constitutes one of the seven ritual trips to be done between Safa and Marwa. Then you will turn back intending to reach Safa. When you reach around the middle of the two green pillars, you will run. After passing them you will walk at ease until you reach Safa; ascending over it you will do

automatically according to the need of Abraham. A long footprint of Abraham, about two inches deep, is marked on this stone. All this was his miracle and constituted a clear proof for the divine nature of the Ka'ba (Qur'ān 3:97). The stone is now enclosed by an ornamental grill. It is covered by a domed kiosk which has six pillars. The believers are commanded by God to perform ritual prayer in the standing place of Abraham (Qur'ān 2:125). This place lies apart from the Ka'ba, but very near to it although outside the stream of those who perform *ṭawāf*. It is at some distance but in front of the door of the Ka'ba; to the right of it, standing parallel, is the high and ornate pulpit (*minbar*), from which the Friday sermons are delivered.

234 Safa and Marwa are just outside the wall of the Sacred Mosque. The pilgrim requires about seventy six paces to reach Safa from the Bāb aṣ-Ṣafā through which he comes out from the Sacred Mosque.

235 Qur'ān 2:158. Those incapable of performing this rite on foot may hire a litter. The origin of the rite of running between Safa and Marwa is: the prophet Abraham's wife Ḥajar made this running when in search of water for her child Ishmael. Abraham received the rite from God that he might pass it on to all men (Qur'ān 22:26-29). Divine revelation came to the prophet Muḥammad, asking the believers to perform this rite; see Qur'ān 2:158.

the same as you did here first. All this makes the second trip between Safa and Marwa. You will complete seven trips, each of which you will start from Safa and end at Marwa, and run in the middle of the distance.

Then you will stay at Mecca in the state of being in *iḥrām*. You will circumambulate the Holy House whenever you find an opportunity. This 'supererogatory' circumambulation is better than 'supererogatory' ritual prayer for those who are not dwellers in Mecca.

On performing the Dawn Prayer (*Salāt āl-Fajr*) at Mecca on the eighth of Dhū l-Ḥijja, you will prepare for going to Mina.[236] You will depart from Mecca after sunrise. It is 'praiseworthy' to perform the Noon Prayer (*Salāt aẓ-Ẓuhr*) at Mina. The reading of the *talbiya* will not be given up in any condition except when one is circumambulating the Ka'ba. In Mina you should stop near Masjid al-Khayf (Khayf Mosque).[237] You will stay at Mina till the performance of the Dawn Prayer there in darkness.[238]

After sunrise you will proceed to the valley of 'Arafa, at a distance of about twenty-two kilometers from the Sacred Mosque, and will stay there. After the sun passes its meridian you will come to Masjid Namira (Namira Mosque) and will, with the greatest imām or his deputy, perform the Noon Prayer and the Late Afternoon Prayer (*Ṣalāt al-'Aṣr*) combinedly, after the imām or his deputy delivers two addresses sitting for a while between them; these two 'obligatory' ritual prayers you will perform with one *adhān* (i.e. call to ritual prayer) and two *iqāmas* (i.e. call to the actual start of a ritual prayer). You will not combine them except if you meet two stipulations, namely, [1] you are in *iḥrām* and [2] performing them with the greatest imām. These two 'obligatory' ritual prayers will not be separated by any 'supererogatory' ritual prayer. If you do not find the greatest imām, perform each of these two ritual prayers in its usual time, do not combine them. On performing ritual prayers with

236 Mina is a stony valley between the bare mountains. It is inside the sacred area.

237 In this mosque the prophet Muḥammad performed ritual prayer. So it is sunna for a pilgrim to do the same. In this mosque seventy of the prophets worshipped God. Among them was Moses. The original mosque is now enlarged and beautified.

238 It is sunna to go to Mina and thence to 'Arafa. During the Farewell Pilgrimage the Prophet slept the night of the ninth day of Dhū l-Ḥijja at Mina, on the way to 'Arafa. In the morning of the ninth day, after sunrise, he departed from Mina and continued on his way. The irreligious shaykh al-ḥajj, also called muṭawwif, neglecting this sunna, sends the pilgrims to 'Arafa direct from Mecca. Pilgrims should insist on going to Mina first and thence to 'Arafa.

the imām, you will depart towards the place of the rite of halting at 'Arafa. The whole of 'Arafa, except the interior of 'Arna, is the place for the rite of halting. In preparation for this rite, you will bathe at 'Arafa just after the sun passes its meridian.[239] You will perform the rite of halting at a place near Jabal ar-Raḥma (the hill of mercy), facing towards the Ka'ba, uttering *Allāhu akbar, lā ilāha illā Allāhu*, the formula of *talbiya*, and other formal prayers for forgiveness, and extending the hands towards the sky like a beggar asking for food. You should make efforts in prayer for yourself, your parents and your Muslim brethren. You should also make an effort to shed tears when praying, for this is an indication that your prayers are accepted by God. You should pray excessively with strong hope that God will accept your prayer. You must not fall short of supplication on this day, for this failure cannot be made good, especially if you are not a dweller in Mecca. Performance of the rite of halting in the state of riding or of being on a transport is better[240] than in the state of standing on the ground which, in turn, is better than the condition of sitting on the ground.

When the sun is set, the imām of the pilgrimage and the people with him will depart from 'Arafa for Muzdalifa, at a distance of eight kilometers, at ease. On finding an opening through the rush of pilgrims you will make haste but not by giving pain to anyone else. You should avoid all that is done by the ignorant — violence in movement, rushing and causing pain to others — for all this is 'unlawful'. On reaching Muzdalifa, you will stop near the Jabal Quzaḥ (Quzaḥ Hill), and will stay at a place high in the interior of the valley in order to leave space for the passersby. At Muzdalifa you will perform the Sunset Prayer (*Ṣalāt al-Māghrib*) and the Evening Prayer (*Ṣalāt al-'Ishā'*) together with one *adhān* and one *iqāma*. If you have performed any 'supererogatory' ritual prayer or have done anything else between these two 'obligatory' ritual prayers, repeat the *iqāma*. It is 'not permissible' by the law to perform the Sunset Prayer on the way from 'Arafa to Muzdalifa. If anyone has performed it on the way, its repetition is essential until the day-break. It is sunna to pass the night at Muzdalifa.[241] On daybreak

[239] From this time starts the ritual of halting at 'Arafa. This rite is the supreme part of the pilgrimage. It is a pillar of the pilgrimage, so that its non-observance makes the pilgrimage invalid. There is a well known Tradition that the Prophet said, "The pilgrimage is *the* rite of halting at 'Arafa."

[240] In the Farewell Pilgrimage (10 A.H./632 A.D.) the Prophet was on camelback atop the stony mountain at 'Arafa (*Jabal 'Arafa*). All his companions were on the boulder-covered slopes of the mountain and on the arid valley surrounding the mountain.

the imām of the pilgrimage will lead the Dawn Prayer very early, when the surroundings are still dark. Then the imām together with the people will perform the ritual of halting at Muzdalifa. The whole of Muzdalifa, except the interior of Muhassar, is the place for the ritual of halting. When observing this ritual, you will try your best in prayer to God.

When the darkness is gone and the dawn is shining fully, the imām of the pilgrimage together with the people will, before sunrise, proceed to Mina. On reaching Mina they will stop. Then you will come to the Jamra al-'Aqaba [242] and throw seven pebbles at it. It is 'praiseworthy' to gather the pebbles from Muzdalifa or from the road to Mina. It is 'disliked' by the law to gather them from those lying at the Jamras. You should not break a piece of stone into several pebbles. You should wash the pebbles in order to make sure that they are clean; casting of unclean pebbles will do, but it is 'disliked' by the law. With the casting of the first of the seven pebbles, you will stop the reading of the formula of *talbiya*.

The procedure of casting the pebbles is as follows. Seven pebbles will be cast at each Jamra. These will be flung one at a time. You will catch a pebble with the edge of your thumb and the forefinger — this is the most correct view — because this is the easiest way and this humiliates Satan most. It is sunna to throw pebbles with the right hand. You will put the pebble on the edge of your thumb and take assistance of your forefinger. If the pebble you have thrown falls upon a place and remains fixed there, you must throw another pebble instead; but if from there it by itself falls on the appropriate place, it will do. When throwing each pebble you will say 'God is the Greatest'(الله اكبر : *Allāhu akbar*).

Then you, who are performing the Ifrād form of pilgrimage, will, if you like, slaughter an animal in sacrifice to God. This will be followed by shaving your head or cutting your hair . A female pilgrim will not do this. Shaving is better; shaving of one-fourth of the head is sufficient. Cutting of hair is such that the hair of the

241 Unfortunately the shaykh al-ḥajj (the guide), also called the muṭawwif, who is mostly an irreligious man and whose only aim is to make money, does not give the pilgrims an opportunity to observe this sunna. His lorry filled with pilgrims stops near Muzdalifa for only a few minutes in order that they may collect pebbles and then leaves for Mina. The pilgrims should insist on passing the night at Muzdalifa.

242 There are three Jamras — al-Ūlā (the first), al-Wusṭā (the middle), and the last which is known as *Jamra al-'Aqaba*. These are three crude stone-and-mortar pillars marking the places in Mina where Satan appeared to Ishmael, son of the prophet Abraham. Cf. al-Bukhārī, *Ṣaḥīḥ*, Ḥajj, 134-8; Ibrāhīm Rif'at, *Mir'at al-Ḥaramayn*, Cairo, 1925, I, 328-29.

measure of the tip of the finger will be cut off. After this rite is completed, everything, except the enjoyment of women, is 'lawful' to you. You are no longer in *iḥrām* and the robes can be put off. The pilgrimage, however, is not yet complete.

After this you will go to Mecca on that very day or the next day or the following day.[243] There you will circumambulate the Holy House seven circuits; this is the Visiting Cirumambulation. On completion of this circumambulation, enjoyment of woman becomes 'lawful' to you. Of these three days of going to Mecca for this *ṭawāf*, the best is the first. Should you not go to Mecca at any time in the three days, which are called the Days of the Sacrifice, but go later, you must offer an ewe in sacrifice as an atonement for delaying in the performance of a 'required' act of pilgrimage.

Then you will return to Mina and stay there. After the sun passed its meridian on the second of the Days of the Sacrifice, i.e. the eleventh of Dhū l-Ḥijja, you will cast pebbles at all three Jamras, starting from the Jamra adjacent to the Khayf Mosque. So you will throw seven pebbles at it on foot, saying *Allāhu akbar* when throwing each pebble. Then you will stand nearby, praying to God by using whatever prayer you like, praising Him by saying *al-ḥamdu li-Allāhi*, and invoking blessings upon the Prophet by saying *Allāh-umma, ṣalli 'alā Muḥammadin, wa 'alā āli Muḥammadin*; you will lift your hands when praying; you will pray for forgiveness of your parents and your Muslim brethren. After this you will cast pebbles at the adjacent Jamra in the same way and will stand near to it, praying. Then you will cast pebbles at the Jamra of 'Aqaba. You will not stand near it but leave the place immediately. On the third of the Days of the Sacrifice, i.e. the twelfth of Dhū l-Ḥijja, you will cast pebbles at all three Jamras after the sun passes its meridian, observing the same rules as observed before.

If you have intended to leave for Mecca, you will have to leave the boundary of Mina by sunset. To stay at Mina to the time of sunset and then to leave for Mecca is 'disliked' by the law, but no atonement for this is required. If the dawn of the fourth day, i.e. the thirteenth of Dhū l-Ḥijja, has appeared while you are still in Mina, it is 'necessary' for you to cast pebbles on this day also. Throwing of pebbles on this day is 'permissible' before the sun passes its meridian, but better after it, and 'disliked' before sunrise. Casting of pebbles at a Jamra after which there is casting at another Jamra, will be accomplished on foot in order that the person casting may be able to pray after casting. If a Jamra is such that after it there is no

243 Qur'ān 2:202.

other Jamra to cast at, then you should cast at this Jamra, and depart after it, without praying. It is 'disliked' to pass the nights outside Mina in the period of throwing of pebbles at Jamras.

Then when you are on the way to Mecca, you will stop for a while at a place called al-Muhassab. On entering into Mecca, you will circumambulate the Holy House without doing *raml* in it and without performing after it the ceremony of running between Safa and Marwa, provided you have once done *raml* and running. This is the Farewell Circumambulation, also called *Ṭawāf aṣ-Ṣadr*. This is 'required' for all pilgrims, except those who are dwellers of Mecca and those who have settled there. On completion of this circumambulation, you will perform two *rak'as* of ritual prayer.

Then you will go to the well Zamzam in order to drink of its water. You will face towards the Holy House and drink much water; you will breathe into the water several times, lifting, at every time, your eyes towards the Holy House. If it is easy, you will pour the water on your body, if not you will only wipe your face and head with it. When drinking the water of Zamzam you will make an intention for whatever purpose you like. 'Abd Allāh, son of 'Abbās,[244] used to pray when drinking this water:

> God, I pray to you for useful knowledge, ample sustenance, and cure of every disease.
> (اللهم انى اسئلك علما نافعا، ورزقا واسعا، وشفاء من كل داء).
> (*Allāhumma, innī as'aluka 'ilaman nāfi'an, wa rizqan wāsi'an wa shifā'n min kulli dā'in.*)

The Prophet said, "The water of Zamzam is effective for any purpose for which it is drunk."[245]

It is 'praiseworthy' to go, after drinking the water of Zamzam, to the door of the Ka'ba for prayer there and for kissing the threshold of the door with full reverence, and then to go to the Multazam which is the wall of the Ka'ba lying between the door and the sacred Black Stone. You will put your chest and face on the Multazam and

245 'Abd Allāh (d. 68 A.H.) and his father 'Abbās were among the Prophet's companions. 'Abbās was an uncle of the Prophet. 'Abd Allāh had vast knowledge of the meaning of the Qur'ān; he is known as the 'Leader of the Commentators of the Qur'ān'. The Prophet once prayed, "God, grant him [i.e. 'Abd Allāh, son of 'Abbās] understanding of the religion" (al-Bukhārī, *Ṣaḥīḥ*, Waḍū', 10; Muslim, *Ṣaḥīḥ*, Faḍā'il aṣ-Ṣaḥāba, 138). For the biographies of 'Abd Allāh and 'Abbās see Ibn 'Abd al-Barr, *al-Istī'āb*, II, 710-17, III, 933-39.

244 Ibn Māja, *Sunan*, Manāsik, 78.

take hold of the veil of the Ka'ba for a while, making humble entreaties to God for all the best things of this world and the Hereafter; you will also pray:

> God, this is Your house which You made blessed, and a means of guidance for the people of the world. God, as You have guided me to it so accept my pilgrimage to it, and do not make this pilgrimage the end of my visit to Your house, but give me the opportunity of returning to it so that You become pleased with me through Your mercy, O the Most Merciful of those who show mercy.
>
> (اللهم، ان هذا بيتك الذى جعلته مباركا وهدى للعالمين. اللهم، كما هديتني له فتقبل مني، ولا تجعل هذا اخر العهد من بيتك، وارزقني العود اليه حتى ترضى عني برحمتك، يا ارحم الراحمين).
>
> (*Allāhumma, inna hādhā baytuka l-ladhī ja'altahu mubārakan wa hudan li l-'ālamīna. Allāhumma, kamā hadaytanī lahu fataqabbal minnī; wa lā taj'al hādhā ākhira l-'ahdi min baytika; wa rjuqnī l-'awda ilayhi ḥattā tarḍā 'annī bi-raḥmatika; yā arḥama r-rāḥimīna*).

The Multazam is one of those places of Mecca where supplication is received by God. These places are fifteen in number. Al-Kamāl ibn al-Humām[246] has copied them from the *Treatise* of al-Ḥasan al-Baṣrī.[247] They are [1] during the circumambulation of the Ka'ba, [2] at the Multazam, [3] below the Mīzāb (water-spout of the Ka'ba),[248] [4] inside of the Holy House, [5] at the well Zamzam, [6] behind the Maqām Ibrāhim, [7] on Ṣafa, [8] on Marwa, [9] during the ceremony of running between Safa and Marwa, [10] at 'Arafa, [11] at Mina, [12-14] near the three Jamras — pebbles are cast at Jamras in four days, i.e. the Day of the Sacrifice and the three following days. [15] Supplication is also accepted by God when

246 Kamāl ibn al-Humām is the author of the *Fatḥ al-Qadīr*, a commentary on the *Hidāya* which is a celebrated work on Ḥanafī jurisprudence. For his deep and accurate knowledge he is given the appellation *muḥaqqiq*.

247 Al-Ḥasan of Baṣra (d. 728 A.D.) was a follower (*tābi'ī*), i.e. a Muslim who did not see the Prophet but saw his companions. Al-Ḥasan was a saint, one drawn near to God, a great ṣūfī, a real ascetic, a sincere preacher and a famous theologian. His statements are often quoted in literature on various Islamic subjects.

248 The pipe through which the rain water falls from the roof of the Holy Ka'ba is called the Mīzāb ar-Raḥma . It exists at that side of the roof of the Ka'ba to which Ḥaṭīm is adjacent. Pilgrims vie with one another to secure the blessed water falling through this pipe when there is rain, and to pray below this pipe, for prayer performed here is received by God.

one sees the Sacred House first in his visit to Mecca.

It is 'praiseworthy' to enter into the Holy House. The person who enters into it should seek the place where the Prophet performed his ritual prayer. This place is in front of him when his back faces the door, so that there is the distance of three cubits between him and the wall in front of him. He will perform ritual prayer in it. If he performs it near the wall, he will put his cheek on it, and pray to God for forgiveness and praise Him. Then he will come to the pillars and praise God, assert His oneness, glorify Him, magnify Him, and pray to Him for whatever he wants. He will behave with the fullest possible courtesy of mind and body. The green slab between the two pillars is not the place where the Prophet performed his ritual prayer.

When you want to return home you should, on completion of the Farewell Circumambulation, move from the precinct of the Holy House in such a state that you walk backwards, keeping your face towards the Holy House, weeping for regret over your separation from the Holy House. You should be in this state until you come out of the Holy House. You will come out of Mecca through the Bāb Banī Shayba (the Gate of Banī Shayba) at ath-Thaniyya as-Suflā.

A female pilgrim will do as a male does in all activities of pilgrimage, except that: she will not bare her head; she will not raise her voice when reading the formula of *talbiya*; nor will she do *raml* when circumambulating the Ka'ba; nor will she run quickly between the two green pillars when performing the ceremony of running between Safa and Marwa — rather she will walk at ease throughout this ceremony —; nor will she shave her head or cut her hair; she will wear sewn clothes; she will not compete with men in kissing the sacred Black Stone.

The above treatment is all that concerns the Ifrād form of pilgrimage.

IFRĀD FORM OF PILGRIMAGE

There are three forms of pilgrimage — Ifrād, Qirān and Tamattu'. The best of these forms is the Qirān; next to this is the Tamattu'; Ifrād is less excellent than the Tamattu'. In respect of a few but important matters they differ from one another. All that is discussed in the preceding section concerns the Ifrād form of pilgrimage. A great part of this discussion, however, is common to the two other forms. The activities where these two forms differ from the Ifrād are mentioned in the two following sections.

THE QIRĀN FORM OF PILGRIMAGE

The Qirān is to combine, through a man's intention the *iḥrām* for *ḥajj* and the *iḥrām* for *'umra*. Thus the pilgrim who has decided to perform the Qirān form of pilgrimage, will, after the performance of the two *rak'as* of ritual prayer for *iḥrām*, make the intention thus:

> God, I intend to perform *'umra* and *ḥajj*. Make them easy for me, and accept them from me.
> (اللهم، انى اريد العمرة والحج؛ فيسرهما لى، وتقبلهما منى).
> (*Allāhumma, innī urīdu l-'umra wa l-ḥajja; fa-yassirhumā lī wa taqabbalhumā minnī*).

Then he will read the formula of *talbiya* and will be observing all restrictions and prohibitions of *iḥrām* we have already described in the preceding section.

On entering into Mecca he will start with the circumambulation of the Ka'ba for *'umra* — he will complete seven circuits, doing *raml* in the first three of them only. Then he will perform the two *rak'as* of ritual prayer for circumambulation.

Then he will come out of the Sacred Mosque through Bāb aṣ-Ṣafā and go to Safa for the ceremony of running seven times between Safa and Marwa. Ascending the hill Safa he will stand up over it, praying and uttering *Allāhu akbar, lā ilāha illā Allāhu*, the formula of *talbiya*, and *Allāhumma, ṣalli 'alā Muḥammadin, wa 'alā āli Muḥammadin*. Then he will descend and proceed towards the hill Marwa at ease; but when passing the distance between the two green pillars he will run; he will complete seven trips between Safā and Marwa, following the methods discussed in the previous section.

All that he will have done so far will constitute the activities of *'umra*. In the Tamattu' form, *iḥrām* is put aside at this stage. But in the Qirān form it continues to the end of *ḥajj*. Then he will perform the Arrival Circumambulation for *ḥajj*. Then he will complete the remaining activities of pilgrimage, as described in the preceding section.

After he has cast pebbles at the Jamra al-'Aqaba on the Day of the Sacrifice, i.e. the tenth of Dhū l-Ḥijja, he is 'required' by the law to slaughter in sacrifice an ewe or one seventh of a camel. In the case of inability to do this, he must, before the arrival of the Days of the Sacrifice, fast three days from the months of pilgrimage, and he must fast seven more days on completion of the pilgrimage even though in Mecca, after the passing of the *Ayyām at-Tashrīq*, (the Days of Drying the Meat).[249] It is 'permissible' to fast these days separately, not consecutively.

THE TAMATTU' FORM OF PILGRIMAGE

The Tamattu' form of pilgrimage is to [a] enter *iḥrām* only for *'umra* at the *mīqāt*. Thus a pilgrim who has decided to perform this form of pilgrimage, will, after the performance of the two *rak'as* of ritual prayer for *iḥrām*, make the intention thus:

> God, I intend to perform *'umra*. Make it easy for me, and accept it from me.
>
> (اللهم، انى اريد العمرة؛ فيسرها لى، وتقبل ها منى).
>
> (*Allāhumma, innī urīdu l-'umra; fa-yassirhā lī, wa taqabbalhā minnī*).

Then he will continue the reading of the formula of *talbiya*, following the methods already mentioned in our discussion of the activities of pilgrimage, until he enters into Mecca.

After entering Mecca he will circumambulate the Ka'ba for *'umra*, doing *raml* in it, and with the start of this circumambulation he will stop the reading of the *talbiya*. On completion of seven ritual circuits of the Ka'ba, he will perform the two *rak'as* of ritual prayer for circumambulation.

Then, after standing on the hill Safa and duly praying to God there, he will perform the ceremony of running between Safa and Marwa — seven courses. Then he will shave his head or cut his hair provided he has not sent the animal for offering in sacrifice to the place of sacrifice. Now everything, including sexual intercourse, is 'lawful' to him, and its lawfulness will persist. If, however, he has sent the animal for offering in sacrifice, he will not dispense with his *'umra*.

[b] On arrival of Yawm at-Tarwiyya, i.e. the eighth day of Dhū l-Ḥijja, he will do *iḥrām* again; but this *iḥrām* is for *ḥajj* and it is to be done from the *ḥaram* (i.e. the sacred area of Mecca); then he will leave for Mina and thence to 'Arafa.

When he has cast pebbles at the Jamra al-'Aqaba on the Day of the Sacrifice, i.e. the tenth of Dhū l-Ḥijja, he is 'required' to slaughter an ewe or one seventh of a camel in sacrifice. In the case of inability to do this, he must fast three days before the arrival of the Day of the Sacrifice and seven more days on returning to his home-

[249] Qur'ān 2:203. In ancient times there was a custom of curing the flesh of the sacrificed animal by drying it in the sun. Following this custom the eleventh, the twelfth and the thirteenth days of the month Dhū l-Ḥijja are called *Ayyām at-Tashrīq*, the Days of Drying the Meat.

land,[250] as in the case of a pilgrim performing the Qirān form of pilgrimage. If he did not fast three days so that the Day of the Sacrifice has arrived, slaughtering of an ewe in sacrifice is 'essential', and now no fasting and no almsgiving as an atonement for it will be of any avail.

'UMRA — THE LESSER PILGRIMAGE

'Umra is sunna.[251] It is the lesser pilgrimage, while *ḥajj* is the greater pilgrimage. *'Umra* is valid at any time of the year. However, on the Day of 'Arafa, i.e. the ninth of Dhū l-Ḥijja, the Day of the Sacrifice, i.e. the tenth of Dhū l-Ḥijja, and the Days of Drying the Meat, i.e. the eleventh, twelfth and thirteenth of Dhū l-Ḥijja, *'umra* is 'disliked' by the law.

The procedure of *'umra* is this. A person already in Mecca will enter *iḥrām* for *'umra* at a place of Mecca considered as *ḥall*, i.e. outside the sacred area.[252] This is not like *iḥrām* for *ḥajj*, because the *iḥrām* for *ḥajj* is taken at a place inside the sacred area (*ḥaram*) of Mecca. As for a person not yet entered into Mecca, he will take *iḥrām* for *'umra* at the *mīqāt*.

Then the person taking *iḥrām* for *'umra* will circumambulate the Ka'ba, and then perform the ceremony of running between Safa and Marwa — both for *'umra*. Then he will shave his head or cut his hair, and by this he will have completed his *'umra*. We have discussed the details of all these acts when we have dealt with the procedure of *ḥajj*.

THE BEST DAY

The best of all days is the Day of 'Arafa, the ninth of Dhū l-Ḥijja, if it happens to be on Friday. Such a day of 'Arafa is more excellent than seventy pilgrimages on days other than Friday. The author of the *Mi'rāj ad-Dirāya* narrated this when he said, "It has correctly been transmitted from the Messenger of God (may God bless him and greet him!) that he said,

'The most excellent of all days is the Day of 'Arafa should it

[250] Qur'ān 2:196.

[251] The Prophet performed *'umra* himself. In the Qur'ān (2:196, 158) *'umra* is recommended.

[252] Part of Mecca is regarded as a sacred area, the rest being called *ḥall*. The sacred places are meant for glorification of the One God. Those who are mentally impure, such as polytheists, are not to be allowed into the sacred area, especially they are not allowed to visit the Sacred Mosque (Qur'ān 9:28). On the way from Jedda to Mecca the sacred ground starts from ash-Shemisi, al-Hudaybia. Beyond this line no non-Muslim can pass.

happen to be on Friday. It is more excellent than seventy pilgrimages.'"

This is mentioned in the *Tajrīd aṣ-Ṣiḥāḥ bi-'Alāmat al-Muaṭṭā'*. Az-Zayla'ī, the commentator of the *Kanz*,[253] has also said this.

According to Imām Abū Ḥanīfa, to live in the neighbourhood of Mecca is 'disliked' by the law, because one who lives there is unable to fulfil the duties towards the Sacred House. The two companions of Abū Ḥanīfa, however, have held the view that it is 'not disliked' to live in the neighbourhood of Mecca.

COMMISSION OF OFFENCES IN PILGRIMAGE

Offences committed in pilgrimage are of two kinds, namely, offences related to *iḥrām* and offences related to the sacred place of Mecca. The latter are not special to those who are in *iḥrām*.

Offences committed by those in *iḥrām* are of several types. Some of them are so grave that sacrifice of animals is necessary for them. Others only require almsgiving of half a *ṣā'* of wheat. There are still others for which almsgiving of less than this measure is 'necessary'. There are some offences which necessitate the payment of the price of any animal, bird, etc. hunted by a person in *iḥrām*. Each person in *iḥrām* who participated in the killing of the hunted animal, will pay the full price.

The offences which require sacrifice of an animal are as follows. A person in *iḥrām* who is major [1] has applied scent to any of his limbs, [2] or has dyed his hair with henna, [3-4] or has applied oil or a similar thing to his body, [5] or has covered his head [254] throughout a day, [6] or has shaved a fourth of his head or his crown or his one armpit or his pubic hair or his neck, [7] or has cut the nails of his hands and feet in one sitting or the nails of his one hand, or one foot, [8] or has left undone any one of the 'required' acts of pilgrimage.

Examples of the offences which require almsgiving of half a *ṣā'* of wheat or its price, are the following. A pilgrim in *iḥrām* [1] has applied scent to a part only of one of his limbs, [2] or has put on a sewn cloth, [3] or has covered his head for less than a day, [4] or has shaved less than one-fourth of his head, [5] or has cut a nail — for cutting each nail the almsgiving of half a *ṣā'* of wheat is 'required'; if

[253] An important later work on Ḥanafī law is the *Kanz ad-Daqā'iq* of Abū l-Barakāt an-Nasafī (d. 710 A.H./1310 A.D.), a synopsis of the same author's *Wāfī*. Several important commentaries are written on the *Kanz*. One of them is the *Tabyīn al-Ḥaqā'iq* of az-Zayla'ī (d. 743 A.H./1342 A.D.)

[254] This is for a male pilgrim. A woman pilgrim will wear sewn cloth and will cover her head.

however, the total number of the nails cut reaches that for which the sacrifice of an animal is necessary, e.g. five nails even though not of one hand or foot, in that case almsgiving is not sufficient; so for almsgiving the total number of the nails cut will be less than that for which an animal must be sacrificed — [6] or has performed the Arrival Circumambulation or the Chest Circumambulation (*ṭawāf aṣ-ṣadr*) in the state of minor legal impurity.

It is 'necessary' to sacrifice an ewe if a pilgrim in *iḥrām* [1] has circumambulated the Ka'ba in the state of major legal impurity, [2] or has left undone a circuit of the Chest Circumambulation — for leaving undone of every circuit one ewe is to be sacrificed if the totality of the circuits left undone is less than the entire Chest Circumambulation — [3] or has left uncast one of the pebbles to be cast at the Jamras — sacrifice of an ewe is 'required' for every pebble left unthrown if the number of the pebbles left unthrown does not reach the total number of pebbles to be thrown on one day; if this number is reached, slaughtering of an animal is 'required' — [4] or has shaved the head of another person, [5] or has cut the nail of another person.

If for an excuse the pilgrim in *iḥrām* has used scent or put on a sewn cloth or shaved, he has the option of slaughtering an animal, or almsgiving of the measure of three *ṣā's* of wheat to six destitute persons, or fasting three days.

The offences requiring the almsgiving of less than half a *ṣā'* of wheat are as follows — killing of a louse or a locust. For an offence of this kind, the offending pilgrim will give away whatever amount of wheat he likes.

The offences which must be atoned for by payment of a price equivalent to the thing hunted, are the following: [1] A pilgrim's killing of a huntable animal or bird, etc. In this case, two upright men will determine its value in the place of its killing or in a place nearby. Should the value be equal to the price of an animal for sacrifice, the offender has the option — if he likes he can buy the animal and slaughter it, or he can buy food with its price and give it as alms at the rate of half a *ṣā'* of wheat to each poor person, or instead of giving food to every poor person he will fast one day. If after giving as alms half a *ṣā'* of wheat to each poor man, there remains less than half a *ṣā'*, this will also be given away as alms, or instead of giving it away the offender will fast one whole day.

[2] It is 'necessary' for a pilgrim in *iḥrām* to pay the price of any injury he caused to a bird or a similar hunted animal by plucking out

its feather with which it does not fly or its hair, or by cutting a limb of it with which it does not repel anything that is harmful to it. [3] Likewise, payment must be made for the injury caused by cutting some of its legs, by plucking out its feather, and by breaking its egg.

For killing a wild animal, sacrifice of an ewe will not do. If the wild animal is killed because it has darted ferociously over the pilgrim in *iḥrām*, killing of it is no offence.

Fasting is of no avail if a person not in *iḥrām* kills a hunted bird or an animal, etc. of the sacred area of Mecca. Nor is fasting of any avail should he cut the grass of the sacred area of Mecca or a tree which grows by itself. In all these cases, the price must be paid.

It is 'unlawful' to pasture animals on the grass of the sacred area of Mecca, or to cut this grass except the grass called idhkhar and mushrooms.

No atonement is necessary for killing of a crow, a hawk, a scorpion, a rat, a snake, a vicious dog, a fly, an ant, a flea, a monkey, a tortoise, and that which is not a hunted thing.

ANIMALS FOR SACRIFICE IN PILGRIMAGE

The lowest degree of animal to be offered up in sacrifice in pilgrimage is the ewe. Animals to be offered up in sacrifice in pilgrimage may lawfully be camels, oxen, cows, goats, sheep, and ewes. The animal which can be sacrified in 'Īd Qurbān (*'Īd al-Aḍḥā*) can be offered up in sacrifice in pilgrimage. It is 'permissible' by the law to offer up an ewe in sacrifice for every offence committed in pilgrimage except [a] the performance of that circumambulation which is a pillar of pilgrimage by a pilgrim who is in the state of major legal impurity, and [b] sexual intercourse done after the ceremony of halting but before shaving. In each of these cases of offence, a camel, not an ewe, is to be offered up in sacrifice.

The law 'permits' that sacrifice of an animal for the Tamattu' form of pilgrimage or for the Qirān form be done only on the Day of the Sacrifice, the tenth of Dhū l-Ḥijja. The law has specified that the slaughtering of every offering animal — except if it is a 'supererogatory' offering — must be accomplished in the sacred area of Mecca. Slaughtering of an animal on the way is a faulty act. It should be done at Mina, and the meat of the slaughtered animal should be eaten.

A necklace may be put upon a camel which is to be sacrificed as an act of 'supererogation', or for the Tamattu' form of pilgrimage, or for the Qirān form. The slaughtered camel in its entirety will be given away as alms. The cost of the butcher cannot be given from the meat. One will not ride the animal unless there is a necessity. It will not be milked. If, however, it is far from the place of sacrifice so that it cannot contain the milk, it will be milked and the milk will be given away as alms. But if it is near, cold water will be sprinkled on its udder.

A person who has vowed to God to perform a pilgrimage on foot, is 'required' to do so. He will not ride or make use of transport until the performance of that circumambulation which is a pillar of pilgrimage. If he rides or makes use of transport before this, he must atone for it by slaughtering an animal. Performance of a pilgrimage on foot has excellence over its performance by using any vehicle only when there is ability to use it.

VISIT TO THE TOMB OF THE PROPHET

A visit to the tomb of the prophet Muḥammad (may God bless and greet him!) at Medina is one of the best works of a man. Indeed it approaches the acts which are graded as those 'required' by the law.

If you have proceeded to visit the tomb of the Prophet you should invoke blessings on him enormously.[255] On seeing the walls of Medina you will invoke blessings on the Prophet by uttering the formula:

> God, bless Muḥammad and the family of Muḥammad, as You blessed Abraham and the family of Abraham. Surely You are All-laudable, Glorious.[256]
> (اللهم، صل على محمد وعلى ال محمد، كما صليت على ابراهيم وعلى ال ابراهيم. انك حميد مجيد).
> (*Allāhumma, ṣalli 'alā Muḥammadin wa 'alā āli Muḥammadin; kamā ṣallayta 'alā Ibrāhīma, wa 'alā āli Ibrāhīma. Innaka ḥamīdun majīdun*)

Then you will supplicate:

> God, here is the sanctuary of Your prophet and the place of the descent of Your revelation. So bestow favour on me by enabling me to enter into this city; make it a means of my safeguard from Hell and my security from punishment in the Hereafter; and make me one of those who will be successful through the intercession of the chosen one [i.e. the Prophet] on the Day of the final return.

255 Qur'ān 35:56. God sends blessing ten times upon a person who invokes blessings upon the Prophet once. See an-Nasā'ī, *Sunan*, Adhān, 37, Sahw, 47.

256 Cf. Qur'ān 11:73.

(اللهم، هنا حرم نبيك ومهبط وحيك. فامنن علي بالدخول فيه، واجعله وقاية لي من النار واماناً من العذاب، واجعلني من الفائزين بشفاعة المصطفى يوم المآب).

(Allāhumma, hunā ḥaramu nabiyyika, wa mahbaṭu waḥyika. Fa-mnun ʿalayya bi-d-dukhūli fīhi, wa jʿalhu wiqāyatan lī mina n-nāri, wa amānan mina l-ʿadhābi, wa jʿalnī mina l-fāʾizīna bi-shafāʿāti al-muṣṭafā yawma l-mʾābi).

You will enter into Medina with humbleness mixed with calmness and dignity, with a consideration of the majesty of the place, and supplicating:

> In the name of God and by the religion of the Prophet (may God bless him and greet him!). 'Lord make my entry a beneficent event and make my coming out also a beneficent event, and grant me from Yourself an authority and a helper.'[257]
>
> God, bless our Prince, Muḥammad, and the family of Muḥammad, as You blessed Abraham and the family of Abraham. Surely You are All-laudable, Glorious.[258] God, forgive me my sins and open for me the doors of Your mercy and Your bounty.
>
> (بسم الله وعلى ملة رسول الله، صلى الله عليه وسلم. "رب ادخلني مدخل صدق، واخرجني مخرج صدق، واجعل لي من لدنك سلطاناً نصيراً." اللهم، صل على سيدنا محمد وعلى آل محمد، كما صليت على ابراهيم وعلى آل ابراهيم. انك حميد مجيد. واغفرلي ذنوبي، وافتح لي ابواب رحمتك وفضلك).
>
> *(Bi-smi Allāhi, wa ʿalā millati rasūli Allāhi, ṣallā Allāhu ʿalayhi wa sallama. Rabbi adkhilnī mudkhala ṣidqin, wa akhrijnī mukhraja ṣidqin, wa jʿal lī min ladunka sulṭānan naṣīran.*
>
> *Allāhumma, ṣalli ʿalā sayyidinā Muḥammadin, wa ʿalā āli Muḥammadin, kamā ṣallayta ʿalā Ibrāhīma, wa ʿalā āli Ibrāhīma. Innaka ḥamdīdun majīdun. Wa ghfir lī dhunūbī, wa ftiḥ lī abwāba raḥmatika wa faḍlika).*

Then you will enter into Masjid an-Nabī (the Mosque of the

[257] Qur'ān 17:80. [258] Cf. Qur'ān 11:73.

Prophet) and perform the two *rak'as* of ritual prayer for greeting the mosque near the *Minbar*, (pulpit), standing in such a way that the pillars of the pulpit are opposite to your right shoulder, because this was the standing place of the Prophet. Between his pulpit and his grave there exists a *Rawḍa* (meadow) from the meadows of Paradise, as the Prophet described it.[259] Aside from the two *rak'as* for greeting the mosque, you will also perform two more *rak'as* in gratitude to God for His help in reaching the Mosque of the Prophet. Then you will supplicate to God for whatever you like.

Then you will go straight to the tomb and stand at a distance of four cubits from the *maqṣūra* (closet) in extreme courtesy, keeping the direction of Mecca at your back, being opposite to the head of the Prophet and to his face, and assuming that he is looking at you, listening to you, returning to you your salutation to him, and saying *āmīn* at the end of your prayer to God. In this state you will read this greeting:

> May peace be upon you O my prince, O messenger of God! May peace be upon you, O prophet of God! May peace be upon you, O beloved to God! May peace be upon you, O prophet of mercy![260] May peace be upon you, O intercessor for the Muslim community! May peace be upon you, O the chief of all messengers of God! May peace by upon you, 'O the last of the prophets!;'[261] May peace by upon you, 'O the one enwrapped in the mantle!'[262] May peace be upon you, 'O the one enwrapped in cloak!'[263] May peace by upon you, upon your good forefathers, and upon the purified members of your family from whom God removed all uncleanness and whom He purified completely.[264] May God grant you such a reward on our behalf as is greater than that which He is to grant to any prophet on behalf of his people, or to any Messenger on behalf of his community!
>
> I bear witness that truly you are a messenger of God and that you conveyed the message,[265] fulfilled your trust, admonished the community, clearly expressed the proof, fought for the sake of God as was your duty, and worked to establish Islam until your death.

259 Aḥmad ibn Ḥanbal, *Musnad*, III, 64. It is in respect of value, nobility and blessings, that the *Rawḍa* is described a meadow from the meadows of Paradise.

260 Cf. Qur'ān 3:159, 21:107, 17:28. 261 Qur'ān 33:40. 262 Qur'ān 72:1.

263 Qur'ān 73:1. 264 Qur'ān 33:33.

265 Cf. Qur'ān 5:67, 33:39, 3:30, 5:99, 13:40, 16:35, 82, 24:54, 29:18, 42:48; also see al-Bukhārī, *Ṣaḥīḥ*, 'Ilm , 30 37; Muslim, *Ṣaḥīḥ*, Īmān, 378.

May God bless and greet you as well as the noblest place which has become noble by the entering of your noble body into it! May blessings and greetings be showered upon you and upon the noble place perpetually from the Lord of all the worlds at the number equal to that of all beings existed in the past, [all beings that are in existence at present], and all beings that will exist in future but are now in God's knowledge — blessings [and greetings] which are unlimited and unending!

Messenger of God, we have come to visit you and to visit your sacred place, and we are honoured by entering in front of you. We have come to you from remote lands and distant places, traversing smooth and rough roads, with the intention of visiting you in order that we may be successful in obtaining your intercession, in looking at the things and places connected with your life, in fulfilling some of our duties towards you, and in asking for your intercession to our Lord — for sins have broken our backs and crimes have overburdened our shoulders — and you are the intercessor granted the right of intercession and the one promised with the greatest intercession,[266] the most laudable station[267] and the means[268] to obtain salvation. God (exalted is He!)

[266] In the Hereafter, angels, prophets, saints, martyrs, and pious religious scholars will intercede to God for doing favour to believers. But they will be able to intercede only with God's permission and only for those believers for the intercession of whom permission will be granted by God (Qur'ān 2:255, 21:28, 10:3, 19:87, 20:109, 34:23, 53:26). This intercession will be in some cases for elevation of ranks in Paradise, in some for admission into Paradise without least suffering in Hell, and in most cases to rescue the sinful believers from Hell after suffering there for sometime. Prophet Muḥammad will be granted permission to intercede for Muslims (Bukhārī, *Ṣaḥīḥ*, Da'wāt, 1, 'Ilm, 33, Riqāq, 51, Anbiyā', 9; Muslim, *Ṣaḥīḥ*, Īmān, 302, 318, 326, 334-45, Zuhd, 38; Ibn Māja, *Sunan*, Zuhd, 37). Every Muslim should pray to God that he might grant the Prophet the permission to intercede for him. Also see *infra*, n., 267.

[267] This is a lofty status in Paradise promised to the prophet Muḥammad (Qur'ān 17:79). By virtue of this station he will intercede for Muslims (Aḥmad ibn Ḥanbal, *Musnad*, II, 441). They invoke this rank to him not only when visiting his tomb, but also five times a day — i.e. through the supplication formula they read at the end of *adhān* for each of the five daily ritual prayers. Also see *supra*, n., 266; *infra*, n., 268.

[268] In general the means to salvation in the Hereafter consists in faith (*īmān*) and good action. There is, however, a special means to salvation, which is the intercession of prophets, saints, martyrs, and pious religious scholars. To find the opportunity of using the prophet Muḥammad as a special means, every Muslim should pray to God for it not only when visiting his tomb, but also after *adhān* for each of the five daily

declared, "If, when they (i.e. believers] had done wrong to their souls, they had come to you [i.e. the Messenger] and asked forgiveness of God and the Messenger also had asked forgiveness for them, they would have surely found God oft-turning with compassion, Ever Merciful."[269] And we have come to you having done wrong to our souls and seeking forgiveness for our sins. So intercede for us to your Lord and pray to Him that He may cause us to die in the state of observing your sunna, that He may include me in your company on the Day of Judgement, that He may allow me to come to your well in Paradise and to drink from its water with your cup,[270] without being humiliated and ashamed. Your intercession I pray for, your intercession, your intercession, O Messenger of God!

'Lord, forgive us and our brethren who preceded us in the faith, and do not permit any feeling of rancour to arise in our minds against those who have believed. Lord, surely You are Compassionate, Ever Merciful.'[271]

(السلام عليك يا سيدى يارسول الله. السلام عليك يا نبى الله. السلام عليك يا حبيب الله. السلام عليك يا نبى الرحمة. السلام عليك يا شفيع الامة. السلام عليك يا سيد المرسلين. السلام عليك يا خاتم النبيين. السلام عليك يا مزمل. السلام عليك يا مدثر. السلام عليك وعلى اصولك الطيبين واهل بيتك الطاهرين الذين اذهب الله عنهم الرجس وطهرهم تطهيرا.

جزاك الله عنا افضل ما جزى نبيا عن قومه ورسولا عن امته. اشهد انك رسول الله قد بلغت الرسالة واديت الامانة ونصحت الامة واوضحت الحجة وجاهدت فى سبيل الله حق جهاده واقمت الدين حتى اتاك اليقين.

صلى الله عليك وسلم وعلى اشرف مكان تشرف بحلول جسمك الكريم فيه صلاة وسلاما دائمين من رب العالمين

ritual prayers. For a detailed discussion of the Islamic conception of the means see Ibn Taymiyya, ***at-Tawassul wa l-Wasīla***, **Bairut, 1970/1390.** Also see Muhammad Abul Quasem, ***The Ethics of al-Ghazālī: a Composite Ethics in Islam***, 2nd ed., New York, 1978, Chap. II, secs. iv-v.

269 Qur'ān 4:64.

270 Qur'ān 108:1; al-Bukhārī, *Ṣaḥīḥ*, Maghāzī, 17, 27, Riqāq, 53; Muslim, *Ṣaḥīḥ*, 53f.; at-Tirmidhī, ***Sunan,*** Qiyāma, 14f.

271 Qur'ān 59:10.

عدد ما كان وعدد ما يكون بعلم الله، صلاة لاانقضاء لامدها.

يا رسول الله: نحن وفدك وزوار حرمك. تشرفنا بالحلول بين يديك. وقد جئناك من بلاد شاسعة وامكنة بعيدة، نقطع السهل والوعر، بقصد زيارتك لنفوز بشفاعتك والنظر الى ماثرك ومعاهدك والقيام ببعض حقك والاستشفاع بك الى ربنا ـ فان الخطايا قد قصمت ظهورنا، والاوزار قد اثقلت كواهلنا ـ وانت الشافع المشفع الموعود بالشفاعة العظمى والمقام المحمود والوسيلة. وقد قال الله تعالى "ولو انهم اذ ظلموا انفسهم جاوءاك، فاستغفروا الله واستغفر لهم الرسول، لوجدوا الله توابا رحيما". وقد جئناك ظالمين لانفسنا، مستغفرين لذنوبنا. فاشفع لنا الى ربك، واسأله ان يميتنا على سنتك، وان يحشرنا فى زمرتك، وان يوردنا حوضك، وان يسقينا بكأسك غير خزايا ولا ندامى. الشفاعة الشفاعة، يا رسول الله!

"ربنا اغفرلنا ولاخواننا الذين سبقونا بالايمان، ولا تجعل فى قلوبنا غلا للذين امنوا، ربنا انك رءوف رحيم".

You will also convey to the Prophet the salutations of those who requested you to do so. So you will say:

> May peace be upon you, O Messenger of God, from so-and-so! He asks for your intercession to your Lord. So intercede for him and for all other Muslims.
>
> (السلام عليك يا رسول الله، من فلان ابن فلان، يتشفع بك الى ربك: فاشفع له وللمسلمين.)
>
> (*As-salāmu ʻalayka yā rasūla Allāhi, min fulānin ibnī fulānin, yatashaffaʻu bika ilā rabbika. Fa-shfaʻ lahu wa li-l-muslimīna.*)

Then you will invoke blessings on the Prophet and pray to God for whatever you like, standing near his countenance in such a way that the direction of Mecca remains behind you.

After this you will move the measure of one cubit so that you will be opposite the head of Abū Bakr aṣ-Ṣiddīq who is buried by the side of the Prophet.[272] Standing here you will read the following salutation:

> May peace be upon you, O successor of the Messenger of

[272] Abu Bakr aṣ-Ṣiddīq (d. 13 A.H.) was the first of all major male persons to accept Islam. Of all companions of the Prophet, he was the most intimate to the

God (may God bless him and greet him!)! May peace be upon you, O companion of God's Messenger, his companion in the cave,[273] his companion in travels, and one who was trusted with his confidence! May God grant you such a reward on our behalf as is better than the reward to be granted to any leader on behalf of his prophet's community!

Indeed you succeeded the Prophet as the best successor, walked on his way and his path in the best manner, fought against the apostates and heretics, arranged the affairs of Islam, and strengthened its pillars. Thus you became a good leader. You did good to your people. Until death you never departed from the way of the just, and from helping the religion and its followers.

Pray to God (Holy is He!) for us so that we may perpetually love you[274], may be included in your company on the Day of Resurrection, and that our visit to you may be accepted by Him.

May peace be upon you and also God's mercy and His blessings!

(السلام عليكم يا خليفة رسول اللهم صلى الله عليه وسلم.
السلام عليكم يا صاحب رسول اللهم وانيسه فى الغارم
ورفيقه فى الاسفارم وامينه على الاسرار. جزاك الله عنا
افضل ما جزى اماما عن امة نبيه.
فلقد خلفته باحسن خلفم وسلكت طريقه ومنهاجه خير

Prophet. As the first successor of the Prophet, he served Islam for two years. His service to the cause of Islam is next to that of the Prophet himself. Hence he deserved to be buried by the side of the Prophet and to be saluted by every visitor who saluted the Prophet. Also see *infra*, n., 101. For his biography see Ibn Ḥajar, *Tahdhīb*, V, 315-16.

[273] This refers to a cave of the mountain Thawr in Mecca. In the night of the Prophet's flight (*hijra*) from Mecca to Medina (622 A.D.) he, accompanied by Abū Bakr, took shelter in this cave (Qur'ān 9:40). This is mentioned in the Qur'ānic verse 9:40.

[274] It is a duty of every Muslim to love all companions of the Prophet (al-Bukhārī, *Ṣaḥīḥ*, Īmān, 103; Muslim, *Ṣaḥīḥ*, 127f.; at-Tirmidhī, *Sunan*. Manāqib, 58), especially the four caliphs — Abū Bakr, 'Umar, Uthman and 'Alī — and all the members of the Prophet's family (at-Tirmidhī, *Sunan*, Manāqib, 20, 31; Ibn Māja, *Sunan*, Muqaddama, 11). One who really loves them may be granted the privilege of being resurrected with them. The prophet said, "A man is with him whom he loves;" see al-Bukhārī, *Ṣaḥiḥ*, Adab, 96; Muslim, *Ṣaḥīḥ*, Birr, 165.

مسلككم وقاتلت اهل الردة والبدعم مهدت الاسلامم وشيدت اركانه. فكنت خير امام. ووصلت الارحام. ولم تزل قائما بالحق ناصرا للدين ولاهله حتى اتاك اليقين. سل الله سبحانه لنا دوام حبكم والحشر مع حزبكم وقبول زيارتنا. السلام عليك ورحمة الله وبركاته).

Then you will move the measure of a cubit so that you will be opposite the head of 'Umar ibn al-Khaṭṭāb who is buried by the side of Abū Bakr.[275] Standing here you will read the salutation:

> May peace be upon you, O the Commander of the Faithful! May peace be upon you, O upholder of Islam! May peace be upon you, O the one who broke the idols! May God grant you the best reward on behalf of us!
>
> Indeed you tremendously helped Islam and the Muslims, conquered most of the territories after the Chief of the Messengers, cared for the orphans, did good to your people, and strengthened Islam. For the Muslims you were a leader with whom they all were pleased, and a guide who was himself guided aright. You reunited them, assisted the needy among them and consoled the broken-hearted of them.
>
> May peace be upon you and also God's mercy and His blessings!
>
> (السلام عليكم يا امير الموءمنين. السلام عليكم يا مظهر الاسلام. السلام عليكم يا مكسر الاصنام. جزاك الله عنا افضل الجزاء.
>
> لقد نصرت الا سلام والمسلمين، وفتحت معظم البلاد بعد سيدالمرسلين، وكفلت الايتام، ووصلت الارحام. وقوى بك الاسلام. وكنت للمسلمين اماما مرضيا وهاديا مهديا. جمعت شملهم، واعنت فقيرهم، وجبرت كسيرهم. السلام عليك ورحمة الله وبركاته)،

Then you will return by the measure of a half cubit and will read the following salutation:

275 Of all the companions of the Prophet 'Umar ibn al-Khaṭṭāb (d. 23 A.H.) was the most intimate to the Prophet after Abū Bakr. His service to Islam during the lifetimes of the Prophet and Abū Bakr was great. He succeeded Abū Bakr, and in the ten years of his caliphate rendered tremendous service to Islam — its propagation and territorial expansion and administration. Thus he deserved to be buried by the side of the Prophet and of Abū Bakr and to be saluted by anyone who visited them. For his biography see Ibn Ḥajar, *Tahdhīb*, VII, 438-41.

May peace be upon you both, O the two most intimate men to the Messenger of God (may God bless him and greet him!), his two special companions,[276] his two viziers, his two counsellors, his two assistants in the establishment of the religion, and the two caliphs who, after him, completely devoted themselves to the welfare of the Muslims! May God grant both of you the best recompense!

We have come to both of you to use you to approach the Messenger of God (may God bless him and greet him!) so that he may intercede to God for us and ask God, our Lord, to accept our efforts, to enable us to live in keeping with his religion and to die with belief in it [when death comes], and to include us in his company on the Day of Resurrection.

(السلام عليكم، يا ضجيعي رسول الله صلى الله عليه وسلم، ورفيقيه ووزيريه ومشيريه، والمعاونين له على القيام بالدين، والقائمين بعده بمصالح المسلمين. جزاكما الله عنا احسن الجزاء.

جئناكما نتوسل بكما الى رسول الله، صلى الله عليه وسلم، ليشفع لنا، ويسأل الله ربنا ان يتقبل سعينا ويحيينا على ملته ويمتنا عليها ويحشرنا فى زمرته).

After this, you will pray to God for the good of yourself, of your parents, of those who requested you to pray for them, and for all other Muslims.

Then you will stand near the head of the Messenger of God in the manner in which you stood first, and will pray:

God, You said — and Your saying is true —, "If, when they [i.e. believers] had done wrong to their souls, they had come to you [i.e. the Messenger] and asked forgiveness of God and the Messenger also had asked forgiveness for them, they would have surely found God Oft-returning with compassion, Ever Merciful."[277] So we have come to You, hearing Your saying, obeying Your command, and asking for the intercession of Your prophet to You.

God, our Lord, forgive us, our fathers, our mothers 'and our brethren who preceded us in the faith, and do not

276 Wherever the Prophet would go he would take both Abū Bakr and 'Umar with him. He was often heard say: 'I and Abū Bakr and 'Umar came out,' 'I and Abū Bakr and 'Umar entered.'

277 Qur'ān 4:64.

permit any feeling of rancour to arise in our minds against those who have believed. Lord, You are Compassionate, Ever Merciful.' [278]

'Lord, grant us the good in this world as well as the good in the Hereafter, and safeguard us against the punishment of Hell.' [279]

'Holy is your Lord, the Lord of honour far above that which they [i.e. the polytheists] describe of Him! May peace be upon the Messengers! Praise be to God, the Lord of all the worlds!' [280]

اللهم، انك قلت ـ وقولك الحق ـ ”ولو انهم اذ ظلموا انفسهم جاوك، فاستغفروا الله واستغفر لهم الرسول، لوجدوا الله توابا رحيما.“ وقد جئناك، سامعين قولك طائعين امرك مستشفعين بنبيك اليك.

اللهم، ربنا اغفر لنا ولابائنا وامهاتنا ”واخواننا الذين سبقونا بالايمان، ولا تجعل فى قلوبنا غلا للذين امنوا؛ ربنا انك رءوف رحيم.“

”ربنا اتنا فى الدنيا حسنة وفى الاخرة حسنة، وقنا عذاب النار. سبحان ربك رب العزة عما يصفون، وسلام على المرسلين، والحمد لله رب العالمين“.)

You will add to this prayer whatever you like; you will pray for that which may come to your mind at that moment and for the prayer of which God may grant you assistance through His bounty.

Then you will come to the Usṭuwāna Abī Lubāba (the column of Abū Lubāba). This is the column to which he tied himself until God turned to him in compassion. [281] It is between the tomb and the pulpit. At the root of this pillar, you will perform 'supererogatory' ritual prayer of whatever number of *rak'as* you like, will turn to Him in repentance, and will pray by reciting whatever prayer formula you like.

Then you will come to the *Rawḍa* (meadow) where you will perform the 'supererogatory' ritual prayer of whatever number of *rak'as* you like, and pray for whatever thing you want. Here you will greatly glorify God, affirm the oneness of God, praise God, and ask

278 Qur'ān 59:10. 279 Qur'ān 20:201.

280 Qur'ān 37:180-82.

281 Abū Lubāba is one of those companions of the Prophet who are called Anṣārs (the helpers). His story, as narrated by Ibn Isḥāq, is as follows. The Jewish clan of

for forgiveness of God, i.e. you will repeatedly utter the following formulae of prayer or similar other formulae with full attention of mind:

> Glory be to God!
> (سبحان الله).
> (*Subḥāna Allāhi*).
>
> There is no god but God.
> (لا اله الا الله).
> (*Lā ilāha illā Allāhu*).
>
> Praise be to God!
> (الحمد لله).
> (*Al-ḥamdu li-Allāhi*).
>
> I pray to God, my Lord, for forgiveness of every sin, and I turn to Him in repentance.
> (استغفرالله العظيم من كل ذنبٍ واتوب اليه).
> (*Astaghfiru Allāha rabbī min kulli dhanbin wa atūbu ilayhi*)]

Then you will come to the *Minbar* (pulpit) and put the hand on [a] the Rummāna (the knob of metal) which was there for the obtain-

Qurayẓa in Medina engaged in secret negotiation with the enemies of Islam. The Prophet, therefore, attacked the clan. The Jews proposed to surrender but were told that they had to surrender unconditionally. They then requested to be allowed to consult Abū Lubāba Anṣārī, a devout Muslim, whose clan was in alliance with them. The Prophet agreed and sent him to them. They asked, "O Abū Lubāba, do you think that we should surrender to the discretion of Muḥammad?" He replied, "Yes", and pointed with his hand to his neck, indicating that it would be slaughter. His feet had not moved from the spot before he realized that he had betrayed God and the Prophet (by indicating the Prophet's intention of putting them to death). Then he departed. He did not, however, go to the Prophet but bound himself to a pillar in the Mosque of the Prophet (which is now called Usṭuwāna Abī Lubāba) and said, "I shall not leave my place here until God pardons me for what I have done," and he swore to God, "I shall never again go to Banū Qurayẓa, and I shall never again go to a district in which I betrayed God and His Messenger." When news of this reached the Prophet he said, "Had he come to me I would have forgiven him; but since he has done as he has done, it is not for me to loose him from his place until God pardons him." Abū Lubāba then remained bound to the pillar except during the times of ritual prayer when his wife (or daughter) untied him. After six days the Prophet announced that God had pardoned him, and at Abū Lubāba's request himself untied him. This happened in May, 627 A.D. Thus the Usṭuwāna Abī Lubāba has become a spot where prayer to God is more likely to be received by God. The visitors to the Prophet's tomb should pray here more than at other spots of the Sanctuary of the Prophet. See Ibn Hishām, *Sīra Rasūl Allāh*, ed. F. Wustenfeld, Gottingen, 1859-60, p. 686f.

ing of blessings from the relic of the Messenger of God,[282] and [b] on the place where he used to put his hand when addressing so that you may gain the blessings of the Prophet. You will invoke blessings upon him and pray to God for whatever you want.

After this you will come to the Usṭuwāna Ḥannāna (the Yearning Column), the column in which remained some of the restlessness which yearned towards the Prophet when he abandoned it and began to address ascending on the pulpit, so that he descended and embraced it and now it became calm.[283]

You will try to gain blessings from the remaining relics of the Prophet and from the holy places of Medina. During your stay there, you will try hard to keep vigil for 'supererogatory' acts of devotion, and will, most of the time, avail yourself of the opportunity of contemplating the prophetic presence and of visiting his tomb.

It is 'praiseworthy' to go out to the al-Baqī', the graveyard of Medina, in order to visit the graves there. You will go to the place of martyrdom and visit the graves of the martyrs, especially the grave of the chief martyr Ḥamza.[284] Then you will go to the last end of al-Baqī' where you will visit the graves of the Prophet's uncle, 'Abbās,[285] and the Prophet's grandson, Ḥasan ibn 'Alī.[286] You will also visit the graves of Amīr al-Mu'minīn 'Uthmān ibn 'Affān,[287] the

282 Laying hands upon the relics of the Prophet with courtesy and reverence with a view to obtaining blessings is 'permissible' by the law. But to kiss them and to prostrate before them, as do the ignorant, are forbidden on the grounds that this is tantamount to worship of relics and not God.

283 Before the construction of the pulpit of his mosque, the Prophet used the Usṭuwāna Ḥannāna. On his abandoing it for the pulpit, the Usṭuwāna began to weep but then became calm after his embracing it. This is one of his many miracles. A number of them is gathered together by al-Ghazālī in his *Iḥyā'*, Bk. XX.

284 Ḥamza ibn 'Abd al-Muṭṭalib, (d. 3 A.H.), an uncle of the Prophet, was killed in the battle of Uḥud. Uḥud is a mountain outside the walls of Medina. At its feet the Prophet and his companions fought against the Quraysh in the third year of the Hijra, and in this battle seventy-three of his companions, one of whom is Ḥamzah, were killed by the Meccan infidels. They all were buried in the foot hills. This graveyard is now surrounded by a low fence. Every pilgrim should visit and pray for those who sacrificed their lives for establishing the oneness of God. For the biography of Ḥamza see Ibn 'Abd al-Barr, al-*Istī'āb*, Cairo, 1960, I, 369-76.

285 For the biography of 'Abbās see Ibn 'Abd al-Barr, *al-Istī'āb*, II, 710-17.

286 Al-Ḥasan ibn 'Alī was a grandson of the Prophet by his daughter Fāṭima. For his biography see *ibid.*, I, 383-92. Al-Ḥasan's brother Imām Ḥusayn was killed at Karbala at the order of the Umayyad ruler Yazīd.

287 He was the third Caliph of Islam and a son-in-law of the Prophet. A rich man, he spent a great part of his wealth for the welfare of Islam during the Prophet's lifetime. For his biography see *ibid.*, III, 1037-53. Pilgrims visit his grave, salute him and pray for him.

Prophet's son, Ibrāhīm,[288] the wives of the Prophet, his aunt Ṣafiyya,[289] his companions and their followers.

You will visit the graves of the martyrs of Uḥud. It is better to visit them on Thursday, if possible. Standing beside them with full reverence and humility, you will say:

> 'May peace be upon you because you were steadfast [in battle]! How excellent is the reward of the Hereafter!'[290]
> (سلام عليكم بما صبرتم، فنعم عقبى الدار)
>
> (*Salāmun 'alaykum bi-mā Ṣabartum, fa-ni'ma 'uqbā d-dāri*)

Here you will also recite the Verse of the Throne[291] and the Sūra of Sincerity[292] eleven times, and also the Sūra of Yā Sīn,[293] if possible. The reward of the recitation of these you will present as gifts to all the martyrs buried there and to all other believers buried in their neighbourhood.

It is 'praiseworthy' to go to Masjid Qubā'[294] (the mosque at Qubā') on Saturday or any other day and to perform ritual prayer in it. At the end of whatever supplication you may read there, you will say:

> 'O Responder of those who cry for succor, O the Help of those who implore for help,'[295] O the Remover of the anxiety of those who are in anxiety, O the Responder to the call of those who are in affliction,[296] bless Muḥammad and his family, and remove my anxiety and grief as You removed the grief and anxiety of Your Messenger at this place. [Accept my prayer], O Compassionate, O Generous, O Doer of immense good and beneficence, O Bestower of perpetual favour, O the Most Merciful of those who show mercy.

288 For his biography see *ibid.*, I, 54-61.

289 For her biography see *ibid.*, IV, 1873.

290 Qur'ān 13:24.

291 Qur'ān 2:255.

292 Qur'ān 112: 1-4.

293 This is the thirty-sixth sūra of the Qur'ān. The benefit of its recitation to the deceased as well as to the reciter is mentioned *supra*, p. 171.

294 Qubā' is a garden village at the distance of a few kilometers from Medina on the camel route from Mecca. After the Prophet, together with Abū Bakr, had fled Mecca and crossed the desert, they arrived at Qubā' (on or about 4th September, 622/12th Rajab, 1 A.H.), where they took rest for a few days. During this pause, the Prophet founded a mosque here and performed in it the first Friday Assembly Prayers. This mosque, known as Masjid Qubā', is the first place of worship founded by the Prophet and his companions after their migration from Mecca.

295 Cf. Qur'ān 8:9.

296 Qur'ān 27:62.

May God bless and greet our Prince Muḥammad, his family and his companions perpetually and eternally! [Accept our prayer], O the Lord of all the worlds. Āmīn.

(يا صريخ المستصرخين، يا غياث المستغيثين، يا مفرج كرب المكروبين، يا مجيب دعوة المضطرين: صل على محمد واله، واكشف كربى وحزنى كما كشفت عن رسولك حزنه وكربه فى هذا المقام. يا حنان، يا منان، يا كثير المعروف والاحسان، يا دائم النعم، يا ارحم الراحمين.

وصلى الله على سيدنا محمد وعلى اله وصحبه، وسلم تسليما دائما ابدا، يا رب العالمين. امين).

VII
QUR'ĀN-RECITATION

ان الذين يتلون كتاب الله واقاموا الصلاة وانفقوا مما رزقناهم
سـرا وعلانية يرجـون تجارة لـن تبور، ليوفيهم اجورهم
ويزيدهم من فضلـه.ـ قران ٣٠ـ٢٩:٣٤

Those who recite the Book of God, observe ritual prayer, and spend out of that which We have provided for them, secretly and openly, are pursuing a commerce that suffers no loss, for God will give them full rewards and will add to them out of His bounty. — Qur'ān 34: 29-30

قـال النبي، صلى الله عليه وسلم: خيركم من تعلم القـران وعلمه.

The Prophet (may God bless and greet him!) said, "The best of you is one who has learnt the Qur'ān and has taught it." [297]

THREE MOTIVES OF QUR'ĀN-RECITATION

Muslims usually recite the Qur'ān with three main motives each of which is relevant to salvation. The first is the motive of performance of a supererogatory act of devotion recommended in the Qur'ān[298] and Tradition.[299] It is with this motive that those Muslims who cannot understand the meaning of the Qur'ān as well as those who can, often recite it, and they do so in the morning after the Dawn Prayer, when keeping vigil at night, and on completion of every ritual prayer. The ṣūfīs also recite the Qur'ān with this motive when they are traversing the ṣūfī path and regard it, in certain circumstances, as the best of all forms of supererogatory worship, and in others as only inferior to their remembrance of God (*dhikr*).[300] Not only recitation, but even a Muslim's looking at a case of the Qur'ān with due respect is a supererogatory act of devotion.[301]

[297] Al-Bukhārī, *Ṣaḥīḥ*, Faḍā'il al-Qur'ān, 21; Ibn Māja, *Sunan*, Muqaddama, 16; ad-Dārimī, *Sunan*, Faḍā'il al-Qur'ān, 2.

[298] Qur'ān 2: 121, 17: 78, 27: 91-92, 34: 29-30.

[299] Al-Bukhārī, *Ṣaḥīḥ*, Faḍā'il al-Qur'ān, 21; Ibn Māja, *Sunan*, Muqaddama, 16.

[300] Al-Ghazālī, *al-Arba'īn*, p. 58.

[301] *Idem.*, *Iḥyā'*, I, 279.

The second motive is to gain the blessings that accrue from uttering the divine speech with due reverence and in the proper manner. The Qur'ān is the speech of God communicated to mankind through the prophet Muḥammad. Its language, like its meaning, is out and out divine: there is no mingling of the language of any of His creatures in it. So one gains blessings from uttering it, believing in its divine origin and exalted status. It is for blessings that Muslims recite the Qur'ān at the start of sermons, in marriage ceremonies, in pious gatherings and on other occasions of similar type. All this forms a point of disagreement between the Qur'ān and the Scriptures of other religions, for the language of none of these Scriptures is divine in the sense in which the language of the Qur'ān is, and none of them is recited for the purpose of gaining any blessings.

The third motive of recitation of the Qur'ān is to understand its meaning, to know the principles of guidance set forth in it. The Qur'ān aims at guiding[302] human being along the right path in every aspect of his life; it contains the core principles of all forms of knowledge needed for the conduct of his life.[303] In order to know these principles those Muslims who can understand Arabic recite the Qur'ān. This motive is cognitive, yet recitation with this motive is an act of devotion, for it is the acquisition of Islamic religious knowledge.[304]

WHEN QUR'ĀN-RECITATION IS 'UNLAWFUL'

Recitation of even a single Qur'ānic verse by a person who has incurred the major legal impurity is unlawful. Touching of it by such a person is also not permitted by God; [305] his touching the exterior of a case which contains the Qur'ān is, however, lawful. Thus a person who has had sexual intercourse but who has not yet bathed, cannot legally recite even a single verse of the Qur'ān, whether from his memory or by touching the *muṣḥaf* — after bathing he is allowed to do so. This is applicable to one who has not actually had sexual intercourse but who has emitted his sperm with excitement, whether in dream or in waking state for any reason and by using any method whatsoever. A menstruating woman and a woman who is bleeding after child-birth are not legally allowed to recite even a single Qur'ānic verse from their memory or by touching it. After the expiry of the period of menstruation or bleeding after child-birth they must bathe and only then can they legally recite or touch the Qur'ān.[306]

[302]Qur'ān 2:2, 26, 97, 159, 185, 3: 16,5: 46,6: 88,9: 33,17: 6,46: 30,72: 2,39: 41,48: 28,61: 9, *passim*.

[303]Qur'ān 6:59. [304]Al-Ghazālī, *Iḥyā'*, I, 13. [305]Qur'ān 56:79.

For a person who has incurred the minor legal impurity it is unlawful to touch the Qur'ān. Such a person's recitation of it, however, is lawful. This has been discussed in the chapter on cleanliness and need not be repeated here. [307]

'REQUIRED' ACTS IN QUR'ĀN-RECITATION

In the Qur'ān there are fourteen verses called verses of prostration (*āyāt as-sajda*). The person who recites anyone of them or hears another person reciting it, is 'required' by the law to prostrate himself before God. Prostration must be made even if the verse recited is in the form of translation into a language other than Arabic. To prostrate due to the recitation of a verse of prostration is the fulfilment of one's obligation to the right (*ḥaqq*) of the verse. Prostration needs to be made immediately, if a verse of prostration is recited inside a ritual prayer; if, however, it is recited outside a ritual prayer, prostration can be delayed. In a section[308] of the chapter on ritual prayer, we have already stated the fourteen verses of prostration together with the sūras in which they occur, the people who are required to prostrate and the people who are not, the circumstances in which prostration can be delayed to a later time, and the cases where it needs to be repeated. We have also discussed there its other aspects, such as its 'pillar', the stipulations for its validity, sunna acts in it, its performance both inside and outside a ritual prayer, and by the imām, his followers and others. Repetition of that discussion here is unnecessary.

SUNNA AND 'PRAISEWORTHY' BODILY TASKS IN QUR'ĀN-RECITATION

There are nine sunna and 'praiseworthy' tasks of the body in Qur'ān-recitation.[309] The first concerns the bodily condition of the reciter. It consists in his being in a state of ablution, politeness and quietness, either standing or sitting, facing the *qibla*, with the head cast down, neither sitting crosslegged nor leaning against anything nor sitting in a haughty manner. He should sit as he would when in front of his teacher.

Of all the the conditions of the reciter the best is that he recites during ritual prayers standing and inside a mosque. In this case ablution is obligatory upon him. If, however, he recites without ablution while reclining on his side on a bed, he also has excellence,

[306] *Supra*, pp. 79f. [307] *Supra*, p. 81. [308] *Supra*, pp. 148-51.

[309] For a detailed account of these tasks see al-Ghazālī, *Iḥyā'*, I,275-80; Muhammad Abul Quasem, *The Recitation and Interpretation of the Qur'ān: al-Ghazālī's Theory*, 2nd ed., Kuala Lumpur, 1979, pp. 34-55.

but this excellence is of a lower grade.[310]

That reading of the Qur'ān which forms part of keeping vigil at night[311] is more excellent than reading it during daytime, for at night the mind is most free from other matters.

The second sunna task concerns the amount of Qur'ān-reading. The best thing in determining it is to rely upon the Prophet's words:

> "One who has read the [entire] Qur'ān in less than three days has not understood it."[312]

This is because swift reading prevents the reader from reading in a slow and distinct manner which is sunna. The Prophet advised 'Abd Allāh ibn 'Umar[313] to read the entire Qur'ān once in every seven days. Likewise a group of the companions of the Prophet used to complete the reading of the entire Qur'ān on every Friday.'[314]

There may be four grades of reading the Qur'ān in its entirety. (1) To read it once in a day and night. This is 'disliked' by the law because it requires too swift a reading. (2) Reading the entire Qur'ān once in every month. This is 'not disliked'. It, however, seems to be an excessive reduction in the amount of reciting in the case of those pious people who have much time to devote to spiritual improvement. Such people should read the entire Qur'ān in less than thirty days. (3) To read the entire Qur'ān once in a week. This is better than the preceding grade, and this is what the Prophet recommended to his companions. If this is adopted, Friday should be the date of completion. (4) To read the entire Qur'ān twice in a week. This is 'not disliked'. In this case it is preferable to complete one reading of the entire Qur'ān on Monday in the Dawn Prayer or just after it, and the other on Friday night in the Sunset Prayer or after it.

More details concerning the amount of Qur'ān-reading are as follows. If the reciter is a devotee traversing the ṣūfī path by performing good acts of the body, he should not do less than read the entire Qur'ān twice a week, because his only task is to do devotional deeds. If, however, the reader is a devotee traversing the ṣūfī path by performing the actions of the soul and by different types of reflection, or if he is one engaged in imparting useful knowledge, then

[310]Qur'ān 3:191.

[311]This is recommended in Qur'ān 17:79.

[312]At-Tirmidhī, *Sunan*, Iqāma, 178.

[313]Ibn 'Umar (d.73/693) was one of the most prominent companions of the Prophet who are very frequently quoted for Traditions, moral qualities and deep piety. For his biography see Ibn Ḥajar, *op. cit.*, II, 338-41.

[314]Friday is selected because in Islam it is considered to be the best of all the days of the week. The blessedness of this day adds to the excellence of a pious act performed on it.

there is no wrong in reducing the reading of the entire Qur'ān to once a week. If the reader is making penetrating reflection on different meanings of verses, it is sufficient for him to complete the reading once in a month, since he needs to repeat the reading of verses and to reflect on them may times. A person busy earning a livelihood or doing worldly deeds should read at least a few pages of the Qur'ān in the morning and evening. By this he will obtain some blessings from the divine speech.

The third 'praiseworthy' task concerns the mode of dividing the Qur'ān into parts for convenience of recitation. The man intending to read the entire Qur'ān once in a week will divide it into seven divisions. The companions of the Prophet used to divide it in this way. It is after their time that the system of division into five parts, ten parts and thirty parts was introduced.

The fourth 'praiseworthy' task is to read from those *muṣḥafs* (i.e. copies of the Qur'ān) in which writing is beautiful and letters are clear and distinct. There is no sin in dotting letters of the Qur'ān and in writing in it different marks with red and other colours, because these colours adorn the Qur'ān, make its letters distinct, and avert its reader from making mistakes. All this is true of marks at the end of verses, marks showing the beginning and end of sūras, and so on. This is the correct view.

The fifth sunna task is to read the Qur'ān in a slow and distinct manner. This is sunna for two reasons. First, the main purpose of reading the Qur'ān is reflection on its meaning, and reading in a slow manner is conducive to it. Second, reading the Qur'ān slowly is nearer to the reverence which the Qur'ān deserves and stronger in its impression on the soul than babbling with haste. For this reason it is sunna even for one, who cannot understand the Qur'ān, to read it slowly and with pauses among sentences. This manner of reading is recommended in the verse,

> "Recite the Qur'ān in a slow and distinct manner "[315]
> (ورتل القران ترتيلا).

The Prophet was very clear and distinct in respect of every letter of the Qur'ān he uttered. His companions as well as their followers were also very particular about this manner of reading, the reward of which is far greater than reading it babbling.

The sixth sunna task is to weep when reading the Qur'ān, The Prophet advised,

> "Recite the Qur'ān and weep. If you do not weep naturally,

force yourselves to weep."[316]

The method of forcing oneself to weep consists in bringing grief to the mind. To do this the reciter should first reflect on the threats, warnings,covenants and promises contained in the Qur'ān; then he should reflect on his shortcomings in respect of its commandments and threats of punishment. Thus he will necessarily be aggrieved and will weep. Should he not feel aggrieved and not weep like those who have purified their souls he should weep for his lack of grief and tears, because this is the greatest of all misfortunes.

The seventh sunna task is to supplicate before, during and after Qur'ān-reading. The supplication formula to be recited before Qur'ān-reading is:

> I seek refuge with God, the All-hearing, the All-knowing, from the rejected Satan. 'Lord, I seek refuge with You from the incitements of Satans; and I seek refuge with You, Lord, lest they should approach me.'[317]
>
> (أعوذ بالله السميع العليم من الشيطان الرجيم. رب، أعوذبك من همزات الشياطين. وأعوذبك، رب، أن يحضرون.)
>
> (*A'ūdhu bi-Allāhi as-samī'i al-'alīmi, min ash-Shayṭāni ar-rajīmi. Rabbi, a'ūdhu bi-ka min hamazāti ash-Shayāṭīni. Wa a'ūdhu bi-ka, rabbi, 'an yaḥḍurūni.*)

Supplication should also be made by reading the Sūra of Man[318] and the Sūra of the Opening of the Book.[319]

The supplication formula to be recited when one is retiring from Qur'ān reading is:

> God (exalted is He!) has spoken the truth, and His Messenger (may God bless and greet him!) has conveyed [it to us]. God, benefit us with the Qur'ān and bless us in it. Praise be to God, the Lord of all the worlds! I seek the forgiveness of God, the Ever Living, the Self-subsisting and All-sustaining.
>
> (صدق الله تعالى، وبلغ رسول الله، صلى الله عليه وسلم. اللهم، انفعنابه، وبارك لنا فيه. الحمد لله رب العالمين، واستغفر الله الحى القيوم.)
>
> (*Ṣadaqa Allāhu ta'ālā, wa ballagha rasūlu Allāhi, ṣalla*

[315]Qur'ān 93:4.

[316]Ibn Māja, *Sunan*, Iqāma, 176, Zuhd, 19. In the Qur'ān 17:109, weeping is praised. The Prophet himself wept when reading the Qur'ān; see al-Bukhārī, *Ṣaḥīḥ*, Faḍā'il aṣ-Ṣaḥāba, 25.

[317]Qur'ān 23:97. [318]Qur'ān 114:1-6. [319]Qur'ān 1:1-7.

Allāhu 'alayhi was sallama. Allāhumma, anfa'nā bi-hi, wa bārik lanā fīhi. Al-ḥamdu li-Allāhi rabbi al-'ālamīna, wa astaghfiru Allāha al-ḥayya al-qayyūma).

During the recitation, when the reciter recites a verse on glorification of God, he will glorify and magnify Him. When he recites a verse on supplication to God and forgiveness of Him, he will supplicate and seek forgiveness. If he reads a verse on frightening matters, he will seek the protection of God from them. He will do these with his tongue or with his mind. Thus in place of glorification of God he will say: glory be to God! (*subḥāna Allāh*); in place of seeking refuge with God he will say: we seek the protection of God (*na'ūdhu bi-Allāh*); and in place of making petition to God he will say: God, grant us sustenance; God, bestow mercy upon us (*Allāhumma arzuqnā, Allāhumma arḥimnā*).

When the recitation of the entire Qur'ān is completed a specific supplication formula should be read. This formula is one which the Prophet used to read on completing the reading of the entire Qur'ān. It is as follows:

> God, bestow mercy upon me through the Qur'ān, and make it for me a leader [who leads to the truth], a light, a guide, and a mercy. God, remind me of that which I have forgotten [when reading the Qur'ān], teach me those parts of the Qur'ān of which I am ignorant, grant me its recitation 'in the hours of the night and different parts of the day,'[320] and make it a point in my favour, O Lord of all the worlds.
>
> (اللهم ارحمني بالقران واجعله لي اماما ونورا وهدى ورحمة.
> اللهم ذكرني منه مانسيت وعلمني منه ماجهلت وارزقني
> تلاوته اناء الليل واطراف النهار. واجعله لي حجة يا رب
> العالمين.)
>
> (*Allāhumma, arḥimnī bi-al-Qur'āni, wa aj'alhu lī imāman wa nūran wa hudan wa raḥmatan. Allāhumma , dhakkirnī minhu mā nasītu, wa 'allimnī minhu mā jahiltu, wa arzuqnī tilāwatahu ānā'a al-layli wa aṭrāfa an-nahāri, wa aj'alhu lī ḥujjatan yā rabba l - 'ālamīna*)

Supplication made on completion of the reading of the entire Qur'ān is received by God, and His mercy descends upon the suppliant.

The eighth 'praiseworthy' task concerns Qur'ān-reading aloud. It

[320]Qur'ān 20:130.

is 'necessary' to read the Qur'ān loud enough so that the reader himself can hear it. As for reading so loud that the reader can be heard by others, it is 'blameworthy' for him who is afraid of ostentation (*riyā'*) and affectation for himself; such a man will read silently. This view is supported by the following Traditions:

> "On who reads the Qur'ān aloud is like one who gives alms publicly, and one who reads it silently is like one who gives alms secretly."[321] "A secret good act is more excellent than a public good act by seventy times." "The best measure of sustenance is that which is sufficient, and the best mode of remembrance of God is that which is secret."[322]

If, however, there is no fear of ostentation and if loud reading does not disturb another devotee, then reading with a loud voice is 'praiseworthy'. There is a Tradition:

> Once the Prophet heard a group of his companions reading the Qur'ān aloud in the supererogatory ritual prayer performed after midnight, and approved of this.[323]

The ninth sunna task is to read the Qur'ān beautifully by controlling the voice, though not with that excessive stretch which changes the prose order. The Prophet advised,

> "Adorn the Qur'ān with your voice."[324] "God does not listen to anything as much as He does to a man's sweet voice at Qur'ān-reading."[325]

The Prophet and his companions used to read the Qur'ān beautifully. On several occasions he earnestly listened to the sweet voices of some of his companions at Qur'ān-recitation, enjoyed it and approved of it.[326]

SUNNA AND 'PRAISEWORTHY' MENTAL TASKS IN QUR'ĀN-RECITATION

[321]Abū Dāwūd, *Sunan*, Taṭawwu', 25; an-Nasā'ī, *Sunan*, Zakā, 68; at-Tirmidhī, *Sunan*, Thawāb al-Qur'ān, 20.

[322]Ibn Ḥanbal, *Musnad*, I. 172, 180, 187.

[323]Al-Bukhārī, *Ṣaḥīḥ*, Maghāzī, 38; Mushin, *Ṣaḥīḥ*, Faḍā'il aṣ-Ṣaḥāba, 166.

[324]Al-Bukhārī, *Ṣaḥīḥ*, Tawḥīd, 52; an-Nasā'ī, *Sunan*, Iftitāḥ, 83; Ibn Māja, *Sunan*, Iqāma, 176; Abū Dāwūd, *Sunan*, Witr, 20.

[325]Al-Bukhārī, *Ṣaḥīḥ*, Tawḥīd, 32, 52, Faḍā'il al-Qur'ān, 19; Muslim, *Ṣaḥīḥ*, Musāfirīn, 232-34.

[326]Al-Bukhārī, *Ṣaḥīḥ*, Faḍā'il aṣ-Ṣaḥāba, 25, Faḍā'il al-Qur'ān, 31, 33, 35; Muslim, *Ṣaḥīḥ*, Musāfirīn, 235, 236; Ibn Māja, *Sunan*, Muqaddama, 11; Ibn Ḥanbal, *Musnad*, I, 7, 26, 38, 445.

There are several sunna and 'praiseworthy' mental tasks in Qur'ān-recitation, the most important of which are as follows:[327]

(1) To understand the origin of the Qur'ān and its greatness. The Qur'ān is God's speech which is His eternal attribute existing with His essence.[238] It is only out of His kindness towards man that He has revealed this attribute to him in the form of letters and sounds which are his attributes, because he is unable to understand God's attributes except through his own attributes. If the inmost majesty of God's speech were not concealed in the garment of letters, neither His throne nor the subsoil would have remained fixed a a result of hearing His speech, and all that is between these two would have been reduced to nothing because of the greatness of His authority and the majesty of His light. All this should be realized by the Qu'rān-reciter when he starts the recitation.

(2) To magnify God Who speaks in the Qur'ān and to realize that what is recited is not the speech of a human being and that in the recitation of divine speech one should be cautious, for just as the Qur'ān can only be touched by those who are physically clean, [329] so also its meaning can only be grasped by the mind which is pure from all defilements and illuminated by the light of magnification and reverence. Such a magnification of the Qur'ān is, in effect, the magnification of God Who speaks in it.

(3) To pay full attention of the mind to the verses recited. There is nothing superior to the Qur'ān, and so no thought of other things should come to the mind when it is read. A verse read without being fully attended to should be read a second time.

(4) To ponder over the verses recited so that their deep meanings may be apprehended. It is sunna to read the Qur'ān in a slow and distinct manner[330] mainly because this manner of reading facilitates pondering over it. Lack of pondering is condemned in the verse:

> "Do they not ponder over the Qur'ān, or is it that their minds are locked up from within?"[331]
> (افلا يتدبرون القران، أم على قلوب اقفالها؟)

Since pondering over verses is strengthened by repetition of them the reciter should do it (except when he is performing a ritual prayer behind the imām). One night the Prophet read the verse, "In the name of God Most Gracious, Ever Merciful,"[332] and repeated it twenty times in order to ponder over its deep meanings. In another

[327]For a very detailed account of all mental tasks see al-Ghazālī, *Iḥyā'*, I, 280-88; Quasem, *Recitation*, pp. 56-85.

[328]This is the Ash'arite view accepted by the main body of Muslims. The heretical view of the Mu'tazilite theologians is that the Qur'ān is 'created', not eternal.

[329]Qur'ān 56:79. [330]Qur'ān 93:4. [331]Qur'ān 87:24. [332]Qur'ān 1:1.

night he kept vigil along with his companions, repeating[333] a single verse: "If You punish them, surely they are Your servants; and if You forgive them surely You are the Mighty, the Wise."[334]

(5) To understand the deep, befitting meaning of every verse recited. The Qur'ān encompasses the description of divine attributes, of divine works, of prophets' circumstances, of the circumstances of their deniers, of divine commandments and threats, and of Paradise and Hell; and the reciter should try to understand each of these properly. Thus from verses on divine attributes and names he should try to understand the deep, hidden meanings of these. The Qur'ān contains the core of all forms of knowledge, the greatest of which is under divine names and attributes; the reciter should try to acquire the knowledge of their depths. From verses on divine works, such as the heavens, the earth and all other things, the reciter should understand the attributes of God and His greatness, since the existence of a work proves the existence of its Agent and the greatness of the former proves the greatness of the Latter. So he should view in the acts the Agent and not the acts. From verses on how prophets were considered false and maltreated he should understand God's attribute of independence from His messengers and their peoples and that if He destroyed all of them this would not affect anything in His kingdom. But from verses on God's help to His messengers in the end he should understand divine power and divine will to further the truth. From the Qur'ānic description of evil to the deniers of God he should understand that God's assault and revenge may overtake himself if he falls short of religious duties. Likewise, from the Qur'ānic description of Paradise, Hell, and all other things, such as promise and threats, hope and fear, he should try to understand the meaning proper to each case.

(6) To make the Qur'ānic teachings specific. This means that the Qur'ān-reader will suppose that every part of the Qur'ān is intended for him (in the sense that the Qur'ānic message is intended for all people and he is one of them). So when he comes across any command or prohibition made in the Qur'ān he will suppose that he is the man commanded or that he is the man to whom the prohibition applies. When he reads a verse on promise of rewards or threats of punishment he will make the same assumption. When reading the stories of previous prophets and their peoples he will know that these are narrated for consideration and deriving lessons. If he thus sup-

[333] An-Nasā'ī, *Sunan*, Iftitāḥ, 69; Ibn Māja, *Sunan*, Iqāma, 179.
[334] Qur'ān 5:118.

poses that every part of the Qur'ān is intended for him, he will not take up mere reading of it as his duty; rather he will try first to understand its deep meaning and then to act in accordance with it.

(7) To feel the Qur'ān, i.e. to be affected by different feelings according to the meanings of different verses recited. Thus the reciter will be in the states of grief, fear, hope, and so on. When reading a verse which warns and restricts divine forgiveness to those who fulfil certain stipulations, he will feel so small as if for fear he is about to die. When, however, a verse on promise of forgiveness is recited he will rejoice as if he flies for joy. When God and His attributes and names are mentioned he will bow his head in submission to His majesty and in awareness of His greatness. When he reads a verse on the infidels' belief in an impossible thing for God — e.g. that He has a child and a consort — he will lower his voice and be brokenhearted in bashfulness because of the evil of what they have believed. When Paradise is described he will long for it, but when Hell is described he will tremble for fear of it. The Prophet felt the Qur'ān so much that his eyes shed tears when 'Abd Allāh ibn Mas'ūd[335] recited the verse, "How will it be when [on the Day of Judgement] We shall bring a witness from every people, and shall bring you [Muḥammad] as a witness against these?"[336]

Mental states of fear, grief, joy and so on should be followed by actions in accordance with them. One who reads the Qur'ān repeatedly but persists in the commission of sins incurs divine hatred. Performance of duties commanded in the Qur'ān and avoidance of sins prohibited in it are the things with which the companions of the Prophet were always occupied.

(8) To rise to a state at which the reciter feels that he is hearing the Qur'ān from God and not from himself. There are three grades of Qur'ān-reading. The lowest grade exists when the reciter feels that he is reading the Qur'ān to God, standing before Him, and He is looking at him and listening to his reading. In this case his mental condition is one of begging to God, praising Him, and entreating Him. The second grade exists when the reciter feels that God is seeing him, addressing him with His kindness, and secretly conversing with him with His gifts and beneficence. So his state is one of reverence, magnification, listening and understanding. The third grade is where the reciter feels that he is seeing God in the

[335]Ibn Mas'ūd (d.32/652-53), a famous companion of the Prophet, was a great narrator of Traditions, an authority on Qur'ān-reading, Qur'ān-exegesis, and legal matters. See Ibn 'Abd al-Barr, *op. cit.*, II, 308-16; Ibn Ḥajar, *op. cit.*, II, 360ff.

[336]Qur'ān 4:41.

Qur'ān and His attributes in its sentences. He does not think of himself, or his Qur'ān-reading, or the relation of divine gifts to him as one upon whom they are bestowed; rather he confines his care to God and concentrates his thought on Him as if he were engrossed in the vision of Him. This last grade is one of those drawn near to God, while the first and second grades are of 'people on the right.'

(9) To get rid of looking at oneself with the eye of satisfaction and purification.[337] Thus when verses on promise to, and praise of, the pious are recited, the reciter will not view himself as one of these; rather he will view those who are the most devout. When, however, he recites verses on divine hatred and divine reproach of those who disobey God, he will view himself here and, fearing and pitying, will suppose that he is the man addressed in these verses. To see oneself as one with shortcomings is the cause of one's nearness to God. If one sees oneself with the eye of satisfaction and purification, one becomes veiled from God by one's self.

[337] Qur'ān 53:32, 4:49, 24:21, where purification of oneself is strictly prohibited.

VIII
REMEMBRANCE OF GOD (*DHIKR ALLĀH*)

فاذكرونى اذكركم، واشكروا لى، ولا تكفرون.— قران ٢:١٥٢

Remember Me and I shall remember you. Be grateful to Me and do not be ungrateful to Me. — Qur'ān 2:152

TWO FORMS OF REMEMBRANCE OF GOD

The phrase *dhikr Allāh* (remembrance of God) is used in the Qur'ān and Tradition in two senses. The first is remembrance of God as a purely mental activity, without the use of the tongue. This consists in *mental* recalling of God by considering His essence, beautiful names and attributes, His favours and His works. Mental recalling of God is possible at any place and at any time. It is often exhorted in the Qur'ān[338] as an act of devotion.

The second is to remember God by uttering, with the tongue, His oneness, His beautiful names and attributes, His majesty and glory, and His greatness and might. This too is exhorted in the Qur'ān as a devotional act of supererogatory type.[339] It is usually regarded as more meritorious than the form just mentioned, on the ground that it involves the tongue in addition to the mind and thus requires a greater degree of labour which earns more merit. It is associated, in the Qur'ān, with specific places, such as mosques, and with specific times, such as after ritual prayers.[340] This is in agreement with other devotional acts of the body. Its association with holy places and noble times is a factor for its being more meritorious in nature.

The Qur'ān contains a few short formulae of remembrance of God to be uttered with the tongue.[341] The Prophet added to them many more and mentioned their merits in this world as well as in the world to come. The use of these formulae is better than the use of one's own words. Whether one uses one's own words or the formulae set forth in the Qur'ān and Tradition, one has to observe certain stipulations.

[338] Qur'ān 2:231, 3: 103, 23: 41, *passim*.

[339] Qur'ān 62:10, 63:9, 7:11, 33:41, 2:152, *passim*.

[340] Qur'ān 2:134, 197-98, 200, 4:103, 22:40, 24:36-37, 33:41.

[341] Qur'ān 1:2, 30:17, 2:163, 255, 3:6, 18, 29:45.

STIPULATIONS FOR REMEMBRANCE OF GOD

The degree of hardship in remembering God by reciting the set formulae with the tongue is comparatively less than that involved in the performance of other bodily acts of devotion. Yet remembrance of God is very meritorious and useful to salvation, and this is so only when *all* stipulations for it are fulfilled.

The stipulations for remembrance of God are three in number. They are: (1) attention of the mind; (2) perseverance in remembrance, and (3) sincerity (*ikhlāṣ*) and truthfulness (*ṣidq*). The first two stipulations are beautifully expressed in the following passage of al-Ghazālī's *Iḥyā'*:

> "What is effective and useful is remembrance of God *constantly* and *attentively*. As for remembrance of God with the tongue, while the mind is inattentive, it is of little use; there are also Traditions which prove this.[342] Attention of the mind to remembrance of God at one moment and then its distraction from Him (powerful and exalted is He!) together with one's entanglement with the world is also of little use. Rather attention of the mind to God (exalted is He!) constantly or most of the time is the preface to acts of devotion. Indeed, it is by it that the rest of devotional acts are honoured. It is the end of the fruit of practical acts of devotion."[343]

The stipulation of sincerity and truthfulness requires that when a man recites, for example, the formula, 'There is no god but God', his mental state must support it. The pronouncement of it with the tongue must not be made for any worldly gain, such as wealth, social approval, and reputation as a religious man; rather it must agree with the state of the mind which is the state of firm conviction in the content of the formula. Disagreement between the outward expression and the inward state is hypocrisy.[344]

MOST IMPORTANT FORMULAE OF REMEMBRANCE OF GOD

The following eleven formulae of remembrance of God are the most important of those which are transmitted from the Prophet and which are often recited by pious Muslims, saints and ṣūfīs, because they are most authentic and because their merit for salvation is very great.

[342] At-Tirmidhī, *Sunan*, Da'wāt, 65. [343] Al-Ghazālī, *Iḥyā'*, I, 301.
[344] *Ibid.*, p. 303; al-Bukhārī, *Ṣaḥīḥ*, 'Ilm, 33, 49; Muslim, *Ṣaḥīḥ*, Ṣalā, 12.

Tahlīl: the Formula of Oneness of God

1. There is no god but God, Who is alone and has no associate (لاالــهالاالله، وحده لاشـــريكلــه).
   (*La ilāha illā Allāhu, waḥdahu lā sharīka lahu.*)

This formula is the best of the teachings of all the prophets of God, including Muḥammad.

2. There is no god but God, Who is alone and has no associate. To Him belongs sovereignty and to Him belongs praise. He is fully powerful over everything.
   (لاالهالاالله، وحده لاشريكله. لهالملك، ولهالحمد. وهو على كل شيء قدير.)
   (*Lā ilāha illā Allāhu, waḥdahu lā sharīka lahu. Lahu al-mulku, wa lahu al-ḥamdu. Wa huwa 'alā kulli shay'in qadīrun.*)

The man who recites this formula a hundred times every day has as good as ransomed ten slaves, and a hundred good deeds are recorded for him and a hundred evil deeds are erased from him; and this formula becomes protection for him against Satan on that day, so that no one can bring a more meritorious deed than what he did except by increasing the same act more than that. The man who recites this formula ten times is like him who has set free four persons from the sons of the prophet Ishmael.[345]

3. I bear witness that there is no god but God, Who is alone and has no associate; and I bear witness that Muḥammad is His servant and messenger.
   (اشهد ان لاالهالاالله، وحده لاشريك له. واشهد ان محمدا عبده ورسوله.)
   (*Ashhadu an lā ilāha illa Allāhu, waḥdahu lā sharīka lahu; wa ashhadu anna Muḥammadan 'abduhu wa rasūluhu.*)

If a man recites this formula after ablution the doors of Paradise will be opened to him on the Day of Judgement, and he will be able to enter through whichever one he likes.[346]

4. There is no God but God, Who is alone and has no associate. To Him belongs sovereignty and to Him belongs praise. He is fully powerful over everything. Glory be to God! Praise be to God! There is no god but God. God is the

[345] Al-Bukhārī, *Ṣaḥiḥ*, Da'wāt, 63; Muslim, *Ṣaḥiḥ*, Dhikr, 10.

[346] Muslim, *Ṣaḥīḥ*; an-Nasā'ī, *Sunan*; Abū Dāwūd, *Sunan*; quoted in al-Ghazālī, *Iḥyā'*, I, 297.

> Greatest. There is no might and no power save in God, the Exalted, the Great.

The man who, on waking up at night, recites this formula and prays to God for forgiveness of sins, is forgiven. If he prays for any other thing, he will be granted it. If he performs ablution and offers ritual prayer, his ritual prayer will be accepted.[347]

> ***Tasbīḥ:*** the Formula of Glorification of God
> ***Taḥmīd:*** the Formula of Praise of God
> ***Takbīr:*** the Formula of Magnification of God

5. Glory be to God! Praise be to God! God is the Greatest.
(سبحان اللهم والحمد للهم والله اكبر.)
(*Subḥāna Allāhi, wa l-ḥamdu li-Allāhi, wa Allāhu akbaru.*)

Each of these three formulae is to be recited thirty-three times after every ritual prayer. Then this formula is to be recited once:

> There is no god but God, Who is alone and has no associate; to Him belongs sovereignty and to Him belongs praise; He is fully powerful over everything.

The result is that all minor sins of the reciter will be forgiven even though they are very many in number.[348]

6. Glory be to God, and praise be to Him!
(سبحان الله وبحمده : *subḥāna Allāhi, wa bi-ḥamdihi.*)

The sins of the reciter of this formula a hundred times a day fall off from him, even though they are of a great number.[349]

7. Lord, praise be to You, excellent and blessed praise!
(ربنام لك الحمدم حمدا كثيرا طيبا مباركا فيه.)
(*Rabbana, laka al-ḥamdu, ḥamdan kathīran ṭayyiban mubārakan fīhi.*)

This formula is so holy that one day, when it was recited by a companion of the Prophet, the Prophet saw that thirty angels were vying with one another as to who should record it first.[350]

8. Glory be to God! Praise be to God! There is no god but God. God is the Greatest.
(سبحان اللهم والحمد اللهم ولااله الا اللهم والله اكبر.)

[347]Al-Bukhārī, *Ṣaḥīḥ*, quoted in al-Ghazāli, *Iḥyā'*, I, 298.
[348]Muslim, *Ṣaḥīḥ*, quoted in al-Ghazālī, *Iḥyā'*, I, 298.
[349]Al-Bukhārī, *Ṣaḥīḥ*, Da'wāt, 64; Muslim, *Ṣaḥīḥ*, Dhikr, 10, 22.
[350]Al-Bukhārī, *Ṣaḥīḥ*, quoted in al-Ghazāli, *Iḥyā'*, I, 299.

(*Subḥāna Allāhi, wa l-ḥamdu li-Allāhi, wa lā ilāha illā Allāhu, wa Allāhu akbaru.*)

The Prophet said that this formula was more liked by him than the world in its entirety. He also said that this formula was the most liked of all utterances to God.[351]

9. Glory be to God and praise be to Him! Glory be to God, the Great!
(سبحان الله وبحمده. سبحان الله العظيم.)
(*Subḥāna Allāhi, wa bi-ḥamdihi. Subḥāna Allāhi al-ʻaẓīmi.*)

"These two sentences are light on the tongue but will be heavy in the Balance on the Day of Judgement and are loved by the Ever Merciful."[352]

10. Glory be to God!
(سبحان الله : *subḥāna Allāhi.*)

A thousand good deeds are recorded for the man who recites this formula a hundred times, or a thousand minor sins are erased from him.[353]

11. There is no might and no power save in God
(لاحول ولاقوة الا بالله).
(*Lā ḥawla wa lā quwwata illā bi-Allāhi.*)

The Prophet called this formula one of the treasures of Paradise.[354]

[351] Muslim, *Ṣaḥīḥ*, Dhikr, 10.
[352] *Ibid.*; al-Bukhārī, *Ṣaḥīḥ*, Da'wāt, 64.
[353] Muslim, *Ṣaḥīḥ*, quoted in al-Ghazālī, *Iḥyā'*, I, 300.
[354] Al-Bukhārī, *Ṣaḥīḥ*, Da'wāt, 49, 66; Muslim, *Ṣaḥīḥ*, Dhikr, 13.

IX
SUPPLICATION (*DU'Ā'*) TO GOD

واذا سألك عبادى عنى، فانى قريب؛ اجيب دعوةالداع اذا
دعان؛ فليستجيبوا لى.— قران ٢:١٨٦

If My servants ask you concerning Me, [say:] I am near; I respond to the supplication of a suppliant when he makes it to Me. So let them call for my response. — Qur'ān 2:186

وقال ربكم: ادعونى استجب لكم. انالذين يستكبرون عن
عبادتى سيدخلون جهنم داخرين.— قران ٤٠:٦٠

Your Lord has said, 'Supplicate to Me and I shall answer you. Surely those who refuse to worship Me out of haughtiness shall enter into Hell in a wretched state — Qur'ān 40:60

THE MEANING OF SUPPLICATION TO GOD

Supplication to God means humble petition to Him for something which may be this-worldly or otherworldly, and which may be positive or negative. Something positive means a desirable thing, while something negative is that which should be avoided. Thus in Islam, supplication to God is equivalent to prayer to God in general, but not to ritual prayer although some of its formulae are included in ritual prayer. The Arabic terms employed for supplication or prayer to God in general are *du'ā'*[355] and *su'āl* (asking),[356] while the word used for ritual prayer is *ṣalā*.[357]

Supplication, whether for something positive or negative, is a supererogatory devotional act. It is regarded in one Tradition as *the* worship,[358] in another as the marrow of all forms of worship,[359] and in still another as something very honourable to God.[360] Why it is so meritorious is explained by al-Ghazālī as follows: supplication is earnest request to God for His grace; it necessarily involves praise of

[355] Qur'ān 2:186, 3:38, 39: 8, 4:60. [356] Qur'ān 14:34, 11:47, 55:29.

[357] Qur'ān 2:3, 43, 45, 83, 110, 153, *passim*.

[358] At-Tirmidhī, *Sunan*, Tafsīr Sūra II, 16; Ibn Māja, *Sunan*, Du'ā', 1; Ibn Ḥanbal, *Musnad*, IV, 267, 271, 276.

[359] At-Tirmidhī, *Sunan*, Du'ā', 1.

[360] *Ibid.*, Da'wāt, 1; Ibn Māja, *Sunan*, Du'ā', 1; Ibn Ḥanbal, *Musnad*, II, 362.

God and secret converse with Him with humility and submission; in all this is present the attention of the mind to God; and it is this attention which is the end of all forms of worship.[361]

Supplication is an expression of man's needs to his Creator, and since needs are many supplications are also many. All the needs can be subsumed under two broad categories; this-worldly and other-worldly. The former are for such things as health, wealth, offspring, and general well-being of life, while the latter are for salvation from punishment of the grave, of the Day of Resurrection and of Hell, and for the attainment of high grades in Paradise. Supplication for the fulfilment of both classes of needs is important: this-wordly needs must be fulfilled, for this world is the place of preparation for the next world. Thus a believer's supplication for the well-being of this life is ultimately supplication for salvation and well-being in the Hereafter. The Qur'ān asks us to pray for both well-beings:

> "There are some who pray: 'Lord, grant us [good] in this world.' These people have no portion in the Hereafter. There are others who pray: 'Lord, grant us good in this world as well as in the world to come, and safeguard us against the punishment of Hell.' It is these people for whom there will be a goodly recompense, because of that which they have earned. God is swift at reckoning."[362]
>
> (فمن الناس من يقول: 'ربنا اتنا فى الدنيا'؛ وماله فى الاخرة من خلاق. ومنهم من يقول: 'ربنا اتنا فى الدنيا حسنة وفى الاخرة حسنة وقنا عذاب النار'؛ أولئك لهم نصيب مما كسبوا؛ والله سريع الحساب.)

There is a Tradition:

> "Most of the supplications of the Prophet were by saying: 'Lord, grant us good in this world as well as in the world to come, and safeguard us against the punishment of Hell.' "[363]

Supplication as a devotional act is perfected by the observance of certain 'praiseworthy' methods known as *ādāb ad-du'ā'*. Supplication made by following these methods becomes an effective means of drawing forth divine grace.

'PRAISEWORTHY' METHODS OF SUPPLICATION

The 'praiseworthy' methods of supplication to God are ten in

[361] Al-Ghazālī, *Iḥyā'*, I, 229. [362] Qur'ān 2:200-202.

[363] Al-Bukhārī, *Ṣaḥīḥ*, Da'wāt, 54; Muslim, *Ṣaḥīḥ*, Dhikr, 9.

number. They are as follows:[364]

(1) To supplicate at noble times, such as the day of 'Arafa from the year, Ramaḍān from the months, Friday from the week, and the hour preceding the day-break from the night time. This hour is especially appropriate to supplication for forgiveness of sins. This is mentioned in a Qur'ānic verse as well as in a Tradition. The verse is:

> "They [i.e. the companions of the Prophet] slept but little at night and sought forgiveness just before daybreak."[365]
> (كانوا قليلا من الليل مايهجعون، وبالاسحارهم يستغفرون.)

The Tradition is:

> "Every night God (exalted is He!) descends to the lowest heaven when the last third of the night remains. Then He (powerful and mighty is He!) says, 'I shall answer him who supplicates to me, and I shall forgive him who asks for forgiveness.' "[366]

(2) To supplicate at noble states, such as after the five ritual prayers, between *adhān* and *iqāma,*[367] the state of fasting, and the states of prostration before God. Concerning this last there is a Tradition:

> "The nearest that a man becomes to his Lord (powerful and mighty is He!) is when he is in prostration. So make many supplications at that state."[368]

(3) To supplicate facing the *qibla*[369] and raising the hands so much that the whiteness of both armpits can be seen by others. The Prophet and his companions used to do this.[370] The suppliant should not look up towards the sky; this was prohibited by the Prophet.[371]

(4) To make the voice neither loud nor silent, but between the two. God hears everything and is very near; so a loud voice is unnecessary — this is what the Prophet said.[372] A low voice is praised

[364]For a very detailed account of these methods see al-Ghazālī, *Iḥyā'*, I, 304-309.

[365]Qur'ān 51:17-18.

[366]Al-Bukhārī, *Ṣaḥīḥ*, Tahajjud, 14; Muslim, *Ṣaḥīḥ*, Musāfirīn, 168-70.

[367]The Prophet said, "Supplication is not rejected between *adhān* and *iqāma*." See at-Tirmidhī, *Sunan*, Ṣalā, 44; Abū Dāwūd, *Sunan*, Ṣalā, 37; Ibn Ḥanbal, *Musnad*, III, 119.

[368]Muslim, *Ṣaḥīḥ*, Ṣalā, 44; Abū Dāwūd, *Sunan*, Ṣalā, 37; Ibn Ḥanbal, *Musnad*, III, 119.

[369]Al-Bukhārī, *Ṣaḥīḥ*, Da'wāt, 24.

[370]*Ibid.*, Da'wāt, 22, 48; Muslim, *Ṣaḥīḥ*, Istisqā', 5.

[371]Muslim, *Ṣaḥīḥ*, Ṣalā, 118; an-Nasā'ī, *Sunan*, Sahw, 40.

[372]Muslim, *Ṣaḥīḥ*, Dhikr, 13.

in certain Qur'ānic verses[373] and commanded in others, [374] one of which is:

> "Supplicate to your Lord humbly and secretly; He does not love those who exceed the limits."[375]
> (وادعوا ربكم تضرعا وخفية· انه لايحب المعتدين.)

(5) To avoid artificiality (*takalluf*) in supplication by using rhyming prose (*saj'*). This is because the suppliant should be humble and submissive to God, but artificiality is against these. Artificiality produced by rhyming prose amounts to transgression of limits in supplication forbidden in the Qur'ān.[376] None of the prayer formulae transmitted from the Prophet transgresses the limits; so man should confine himself to them. If, however, he uses his own words, he should beg God with the tongue of humility and not with the tongue of eloquence and unrestraint. The companions of the Prophet avoided this kind of tongue.[377]

(6) To supplicate to God with humility and submission, and hope and fear. Two Qur'ānic verses may be quoted in this connection:

> "They supplicated to Us in hope and fear, and humbled themselves before Us."[378]
> (وادعوننا رغبا ورهبا، وكانوا لنا خاشعين.)
>
> "Supplicate to Your Lord humbly and secretly; He does not love those who exceed the limits."[379]
> (وادعوا ربكم تضرعا وخفية· انه لايحب المعتدين.)

(7) To supplicate unconditionally and believing firmly in response from God. On this theme there are two Traditions:

> "Let not anyone of you say in supplication, 'God, forgive me if You please and bestow mercy upon me if You please.' He should ask God unconditionally, since there is no one who can compel Him."[380]
>
> "Supplicate to God with firm conviction in His response. Know that God (powerful and mighty is He!) does not answer the supplication of one whose mind is inattentive."[381]

[373] Qur'ān 19:3.
[374] Qur'ān 17:110, 7:55. [375] Qur'ān 7:55. [376] Qur'ān 7:58.
[377] Al-Bukhārī, *Ṣaḥīḥ*, Da'wāt, 20; Ibn Ḥanbal, *Musnad*, VI, 217.
[378] Qur'ān 21:90. [379] Qur'ān 7:55.
[380] Al-Bukhārī, *Ṣaḥīḥ*, Da'wāt, 20; Muslim, *Ṣaḥīḥ*, Dhikr, 3, 7.
[381] At-Tirmidhī, *Sunan*, Da'wāt, 64.

(8) To supplicate very earnestly and to repeat the supplication three times. There is a Tradition which runs thus:

> "When the Prophet (may peace be upon him!) supplicated to God he supplicated three times, and when he asked God for anything he asked three times."[382]

One should not be impatient and irritated about the delay in response from God. There is a Tradition prohibiting this:

> "Anyone of you will be answered so long as he is not so anxious as to complain saying, 'I have prayed to God but He did not answer.' So when you supplicate ask God much, for you are supplicating to a Gracious One."[383]

(9) To start supplication to God with glorification of Him and not with petition. At the beginning of supplication, one should recite such formula as:

> "Glory be to my Lord, the Supreme, the Most Exalted, the Generous Giver!" (سبحان ربى العلى الاعلى الوهاب).
> (*Subḥāna rabbī l-'aliyyī l-a'lā l-wahhābi*)

(10) The last 'praiseworthy' method concerns, for the most part, the mind of the suppliant. This method is the root of response from God. It consists in confession of sins and repentance of them, compensation of injustice and oppression to those to whom these were done, and turning to God with the inmost desire. All this is the most effective means of response from God. This method should be used especially in prayer for serious matters, such as rain at a time of severe drought.[384]

MOST IMPORTANT SUPPLICATION FORMULAE

Supplication Formulae of taking Refuge with God

One can use one's own words when supplicating to God for refuge with Him. It is, however, better to use those formulae which the Prophet himself recited. A few of these formulae may be cited here as follows.

(1) God, verily I take refuge with You from miserliness; I take refuge with You from cowardice: I take refuge with You that I should not be thrown back to the most contemptible life; I take refuge with You from the disturbance (*fitna*) of

[382] Al-Bukhārī, *Ṣaḥīḥ*, Da'wāt, 53; Muslim, *Ṣaḥīḥ*, Jihād, 107.
[383] Al-Bukhārī, *Ṣaḥīḥ*, Da'wāt, 21; Muslim, *Ṣaḥīḥ*, Dhikr 25.
[384] See *Supra*, pp. 160ff.

this world; and I take refuge with You from the punishment of the grave.[385]

(اللهم انى أعوذبك من البخل، واعوذبك من الجبن، واعوذبك
من ان ارد الى ارذل العمر، وأعوذبك من فتنة الدنيا، واعوذبك
من عذاب القبر.)

(Allāhumma, innī a'ūdhu bika min al-bukhli; wa a'ūdhū bika min al-jubni; wa a'udhu bika min an arudda ilā arzali al-'umri; wa a'ūdhu buka min fitnati ad-dunyā; wa a'ūdhu bika min 'adhābi al-qabri.)

(2) God I take refuge with You from the evil of the works I have done as well as from the evil of the works I have not done.[386]

(اللهم انى اعوذبك من شرما عملت، ومن شر مالم اعمل.)

(Allāhumma, innī a'ūdhu bika min sharri mā 'amiltu, wa min sharri mā lam a'mal.)

(3) God, I take refuge with You from harsh trial, affliction, ill luck, and the malicious joy of enemies.[387]

(اللهم انى اعوذبك من جهد البلاء، ودرك الشقاء، وسوء القضاء
وشماتة الاعداء.)

(Allāhumma, innī a'ūdhu bika min juhdi al-balā'i, wa daraki ash-shaqā'i, wa sū'i al-qaḍā'i, wa shamātati al-a'dā'i.)

(4) God, I take refuge with You from the punishment of the grave, from the punishment of Hell, and from the evil of the disturbance of the Antichrist, the False Messiah.[388]

(اللهم انى اعوذبك من عذاب القبر، وعذاب جهنم، ومن شر
فتنة المسيح الدجال.)

(Allāhumma, innī a'ūdhu bika min 'adhābi al-qabri wa 'adhābi jahannama, wa min sharri fitnati al-Masīḥi ad-Dajjāli.)

(5) God, I take refuge with You from the withdrawal of Your protection, from Your sudden revenge, and from all Your displeasure.[389]

(اللهم انى أعوذبك من زوال نعمتك، ومن فجأة نقمتك، ومن
جميع سخطك.)

(Allāhumma, innī a'ūdhu bika min zawāli ni'matika wa

[385] Al-Bukhārī, *Ṣaḥīḥ*, Da'wāt, 36, 40; Muslim, *Ṣaḥīḥ*, Dhikr, 15.
[386] Muslim, *Ṣaḥīḥ*, Dhikr, 18. [387] *Ibid.*, 16; al-Bukhārī, *Ṣaḥīḥ*, Da'wāt, 27.
[388] Al-Bukhārī, *Ṣaḥīḥ*, Da'wāt, 38; Muslim, *Ṣaḥīḥ*, Dhikr, 14.
[389] Muslim, *Ṣaḥīḥ*, quoted in al-Ghazālī, *Iḥyā'*, I, 322.

min taḥawwuli 'āfiyatika, wa min fuja'ti niqmatika, wa min jamī'i sukhtika.)

(6) God, I take refuge with You from the punishment of Hell and the trial of Hell, from the punishment of the grave and the trial of the grave, from the evil of the disturbance of riches and of poverty, and from the evil of the disturbance of the Antichrist, the False Messiah; and I take refuge with You from debt and sin.[390]

(اللهم، انى أعوذبك من عذاب النار و فتنة النار، وعذاب القبر وفتنة القبر، وشر فتنة الغنى وشر فتنة الفقر، وشر فتنة المسيح الدجال؛ وأعوذبك من المغرم والمأثم.)

(Allāhumma, innī a'ūdhu bika min 'adhābi an-nāri wa fitnati an-nāri, wa 'adhābi al-qabri wa fitnati al-qabri, wa min sharri fitnati al-ghinā wa min sharri fitnati al-faqri, wa min sharri fitnati al-Masīḥi ad-Dajjāli. Wa a'ūdhu bika min al-maghrami wa al-ma'thami.)

(7) God, I take refuge with You from a mind which is not humble, from a carnal soul which is not satisfied, from an action which is not lifted up [to You as being accepted], from a supplication which is not received [by You] and from a ritual prayer which is not useful.[391].

(اللهم، انى أعوذبك من قلب لايخشع، ونفس لاتشبع، وعمل لايرفع، ودعوة لايستجاب لها، وصلاة لاتنفع.)

(Allāhumma, innī a'ūdhu bika min qalbin lā yakhsha'u, wa nafsin lā tashba'u, wa 'amalin lā yurfa'u, wa da'watin lā yustajābu lahā, wa ṣalatin lā tanfa'u.).

Supplication Formulae for Forgiveness of Sin

(1)The best of all supplication formulae for forgiveness of sins is one known as *sayyid al-istighfār*. It is as follows:

God, You are my Lord and I am Your creature — You have created me. I am observing my covenant with, and promise to, You as much as I can. I take refuge with You from the evil of what I have done. I acknowledge to You Your favour to me, and I acknowledge to myself my sins. So forgive me; verily no one, except You, can forgive sins.[392]

(اللهم، انت ربى وانا عبدك، خلقتنى. وانا على عهدك ووعدك

[390] Al-Bukhari, *Ṣaḥiḥ*, Da'wat, 38; Muslim, *Ṣaḥīḥ*, Dhikr, 14.

[391] Muslim, *Ṣaḥīḥ*, Dhikr, 73.

[392] Al-Bukhārī, *Ṣaḥīḥ*, Da'wāt, 1, 15.

ماااستطعت، أعوذبك من شر مــاصنعت، ابوءلك بنعمتك علي، وابوء على نفسي بذنبي. فاغفرلي، فانه لايغفر الذنوب الا انت.)

(*Allāhumma, anta rabbī wa anā 'abduka khalaqtanī. Wa anā 'alā 'ahdika wa wa'dika mā astaṭa'tu. A'ūdhu bika min sharri mā ṣana'tu. Abū'u laka bi-ni'matika 'alayya wa abū'u 'alā nafsī bi-dhanbī. Fa-ghfir lī; fa-innahu lā yaghfiru adh-dhunūba illā anta.*)

(2) There is a prayer formula which was frequently recited by the Prophet. It is:

> Glory be to You! God, praise be to You! God, forgive me.[393]
> (سبحانك اللهم وبحمدك، اللهم اغفرلي.)
> (*Subḥānaka, Allāhummma, wa bi-ḥamdika, Allāhumma, aghfir lī.*)

(3) The minor sins of a man who recites the following prayer formula are forgiven even though they are as many as the leaves of trees or the days of the world:

> I beg forgiveness from God, the Great, except Whom there is no god, the Ever Living, the Self-subsisting and All-sustaining; and I turn to Him in repentance.[394]
> (استغفرالله العظيم، الذى لااله الا هوالحى القيوم، واتوب اليه.)
> (*Astaghfiru Allāha al-'aẓīma, al-ladhī lā ilāha illā hua al-ḥayyu al-qayyūmu. Wa atūbu ilayhi.*)

(4) In prayer for forgiveness the Prophet used to recite the following supplication formula:

> God, forgive me my mistake, my ignorance, my intemperance in my affairs, and that which You know better than I. God, forgive me my flippancy and my over-seriousness, my error, my evil intention, and anything like this which I have. God, forgive me what I did in the past and what I shall do in the future, what I did in secret and what I did in public, and what You know better than I. You are the hastener and the postponer; You are fully powerful over everything.[395]
> (اللهم، اغفرلى خطيئتي، جهلي و اسـرافي في امري، وماانت اعلم بـه مني. اللهم، اغفرلي هزلي، وجدي، وخطىء، وعمدي،

[393] Al-Bukhārī, *Ṣaḥīḥ*; Muslim, *Ṣaḥīḥ*; quoted in al-Ghazālī, *Iḥyā'*, I, 311.
[394] Al-Bukhārī, *Tārīkh*, quoted in al-Ghazālī, *Iḥyā'*, I, 311.
[395] *Idem.*, *Ṣaḥīḥ*, Da'wāt, 59; Muslim, *Ṣaḥīḥ*, Dhikr, 18.

وكل ذلك عندي. اللهم اغفرلي ما قدمت وما اخرت وما اسررت وما اعلنت وما انت اعلم بـه مني. انت المقدم انت الموءخر وانت على كل شيء قدير.)

(*Allāhumma, aghfir lī khaṭi'atī wa jahlī wa isrāfī fī amrī wa mā anta a'lamu bihi minnī. Allāhumma, aghfir lī hazlī wa jiddī wa khaṭa'ī wa 'amdī wa kulla dhālika 'indī. Allāhumma, aghfir lī mā qaddamtu wa mā akhkhartu, wa mā a'lantu wa mā anta a'lamu bihi minnī. Anta al-muqaddimu wa anta al-mu'akhkhiru; wa anta 'alā kulli shay'in qadīrun.*)

(5) There is a Tradition which runs thus:

> "When a man commits a sin and says, 'God, forgive me' (اللهم اغفرلي : *Allāhumma, aghfir lī*), God says, 'My servant has committed a sin but he knows that he has a Lord Who catches man for his sins and also forgives sins. My servant, do what you want; I have forgiven you.'"[396]

Formulae of Invoking Blessings upon the Prophet

When asked by his companions as to how they should invoke blessings upon him, the Prophet replied that they should recite the formula:

> God, send blessings upon Muḥammad and upon his family, as You sent blessings upon Abraham and upon his family. Verily, [You are All-laudable, All-gracious]. God, send grace upon Muḥammad and upon his family, as You sent grace upon Abraham and upon his family. Verily You are All-laudable, All-gracious.[397]

(اللهم صل على محمد وعلى ال محمد كما صليت على ابراهيم وعلى ال ابراهيم. اللهم بارك على محمد وعلى ال محمد كما باركت على ابراهيم وعلى ال ابراهيم. انك حميد مجيد.)

The Prophet said that in the Hereafter it would be lawful for him to intercede[398] for the salvation of those who recited the following formula when the *mu'adhdhin* ended his *adhān:*

> God, the Lord of this completed call and initiated ritual prayer, send blessings upon Muḥammad, Your servant and Your messenger, and give him the right of mediation, excellence, and the exalted rank on the Day of

[396] Al-Bukhārī, *Ṣaḥīḥ*; Muslim, *Ṣaḥīḥ*; quoted in al-Ghazālī, *Iḥyā'*, I, 312.

[397] Al-Bukhārī, *Ṣaḥīḥ*, Da'wāt, 31; Muslim, *Ṣaḥīḥ*, Dhikr, 7.

[398] *Supra* nn. 266-68.

Resurrection.[399]
(اللهم، رب هذه الدعوة التامة والصلاة القائمة، صل على محمد عبدك ورسولك، وأعطه الوسيلة والفضيلة والدرجة الرفيعة يوم القيامة.)

[399] Al-Bukhārī, *Ṣaḥīḥ*; Adhān, 7; Muslim, *Ṣaḥīḥ*, Ṣalā, 10f.

CONCLUSION

The preceding chapters form a study of the Islamic doctrine of salvation, as contained in the Qur'ān and Tradition, and of the acts of devotion prescribed by Islam as a means to salvation. The study may be concluded by pointing out some of our important findings. Thus the terms usually used for salvation in the Qur'ān and Tradition have been found to be: *najāt, fawz, falāḥ* and *sa'āda,* together with their derivatives. The forms of salvation have been found to be (a) that which occurs in the life of this world and (b) that which takes place in the life of the world to come. The former means escape from things which threaten life in this world, and the latter, in addition to escape from misery or punishment in the Hereafter, includes the element of obtaining reward or happiness in different forms. It is this eschatological salvation which is usually meant when the term 'salvation' is used in the context of the Qur'ān and Tradition and of the belief-system of the Islamic religion, and which is most intimately connected with Islamic devotions.

Two general features of salvation have been found to exist in the Qur'ān and Tradition. One is that salvation is of both the soul and the body, but there is an important sense in which it can be said to be of the soul only, even though the body is also saved. The other feature is that salvation and damnation occur by stages, the last of which is man's dwelling in Paradise or in Hell. At this last stage salvation and damnation will take place in their full form, while the stages which precede it are only foretastes of what will be experienced at the last stage. Salvation is individualistic — a reason why Islam, like all other revealed religions, is regarded as individualistic in nature. Declaration of salvation and damnation will be made on the Day of Judgement, following the weighing of acts in the Balance. Two forms of salvation will take place: (a) salvation free from damnation, which means obtaining a reward in Paradise without suffering in Hell at all, and (b) salvation after damnation, which consists in entitlement of reward in Paradise after suffering in Hell for some time. There are grades of salvation and damnation. Major grades of damnation in its full form are to be found in the major grades of Hell. All grades of salvation can be subsumed under a lower and a higher grade. The former lies in physical enjoyment in Paradise, the latter in beatific vision forevermore.

The means to salvation have been found to exist on the human side as well as on the divine side. The former are faith and action, while the latter are intercession and divine mercy. Faith precedes action in order as well as in importance for salvation. Faith and action are both needed for salvation free from damnation. Without faith even salvation after damnation cannot be achieved, but it can be achieved without action. Faith has three basic ingredients together with their associates. Action is very comprehensive in scope in as much as it includes man's practical life in its entirety; it is commonly divided into man-directed acts and God-directed acts which are identical with devotional acts or simply devotions. Justice in man-directed acts and correct performance of devotions are both essential for salvation. Intercession will be made by human beings and the angels, but there is a sense in which it can be included in the means on the divine side. Intercession and divine mercy will both take place in two stages — on the Day of Judgement and after the sinners' entry into Hell — resulting, respectively, in salvation free from damnation and salvation after damnation. Intercession and divine mercy are appropriate to believers only — for disbelievers there is no salvation. Thus faith is the most basic requirement of salvation. Action will facilitate intercession and divine mercy and thus be involved in them. Divine mercy plays a great role in salvation even where the means to it are worked out through human endeavour.

The Qur'ānic teaching on the meaning of salvation and means to it has been found to be followed very closely by Muslim jurists, theologians and ṣūfīs, and only partly by medieval Muslim philosophers. Its agreement with Christian and Judaic teachings on certain points and disagreement with them on others have also been noted.

Devotional acts are of two categories: (a) 'obligatory' which are ritual prayer, fasting, divine tax and the pilgrimage, and (b) 'supererogatory' which are Qur'ān-recitation, remembrance of God, and supplication to Him. 'Obligatory' acts can also be performed as 'supererogatory'. Of all aspects of devotions it is their correct performance which has been found to be closely linked with salvation. The prerequisite to such performance, in the case of most of them, is physical and legal purity which has two aspects, namely, that of things with which purity of the body, clothes, etc. can be achieved and that of the methods by which such purity can be effected. Legal treatment of the methods of achievement of purity and of correct performance of 'obligatory' devotions has been found to be most comprehensive — so comprehensive that a simple act of achieving purity by bathing, for example, is treated in its eight aspects, and ritual prayer, fasting, divine tax and the pilgrimage are dealt with in forty-three, fifteen, three and fifteen aspects respectively. In the case of many of these aspects discussion is made by dividing an aspect into a number of parts. Such meticulous, detailed formulation of methods of correct performance of 'obligatory' devotions is owing to the fact that without these devotions salvation, even though of the lower grade, cannot be achieved.

In the case of purely 'supererogatory' devotions, however, legal treatment of the methods of their correct performance has been found comparatively less meticulous, and this is owing to the nature of these acts. Thus in Qur'ān-recitation three sound motives, one 'required' act, two sets of sunna and 'praiseworthy' acts — one related to the body and one to the mind — and one or two 'unlawful' cases of recitation have been found. In remembrance of God two forms of it are recorded: one is purely mental and the other is that in which the tongue is also involved. The stipulations which must be fulfilled if remembrance of God is to be useful to salvation are attention of the mind, perseverance in remembrance and sincerity. *Tahlīl, tasbīḥ, taḥmīd* and *takbīr* are the four categories of formulae of remembrance of God; and of the numerous formulae, falling under these categories, which are transmitted from the Prophet, eleven have been found to be extremely important for salvation and to be those which are often recited by pious Muslims, saints and ṣūfīs. In supplication to God it has been found that one can legally supplicate for well-being in this world as one can do so for well-being in the world to come. The meaning of the words of the Prophet, "Supplication is the marrow of all forms of worship," has been determined. The 'praiseworthy' methods of supplication are ten in number. The most important supplication formulae are: the formulae for taking refuge with God, the formulae for seeking forgiveness of sin, and the formulae for invoking blessings upon the Prophet. The best of all formulae for seeking forgiveness of sin is one called *sayyid al-istighfār*. The best of all formulae for invoking blessings upon the Prophet have been found to be those two which he taught to his companions himself. One of them is especially important for salvation, since the man who recites it when the *mu'adhdhin* ends his *adhān* will be entitled to intercession by the Prophet in the Hereafter.

The 'obligatory' acts of devotion aim only at making salvation possible. The 'supererogatory' acts are recommended in order to make good for the imperfections that usually occur in 'obligatory' devotions and also in order to elevate one's grade of salvation. Each devotional act, whether 'obligatory' or 'supererogatory', consists of different parts — 'obligatory', 'required', sunna, 'praiseworthy', and so on — which constitute its positive aspect, its negative aspect being those things which are 'unlawful' and 'disliked' in it. The 'obligatory' and 'required' parts aim at bare soundness of the act which only makes salvation possible, while the other parts of the positive aspect aim at compensating for the imperfections that usually occur in the 'obligatory' and 'required' parts and also at enhancing the merit of the act so that a higher degree of salvation may be achieved.

BIBLIOGRAPHY

(The Arabic article *al-*, with its variants, such as *an, ad, ash,* is disregarded in the alphabetical arrangement of this bibliography.)

Abū Dāwūd, Sulaymān Ibn al-Ash'ath as-Sijistānī. *Sunan*. 2 vols. Cairo, 1935.

Abū Zahra, Muḥammad. *Tārīkh al-Madhāhib al-Islāmiyya*. Cairo, 1963.

Ahmad, M.B. "Theory and Practice of Law in Islam". *J.P.H.S.*, VIII (1960), 184-205, 271-86, IX(1961), 8-22.

Al-'Asqalānī, Ibn Ḥajar. *Tahdhīb at-Tahdhīb*. 12 in 6 vols. Hyderabad, India, 1325-27 A.H.

Bey, Muḥammad Zayd al-Ibyānī. *Sharḥ al-Aḥkām ash-Shar'iyya*. 3 vols. Cairo, 1342/1924.

Al-Bukhārī, Muḥammad Ibn Ismā'īl. *Ṣaḥīḥ*. 9 vols. Egypt, 1377 A.H.

Coulson, Noel J. *Conflict and Tensions in Islamic Jurisprudence.* Chicago, 1969.

Ad-Dārimī, 'Abd Allāh Ibn 'Abd ar-Raḥmān. *Sunan*. 2 vols. Damascus, 1349 A.H.

Al-Fīrūzābādī, Muḥammad Ibn Ya'qūb. *Al-Qāmūs al-Muḥīṭ*. 4 vols. 3rd ed. Cairo, 1344/1925.

Fyzee, A.A.A. *Outlines of Muḥammadan Law*. 3rd ed. London, 1964.

Al-Ghazālī, Abū Ḥāmid. *al-Arba'īn fī Uṣūl ad-Dīn*.Egypt,1344 A.H.

__________. *Ayyuhā l-Walad*. Beirut, 1933.

__________. *Bidāyat al-Hidāya*. Egypt, n.d.

__________. *Iḥyā' 'Ulūm ad-Dīn*. 5 vols. Beirut, n.d.

__________. *Jawāhir al-Qur'ān*. 2nd ed. Cairo, 1933

__________. *al-Munqidh min aḍ-Ḍalāl*. Edited by 'Abd al-Ḥalīm Maḥmūd. Cairo, 1955.

__________. *Tahāfut al-Falāsifa*. Edited by al-Yasū'ī. Beirut, 1962.

Heffening, W. "Shahīd". *E.I.(S)*, pp. 515-18.

__________. "Al-Shaibānī". *E.I.* (*S*), pp. 518f.

Hoenerbach, W. "Some Notes on the Legal Language of Christian and Islamic Deeds". *J.A.O.S.*, LXXI (1961), 34-38.

Hourani, G.F. "The Basis of Authenticity of Consensus in Sunnite Islam". *S.I.*, XXI (1964), 13-60.

Ibn 'Abd al-Barr. *Al-Istī'āb.* 4 vols. Egypt, 1960.

Ibn 'Āshūr, Muḥammad Ṭāhir. *Maqāṣid ash-Sharī'a al-Islāmiyya.* Tunis, 1366/1947.

Ibn al-Ḥajjāj, Muslim. *Ṣaḥīḥ.* 16 vols. Cairo, 1929.

Ibn Ḥanbal, Aḥmad. *Musnad.* 6 vols. Cairo, n.d.

Ibn Hishām. *Sīrat Rasūl Allāh.* 2 vols. Edited by F. Wustenfeld. Gottingen, 1858-60.

Ibn al-'Imād al-Ḥanbalī. *Shadharāt adh-Dhahab fī Akhbār man Dhahab.* Cairo, 1950.

Ibn Māja, Muḥammad Ibn Yazīd al-Qazwīnī. *Sunan.* 2 vols. Edited by Muḥammad Fu'ād 'Abd al-Bāqī. Cairo, 1952-53.

Ibn an Nadīm, Muḥammad. *Kitāb al-Fihrist.* Translated by Bayard Dodge. 2 vols. New York, 1970.

Ibn Nujaym, Zayn al-'Abidīn Ibn Ibrāhīm. *Al-Ashbāh wa an-Naẓā'ir.* Edited by 'Abd al-'Azīz Muḥammad al-Wakīl. Cairo, 1968.

Ibn Qayyim, Shams ad-Dīn Abū 'Abd Allāh Muḥammad. *Zād al-Ma'ād.* 2nd ed. 3 vols. Egypt, 1369/1950.

Ibn Sa'd. *Ṭabaqāt al-Kubrā.* Edited by E. Sachau. 9 vols. Leiden, 1905-21.

Ibn Taymiyya, Taqī ad-Dīn. *At-Tawassul wa al-Wasīla.* Beirut, 1390/1970.

Al-Kāsānī, 'Alā' ad-Dīn Abū Bakr. *Badā'i' aṣ-Ṣanā'i'.* Egypt, 1328/1910.

Al-Khuḍri, Muḥammad. *Tārīkh at-Tashrī' al-Islāmī.* 7th ed. Cairo, 1961.

Macdonald. D.B. *Development of Religious Attitude and Life in Islam.* Beyrouth, 1965.

__________. and Masse, H. *et al.* "Djinn". *E.I.²*, II, 546-50.

Maḥmasānī, Ṣubḥī. *Falsafa at-Tashrī' fī al-Islam.* Beirut, 1946.

Al-Makkī, Abū Ṭālib. *Qūt al-Qulūb.* 2 vols. Cairo, 1961.

Al-Marghīnānī. *Al-Hidāya.* Translated by Charles Hamilton. 4 vols. 1st ed. London, 1791.

An-Nasā'ī, Abū 'Abd ar-Raḥmān Ibn Shu'ayb. *Sunan.* 8 vols. Egypt, 1383/1964.

Nawawī. *Minhāj aṭ-Ṭālibīn.* Translated into English from the

French by E.C. Howard. London, 1914.

Quasem, Muhammad Abul. *The Ethics of al-Ghazālī: a Composite Ethics in Islam.* Foreword by W. Montgomery Watt. 2nd ed. New York, 1978.

____________.*The Jewels of the Qur'ān:al-Ghazālī's Theory*. 2nd ed. Kuala Lumpur, Malaysia, 1980.

____________.*The Recitation and Interpretation of the Qur'ān: al-Ghazālī's Theory*. 2nd ed. Kuala Lumpur, Malaysia, 1979.

____________."Al-Ghazālī's Conception of Happiness." *Arabica*, XXII, No. 2 (1976), 153-61.

____________."Al-Ghazālī's Theory of Devotional Acts." *I.Q.*, XVIII, Nos. 3/4 (1978), 48-61.

____________."Al-Ḥasan al-Baṣrī on the Recitation of Idrisite Divine Names:an Unpublished Treatise Ascribed to Him." *M.W.*, (in press).

Qudūrī. *Al-Mukhtaṣar*. Partly translated by G.H. Bousquet and L. Bercher under the title *Le statut personnel en droit musalman hanafite.* Paris, 1952.

Rahman, A.F.M. Abdur. *Institutes of Mussalman Law: a Treatise on Personal Law.* Calcutta, India, 1907.

Rif'at, Ibrāhīm. *Mir'at al-Ḥaramayn*. Cairo, 1925.

Ritter, H. "On the Treatise of Ḥasan al-Baṣrī". (text) *D.I.*, XX (1932), 67-83.

Robson, J. "Ḥadīth Ḳudsī". *E.I².*,III, 28-29.

Rosenthal, F. "Gifts and Bribes: the Muslim View". *P.A.P.S.*, CVIII (1964), 135-44.

Rousseau, S. *A Dictionary of Mohammedan Law*. London, 1802.

Al-Sanhūrī, 'Abd ar-Razzāq Aḥmad. *Maṣādir al-Ḥaqq fī l-Fiqh al-Islamī.* Cairo, 1954-59.

As-Sarakhsī, Shams ad-Dīn. *Al-Mabsūṭ*. 30 vols. Egypt, 1324-33 A.H.

Schacht, S.J. "Abū Yūsuf".*E.I².*, I, 164f.

____________ "Abū Ḥanīfa".*E.I².*, I, 123f.

____________"'Aṭā' b. Abī Rabāḥ".*E.I².*,I, 730.

Ash-Shāfi'ī, Imām. *Riṣāla.* Translated by Mājid Khaddūrī. Baltimore, 1961.

Ash-Shaybānī, Imām Muḥammad. *Kitāb al-Makhārij fī l-Ḥiyal.* Leipzig, 1930.

Shaykh Zāde, 'Abd ar-Raḥmān Ibn Shaykh Muḥammad Ibn Sulaymān. *Majma' al-Anhur fī Sharḥ Multaqā al-Abḥur.* Egypt, 1305 A.H.

Ash-Shurunbalālī, Ḥasan Ibn 'Ammār. *Matn Nūr al-Īḍāḥ*. Cairo, 1389/1969.

Ash-Shurunbalālī, Maḥmūd 'Abd al-Wahhāb. *Marāqī al-Falāḥ: Sharḥ Matn Nūr al-Īḍāḥ*. Egypt, n.d.

As-Suyūṭī, Jalāl ad-Dīn. *Al-Itqān fī 'Ulūm al-Qur'ān*. 3rd ed. Cairo, 1370/1951.

Aṭ-Ṭabarī, Abū Ja'far Muḥammad Ibn Jarīr. *Tārīkh al-Umam wa l-Mulūk*. Egypt, n.d.

At-Tahānawī, Muḥammad A'lā Ibn 'Alī. *Kashf* (or *Kashshāf*) *Iṣṭilāḥāt al-Funūn*. Bayrut, 1966.

Wakī'. *Akhbār al-Quḍāt*. Edited by 'Abd al-'Azīz Muṣṭafā al-Marāghī. Cairo, 1947-50.

Walī Allāh, Shāh. *Ḥujjat Allāh al-Bāligha*. Edited by as-Sayyid Sābiq. Cairo, n.d.

Az-Zamakhsharī, Abū l-Qāsim Jār Allāh. *Al-Kashshāf*. 4 vols. Egypt, 1385/1966.

Zayd, Muṣṭafā. *Al-Maṣlaḥa fī t-Tashrī' al-Islāmī*. 2nd ed. Cairo, 1384/1964.

The Bible. Authorized version. Oxford, England, n.d.

Qu'rān Karīm.(Bi-r-rasm al-'Uthmānī.) Egypt, n.d.

(The meaning of abbreviations used in this bibliography is given on p.17.)

INDEX

(The Arabic article *al-*, with its variants such as *an-*, *ash-*, etc., is disregarded in the alphabetical arrangement. The article 'The' before English language titles is also not taken into consideration. Journals and encyclopaedias are listed by their abbreviations, the meaning of which is given on p. 17.)

'Abbās, 203, 223, 243
abbreviations, 6
'Abd Allāh, 223
Abiar 'Ali, 209
ablution (*waḍū'*), 40, 51ff., 55, 58-66, 69-79, 81ff., 89, 107, 113f., 127ff., 164f., 191, 195, 201, 214, 248, 260.; with clean sand (*tayammum*), 52f., 71-75, 80, 107, 113, 165
Abraham, 32f., 105, 213, 216ff., 221, 232f., 271
Absolute, 32
Abū Bakr, 237-40, 244
Abū Ḥanīfa, Imām, 86, 126, 131f., 151, 159, 190, 199, 201f., 229
Abū l-Layth, 187
Abū Lubāba al-Anṣārī, 241f.
Abū Qatāda, 204
Abū Ṭalḥa al-Anṣārī, 204
Abū Ṭālib, 203
Abū Yūsuf, Imām, 80, 123, 126, 132, 151, 159, 190, 199, 201f., 229
action (*'amal*), as means to salvation, 13, 21, 25, 28f., 35-38, 85-272, 274ff.; weighing of, 44, 46, 273
Adam, 32f., 210
adhān, 64, 72, 88-91, 144, 154f., 160f., 219f., 235, 265, 271, 275
Ahl as-Sunna wa l-Jamā'a, 13
Albo, Joseph, 27
'Alī, 203f., 238
Alms (*ṣadaqa*), 156ff., 161, 192ff., 198, 204, 228ff., 232, 253
'amial, see action
'Amr, 194
analogy, 50
ancestral merit, 30
angel, 23f., 32, 34, 44, 46, 59, 99, 196, 213, 235, 261; guardian, 99f., 274
Anṣār, al-Anṣārī, 204f., 241f.
Antichrist, 268f.
apostasy, apostate, 122, 238
'aql, see sanity, intellect
'Aqīl, 203
Arabic, 12ff., 27f., 89, 101, 247f., 263
'Arafa, 64, 70, 86, 88, 97, 103, 181, 209, 211ff., 219f., 224, 227, 265
al-Arba'īn fī Uṣūl ad-Dīn, 30, 246
Armenian, 187
'Arna, 220
Arrival Circumambulation (*Ṭawāf al-Qudūm*), 211, 218, 226, 230
ascetic, 20, 38, 224
Ash'arite, 25f., 254
al-'Asqalānī, Ibn Ḥajar, 104, 196, 238, 249, 256
'Aṭā' ibn Abī Rabāḥ, 196
atonement, 30f., 128, 180, 183f., 187-90, 214, 222, 228, 230
autumnal equinox, 182
'Awf ibn Mālik, 168
'awra, see private parts
al-Ayyām al-Biḍ, 181
Ayyām Minā, 212
Ayyām at-Tashrīq, see Days of Drying Meat
Ayyuhā l-Walad, 30
al-Azhar, 14
'Azrā'īl (Azrael), 32

Bāb Banī Shayba, 225
Bāb al-Mu'allā, 211, 216
Bāb Sabīka, 214
Bāb aṣ-Ṣafā, 218, 226
Bāb aṣ-Ṣalām, 216
backbiting, 64, 186f.

Badā'i' aṣ-Ṣanāi', 138
Balance, 25, 44, 46, 262, 273
bāligh, see major
Bangladesh, 14
Banū Qurayẓa, 242
Baqī', 243f.
barrier (*sutra*), 120, 133
barzakh, 22
bath, 51, 55, 66-71, 75f., 80, 156, 191, 210f., 214ff., 220, 247, 275
bayt Allāh, see Ka'ba
belief, believer, *see* faith
Biblical, 29
al-Birr wa ṣ-Ṣila, 204
Bish ibn al-Ḥārith, 186
Black Stone (*Ḥajar Aswad*), 103, 210, 214, 216ff., 223, 225, 232
blessings upon Prophet, *see* Muḥammad
bliss, *see* salvation
Book, 34, 39
Bridge, 25, 46
al-Bukhārī, *see Ṣaḥīḥ*
al-Burāq, 217

Chest Circumambulation (*Ṭawāf aṣ-Ṣadr*), 230
childbirth, 50, 60, 65, 67, 70, 74, 78-82, 91, 149, 164, 175, 178f., 188, 190, 211, 214, 247
Christ, Christian, Christianity, 20f., 25, 28, 30f., 35, 38, 43f., 191, 274
circumambulation (*ṭawāf*), 59, 64, 71, 80f., 87f., 210f., 217, 219, 222-28, 230ff.; *see also* Chest, Visiting, Farewell, Arrival
cleanliness (*ṭahāra*), 49-85, 154, 159, 167, 214, 221, 248, 254, 274f.
collective obligation (*farḍ kifāya*), 67, 133, 167
companions of the Prophet, 63, 75, 104, 124, 128, 130, 168, 191, 214, 220, 223f., 237-41, 243ff., 249f., 253, 255f., 261, 265f., 271, 275
congregation, 80, 90, 92, 95, 99f., 101f., 105-11, 118f., 123, 125, 133f., 136, 142-45, 153, 156, 159ff., 170, 194
consensus, 50, 131
Corinthians I, 21, 27 ; II, 38
Crouch, H., 15

Damascus, 217
damnation, *see* punishment
David, 181
Dawn Prayer (*Ṣalāt al-Fajr*), 85, 87-90, 96, 98, 114, 124, 131, 141-47, 157, 159, 219, 221, 246, 249
day, best, 228f., 249
Day of 'Arafa, 159, 211f., 228
Days of Bright Nights, 181
Day of Doubt, 183ff.
Days of Drying the Meat, 158f., 182, 188, 193, 211, 226ff.
Day of Judgement, Doomsday, Day of Resurrection, 12-48, *passim*, 89, 91, 178, 202, 232, 236, 238, 240, 256, 260, 262, 264, 271, 273f.
Days of Minā, 212
Day of Quenching Thirst, 212, 227
Day of Sacrifice of Animals, 71, 212f., 222
Deluge, 216
Development of Religious Attitude and Life in Islam, 99
device (*ḥīla*), 202
devotion (*'ibāda*), devotional, 6, 12ff., 19f. 30-50, *passim*, 60, 62, 70ff., 85-275; and salvation, 35-43, 48f., 273; parts of and salvation, 40-43, 276; al-Ghazālī on, 43; aims of, 38f., 43, 276
Dhat 'Irq, 209
dhikr Allāh, see remembrance
Dhū l-Ḥijja, 71, 130, 158f., 181, 188, 207, 209, 212f., 219, 222, 226ff., 231
Dhu l-Hulayfa, 209
Dhū l-Qa'da, 181, 207
divorce, 116, 199, 208
dog, 21, 52f., 82, 84, 116f.
Dome of the Rock, 161
du'ā', 263
dualism, 21

eclipse, 71, 160
Edinburgh, 14
Egypt, Egyptian, 13f., 194, 209
EI, 86
EI², 99, 180, 196
English, 14, 101
Enoch, 33
ERE, 20
eschatology, 20, 273
The Ethics of al-Ghazālī: a Composite Ethics in Islam. 19, 21, 236
Evening Prayer (*Ṣalāt al-'Ishā'*), 86ff., 96ff., 116, 119, 122, 125f., 133, 141, 144, 212, 220
excuse, 57f., 63f., 72f., 80f., 86, 106ff., 113f., 117f., 130f., 15 2, 155, 158f., 167, 171, 192f., 210, 230
extremism, extremist, 182, 191

faith (*īmān*), belief, believer, 12, 20-26, 28f., 33, 36ff., 40, 43f., 46f., 50, 70,

82, 85, 91, 113, 117, 152, 154, 163, 167, 171, 174, 180, 188, 204, 218, 235f., 240f., 264, 273; as means to salvation, 13, 20, 29-35, 274; only valid, 34; ingredients of, 31-34, 274; sentences of, 63, 89, 154, 163
falāḥ, 20, 28, 82, 152, 273
False Messiah, 268f.
Farewell Circumambulation (*Ṭawāf al-Wadā'*),210f., 223, 225
Farewell Pilgrimage, 219f.
fasting (*ṣawm*), 36f., 48f., 56, 62, 79ff., 92, 122, 139f., 177-196, 189, 191, 226ff., 230f., 274f.; new moon for, 183-185; aim of, 177
Fatḥ al-Qadīr, 224
al-Fātiḥa, see Opening Sūra
Fātima, 243
Fawz, 20, 273
Festival Day on expiry of Ramaḍān (*'Īd al-Fiṭr*), 70, 181, 188, 193; divine tax of, 204f.; new moon for, 183-85; ritual prayer on, *see* 'Īd Prayer
Festival Day of Sacrifice of Animals (*'Īd al-Aḍḥā*), 70, 182, 188, 193, 209f.; new moon for, 183ff.; ritual Prayer on, *see* 'Īd Prayer
fidya, *see* ransom
Fihrist, 86, 99
fiqh, 54
follower, 63, 224, 244, 250
forgiveness, 44, 82, 91, 105, 111f., 123, 126, 129f., 154, 161, 163, 168ff., 193, 196, 199, 220, 222, 225, 233, 236, 240, 242, 251f., 256, 261, 265f., 269-71, 275
Friday, 90, 156, 181f., 218, 228f., 249, 265
Friday Assembly Prayer, 70, 73, 89, 96, 106, 114, 116, 125, 142f., 145, 152-56, 160, 166, 195

Gabriel (Jibrā'īl), 213, 217
Galatians, 30
gambling, 82
al-Ghazālī, Abū Ḥāmid, 14, 21f., 24-30, 32, 38, 42-45, 47, 112, 121f., 179-86, 189, 191, 194f., 202, 204, 206, 243, 246ff., 254, 259-65, 268, 270f.
glorification of God (*tasbīḥ*), 70, 98, 101ff., 110-13, 120, 127, 129f., 133, 153, 157f., 225, 228, 241f., 252, 260ff., 267, 270; formulae of, 261f.
God, divine, 6-276, *passim*; veil from, 21, 26; throne of, 24; love of, 39; nearness to, 21, 24, 39, 43, 45, 60, 125, 128, 224, 257; oneness of, 31-34, 99, 153, 163, 225, 241, 243, 258, 260; *see also* glorification, grace, gratitude, vow, vision, wrath, praise, remembrance, mercy, prostration.
Gospels, 33
grace of God, *see* mercy
gratitute to God, 15, 123, 181, 234
grave, graveyard, 22ff., 33, 72, 118, 163-76, 168f., 171-74, 214, 264, 268f.
Greek, 30
ḥadath, *see* impurity
ḥadīth, *see* Tradition
haemorrhage, 81, 106
Hajar, 213, 217f.
Ḥajar Aswad, *see* Black Stone
Ḥākim ash-Shahīd, 138
al-Ḥalabī, Ibrāhīm, 138
Ḥalwānī, Shams al-A'imma, 111
Ḥamza ibn 'Abd al-Muṭṭalib, 243
Ḥanafī school (*madhhab*), 86, 125, 135, 138, 173, 224, 229
Ḥanbalī, 135
hands, use of, 57f., 63
happiness, *see* salvation
Ḥāris, 203
Hārūn ar-Rashīd, 86
Ḥasan al-Baṣrī, 224
Ḥasan ibn 'Ali, 243
Hāshim, 203
Ḥassān ibn Thābit, 204
Hastening Circumambulation (*Ṭawāf al-Ifāḍa*), 209, 211
Ḥaṭīm, 217, 224
Hebrews, 21
Heffening, W., 86
Hell, 22f., 25f., 28, 33, 44-47, 99, 113, 124, 168, 211, 232, 235, 241, 255f., 264, 268f., 273f.
Hereafter, world to come, 12f., 19-21, 24f., 28f., 33ff., 40ff., 59, 122, 124, 168, 175, 179, 202, 212, 224, 232, 235-44, 258, 263f.; bodily and spiritual nature of, 23-27, 271, 273, 275
heretic, heretical, 25f., 29, 109, 238, 254
hermaphrodite, 165, 170
Hidāya, 14, 138, 199, 203, 205, 224
Hijaz, 153
Ḥijr, 217
ḥīla, *see* device
House, Holy, Sacred, Most Ancient, *see* Ka'ba
al-Hudaybia, 228
Ḥujjat Allāh al-Bāligha, 14, 177, 181f., 196

ḥurīs, 26
Ḥusayn, Imām, 243
hypocrite, 23, 259

'ibāda, see devotion
Ibn 'Abd al-Barr, 168, 223, 243, 256
Ibn Ḥishām, 242
Ibn al-'Imād, 186
Ibn Isḥāq, 241
Ibn Mas'ūd, 'Abd Allāh, 104, 256
Ibn al-Mubārak, 'Abd Allāh, 204
Ibn an-Nadīm, 86, 99
Ibn Qayyim, 14
Ibn Sa'd, 186
Ibn Taymiyya, 236
Ibn 'Umar, 'Abd Allāh, 249
Ibrāhīm, Prophet's son, 244
Ibrāhīm, prophet, *see* Abraham
Ibrāhīm, Rif'at, 221
'Īd Prayer, 73, 88, 96, 102f., 106, 114, 130f., 145, 156-66; *see also* Festival
Idrīs, 33
Iḍṭibā', 211, 217
Ifrād, 213, 221, 225
iḥrām, 70, 86, 159, 209, 211, 214f., 219, 222, 226-30
iḥtilām, 66, 70
Iḥyā', 14, 21, 24-27, 32, 38, 42, 44f., 47, 112, 122, 161, 179-86, 189, 191, 194f., 204, 206, 243, 246ff., 254, 259-62, 264f., 268, 270f.
ikhlāṣ, *see* sincere
imām, 86, 88, 92, 96-102, 104-111; 114f., 123ff., 134, 136, 142-46, 148ff., 153, 155-62, 167-70, 185, 211, 219ff., 248, 254
īmān, see faith
impurity: major (*janāba*), 51, 55, 64, 66, 68, 70, 72, 75f., 79ff., 91, 114, 149, 164, 175, 179, 186, 210, 230f., 247; minor (*ḥadath*), 50f., 60, 63f., 72, 74, 76, 81, 90f., 114f., 148, 210, 230, 248
India, 14
infidel, infidelity, disbeliever, 22ff., 26, 33, 47, 123, 149, 171, 190, 203, 243, 256, 274
injection, 67, 189
injustice, unjust, 13, 19, 37, 39, 47, 166, 171, 176f., 238, 267
insanity, *see* sanity
intellect (*'aql*), 90, 169, 192
intention (*niyya*), 43, 51, 62f., 68, 71f., 78, 92, 100f., 106, 108, 114f., 127, 129, 134-37, 150, 157, 177, 179, 182ff., 189f., 193ff., 198f., 204, 214., 217, 223, 226f.
intercession, intercessor, mediation, 25f., 43-47, 91, 163, 169, 232, 234-37, 240, 271, 274f.
IQ, 43
iqāma, 64, 72, 88ff., 101, 119, 154, 160f., 219f., 265
Iraq, 205, 209, 217
Isaiah, 27
Ishmael (Isma'īl), 213, 216ff., 221, 260
Islam, Islamic, 12ff., 19, 21f., 25, 29-32, 34-40, 43-46, 48ff., 52, 54, 57, 59f., 70, 72, 82, 84ff., 92, 106, 108, 113, 135, 138, 142, 163, 171, 177f., 180ff., 185, 190, 196, 202, 204, 207-10, 224, 234, 236-39, 242f., 247, 249, 263, 273
al-isrā', 217
Isrāfīl, 32
al-Istī'āb, 168, 223, 243
istiḥāḍa, 71, 78-81
istinjā', 55f., 58
i'tikāf, 193-96

Jabal 'Arafa, 220
Jabal Quzaḥ, 220
Jabal ar-Raḥma, 220
Ja'far, 203
Jamra, 71, 103, 209, 212f., 221-24, 226, 230
James, 21, 29
janāba, see impurity
Jeremiah, 38
Jerusalem, 161, 217
Jesus, 30ff.
Jew, Jewish, 20, 191, 241f.
The Jewels of the Qur'ān:al-Ghazālī's Theory, 31
Jibrā'īl, *see* Gabriel
jinnī, 23f., 36, 89, 99f.
Joseph, M., 20
Judaic, Judaism, 20f., 30f., 38
journey, travel, 71, 77f., 86, 89, 107f., 116, 122, 134-37, 139, 153, 155, 159, 179, 182, 185, 189f., 192, 199, 202, 207, 217
Judaic, Judaism, 20f., 30f., 38, 274
Judgement Day, *see* Day of Judgement
'Judge of Judges', 86
Juhfa, 209
July, 141
jurist, jurisprudence, juristic, 12ff., 19-22, 29, 86, 108, 119f., 123, 131f., 135, 138, 145, 149, 157, 163, 173, 187, 190, 202f., 206, 224, 274
'justification', 30, 35

Ka'ba, Holy House, Sacred House, Most

Ancient House, *bayt Allāh*, 58f., 62ff., 69, 71f., 80f., 87ff., 91, 94-96, 99, 101, 103, 113, 118, 121, 132ff., 138, 147f., 160f., 163, 170, 172f., 207, 209ff., 213f., 216-20, 223-230
al-Kāfī, 138, 152
al-Kamāl ibn al-Hummām, 224
Kanz ad-Daqā'iq, 229
al-Kāsānī, 138
kashf, 35, 71
al-Khāniyya, 125
Kilpatrick, T.B., 20
kiss, 103, 116, 166, 187, 190f., 210, 214, 216ff., 223, 225
knowledge, 12, 14, 21, 29, 64, 71, 93, 128, 178, 183, 204, 223f., 235, 247f., 255; by mystical intuition, 35, 71
khul'a, 199
al-Khulāṣa, 138

lāḥiq, 145
Late Afternoon Prayer (*Ṣalāt al-'Aṣr*), 86ff., 97f., 114, 126, 140ff., 144ff., 159, 212, 219
lavatory, 57f.
Laylat al-Barā'a, 70
Layiat al-Qadr, 70, 194ff.
Layth ibn Abī Sulaymān, 186
Leaves, 33
Luke, 38

Macdonald, 99
madhhab, see Ḥanafī
madhī, 119
Maimonides, 21, 27
al-Majma' al-Anhur, 138
major, mature (*bāligh*), maturity, 52, 59, 65, 70, 79, 85, 106, 135, 169, 178, 190, 205, 207f., 229
al-Makkī, Abū Ṭālib, 22, 27f., 45
Malaysia, 15
Mālikī, 135
Maqām Ibrāhim, 217, 224
Marāqī al-Falāḥ; Sharḥ Matn Nūr al-Īḍāḥ, 14, 53, 55, 57, 65, 110, 163, 189
Mārghinānī, 14
Mark, 38
martyr, 82, 174ff., 235, 243f.
Marwa, 64, 103, 210f., 213, 217ff., 223-28
Mary, 32
masbūq, 100, 102, 107, 115, 145
Mash'ar Ḥarām, 209, 224
al-Masjid al-Aqṣā, 161
al-Masjid al-Ḥarām, *see* Sacred Mosque
Masjid al-Khayf, 212, 219, 222
Masjid an-Nabī, 161, 235, 242f.
Masjid Namira, 219
Masjid Qubā', 244
Masse, H., 99
Matthew, 21, 31
Means, 90f., 163, 235f.
Mecca, 37, 62ff., 71, 80f., 91, 129, 153, 161, 194, 196, 202f., 207ff., 211-14, 216-20, 222-29, 231, 234, 237f., 243f.
Medina, 55, 71, 161, 180, 209, 217, 232f., 238, 242ff.
menstruation, 55, 60, 67, 70, 73f., 78-82, 91, 149, 164, 175
mercy of God, 25, 29, 43-47, 104f., 110, 113, 123f., 129, 152, 161, 163, 168, 224, 233f., 266, 274
Mikā'īl (Michael), 32
Mina, 103, 153, 209, 212f., 219, 221-24, 227, 231
mīqāt, 209, 214, 217
Mi'rāj ad-Dirāya, 228
Mir'at al-Ḥaramayn, 221
miserliness, 63, 69, 75, 202, 267
miswāk, see tooth-stick
Mīzāb ar-Raḥma, 224
moderation, 54, 69, 134, 177ff., 183, 188, 190f. 208, 211, 214, 247
Monday, 181, 249
monism, 21
monotheism, 32
Moony, P., 15
Moses, 30, 32, 219
mosque, 72, 79f., 95, 108, 114ff., 119, 127, 130, 143f., 154f., 157, 161, 170, 193-96, 203, 234, 244, 248, 258; of Prophet, 161, 235, 242f.; *see also* masjid
mu'adhdhin, 89f., 144, 271, 275
muftī, 153, 184
Muḥammad, Imām, 80, 123, 126, 132, 151, 159, 199, 201f.
Muḥammad, Prophet, prophetic, Messenger, 12, 19ff., 23, 27ff., 32-35, 37ff., 41, 43-46, 48, 50, 52, 54f., 57ff., 61ff., 69ff., 75, 79, 82, 85, 89, 91f., 100, 104ff., 108-112, 116, 118ff., 123-30, 135, 151f., 154, 156, 160, 162ff., 168, 172, 178, 180ff., 186f., 189, 191, 194-97, 203f., 207, 210f., 213, 216-20, 223-26, 237-46, 249-54, 256, 258ff., 261f., 264-67, 270, 275f.; visit to tomb of, 64, 89f., 214, 232-45; blessings upon, 70, 91, 99, 104f., 110, 123f., 129f., 133, 154, 158, 167, 211, 216, 222, 234-37, 244, 271f., best formulae of, 104f., 271f., 275; *see also*

companions
Muḥarram, 15, 180f., 208
Muhassab, 213, 223
Muhassar, 221
al-Muḥīṭ, 138
Mujāhid, 186
mukallaf, 59
Multaqā al-Abḥur, 138
Multazam, 213f., 223f.
Munkar, 22f.
muqīm, see stationary
muṣḥaf, 115, 247, 250
musk, 84
Muslim, 12ff., 20ff., 24, 26f., 35-38, 50, 60, 67, 70, 72, 85, 89, 106, 112f., 116, 122, 125, 131, 136, 142, 154, 159, 162, 167, 169ff.. 173, 175, 178, 180, 192, 194, 202, 204f., 208f., 212, 220, 222, 224, 234f., 237-40, 242, 274f.
Musnad, 23, 28, 30, 37, 39, 43-46, 61, 80, 85, 174, 234f., 263, 265f.
mutawātir, 75
muṭawwif, 219, 221
Mu'tazila, 13, 21, 25f., 163, 254
Muzdalifa, 71, 86, 88, 103, 209, 212, 220f.

nafs, see soul
Naḥr al-Ḥayāt, 47
Najāt, see salvation
an-Nakīr, 22f.
an-Nasafī, Abū l-Barakāt, 152, 229
Nejd, 209
New Year's day, 182
Night of Decree, 70, 194ff.
Night of Immunity, 70
niṣāb, 197-203, 205
niyya, see intention
Noah, 216
Nocturnal emission, 66, 70
non-Muslim, 36, 142, 178, 208, 228
Noon Prayer (*Ṣalāt aẓ-Ẓuhr*), 73, 85ff., 90, 97f., 125, 140-44, 155f., 211ff., 219
November, 15
Nūr al-Īḍāḥ wa Najāt al-Qulūb, 13f.

oath, swearing, 140, 193
Odd Prayer (*Ṣalāt al-Witr*), 81, 86f., 92, 96f., 103, 122-25, 131, 133, 140f., 146
Opening Sūra (*al-Fātiḥa*), 96-99, 102, 104, 120, 122, 136, 157f., 251
opthalmia, 78
ostentation, 253
Ottoman Empire, 138

pagan, 210
Pakistan, 14
Paradise, 22f., 25-28, 33, 44, 46, 91, 99, 113, 125, 163, 168, 207, 234ff.; gates, doors of, 26, 44, 47, 180, 211, 260, 273f.
People of the Book, 191
'people of the right', 217
People of Sunna and Jamā'a, 175
Persian, 87, 148f.
Peter II, 38
philosophy, philosophic, philosopher, 12f,. 19f., 22, 24, 27, 29f., 32, 54, 274
piety, pious, 20, 25, 44f., 89f., 99f., 104, 109, 129, 196, 204, 211, 235, 247, 249, 259, 275
pig, 52f., 82, 84
pilgrimage, 36f, 48f., 64, 70f., 86, 92, 129, 153, 159, 202, 207-45, 274f.; for female, 210f., 219ff., 225, 229; Farewell, 219f.
pillar, 58f., 74, 91, 93, 96, 108, 115, 145, 147f., 167, 179, 209, 218, 220, 231f., 238, 248
polytheist, 248, 241
poor, definition of, 202
praise of God, 58, 62, 64, 69, 97f., 101ff., 111ff., 119, 123, 127, 129, 133, 153ff., 157, 159, 167, 172, 215, 217, 220, 222, 225, 241, 256, 260f., 262ff., 270
prayer, *see* suplication,
prayer, ritual (*ṣalā*), 35, 37, 40, 45, 48f., 52f., 57-61, 63-66, 68, 70-75, 80-176, 193ff., 197, 211, 214, 216-19, 223, 225ff., 235f., 244, 246, 248, 253f., 258, 261, 263, 265, 269, 271,274f.; over bier, 64f., 67, 72f., 79, 88, 131, 164, 167ff., 176, 195; spirit of, 117; combination of, 86, 88, 97, 212, 219f.; *see also* Afternoon, Dawn, Evening, Late Afternoon, Odd, Prayer, rain, Sunset, Tahajjud, Tarāwīḥ, Supererogatory, Noon
Prayer (ritual) after Sunrise, 127, 158
Prayer for Geeting the Mosque, 127, 234
pregnant, 79, 192
private parts (*'awara*), 53, 56ff., 69, 91, 94f., 106, 114f., 148, 154, 164, 166, 210
prophecy, prophet, messenger, 23, 25, 30ff., 34f., 57, 105, 163, 173, 180f., 216f., 219, 234f., 247, 255, 260; greatest, 33
Prophet, prophetic, *see* Muḥammad
prosperity, 20, 28, 82, 152
prostration: due to forgetfulness, 40f., 97, 115, 124, 126, 131, 144-56; due to Qur'ān-reeitation, 64f., 87f., 148, 152,

248; for gratitude to God, 151, 265
Psalms, 33, 46
psychology, 13
punishment, misery, damnation, 6, 12-48, *passim*, 122ff., 168, 174, 202, 232, 241, 250, 255-64, 268f., 273f.

qaḍā', 73, 136, 138, 140ff., 150
Qāḍīkhān, 125, 138
Qāḍī al-Quḍāt, 86
Qarn, 209
qibla, 57, 91, 248, 265
Qirān, 209f., 213, 216ff., 225-28, 231
Quasem, M.A., 15, 19, 21, 31, 43, 236, 234, 248
Qubā', 55, 244
Qunūt, 70, 96, 103, 122-25
Qur'ān, Qur'ānic, 6f., 12-15, 19-22, 24-39, 41, 43-47, 50, 52, 54f., 58f., 61f., 64, 68, 70ff., 78ff., 82, 85, 89f., 92f., 95ff., 99, 101f., 105f., 109, 111, 113ff., 117-22, 124, 126f., 130, 133, 135 f., 144, 146, 152, 154, 157-62, 164, 172, 174, 177, 178, 180, 182, 191, 195, 197, 202, 204, 209f., 222f., 227f., 232-36, 238, 240, 244, 258; aim of, 31, 247, 273f.; touching of, 57, 59, 64, 72, 79ff., 116f., 247f.; recitation of as supererogatory act, 49, 246-57, 186, 194, 274f.; exegesis of, 79, 256; leader of commentators of, 223; *see also* prostration
Quraysh, 243
Qurayẓa, 242
qurba, 60
Qūt al-Qulūb, 22, 27, 45
Quzaḥ Hill, 212

Rabbinic, 26
Rabigh, 209
rafath, 215
rain, ritual prayer for, 71, 103, 160ff., 267
Rajab, 181, 194, 217
Ramaḍān, 37, 48, 70f., 97, 122f., 125, 130, 133, 139, 142, 156, 177-85, 188, 190ff., 194ff., 204f., 265
raml, 211, 217, 223, 225ff.,
ransom, redemption (*fidya*), 28f., 44, 139f., 192f., 202
Raphel, 32
Rawḍa, 234, 241
Rayyān, 180
redemption, *see* ransom
religion, religious, 12, 14, 19, 25, 30ff., 34ff., 39, 41, 44, 50, 52, 54, 59, 64, 86, 99, 109, 128f., 135, 138, 163f., 169, 172, 178ff., 182, 185, 195ff., 219, 223, 233, 255, 259, 273
remembrance of God, (*dhikr Allāh*), 36, 38f., 49, 82, 152, 160, 186, 194, 209, 246, 253, 258-62, 274f.
repentance (*tawba*), 29, 37f., 45, 63, 71, 123, 184, 194, 241f., 267
Resurrection, Day of, *see* Day of Judgement
revealed, revelation, 84, 218, 232, 273
reward, 6, 12, 20-24, 26ff., 32-35, 38, 44ff., 59f., 64, 108, 113, 143, 151, 164, 169, 173f., 179ff., 194, 207, 234, 238ff., 244, 246, 255, 264, 273
righteous, righteousness, 6, 28, 34
riyā', 253
River of Life, 47
Robson, J., 180
Romans, 21, 30, 38
Rummāna, 242

sa'āda, sa'īd, see salvation
Sacred Mosque (*al-Masjid al-Ḥarām*), 91, 95, 161, 216, 218f., 225f., 228
sacrifice, 209f., 213, 221, 226-32
ṣadaqa, see alms
Safa, 64, 103, 210f., 213, 217ff., 223-28
Ṣafiyya, 244
ṣāḥib ash-shimāl, 59
ṣāḥib al-yamīn, 59
Ṣaḥīḥ: of al-Bukhārī, 14, 20, 23ff., 27f., 30, 32, 35, 39, 43-46, 48, 50, 52, 54-57, 59, 62, 64, 70, 89-92, 100, 104ff., 108ff., 112, 116, 118ff., 127f., 130, 156, 160, 163, 177, 180ff., 186, 191, 194f., 204, 207, 210, 217, 221, 223, 234ff., 238, 246, 251, 253, 259-62, 264-72; of Muslim, 14, 20, 23ff., 27, 30, 44ff., 48, 50, 52, 54, 56, 70, 80, 83, 89-92, 100f., 105, 108ff., 112, 116, 119, 125, 127, 152, 160, 163, 168, 177, 180ff., 186, 191, 194, 203f., 207, 210, 217, 223, 234ff., 238, 253, 259, 260ff., 264-72
sa'ī, 103, 188, 192f., 205, 210, 213, 229f.
saint, 25, 38, 44, 99, 224, 235, 259, 275
ṣalā, see prayer, ritual, Prayer, *Ṣalāt*
Ṣalāt al-Awwābīn, 126
Ṣalāt al-Ḥāja, 129f.
Ṣalāt al-Istikhāra, 128f.
salvation (*najāt*), safety, happiness (*sa'āda*), well-being, bliss, 6, 12, 16, 19-47, *passim*, 99, 124, 154, 164, 180, 246, 259, 264, 271, 273, 275; terms of,

20, 273; meanings of, 12, 15, 19f., 29, 273f.; forms of, 19, 273; means to, 13, 15, 20, 34, 40, 43, 51-272; on human side, 29-43, 48, 274ff.; on divine side, 43-47; indication of, 28; declaration of, 25, 28, 44, 273; general features of, 21f., 273; foretaste of, 22, 24f., 273; in Christianity, 28, 274; grades of, 24-28, 30, 35, 37-40, 44, 273ff.; basic idea in, 28; *see also* action
sam'iyyāt, 20
Samuel II, 210
'sanctification', 30, 35
sanity (*'aql*), sane, insanity, 59, 65, 70, 72, 85, 90, 106, 114, 139, 149, 169, 178, 207f.
as-Sarakhsī, Fakhr al-Islām, 138
Satan, Satanic, 24, 38, 57, 82, 97, 100, 102f., 110, 118, 251, 260, 271
Saturday, 182, 244
ṣawm, see fasting
sayyid al-istighfār, 269, 275
Schacht, J., 86, 196
Scripture, 19-22, 27, 32f., 38f., 247
Seth, *see* Shīth
sex, sexual, 56, 60, 64, 66ff., 80f., 114, 116, 177, 179, 185-91, 195, 209f., 215-17, 227, 231, 247
Sha'bān, 70, 130, 181, 183f., 194
Shadharāt adh-dhahab, 186
shahāda, 33
Shāfi'ī, Imām, 135, 186
Sharī'a, 84, 163, 49
Shaykh Abū Ḥafṣ al-Kabīr, 204
Shaykh Aḥmad az-Zāhid, 62
shaykh al-ḥajj, 219, 221
Shaykh al-Islām Khawāhir Zāde, 138
saving, 61, 210, 221, 227f., 230
Shawwāl, 181, 184, 207
ash-Shemisi, 228
Shīth(Seth), 33
ash-Shurunbalālī, Maḥmūd 'Abd al-Wahhāb, 13f., 53, 55, 57, 65, 69, 110, 163, 189
sin, sinner, 26ff., 31, 37f., 44ff., 64, 69, 71, 105, 109, 111f., 116, 128ff., 133f., 154, 159, 161, 166, 168f., 170ff., 178, 194, 210, 215, 233, 236, 242, 250, 256, 261f., 265, 267, 269ff., 274f.
sincere, sincerity (*ikhlāṣ*), 43, 195, 224, 259, 275
Sīra Rasūl Allāh, 242
slave, 94, 109, 152f., 184, 188, 193, 202f., 204, 207, 260
sociology, 13
soul, carnal (*nafs*), 38, 181, 191, 269
stationary (*muqīm*), 76f., 89, 98, 107, 134-37, 152f., 159, 177f., 182, 188f., 192
stipulation, 59f., 71f., 74, 76, 81, 85, 91, 93, 95, 106ff., 135, 151f., 156, 167, 177ff., 183ff., 192-95, 197f., 207ff., 219, 248, 256, 258f., 275
success (*fawz*), 6, 20, 28, 117, 232, 235
suckling, 192, 208
The Sufficient, 138, 152
ṣūfī, ṣūfism, mystical, 12, 19-23, 27-30, 35, 44, 54, 224, 246, 249, 259, 274f.
suḥuf, 33
Sunan: Abū Dāwūd, 23, 44, 46, 58, 69, 79f., 83, 91, 110, 112, 119f., 125, 152, 163, 170, 174, 182, 195, 198, 204, 253, 260, 265; of ad-Dārimī, 23, 32, 50, 101, 246; of Ibn Māja, 20, 24, 27, 38, 44ff., 55-58, 61, 79, 83, 96, 106, 108, 112, 120, 122, 127, 129, 152, 160, 163, 168, 178, 180, 194, 207, 223, 238, 246, 251, 253, 255, 263; of an-Nasā'ī, 23f., 46, 59, 62, 64, 69f., 83, 104, 106, 108, 110, 112, 116, 118, 120, 127, 160, 168, 181, 191, 203, 207, 232, 253, 255, 260, 265; of at-Tirmidhī, 23f., 27, 30, 44f., 56-59, 64, 79, 83, 96, 108f., 112, 116, 118, 120, 122, 125, 127ff., 152, 168, 170, 174, 181f., 204, 207, 236, 238, 249, 253, 259, 263, 265f.
Sunset Prayer (*Ṣalāt al-Maghrib*), 70, 86f., 90, 96ff., 125f., 144, 162, 212, 220, 249
Supererogatory Ritual Prayer after Sunrise (*Ṣalāt aḍ-Ḍuḥā*), 127, 158
supplication, prayer, 14, 49, 57f., 62f., 72, 74, 90ff., 97ff., 101-105, 110ff., 122ff., 126-30, 133, 154, 157, 161, 164, 167-70, 174, 179, 211-18, 220, 222, 251f., 258-63, 267-72, 274f.
Sūra of Abū Lahab, 118
Sūra of Man, 251
Sūra of Opening, *see* Opening
Sūra of Sincerity, 31, 117, 244
Sūra of Thunderbolt (*ar-Ra'd*), 149, 164
Sūra of Ya Sīn, 163, 174, 244
sutra, see barrier
swearing, *see* oath
Syria, 209

Ṭabaqāt, 186
aṭ-Ṭabarī, Abū Ja'far Muḥammad ibn Jarīr, 33
Tabyīn al-Ḥaqā'iq, 229

Tahāfut al-Falāsifa, 21f., 24
Tahajjud Prayer, 125
ṭahāra, see cleanliness
aṭ-Ṭaḥāwī, Imām Abū Ja'far, 86, 203
Tahdhīb at-Tahdhīb, 104, 196, 238f.
tahlīl, 260f., 275
taḥmīd, 261f., 275; *see also* praise
at-Tajnīs wa l-Mazīd, 138
Tajrīd aṣ-Ṣiḥāḥ bi 'Alāmat al-Mu'aṭṭā', 229
talbiya, 159, 211, 215f., 218-21, 222ff.
Tamattu', 209f., 213, 225-28, 231
Tarāwīḥ Prayer, 96, 116, 132f.
Tārīkh, 270
Tārīkh al-Umam wa l-Mulūk, 33
tasbīḥ, 261f., 275; *see also* glorification
ṭawāf, 213, 217, 218; *see also* circumambulation, Visiting, Arrival, Farewell, Chest, Hastening
at-Tawassul wa l-Wasīla, 236
tawba, see repentance
tax, divine (*zakā*), 36f., 48f., 92, 197-204, 206, 274f.
tayammum, see ablution
thanā', 103, 133, 167
ath-Thaniyya as-Suflā, 214, 225
Thawr, 238
ath-Thawrī, Sufyān, 186
theology, theologian, theological, 12, 19, 21f., 25f., 29, 35, 86, 224, 254, 274
Thursday, 182, 244
Timothy II, 38
tooth-stick (*miswāk*), 61f., 156, 191
Torah, 33
Tradition (*ḥadīth*), 12-15, 19-24, 26f., 29-33, 35, 43, 54, 59, 61, 64, 75, 83, 99, 105, 108, 112, 135, 151, 170, 174, 180, 187, 189, 220, 273; 'holy Tradition,' 39, 180
transliterations, 6, 14
Treatise, 224
Tuḥfat as-Sālik fī Faḍā'il as-Siwāk, 62

Uḥud, 243f.
'Umar ibn al-Khaṭṭāb, 239f., 243
Umayyad, 243
'umra, 70, 209, 216, 227f.
unjust, *see* injustice
upright, 53, 148, 184f., 192, 230
Usṭuwāna Abī Lubāba, 241f.
Usṭuwāna Ḥannāna, 243
'Uthmān ibn 'Affān, 248

veil from God, *see* God
Verse of the Throne, 111, 244
vigil, 127, 130, 243, 246, 248, 255
vision, beatific, 27, 30, 257, 274
Visiting Circumambulation (*Ṭawāf az-Ziyāra*), 71, 210, 222
vomiting, 65f., 82, 107, 186, 190
vow to God 87f 131, 180 182f., 192-95, 232

wadī, 67, 82
waḍū', see ablution
al-*Wāfī*, 229
Walī Allāh, Shāh, 14, 177, 181f., 196
al-Walwālijī, 38
well-being, *see* happiness
Western, 12
will, 139f., 169, 175, 192, 201
wine, 53, 82
wiping, 40, 53, 56f., 59, 61-64, 68, 73ff., 83, 107, 112, 119ff., 164f.; over boots, 75-80, 107, 114; over bandage, 78, 107, 114
Witnessing (*at-tashahhud*), 93, 96, 99, 104, 110f., 115, 118, 122, 126, 131, 133, 135, 142, 144-48, 151, 156
world to come, *see* Hereafter
worship, worshipper, 36f., 42, 100, 123, 194ff., 210, 213, 216, 219, 244, 246, 263f., 275
wrath of God, 45

zakā, see tax, divine

Yaḥyā, 113
Yalamlam, 209
al-Yanābī', 138
Yawm 'Arafa, 159, 211f., 228
Yawm an-Naḥr, 71, 212f., 222
Yawm at-Tarwiyya, 212, 227
Yazīd, 243
Yemen, 209

Zād al-Ma'ād, 14, 194, 196
az-Zāhid, Shaykh Aḥmad, *see* Shaykh
aẓ-Ẓāhiriyya, 138
Zamzam, 213, 223
Zayd, 94
az-Zayla'ī, 229

For Product Safety Concerns and Information please contact our EU
representative GPSR@taylorandfrancis.com
Taylor & Francis Verlag GmbH, Kaufingerstraße 24, 80331 München, Germany

www.ingramcontent.com/pod-product-compliance
Lightning Source LLC
Chambersburg PA
CBHW050626300426
44112CB00012B/1676
9781032514635